The Collected Courses of the Academy of European Law
Series Editors: Professor Philip Alston,
New York University School of Law;
Professor Gráinne de Búrca, and
Professor Bruno de Witte,
European University Institute,
Florence

006

VOLUME XII/2

Gender and Human Rights

WITHDRÁWN

The Collected Courses of the Academy of European Law
Edited by Professor Philip Alston, Professor Gráinne de Búrca, and Professor Bruno de Witte

This series brings together the Collected Courses of the Academy of European Law in Florence. The Academy's mission is to produce scholarly analyses which are at the cutting edge of the two fields in which it works: European Union law and human rights law. A 'general course' is given each year in each field, by a distinguished scholar and/or practitioner, who either examines the field as a whole through a particular thematic, conceptual, or philosophical lens, or who looks at a particular theme in the context of the overall body of law in the field. The Academy also publishes each year a volume of collected essays with a specific theme in each of the two fields.

Gender and Human Rights

Edited by

KAREN KNOP

Academy of European Law
European University Institute

OXFORD
UNIVERSITY PRESS

OXFORD

UNIVERSITY PRESS

Great Clarendon Street, Oxford OX2 6DP

Oxford University Press is a department of the University of Oxford.
It furthers the University's objective of excellence in research, scholarship,
and education by publishing worldwide in

Oxford New York

Auckland Bangkok Buenos Aires Cape Town Chennai
Dar es Salaam Delhi Hong Kong Istanbul Karachi Kolkata
Kuala Lumpur Madrid Melbourne Mexico City Mumbai Nairobi
São Paulo Shanghai Singapore Taipei Tokyo Toronto

Oxford is a registered trade mark of Oxford University Press
in the UK and in certain other countries

Published in the United States
by Oxford University Press Inc., New York

© the various contributors, except where indicated, 2004

The moral rights of the author have been asserted
Crown copyright material is reproduced under
Class Licence Number CO1P0000148 with the permission of
HMSO and the Queen's Printer for Scotland

Database right Oxford University Press (maker)

First published 2004

British Library Cataloguing in Publication Data
Data available

Library of Congress Cataloging in Publication Data
Data available

ISBN 0-19-926090-7 (hbk.)
ISBN 0-19-926091-5 (pbk.)

1 3 5 7 9 10 8 6 4 2

Typeset by Kolam Information Services Pvt. Ltd, Pondicherry, India
Printed in Great Britain
on acid-free paper by
Biddles Ltd, King's Lynn

Contents

Acknowledgements   vi
Notes on Contributors   vii

1 **Introduction**   1
   Karen Knop

2 **Feminist Legal Theory and the Rights of Women**   13
   Nicola Lacey

3 **Take a Break from Feminism?**   57
   Janet Halley

4 **Citizenship in Europe and the Construction of Gender
   by Law in the European Charter of Fundamental Rights**   83
   Susanne Baer

5 **Constitutional Domestication of International Gender
   Norms: Categorizations, Illustrations, and Reflections
   from the Nearside of the Bridge**   113
   Ruth Rubio-Marín and Martha I. Morgan

6 **Individual(s') Liability for Collective Sexual Violence**   153
   Patricia Viseur Sellers

7 **'The Appeals of the Orient': Colonized Desire and
   the War of the Riff**   195
   Nathaniel Berman

8 **Toward an Understanding of Transnationalism and Gender**   231
   Ruba Salih

Index   251

Acknowledgements

This collection developed from a series of lectures given at the European University Institute in Florence as part of the Academy of European Law's annual summer course in the field of international human rights law. The shape of the collection owes much to the remarkable environment created by the course. I am especially grateful to Philip Alston for his commitment to the idea of specialized lectures on gender and international human rights that would bring together feminists and internationalists from outside the field, and to Christine Chinkin, who gave the general lectures on international human rights and whose generous collaboration added greatly to the experience and the synergy of the course as a whole. This book also benefited from exchanges with students and from the presence in Florence of a number of feminist legal scholars including, in addition to those directly involved in the course, Gráinne de Búrca, Mayo Moran, Thérèse Murphy, and Wendy Williams.

For assistance in the preparation of the volume, I should like to thank Kevin-Paul Deveau and the Cecil A. Wright Foundation for Legal Scholarship of the University of Toronto Faculty of Law, which funded his work.

Portains of Chapter 3 were published in Cossman *et al.*, 'Gender, Sexuality, and Power: Is Feminist Theory Enough?', 12 *Columbia Journal of Gender and Low* (2003) 601. An earlier version of Chapter 8 was published as Salih, 'Moroccan Migrant Women: Transnationalism, Nation-States and Gender', 27 *Journal of Ethnic and Migration Studies* (2001) 655, reproduced in revised form by kind permission of Taylor & Francis Ltd. The website for the *Journal of Ethnic and Migration Studies* is http://www.tandf.co.uk/journals/carfax/1369183X. html.

Karen Knop
Toronto

Notes on Contributors

Susanne Baer is Professor of German and Comparative Constitutional and Administrative Law, Legal Theory, and Gender Studies at Humboldt University. She is Director of the Centre for Transdisciplinary Gender Studies (http://www.gender.hu-berlin.de) and advises government agencies and the European Commission on discrimination law. She also teaches at Central European University, Budapest. Her recent publications include *Comparative Constitionalism* (West, 2003) with Norman Dorsen, Michel Rosenfeld, and András Sajó; and 'Equality: The Jurisprudence of the German Constitutional Court', 5 *Columbia Journal of European Law* (1999) 249.

Nathaniel Berman is Professor of Law at Brooklyn Law School, where his courses include public international law, European Union law, international trade law, and human rights. His scholarship focuses on the relationship between nationalism, colonialism, and international law. He has written on international legal responses to nationalist conflicts, ranging from Upper Silesia and Morocco in the 1920s to Bosnia and Jerusalem in the 1990s. More recently, he has turned to the law of war, analysing the history of the field in light of developments such as 9/11 and Iraq. His work is broadly interdisciplinary, drawing on literary theory, cultural history, feminism, and postcolonial studies.

Janet Halley is Professor at Harvard Law School. She has published widely on gay rights, sexuality, and feminism in legal journals and elsewhere. Her most recent books are *Left Legalism/Left Critique*, co-edited with Wendy Brown (Duke University Press, 2002), and *Don't: A Reader's Guide to the Military's Anti-Gay Policy* (Duke University Press, 1999). The chapter included here is a progress report towards two books, currently in the final stages of composition: *Governance Feminisms and their Critiques*, and *Sexuality Harassment*.

Karen Knop is Associate Professor at the Faculty of Law, University of Toronto, and Director of the JD/MA (International Relations) Programme at the University of Toronto. Her book *Diversity and Self-Determination in International Law* (Cambridge University Press, 2002) was awarded a Certificate of Merit by the American Society of International Law. She is editor, with Sylvia Ostry, Richard Simeon, and Katherine Swinton, of *Re-Thinking Federalism: Citizens, Markets and Governments in a Changing World* (University of British Columbia Press, 1995). As rapporteur for the International Law

Association's Committee on Feminism and International Law, she was responsible for the ILA's report on gender and nationality (2000).

Nicola Lacey is Professor of Criminal Law at the London School of Economics and Adjunct Professor of Social and Political Theory at the Research School of Social Sciences of the Australian National University. She is the author of *State Punishment* (Routledge, 1988); with Elizabeth Frazer, *The Politics of Community: A Feminist Analysis of the Liberal-Communitarian Debate* (Harvester, 1993); *Unspeakable Subjects: Feminist Essays in Legal and Social Theory* (Hart, 1998); and with Celia Wells and Oliver Quick, *Reconstructing Criminal Law* (3rd edn, Butterworths, 2003). She is a Fellow of the British Academy and was in 2001 and 2003 visiting member of the Hauser Global Law Faculty at New York University.

Martha I. Morgan is the Robert S. Vance Professor of Law at the University of Alabama School of Law, teaching courses in constitutional law, civil rights legislation, and comparative constitutional law. She has done field research and writing on women and constitution-making in Colombia and Nicaragua, as well as on other law reform efforts by women in Costa Rica, Guatemala, and Nicaragua. Recently, her research and publications have focused on the emerging gender jurisprudence in Latin America and on the domestic incorporation of gender rights contained in international human rights law. She serves as a consultant to the Women, Justice, and Gender Program of the United Nations Latin American Institute for the Prevention of Crime and Treatment of Delinquency in San José, Costa Rica.

Ruth Rubio-Marín is Professor of Constitutional Law at the University of Seville, Spain. She is author of *Immigration as a Democratic Challenge* (Cambridge University Press, 2000) and of several articles on language rights, nationality, immigration, antidiscrimination, and gender in the law. She has taught at different North American academic institutions, including Princeton University and Columbia Law School, and is currently part of the Hauser Global Law Faculty at New York University.

Ruba Salih is a social anthropologist currently based at the University of Bologna. Her research interests cover issues of transnational migration, gender, Islam, and citizenship in Europe and the Middle East. She has published extensively on the subject in several international journals. She is the author of *Gender in Transnationalism. Home, Longing and Belonging among Moroccan Migrant Women* (Routledge, 2003). Currently she is undertaking research on membership, identity, and citizenship among the Palestinian diaspora in Jordan.

Patricia Viseur Sellers is the Legal Advisor for Gender-related Crimes and Trial Attorney in the Office of the Prosecutor for the International Criminal Tribunal for the Former Yugoslavia. She also advises the Prosecutor on gender matters at the Rwanda Tribunal. She is the recipient of the American Society of International Law Outstanding Women in International Law award, and has received an honorary doctorate in law from City University of New York and the Martin Luther King Award from Rutgers University Law School. She is the author of various articles on gender and has lectured extensively on international criminal law.

1

Introduction

KAREN KNOP

A working bibliography on women's international human rights published in 1989 contained 142 publications, ten cases, and a list of 15 international governmental and non-governmental organizations and other sources of information.[1] By 2003, it had grown into a website[2] that includes approximately 700 articles, over 766 treaties, cases, and other legal documents, and 346 links to other websites.[3] Not only have women's international human rights come to receive significant attention in the literature, but a comparison of some of the main edited works over the past ten years indicates that the subject is now firmly established as a field of study. *Human Rights of Women*[4] and *Women's Rights/Human Rights*,[5] two groundbreaking collections from the mid-1990s, are each single volumes of average length, intended to introduce and organize women's international human rights as a field. In contrast, the three-volume, nearly 2,500-page *Women and International Human Rights Law*,[6] published between 1999 and 2001, is divided into specialized entries written by over 80 leading authorities and will soon be supplemented by a fourth volume.

Consolidation, categorization, and heft do not mean that issues of women's international human rights have lost their urgency. If anything, they prove the contrary. In this collection, we have only to read, for example, the deeply disturbing accounts of collective sexual violence that Patricia Viseur Sellers quotes from judgments of the International Criminal Tribunal for the Former

---

[1] Cook, 'The International Right to Nondiscrimination on the Basis of Sex: A Bibliography', 14 *Yale Journal of International Law* (1989) 161.

[2] *Women's Human Rights Resources*, at http://www.law-lib.utoronto.ca/diana/mainpage. htm.

[3] International Programme on Reproductive and Sexual Health Law, Faculty of Law, University of Toronto, *2002 Annual Report* (2003), at 30.

[4] R. J. Cook (ed.), *Human Rights of Women: National and International Perspectives* (1994).

[5] J. Peters and A. Wolper (eds), *Women's Rights/Human Rights: International Feminist Perspectives* (1995).

[6] K. D. Askin and D. Koenig (eds), *Women and International Human Rights Law*, 3 vols (1999–2001).

Yugoslavia (ICTY). The corollary of moulding women's international human rights into a field, however, is that the literature becomes increasingly self-contained. It acquires its own dynamics, the positions in the literature come to be classifiable as majority or minority views, and debates are internalized. In the process, ideas received or adapted from other fields take on a life of their own and to some extent lose touch with their fate in those other fields. The emergence of women's international human rights as an independent subject of inquiry also has the effect of separating it from developments in fields that it takes for granted, or in fields that share some subset of its concerns but have not figured much in thinking about women's international human rights thus far.

Although specialization and the intellectual and practical energies that it concentrates continue to be vital to women's international human rights, the premiss of this collection is that we have reached a stage where it is both possible and fruitful to reflect fundamentally on the field *from outside*: to benefit from lines of inquiry in related fields, to examine the field's interfaces from the other side, and to study the field against a number of broader fields. In this spirit, the contributors to the collection are all authors working on issues of gender in other areas who have been invited to engage with women's international human rights. Along with other areas of international law (Patricia Viseur Sellers, Nathaniel Berman), these areas include philosophies of rights (Nicola Lacey), queer theory (Janet Halley), ideas of citizenship (Susanne Baer), constitutional law (Ruth Rubio-Marín and Martha Morgan), and migration studies (Ruba Salih). The result is a group of essays that aims not to offer ready-made solutions from elsewhere, but to begin, resume, or deepen a conversation across types and topics of inquiry related to gender and human rights.

While valuable cross-cutting exchanges already exist on some issues such as gender and cultural relativism,[7] and sexuality and trafficking in women,[8] the aim of this collection is structurally broader. It takes three sets of ideas basic to women's international human rights law—ideas about *feminism*, about *rights* and how they operate, and about the organization of *international society*—and explores these ideas and the relationships between them from a variety of interdisciplinary perspectives. The collection thus encourages us to revisit some of the fundamentals of women's international human rights law: to consider hard questions about core concepts, to re-evaluate accepted methods, to probe the limits of central paradigms, and to ask where familiar critiques may ultimately lead. It is at this level that the collection's heterogeneity seeks to enhance our understanding of the field.

[7] See e.g. S. Moller Okin with Respondents, *Is Multiculturalism Bad for Women?*, J. Cohen, M. Howard, and M. C. Nussbuam (eds) (1999).
[8] Compare e.g. K. Barry, *Female Sexual Slavery* (1979), with K. Kempadoo and J. Doezema (eds), *Global Sex Workers: Rights, Resistance, and Redefinition* (1998).

Part of the Collected Courses of the Academy of European Law, the volume features a number of authors and themes based in Europe. While the hope is that its diversity of European scholarship and issues will further the analysis of gender and human rights generally, the collection does not pretend to be either global or comprehensive. As a contribution to a women's international human rights literature that has often concentrated on the portability of a few Western-inspired feminist approaches and struggled to make visible a range of non-Western alternatives, this collection also seeks to illustrate that, on the Western side, there are many different European perspectives on gender and human rights. Indeed, there are many different Europes. What emerges from the chapters by Nathaniel Berman, Susanne Baer, and Ruba Salih is a Europe with a history of empire and a present shaped by the circuits of migrants that cross its borders. Berman's Europe is a historical, imperial one; Baer's, the multicultural Europe to which the European Union aspires; and Salih's, a contemporary Europe redefined by transmigration. The encounters within each of these Europes hold important lessons for key issues of gender and human rights.

***

Nicola Lacey's chapter 'Feminist Legal Theory and the Rights of Women' and Janet Halley's chapter 'Take a Break from Feminism?' together introduce the collection by asking two fundamental questions about gender and human rights. Assuming that we want to use the framework of human rights to secure justice, autonomy, or equality for women, what are the limitations as well as the potential of rights? Lacey explores this question through a subtle treatment of feminist legal theory, theories of rights, and the relationship between them. With innovative rigour, she breaks down the question analytically into parts: what do we mean by feminism (including the sex/gender distinction), what do we mean by rights, what is the feminist critique of rights, and what ideas exist for reconstructing rights in a more satisfactory way? Each of these inquiries is open-ended and has implications for the next. By drawing on the fullness of theories and debates that have developed about feminism, rights, and the implications of one for the other at the level of national law, Lacey brings a richer and more precise conceptual vocabulary to the international level. She shows why such a normative language is important for women's international human rights and how it moves us beyond the choice between a commitment to rights as an article of faith or a pragmatic strategy on the one hand, and an outright rejection of rights on the other. Indeed, she demonstrates that the United Nations Convention on the Elimination of All Forms of Discrimination against Women[9] already reflects certain ideas for reconstructing rights

---

[9] Convention on the Elimination of All Forms of Discrimination against Women, New York, adopted 18 December 1979, in force 3 September 1981, 1249 UNTS 13.

in ways responsive to the feminist critique of rights and, further, that these ideas do not exhaust the possibilities.

In her chapter, Janet Halley poses a question about feminism analogous to the one that Lacey asks about rights: what are the limits of feminism? While Halley affirms that there are many places in national locales and in inter-national/global left-wing politics where feminism is indispensable, she asks whether there are also aims, constituencies, freedoms, or pleasures that could become articulate and to which we could measure our commitment only if we let ourselves 'take a break from feminism'. Halley builds on the insights of queer theory as it has developed in the United States to challenge the presup-position that feminism will always be the origin and destiny of left politics on sexuality.

In Susanne Baer's chapter 'Citizenship in Europe and the Construction of Gender by Law in the European Charter of Fundamental Rights' and Ruth Rubio-Marín and Martha Morgan's chapter 'Constitutional Domestication of International Gender Norms: Categorizations, Illustrations, and Reflections from the Nearside of the Bridge', we see the theoretical and practical power of the sorts of feminist analysis for which Lacey argues. In her chapter, Lacey describes four influential attempts to construct a coherent theory of legal rights and draws out the implications of each, including for the typical subject of legal rights. She maintains this focus on the subject in her outline of the feminist critique of rights and her examination of a number of efforts to reconstruct rights in ways that seek to escape the problems identified by feminists. Baer further develops our understanding of the constitution of the subject of legal rights as sexed and gendered. Whereas Lacey looks at theories of rights, Baer shifts our attention to actual codes of rights, whether national human rights legislation, constitutional bills of rights, international human rights treaties, or other international instruments. Together with the model of feminist legal theory that Lacey distinguishes as 'difference feminism', Baer employs theories of citizenship to identify the subject assumed by, and thus brought into being by, such texts. Baer shows convincingly that gender-neutral language is not enough in a human rights instrument. The choice, configur-ation, and expression of rights in the document produce and thereby privilege a certain type of citizen. An understanding of the various theories of citizen-ship helps us to recognize what that type of citizen is and what the alternatives might be, while feminist methods enable us to discern the consequences of that type of citizenship for inclusion and equality. Baer offers a set of tools for 'reading' any human rights instrument, by which she means apprehending the given and hidden meanings of the text, reconstructing what is said and what is left out, and building a case from the text alone. She then uses these tools to read the European Convention for the Protection of Human Rights and Fundamental Freedoms (European Convention on Human Rights) and par-ticularly to reread the newer Charter of Fundamental Rights of the European

Union (European Charter of Fundamental Rights).[10] If reading in her sense is a critical process, it is also a potentially reconstructive one. Working out who the citizen is can be part of the undertaking that Anne Phillips calls 'gendered substitution':[11] the reshaping of a term in a gender-sensitive way, rather than its rejection as discriminatory.

Lacey argues that to appreciate the potential and the limitations of rights for achieving women's empowerment and equality, we must consider the complex institutional issues involved as well as the theoretical and normative ones. This requires extensive social science research into the interaction between legal, political, economic, and cultural institutions in specific societies, both as it gives rise to sex-based disadvantage and as it affects the efficacy of the international norms designed to remedy such disadvantage. In the latter mode, the chapter by Ruth Rubio-Marín and Martha Morgan contributes substantially to our understanding of the relationship of international gender norms to domestic constitutions. Like Baer's chapter, their chapter takes a working assumption in women's international human rights law and subjects it to close scrutiny from outside the field. Just as Baer demonstrates that gender-neutral language is not enough in an international human rights document, Rubio-Marín and Morgan demonstrate that the usual focus on the formally binding status of international gender norms in domestic legal systems neither exhausts their potential to affect the system nor tells us what that effect will be. As Rubio-Marín and Morgan illustrate, there has been more to the domestic application of women's international human rights than whether these rights are enforceable domestically. Based on the constitutional experience in a number of countries, particularly Spanish-speaking countries, they propose a typology for identifying and describing the primary processes through which international human rights treaty law interacts with domestic constitutional law. They then proceed to categorize and examine some of the main effects that these various processes have had upon gender jurisprudence in domestic constitutional law. While the resulting analysis may lack the clarity of the familiar accounts, Rubio-Marín and Morgan argue that their classification scheme is descriptively more accurate, draws attention to a wider range of strategies for incorporation, and engages more openly with the issues of contextualization and legitimation raised by incorporation.

The chapters by Patricia Viseur Sellers, Nathaniel Berman, and Ruba Salih contain lessons for gender and human rights derived from different international and transnational fields of study. Sellers's chapter, 'Individual(s') Liability for Collective Sexual Violence', describes one aspect of what surely ranks among the most significant legal achievements for women, nationally or

---

[10] Charter of Fundamental Rights of the European Union, OJ 2000 C 364, at 1.
[11] Phillips, 'Citizenship and Feminist Theory', in G. Andrews (ed.), *Citizenship* (1991) 76, at 77.

internationally, over the last decade: the prosecution and legal reconception of sexual violence in wartime. Together, the ICTY and the International Criminal Tribunal for Rwanda (ICTR) have held that rape and other forms of sexual violence constitute acts of genocide, crimes against humanity, violations of the laws or customs of war (that is, war crimes), and grave breaches of the Geneva Conventions.[12] In her chapter, Sellers focuses on one line of the ICTY's sexual assault cases: the cases that shape the emergence or application of common purpose or joint criminal liability as interpreted in Article 7 of the ICTY Statute.[13] Sellers demonstrates the significance of this doctrinal development in terms of its definitive destruction of two myths that have discouraged, hindered, or obscured the prosecution of wartime sexual violence. The one myth is that soldiers who rape have, as a psychological matter, succumbed to their natural sexual urges and have, as a legal matter, committed a wrong that is beyond the reach of international humanitarian law. The other myth recognizes the possibility of prosecution, but alleges that the inevitable sexual violence cannot be prosecuted unless it is systematic or committed on a superior's order. Under the doctrine of common purpose, it is precisely the inevitability that makes such acts indictable. The doctrine encompasses a single, one-act crime by multiple perpetrators and an act that is part of a system of ill-treatment or a foreseeable consequence of that system.

The discussion by Sellers of these two myths contains a caution about one of the feminist methods imported from national into international law and, perhaps, more generally about the limits of borrowing from other fields of study. In the context of national society, the public/private distinction refers to the notional division that sees legal regulation as appropriate to the public sphere and ordinarily inappropriate to the private sphere, where the line between public and private is most often drawn either between the state and civil society or within civil society so as to mark off the domestic space of family life as private. As feminist legal analysis has shown, women are more vulnerable than men to serious harm, injustice, and discrimination in the private sphere, and the public/private distinction has prevented the law from remedying the situation. Feminists have imported this critique into international human rights law, where it operates directly in areas such as state

---

[12] The four Geneva Conventions, signed 12 August 1949, in force 21 October 1950, are the Geneva Convention (I) for the Amelioration of the Condition of the Wounded and Sick in Armed Forces in the Field, 75 UNTS 31; Geneva Convention (II) for the Amelioration of the Condition of Wounded, Sick and Shipwrecked Members of Armed Forces at Sea, 75 UNTS 85; Geneva Convention (III) Relative to the Treatment of Prisoners of War, 75 UNTS 135; and Geneva Convention (IV) Relative to the Protection of Civilian Persons in Time of War, 75 UNTS 287.

[13] Statute of the ICTY, attached to the Report of the Secretary General Pursuant to Paragraph 2 of the Security Council Resolution 808, UN Doc. S/25704, Annex (1993), reprinted in 32 ILM 1159 (1993).

responsibility for domestic violence,[14] and also into public international law, where it operates by analogy in areas such as intervention in matters within the domestic jurisdiction of states.[15] Some strands of the debate among feminists in public international law over the implications of the critique are traceable to the importation of different versions of the public/private distinction[16] or different versions of the critique.[17] Other strands are concerned with the downside of any such distinction and critique.[18] In the field of international humanitarian law, Sellers makes a different point: namely, that the public/private distinction may have been more mystifying than useful. Feminists have introduced the public/private distinction as a criticism of the scope of international humanitarian law: rape, or some rapes, by combatants are private acts that are outside the public conduct of the conflict. But Sellers argues that this broad private sphere is an illusion created primarily by gross under-prosecution and compounded by the lesser status of the prohibition of sexual violence in the hierarchy of war crimes historically. Although these other problems might well reflect a public/private distinction at the level of political priorities and social attitudes, her view leads us to ask whether they are not better explored without the labels. Sellers also shows that if the public/private distinction is a criticism of the law itself, then there is no standard notion of what is private in international humanitarian law. Accordingly, we need to do so much work to operate the public/private distinction that again we may wonder about the value of the exercise.

As the analysis of a doctrinal development that represents major progress for the feminist project in international law, Sellers's chapter returns us to the questions that Halley asks about the limits of feminism. Are the theories of gender oppression that contributed to this and related law reforms also

---

[14] See e.g. Romany, 'State Responsibility Goes Private: A Feminist Critique of the Public/Private Distinction in International Human Rights Law', in Cook (ed.), *supra* n. 4, 85.

[15] See e.g. H. Charlesworth and C. Chinkin, *The Boundaries of International Law: A Feminist Analysis* (2000), at 30–1, 56–7; Walker, 'An Exploration of Article 2(7) of the United Nations Charter as an Embodiment of the Public/Private Distinction in International Law', 26 *New York University Journal of International Law and Politics* (1994) 173.

[16] Karen Engle, for example, maps onto public international law the public/private distinction that demarcates bodily autonomy as private, and this distinction carries different implications for legal intervention. Engle, 'After the Collapse of the Public/Private Distinction: Strategizing Women's Rights', in D. G. Dallmeyer (ed.), *Reconceiving Reality: Women and International Law* (1993) 143, at 148–50. See also Knop, 'Re/Statements: Feminism and State Sovereignty in International Law', 3 *Transnational Law and Contemporary Problems* (1993) 293, at 328–32.

[17] See e.g. Engle, *supra* n. 16; Knop, *supra* n. 16; Olsen, 'International Law: Feminist Critiques of the Public/Private Distinction', in Dallmeyer (ed.), *supra* n. 16, at 157.

[18] See e.g. Buss, 'Going Global: Feminist Theory, International Law, and the Public/Private Divide', in S. B. Boyd (ed.), *Challenging the Public/Private Divide: Feminism, Law, and Public Policy* (1997) 360, at 366–73.

capable of furnishing an adequate theory of sexuality? And, more controver-
sially, do they come at a cost that we are reluctant to name, let alone confront?
The very success that Sellers tracks seems to lend support to Halley's points,
notably her point that feminism has become a powerful constitutive discourse.
If Halley is right—if feminism, and no longer just the discourses that it
criticizes, helps to form our sense of reality—then must we consider whether
'it might well have a shaping contribution to make *to women's suffering*'?[19]
Halley raises the uncomfortable possibilities that the feminist discourses
which present the rape victim as devoid of agency may contribute to this
result by leading women to believe that they can never recover from rape, and
that the feminist discourses which seek to describe and oppose the social and
psychic trauma of rape may instead cause men to choose rape as the form of
aggression because its effect will be the most devastating. Then again, Halley's
challenge is hard even to contemplate when set against the detailed judicial
narratives of sexual injury and humiliation in the Yugoslav conflict that Sellers
includes in her chapter.[20] It is precisely because the sexual violence that occurs
in war is so shockingly brutal and pervasive that it tests Halley's proposal to
'take a break from feminism' as much as her proposal tests the feminism that
contributed to its strenuous prosecution.

Shifting the international setting from war to colonialism, Nathaniel Berman's chapter, ' "The Appeals of the Orient": Colonized Desire and the War of
the Riff', explores the role of gendered desire in international debate. Berman's
chapter uses the language of desire and the language of law to understand the
positions taken by a variety of political and cultural figures on the 1925 'War
of the Riff' between France and a group of Riffan rebels fighting against
increasing European encroachment on their region of Morocco. In his study
of the public discourse of the war, Berman focuses on the relationships among
French images of the colonized world, notions of international legal order
associated with those images, and images of anti-colonial struggle claimed and
evoked by the leader of the rebellion, Mohamed ben Abd el-Krim el-Khattabi.
In analysing French images of the colonized world, Berman highlights the
prominence of gender imagery and the expression of libidinal desires, and
traces the ways that these fantasies inform the positions taken on the war and
the international legal order appropriate to colonialism more generally. While
some post-colonialists have similarly argued that the gendering of the Occi-
dent/Orient or colonizer/colonized dichotomy in the Western mind has lent
persuasive power to the international law and politics of colonialism, and there

[19] *Infra*, at p. 68.
[20] The critical bite of Halley's questions varies, of course, with the interpretation of the
ICTY's judgments. For a positive reading of the judgments as resisting 'the pull to characterize
the wrong of these violent acts as predominantly sexual in nature' and instead demonstrating
'how sex can be used as a tool in the service of race, ethnicity, or religion-based war crimes', see
Franke, 'Putting Sex to Work', 75 *Denver University Law Review* (1998) 1139, at 1143.

are feminists who have discerned such stereotypes in arguments for humanitarian, specifically military, intervention, Berman's study both contributes to and reflects on this methodology. Anne Orford, for example, has shown in the context of Kosovo that the international discourse justifying intervention relied on narratives ingrained in the popular imagination of the West to cast the international community as masculine action hero and the state targeted for intervention as helpless feminine victim.[21] Whereas Orford's focus is on the position that ultimately prevailed and its dependence on pre-programmed gender imagery, Berman explores a variety of positions taken on the War of the Riff and their association with a variety of gendered images of 'the Orient' and sexualized configurations of the relationship between the Occident and the Orient. Thus, in contrast to Orford, whose interest is in why one possibility won the day, Berman seeks to recuperate a range of political and cultural possibilities available at a given historical moment. In this vein, he also explores the possibilities for resistance deployed by the leader of the Riffan rebellion.

The deeper contrast between Orford and Berman goes, however, to what Halley terms essential elements of US feminism: the distinction between m and f (whether defined as men/women, male/female, or masculine/feminine) and the $m > f$ hypothesis that f is disadvantaged or subordinated relative to m. Orford documents the power of $m > f$ stereotypes as mapped onto the stance for humanitarian intervention in Kosovo, and Berman too finds 'the chivalrous Socialist desire to save the damsel in distress, in the guise of the chaotic and fragmented Moroccan countryside'. But he also finds, for instance, 'the homoerotic Communist desire to instruct "barbarian" virility, in the guise of the urbanized Moroccan worker'.[22] More generally, Berman shows that the French Socialists, Communists, and Surrealists each assigned m and f differently to the Occident and the Orient, each desired a different relationship between them, and, accordingly, each advocated a different French approach to the War of the Riff. He argues that colonialism does not rely on a certain projection of gender roles in fixed combination with a certain projection of sexualized desire, but can be supported—or opposed—by a variety of such roles and desires in a variety of combinations.

Berman's account of 'colonized desires' also provocatively engages an issue that is fundamental to work in the field of women's international human rights: our relationship with the Other. By showing that these desires are separable from both their gendered expression and their politics, Berman identifies a similarity between the French Socialists' double tactic of splitting and seduction, and ideas of coalition-building found in women's international

[21] Orford, 'Muscular Humanitarianism: Reading the Narratives of the New Interventionism', 10 *EJIL* (1999) 679.
[22] *Infra*, at p. 213.

human rights. Much as the Socialist approach was to oppose the Sultan of Morocco and form an alliance with the more independent tribes in order to win them over to France, post-Cold War global feminists have proposed a strategy of disaggregation in relation to other societies whereby international law would recognize and lend support to women's groups seeking to contest their patriarchal religion or culture from within.[23] In alluding to the persistence of this strategy, Berman is not condemning it. His position is that desire is inescapable, and the question therefore is to what it lends itself. He thus parts company with the ideal implicit in much of the women's international human rights literature, which imagines that an authentic unmediated encounter between women in different societies is possible if Western feminists overcome the tendency to engage with women in other cultures as exotic victims and instead recognize and respect their agency.[24] Berman presumes that such an encounter is never possible, let alone across great differences of power, wealth, and culture. 'Fears and fantasies about others, marked by shifting and ambivalent configurations of gender and sexuality, are an irreducible element of human experience.'[25] At the same time, he suggests that this irrationality is not cause for pessimism because fears and fantasies have promoted, and can promote, a variety of positive alliances and projects.

The collection's final chapter by Ruba Salih, 'Toward an Understanding of Transnationalism and Gender', is paradoxically perhaps both the farthest removed from and the most immediate to women's international human rights. Salih's is the only contribution by a non-lawyer; she is a social anthropologist. But, as her title suggests, she reflects on the organization of international society, on citizenship, law, and rights, and on their gendered dimensions as they are actually experienced by migrant women, specifically Moroccan women in Italy. Salih's chapter emphasizes and thus directs us to places and junctions that have received relatively little attention in the women's international human rights literature, although not necessarily elsewhere. Salih begins with Zygmunt Bauman's observation that 'access to global mobility' is becoming one of the most important factors in social stratification, to which she adds that access to global mobility is gendered. She thus immediately invites us to substitute a transnational paradigm for the international/national paradigm usual to international human rights law. Migrant women are increasingly likely to participate in the political and social lives of two countries, and the set of mobility-related rights that permits and facilitates

---

[23] See e.g. Sunder, 'Piercing the Veil', 112 *Yale Law Journal* (2003) 1399.

[24] On this tendency, see e.g. Kapur, 'The Tragedy of Victimization Rhetoric: Resurrecting the "Native" Subject in International/Post-Colonial Feminist Legal Politics', 15 *Harvard Human Rights Journal* (2002) 1. See also Mahmood, 'Feminist Theory, Embodiment, and the Docile Agent: Some Reflections on the Egyptian Islamic Revival', 16:2 *Cultural Anthropology* (2001) 202.

[25] *Infra*, at p. 229.

this lifestyle therefore takes on increasing importance. Salih proceeds from the social and economic dimensions of the everyday more than the cultural dimension that occupies centre stage in prominent debates about gender and cultural relativism or multiculturalism.[26] She similarly shows that the women she interviewed construct a home spanning Italy and Morocco not only through what we might romantically code as 'cultural' objects and practices, but through such consumer routines as shopping in Italy for home appliances, bedding, nappies, and other goods to take with them to Morocco when they return each summer. In a final difference from much of the culture-oriented literature, Salih relates migrant women to Italian women within a socio-economic frame. Gender and multiculturalism debates are concerned with the inequality of women within minority cultures, while the inequality of minority women within the larger society is examined as discrimination on the basis of race, ethnicity, or origin alone, or its intersection with gender-based discrimination. In contrast, Salih positions migrant women so that their status is neither separated out from that of Italian women by multiculturalism's frame of culture,[27] nor grouped with that of Italian women in the larger society as against all men: she makes the point that the ability of Italian women to participate in the labour market has relied on the assumption of their traditional care-related family roles by migrant women.[28]

By touching on the interaction of Italian and Moroccan law, Salih also adds to the theme of citizenship introduced by Baer and the theme of the domestic application of international gender norms treated by Rubio-Marín and Morgan. For Moroccan spouses in Italy, Italian private international law refers questions of personal status to the laws of Morocco unless the applicable Moroccan law is judged to be a threat to public order, or a violation of human rights as defined by the European Convention on Human Rights. In addition, Moroccan women marrying in Italy are mindful of the requirements of Moroccan marriage laws and customs because compliance is necessary to the legal and social realities of returning to Morocco. Thus, Italian and Moroccan law together, along with transnationalism, produce the differentiated position

[26] Compare Volpp, 'Feminism Versus Multiculturalism', 101 *Columbia Law Review* (2001) 1181, at 1204–5, 1208–10 (criticizing the excessive focus on minority and Third World sex-subordinating cultural practices to the exclusion of other social and economic issues affecting women).

[27] While there is an important literature that seeks to show that 'culture' is not the exclusive habitat of minority or Third World women, such work aims more to establish women in their respective cultural frames as comparable. See e.g. Abu-Odeh, 'Comparatively Speaking: The "Honor" of the "East" and the "Passion" of the "West"', *Utah Law Review* (1997) 287; U. Narayan, *Dislocating Cultures: Identities, Traditions, and Third World Feminism* (1997), at 81–117.

[28] Compare S. H. Razack, *Looking White People in the Eye: Gender, Race, and Culture in Courtrooms and Classrooms* (1998), at 8–14 (arguing for an analysis of interlocking systems of oppression and using the example of professional women and domestic workers).

of the Moroccan woman within Italian society. This result also highlights the relevance of the impact of international gender norms on a state's private international law.

***

Although the field of women's international human rights law depends in every aspect on some combination of ideas about feminism, rights, and international society, these ideas and the relationships between them have received more sustained analysis outside than inside the field. By bringing a variety of vantage points and methodologies from other disciplines and areas of law to bear on gender and human rights, this collection seeks to draw attention to the theoretical and practical importance of revisiting the basic concepts, how they work, and how they interact.

2

Feminist Legal Theory and the Rights of Women

NICOLA LACEY*

In this chapter, I shall consider the relationship between feminist analyses of law and contemporary campaigns seeking to use codes of human rights as vehicles to secure justice, autonomy, or equality for women. I shall begin by sketching out the varieties of methods developed by and issues taken up within feminist legal theory. I shall then move on to consider theories of legal and political rights, and feminist critiques of the ways in which rights as often articulated—both conceptually and substantively—fail satisfactorily to accommodate the dynamics of gender. Lastly, I shall consider models developed within both feminist and critical race theory aimed at reconstructing rights in a more satisfactory way, examining in particular how far critiques developed primarily in relation to conceptualizations and institutionalizations of rights at the national level might be brought to bear on the debate about human rights at the international level.

1. FEMINIST LEGAL THEORY

A. The History of Feminist Thought about Law

Reading many contemporary feminist texts on law, one could be forgiven for thinking that legal feminism is the creation of the late twentieth century. This, however, would be a mistake, for feminist thought about law stretches back for many centuries. In the modern era, it includes the arguments for women's rights and equal legal and political status resoundingly articulated by Mary

* I should like to thank Emily Jackson for discussion of and comments on the first part of this chapter; Karen Knop for her astute comments on an earlier draft; and Radu Popa for his generous assistance in gathering research materials.

Wollstonecraft in the eighteenth century[1] and, of course, the suffragists of the nineteenth and early twentieth centuries. Though it is true that liberal and Enlightenment thinking has been associated with an intensification of feminist analysis, there is a strong case for thinking of the feminist tradition as distinctive and important in its own right. On the other hand, a useful way of thinking about feminist critique of modern law is undoubtedly its status as an immanent critique of liberalism: as part of the conscience of a liberal order which has been slow to deliver the universalism which it promised.[2]

It cannot be doubted, of course, that the second wave women's movement of the late 1960s and 1970s gave a fresh impetus to feminist thought, and in particular stimulated the gradual entry of feminist ideas into the academy. The most receptive disciplines, originally, were sociology and literary studies; however, the capacity of feminist analysis to cross the boundaries of established disciplines led relatively quickly to the establishment of specific programmes and even departments of women's or gender studies—a disciplinary innovation which was arguably bought at the cost of keeping feminist issues relatively marginalized in the academy. Nonetheless, the intellectual work done in this era of the women's movement not only affected popular consciousness and culture, but put on the intellectual agenda a range of issues formerly ignored: sexual violence; the gendered division of labour; questions of pay equity; and sex discrimination, to name only the most obvious.

These developments were, however, rather slow to reach legal scholarship and education. On the face of it, this is surprising: many of the political and analytic issues raised by the women's movement had, after all, centrally to do with women's legal and civic status. The earliest feminist legal scholarship pointed out and deplored the absence of women and women's issues from the agenda of legal study; questions such as domestic and sexual violence began to find their way into family and criminal law courses and texts; women's distinctive position in the economy began to be acknowledged in labour law and social welfare law courses; and sex discrimination law—already an important part of civil rights law in many countries—found a curiously tentative position in legal education, hovering somewhere between labour law and civil rights. This initial move to include in the curriculum issues where women or gender questions were particularly visible soon led on to more searching work which identified gender issues in a far wider range of legal arrangements, with property laws, medical law, and pensions law becoming a focus for analysis of 'indirect discrimination', broadly understood as the existence of arrangements which, though facially neutral, in fact serve to exclude or disadvantage a disproportionate number of women (or indeed men).[3] And this in turn led

---

[1] M. Wollstonecraft, *A Vindication of the Rights of Woman* (first pub. 1792; 1988).
[2] M. Thornton, *The Liberal Promise* (1990).
[3] See e.g. S. Atkins and B. Hoggett, *Women and the Law* (1984).

to a more radical set of theoretical arguments, with the feminists of the Oslo school, led by the late Tove Stang Dahl, setting up a department of women's law and reorganizing the very conceptualization of subjects around women's lives—birth law, money law, housewives' law.[4]

Central to these early feminist approaches was a rather sharp distinction between sex and gender, with sex understood as a bodily or biological category, and gender as the socially constructed meaning of sex. Though this distinction, as we shall see, soon came under intense critical scrutiny, it had an important (and controversial) effect in shifting the political and intellectual focus towards an exploration of the role of law in constituting social meanings of gender. For while 'women and law' work tended to leave both categories intact, and appeared to assume that a particular 'women's' perspective could be identified, the 'law and gender' approach presented the framework of sex/gender divisions as a general category for critical legal analysis, and opened up the possibility that law's contribution to the sexing or gendering of its subjects might interact with other social forces, hence constituting multiple female subject positions.[5] It assumed both a powerful, dynamic role for law in the constitution of gender, and, hence, a wide-ranging and potentially radical law reform agenda.[6] Furthermore, it opened up the possibility of incorporating sexual orientation in the critical analysis of law's constitution of gender, and of analysing the gendering of men, hence promising finally to explode the myth of sex/gender as exclusively a 'woman problem'.

The move from 'women and law' to 'law and gender' was not, however, without its critics. A pervasive objection was that the shift threatened to make women, and issues of particular concern to women—the 'woman-centred-ness of feminism'[7]—disappear again just as they had seemed to be gaining a foothold. Furthermore, there was some concern about whether the analytic frame of gender analysis would submerge or displace feminism's traditionally political and ethical concerns in favour of a scientistic approach. And finally, the question had to be asked whether the shift to gender could really make the problem of sex disappear: granted that gender roles are socially constructed (which is not to say easy to change), why had they happened to be ascribed to men and to women in the way they had?

These concerns about the move to 'law and gender' prompted what can be identified as a third phase in the development of feminist legal scholarship, which might be called the move to 'feminist legal theory'. In this phase, the concern has been to reprioritize the political commitments of feminist

---

[4] T. S. Dahl, *Women's Law* (1986).

[5] See K. O'Donovan, *Sexual Divisions in Law* (1985).

[6] See D. L. Rhode, *Justice and Gender* (1989); R. Graycar and J. Morgan, *The Hidden Gender of Law* (1990); K. Bartlett and R. Kennedy (eds), *Feminist Legal Theory* (1990).

[7] Conaghan, 'Reassessing the Feminist Theoretical Project in Law', 27 *Journal of Law and Society* (2000) 351.

scholarship, emphasizing the combination of analytic and normative/ethical concerns on which feminist work is founded, while holding to a close engagement with particular legal issues and institutions.[8] Within this framework, feminist legal theory has come of age, and has interacted fruitfully with other important theoretical and political-academic movements such as critical race theory, post-structuralism, postmodernism, postcolonialism, and psychoanalysis. Perhaps the defining feature of this phase of intellectual development is its theoretical ambition to produce a feminist jurisprudence—a general feminist account of legal method and of the substantive development of modern legal orders. It is this project that has generated a critical analysis of not merely the substance but also the conceptual framework of legal rights.

Contemporary feminist legal theory is constructed out of a combination of *analytic and political-ethical claims*. Analytically, the claim is that sex/gender is one important social structure or axis of social differentiation, and is hence likely to characterize and influence the shape of law. Politically and ethically, feminist theory starts out from the assumption that the ways in which sex/gender has shaped the world, including through law, have been unjust. In other words, sex/gender consists not just in differentiation but in domination, oppression, or discrimination. Legal sex differentiation, in short, on the whole disadvantages women. This political stance is often combined with an incipient utopianism in legal feminism: its social constructionist methodology, which seeks to identify the historical bases of discrimination in social decision-making and action rather than in biology, implies a contingency which opens up radical possibilities for political and social change. This is so notwithstanding the fact that what has been socially constructed as 'real'—sex-role expectations for example—is sometimes harder to change than biological or 'natural' features such as the possession of certain sexed physical characteristics.

Another important feature of feminist legal theory has to do with its *methodology*. We often think of legal theories as dividing roughly into the internal and the external—theoretical approaches which seek to rationalize and explicate the nature of law and legal method from the point of view of legal reasoning or legal practice itself, contrasting with theoretical approaches which self-consciously stand outside legal practices, subjecting them to an analysis from the point of view of a particular social scientific method or from distinctive normative points of view. We can see, however, that a large section of feminist theory in fact occupies a third perspective, which might be called interpretive. In other words, feminist legal theories do not merely seek to rationalize legal practices; nor, conversely, do they typically engage in entirely external critique and prescription. Rather, they aspire to produce a critical

---

[8] See e.g. N. Naffine and R. Owens (eds), *Sexing the Subject of Law* (1997); A. Bottomley (ed.), *Feminist Perspectives on the Foundational Subjects of Law* (1996).

interpretation of legal practices: an account which at once takes seriously the legal point of view yet which subjects that point of view to critical scrutiny on the basis of both its own professed values and a range of other ethical and political commitments. For this reason among others (notably the political antecedents of the social movements which generated feminist scholarship) feminist legal scholarship is characterized by a particularly intimate linkage between theory and practice: both with a rejection of any strong division between the two, which sometimes in fact implies a certain scepticism about theory; and with an impulse to have effects beyond the academy. Hence feminist theory is firmly grounded in particular legal issues.

B. Varieties of Feminist Legal Theory

So far, I have been speaking as if feminist legal theory constituted a relatively unitary genre. This is at one level both a necessary and a useful device: we need to generalize among feminist theories if we are going to engage in the project of characterizing the genre. However, this convenient technique of generalization should not mislead us about the true variety of legal feminisms. It is therefore important to be clear about identifying the main axes of differentiation between feminist legal theories. In this section, I shall distinguish four main theoretical points of distinction between feminist theorists—each of them of relevance to the use of rights as a political strategy—before going on to identify a number of distinctive genres of feminist scholarship.

A first—striking though insufficiently analysed—difference between feminist writers on law has to do with a mixture of *methodology and written style*. For example, Catharine MacKinnon's written style is rhetorical and polemical: her arguments are advanced by striking elisions and rhetorical tropes which are interspersed with more detailed analysis of particular legal institutions.[9] In Patricia Williams, we also find a genre of rhetoric, but realized through narratives which deliver an analytic or political point obliquely, indirectly.[10] Both of these styles contrast sharply with, for example, the more classically academic style of Ngaire Naffine, whose writing deploys the techniques of analytical legal scholarship and political theory.[11] Moving on, Luce Irigaray writes in a seamlessly metaphorical style, weaving social critique with utopian visions and elliptical, poetic meditations,[12] while Drucilla Cornell moves between each of the techniques of the other four.[13]

---

[9] See especially C. A. MacKinnon, *Feminism Unmodified* (1987).
[10] P. J. Williams, *The Alchemy of Race and Rights* (1991).
[11] N. Naffine, *Law and the Sexes* (1990).
[12] See especially L. Irigaray, *J'aime à toi* (1992).
[13] See e.g. D. Cornell, *Beyond Accommodation* (1991).

These differences are not just a matter of style. The resort to polemical or self-consciously literary forms of expression also reflects the idea that the very conceptual framework of legal scholarship makes it impossible to say certain kinds of things: that the way in which particular intellectual disciplines and discourses have developed makes it impossible to conceptualize certain types of harm or wrong, or to reveal certain kinds of interest or subject position. To take a well-known example, the concept of harassment was developed (by MacKinnon)[14] to identify a form of abuse of power which fell between a number of existing social and legal concepts such as rape, assault, and sex discrimination.

A second important axis of differentiation among feminist legal theories has to do with their *underlying theories of sexual difference.* In MacKinnon's work, for example, we find a structural, material theory of women's oppression analogous to the theory of class difference to be found in Marxism. As MacKinnon herself puts it, sex is to feminism what work is to Marxism—that which is most one's own and yet most taken away.[15] This theory has a unitary view of sex difference: since the origins and maintenance of sex difference lie in domination grounded in the abuse of sexual power and the exercise of sexual violence. This in turn implies that the kinds of issues which feminist legal theory should focus on are rather distinctive: pornography, sexual violence, abortion, sexual harassment. This contrasts with the more pluralistic approach of, for example, Carol Smart, who emphasizes not only these issues but also the economic position of women, the construction of women and femininity in legal discourse, and the effect of legal arrangements on family structure.[16] To take a different example again, Cornell's approach is more eclectic than MacKinnon's in terms of subject matter, but is unified within a psychoanalytic account of the acquisition of identity which is structurally gendered and which has consequences for the power of women's speech and the status of women as legal and political subjects.[17] A different position would be that of some radical or cultural feminists who see sexual difference as rooted in women's distinctive bodily experiences and relationships which generate a particular female culture or ethic; these feminists therefore argue not for a repositioning of women but rather for a revaluation of the feminine.[18] Yet other feminists would deny the need for any theory of the causes or origins of women's oppression.

[14] C. A. MacKinnon, *The Sexual Harassment of Working Women* (1979).

[15] MacKinnon, *supra* n. 9, at 48.

[16] C. Smart, *Feminism and the Power of Law* (1989); L. Weitzman, *The Divorce Revolution* (1985).

[17] D. Cornell, *The Imaginary Domain* (1995).

[18] See e.g. S. Ruddick, *Maternal Thinking: Toward a politics of peace* (1990); West, 'The Difference in Women's Hedonic Lives', 3 *Wisconsin Women's Law Journal* (1987) 81.

A third axis of differentiation between feminist theories has to do with the degree to which they exhibit *substantive or methodological continuities with other legal and social theories*. On one view, feminist legal theory is not so much an autonomous theoretical or methodological approach but rather a genre which places distinctive substantive issues on the agenda of legal scholarship and legal theory, using analytic and critical methods shared with, for example, the sociology of law or critical or Marxist legal theory to illuminate sex/gender issues. On this view, law is seen as both a force within and a product of the social construction of reality. Feminist legal theory is conceptualized as an interpretive approach which seeks to get beyond the surface level of legal doctrine and legal discourse, and which sees traditional jurisprudence as ideological—and hence as an apologia for the status quo. Radical and cultural, and to some extent psychoanalytic feminists, however, would be more inclined to insist upon the autonomy of feminist theory at the level of method.

The final, and certainly the most obvious, axis of differentiation among feminist theories, and one which is of particular importance in considering feminist deployment of rights, is their *political orientation*. I shall therefore now move on to sketch four different political versions of feminist theory. Again, it is important to realize that these are models rather than detailed taxonomies: some writers fall between several of the classifications. The categories are nonetheless useful both in understanding the development of feminist thought and in seeing how different political orientations have led feminists to take up very different positions on the deployment of legal rights as a framework of analysis or political strategy.

C. Liberal Feminism

Liberal feminism finds its roots in the emergence of liberal political thought with the Enlightenment. Liberalism has become the dominant political expression of progressive thought in the modern age, but itself encompasses a range of doctrines. Most would agree that liberalism centres on core ideas of autonomy, of universal rights, of equal citizenship, and of democracy—but exactly what these ideas amount to has varied over the decades. Early liberals, as well as taking a more parsimonious view than their late twentieth-century counterparts of the proper role of the state in securing the conditions for human welfare,[19] were far from endorsing the principles of universal suffrage, property, and other civil and political rights which are now taken to be intrinsic to liberalism. One way of looking at the development of liberal thought is that its universalist ideals have provided the basis for an immanent critique of its own forms: the liberal promise has come later for some groups

[19] J. Rawls, *A Theory of Justice* (1971).

than for others, and for some is still far from being a reality. Liberal feminism is simply the idea that those liberal ideals of equality and rights or liberties apply to women. In this sense, it is not so much a distinctively feminist theory as liberalism applied to women. Liberal feminism has been particularly associated with the ideas of formal equality and of equality of opportunity, although contemporary liberal theories such as that of Ronald Dworkin also subscribe to stronger principles of equality, such as equality of resources or equality of concern and respect.[20]

Liberalism has often been associated with the birth of feminism. Although this is indeed a strong association, it is historically crude: some early feminists, like Mary Astell, were rather conservative in their general political views, and took a much more distinctively feminist or woman-oriented stance than is implied in the idea of liberal feminism. And even early feminists who were more sympathetic with developments such as declarations of universal human rights in the French and American Revolutions were quick to point out that women were all too often implicitly or explicitly excluded from the definition 'human' in the delineation and interpretation of those rights.[21] There have always, in short, been feminisms outside liberalism, and it is therefore important to analyse some of the arguments made by feminist critics of liberalism.

A key limitation of liberalism from a feminist point of view has been argued to be its *individualism*. Though this has become a mantra of contemporary feminist critique, it is extremely important to distinguish at least three different kinds of feminist objection to unmodified liberal individualism.

The first two objections are to the implicit individualism of the liberal legal subject. In the first place, it is argued that the liberal focus on the interests, rights, and entitlements of individuals is argued to obscure our vision of systematic patterns of exclusion and disadvantage such as those which characterize women's subordination. Differently patterned outcomes—for example, women's under-representation in various occupations and spheres of life—can be explained away as the product of autonomous individual choices and hence legitimated within a liberal world-view. In the context of rights, this bears upon a number of important issues. One is the question of whether women's interests can be fully articulated within a classic model of individual rights, or of whether rights specific to particular social groups need also to be developed, at least as an interim measure. Another is the question of how the framework of rights can provide not only a formal articulation of individual entitlements, but also accommodation of the contextual factors which shape the capacities of differently situated subjects to take up and realize their rights.

---

[20] R. M. Dworkin, 'What is Equality? Part I', 10 *Philosophy and Public Affairs* (1980) 185; R. M. Dworkin, 'What is Equality? Part II', 10 *Philosophy and Public Affairs* (1980) 283; A. Phillips, *Which Inequalities Matter?* (1999).

[21] Wollstonecraft, *supra* n. 1.

Secondly, it is argued that liberal theory tends to operate with a pre-social conception of the individual. Liberal rights and limits on governmental power are derived from an *a priori* idea of the nature of the human being which underplays the extent to which social and political institutions shape individual preferences, attitudes, and dispositions. The screen brought in by an implicit, purportedly gender-neutral image of human nature obscures the assumptions being made about women and about sexual difference which feminism wants to reveal and criticize. This gives rise to concerns about the appropriateness of universal rights, and about the capacity of such a framework to deliver justice to differently situated subjects.[22]

A third aspect of the critique of liberal individualism has to do with its conception of political value. Here it is argued that liberalism's focus on the individual has realized itself in terms of a primary concern with individual entitlements at the expense of a proper appreciation of the importance of collective and public goods. Once again, feminists have argued that these may be of particular importance to women, and that there is a need for a searching analysis of the ways in which the objects, as well as the subjects, of rights should be defined.

A second general criticism of the limits of liberalism focuses on *liberal conceptions of freedom*. Many liberal political frameworks operate with a basically negative conception of freedom: in other words, freedom is understood as consisting in being free from outside interference, particularly by the state. Hence the positive capacity to exercise freedom or rights, which may depend on goods or resources, is underplayed. This has important implications for feminist arguments, which often invoke entitlements to empowering and facilitating resources. To take an example, MacKinnon's and Andrea Dworkin's argument about the threat that pornography poses to women's civil rights depends on the idea that a centrally important question about freedom of speech is just how much this freedom is worth to different social groups: negative freedom of speech may be of little value to those whose capacity to speak or to be heard is systematically undermined by, for instance, the exercise of others' freedom to speak.[23] In other words, there is a question about the material and symbolic conditions under which rights are meaningful to those who, formally, possess them.

A third general feminist criticism of liberal theory has to do with the reliance which it places on a distinction between *public and private spheres*. Typically, liberal political thought assumes the world to be divided into public

---

[22] For a contemporary analysis which places particular emphasis on interpreting the liberal tradition in social constructionist terms and on tracing its implications for human rights, see M. C. Nussbaum, *Sex and Social Justice* (1999); D. Cornell, *At the Heart of Freedom: feminism, sex and equality* (1998).

[23] See C. A. MacKinnon, *Only Words* (1993); A. Dworkin, *Pornography: Men Possessing Women* (1981).

and private spaces and issues: governmental action, and hence liberal principles, apply primarily to the public world, while private lives and private
spheres are properly subject to the regime of individual autonomy and
negative freedom. This distinction is, of course, reflected in many codes of
human rights such as the US Bill of Rights or the European Convention on
Human Rights (ECHR), which concern themselves exclusively with state or
public actions. It is a division that has been criticized on both analytic and
historical grounds.[24] Analytically, it has been doubted whether a clear public/
private boundary can be delineated; for example, most liberals would see the
home and the family as quintessentially private spheres, but would hesitate
about the implications of the classification when confronted with questions
such as child abuse or domestic violence. Furthermore, it seems evident
that disadvantages within the allegedly private sphere—unequal divisions of
domestic labour for example—spill over into entitlements and opportunities
in the public world. Historically and empirically, it has been argued that the
received view of public and private tends to consign women's lives and
concerns to the private sphere, thus defining them as outside the scope of
political intervention, and even rendering them invisible as political issues. It
has been further argued that this explains the tardy reception of issues such as
domestic violence, marital rape, domestic work, and child abuse onto the legal
and political agenda. From a critical race theory perspective, it has further been
argued that the association of femaleness and the private is one which has
marked white women's to a far greater extent than black women's experience.[25]

Finally, though perhaps most radically of all, feminists have questioned
both the political advisability and the analytic integrity of liberalism's commitment to *gender-neutrality* in law and legal analysis. In a world in which sex/
gender is indeed a basic axis of social differentiation—albeit mediated through
other axes such as class, race, age, ethnicity, geography, and so on—can legal
subjects generally be constructed as gender-neutral? And can this alchemy be
effected by the mere palliative of gender-neutral language? In relation to
rights, this raises once again the question of whether a gender-neutral set of
universal human rights might need to be replaced or supplemented in certain
areas by special rights for women or members of other groups. In this context,
as we shall see below, the UN Convention on the Elimination of All Forms of
Discrimination against Women (CEDAW)[26] is of particular interest, subtly
positioned as it is between a universal conception of human rights and a
woman-centred political focus.

[24] For more detailed discussion, see N. Lacey, *Unspeakable Subjects* (1998), at Chapter 3;
Olsen, 'The Family and the Market', 96 *Harvard Law Review* (1983) 1497.
[25] Harris, 'Race and Essentialism in Feminist Legal Theory', 42 *Stanford Law Review* (1990)
581.
[26] Convention on the Elimination of All Forms of Discrimination against Women, New
York, 18 December 1979, in force 3 September 1981, 1249 UNTS 13.

D. Radical Feminism

Radical feminism can perhaps claim to be the most autonomous and distinctive conception of feminism, in that it is exclusively a feminist theory. Having
said that, beyond identifying actual feminists who have claimed the label, it is
more difficult to set out any unifying features of radical feminism. At the risk
of stereotyping, we could say that radical feminists see sexual difference as
having a certain priority in social life: they see sex difference as more 'radical'
or basic than, say, class difference, or racial, or ethnic difference. To radical
feminists, sex difference is structural in just the way class difference is structural to Marxists.[27] Radical feminists have tended to stay within the analytic
framework of sex rather than moving to that of gender: some radical feminists
explicitly embrace the idea of an 'essential' sex difference (anathema to most
other feminisms) and seek to explore and effect the re-evaluation of repressed
aspects of women's culture, women's values, and so on. There is also an
ecological branch of radical feminism, sometimes known as 'cultural feminism': this genre of feminism argues, for instance, that women's natural nurtur-
ing role in bearing and rearing children gives them a distinctive empathy with
others and with the natural world.[28] But many forms of radical feminism do
not embrace essentialism in this way: their assertion of the primacy of sex
difference is based on historical or psychoanalytic arguments which are, in
principle, constructionist. Institutionally, radical feminists have been inclined
to pursue separatist politics; and radical feminism has also had a strongly
utopian strand.[29]

One useful way of illustrating the differences between radical and liberal
feminism has been provided by Frances Olsen.[30] Olsen starts out by noting
the power of a number of binary divisions in Western thought: male and
female; subject and object; public and private; form and substance; mind and
body; active and passive; reason and emotion. Feminists in general have
asserted that these dichotomies are both hierarchized and sexualized: man is
associated with the first half of each pair, and that half has been valued over and
above the other. But strategic responses to this analysis differ as between
radical and liberal feminists. Radical, and particularly cultural, feminists
accept the sexualization of the divisions, but seek to reverse the valuation,

[27] For the most persuasive statement of radical feminism in a legal context, see C. A. Mac-
Kinnon, *Toward a Feminist Theory of the State* (1989); West, 'Jurisprudence and Gender', 50
University of Chicago Law Review (1988) 1.
[28] See e.g. N. Noddings, *Caring: A feminist approach to ethics and moral education* (1984);
Ruddick, *supra* n. 18.
[29] See e.g. S. Griffin, *Pornography and Silence* (1981).
[30] Olsen, 'Feminism and Critical Legal Theory', 8 *International Journal of the Sociology of
Law* (1990) 199.

arguing for the greater recognition of the emotive, the affective, the feminine in social practice.[31] Liberals, by contrast, often accept the hierarchical ordering, but seek to reverse the sexualization of the dichotomies, arguing that women are every bit as capable of reason, as entitled to inhabit the public sphere, as capable of activity and intellectual power and objectivity, as are men. As Kate Nash has put it, there is a distinction here between the project of revaluing the feminine on the one hand and de-gendering strategies on the other.[32]

Radical feminism has been an influential and intellectually powerful strand in contemporary feminist legal scholarship. Like liberal feminism, however, it has been subject to a persuasive critique. The main criticisms of radical feminism focus on four features. First, critics have noted the dangers of its actual or apparent *essentialism*: if women's position is, or is seen to be, related to 'natural' sex difference, may this not undercut the main basis for feminist political advance? Even if not in principle essentialist, does radical feminism fall into the trap of replaying images and assumptions which are very hard to distinguish from those of a patriarchal social order? A good example here might be the position on women's sexuate rights defended by Irigaray and discussed later in this chapter.[33]

A second point of criticism has been the relatively *limited substantive focus* of radical feminism. Most radical feminist lawyers focus on a very particular set of issues—i.e. those around sex, sexuality, reproduction, ecology. Typically, and as a direct result of their analysis of the roots of women's oppression, they show less interest in economic and political inequities which, one might argue, the law plays a central role in constituting and sustaining.

A third object of critique has been the status of radical feminism as so-called *grand theory*. More eclectic or pluralistic feminists have objected to radical feminism's monolithic theory of 'patriarchy', which is insensitive to comparative social differences around axes such as ethnicity and class and again courts essentialism. Lastly, hence, it has been argued that radical feminism's typically separatist stance risks *blunting the potential for possible political alliances* and continuities around issues of class, ethnicity, and so on.

---

[31]   Once again, this is a typology which is meant to be useful for analytic purposes rather than an accurate description of all contributors to the field. MacKinnon, for example, though espousing a version of radical feminism, is sceptical about the argument that 'the feminine' should be revalued, on the basis that 'feminine values' are themselves the product of a history of oppression. As she graphically puts it, the 'woman's voice' is spoken 'with a foot on its neck'. MacKinnon, *supra* n. 9.

[32]   Nash, 'Human rights for women: an argument for "deconstructive equality"', 31 *Economy and Society* (2002) 414.

[33]   L. Irigaray, *Thinking the Difference*, trans. K. Montin (1994).

E. Marxist and Socialist Feminism: Socio-Economic Structure and Women's Oppression

Like liberal feminism, we might see Marxist and socialist feminism as not so much a distinctively feminist position but rather an immanent critique of Marxism which subtly transforms Marxist arguments by pointing out the implications of incorporating women specifically into the analysis. The relevant aspect of the traditional Marxist position is that the fundamental social division as based on class, and sex or other (for example, racial) subordination is epiphenomenal—in other words, is a side effect of class difference. Feminists have pointed out that this analysis is incapable of accommodating the sense in which all men—even poor men—benefit from the exploitation of women. Nonetheless, Marxist and other materialist feminists have sought to extend and modify the Marxist position by constructing an imaginative argument which twins exploitation in the system of economic production with exploitation in the process of reproduction. According to this 'dual systems' theory, women's reproductive labour is exploited by men in just the same way as the working class's productive labour is exploited by capitalists.[34]

Marxist feminism suffers some important weaknesses, however, particularly as applied to law. Of these, perhaps the most important is its class reductionism: can all exploitation of women be accommodated within the model of reproductive exploitation? There is a real problem here, because women experience disadvantage and discrimination—for example in the labour market—which is neither exclusively based on assumptions about their reproductive lives nor a form of class exploitation. Furthermore, Marxist feminism suffers from all the general problems of Marxist theory: a unitary and monolithic analysis of oppression as based on economic relations; obscurity in its analysis of the actual processes whereby the ownership of the means of production realizes itself in particular relations of production and in distinctive ideological, superstructural formations such as law; and, particularly at the start of the twenty-first century, the implausibility of the Marxist theory of history.

F. Difference Feminism and the Critique of Liberal Legal Feminism

These criticisms of the main genres of political feminism have led to the gradual emergence of a somewhat different set of models for feminist legal theory which can conveniently be grouped together under the label 'difference feminism'.[35] These 'difference feminisms' have in common a certain

---

[34] M. Barrett, *Women's Oppression Today* (1991).
[35] For a fuller analysis of 'difference feminisms', see Lacey, *supra* n. 24, at Chapter 7.

engagement both with theoretical preoccupations of *postmodernism* and the sociological category of *postmodernity*. Like postmodernism, they typically engage in a philosophical rejection of 'meta-theories' and 'grand narratives'; while their concern with multiple identities and subjectivities is also informed by a sociological analysis of a stage in the development of late modern societies, in which social and geographical mobility, the fragmentation of values, identities and traditional institutions, and consequent feelings of anxiety and insecurity have become key objects of social analysis.[36]

2. BEYOND GENDER NEUTRALITY?

Difference feminism moves beyond standard rule of law values such as formal equality. Like radical feminism, it criticizes liberal feminism as being limited by its essentially comparative standard, the underlying strategy of which is said to be assimilation of women to a standard set by and for men: wherever a woman can make herself look sufficiently like a man, can conform her life to male patterns or standards, she will be treated equally. Within this liberal model, it is argued, it is impossible to recognize or accommodate differences between the lives of women and men without reinforcing views of woman which should be challenged. Liberalism accords no space for the revaluation of the feminine envisaged by radical feminism, and courts the constant danger of subtler disadvantage and discrimination being hidden behind the veil of neutrality.[37]

Difference feminism is therefore associated with a shift of emphasis towards a questioning of the very idea of gender neutrality, both as ideal and as possible. However, in seeking also to avoid the difficulties of radical feminism, it has shifted towards a focus not only on law's reflection of 'pre-legal' sexual difference, but also on law's dynamic role in constructing, under-pinning, and maintaining sexual difference and sexed identities. Evidently, both this scepticism about gender neutrality and the emphasis on law's identity-constituting role raise important questions about the espousal of rights frameworks at both national and international levels. Difference femi-nism is a more complex and a more radical legal critique than was liberal feminism, and it is now the dominant approach within feminist legal theory. At a schematic level, difference feminism may be characterized in terms of the following themes.

---

[36] See e.g. Z. Bauman, *Postmodern Ethics* (1993); Featherstone, 'In Pursuit of the Post-Modern', 5 *Theory, Culture and Society* (1988) 195; J.-F. Lyotard, *The Post-modern Condition: A Report on Knowledge* (1984).

[37] See e.g. Cornell, *supra* n. 13. For further discussion, see Lacey, *supra* n. 24, at Chapter 7.

A. The Substance of Law as Reflecting, Implicitly, a Male Point of View

The theoretical move here is beyond explicit exclusion to implicit partiality: digging under the surface of the law to look at its implicit assumptions. The law of rape is a rare case where law contains sexual differentiation on its surface; yet even though rape law might be taken as specifically concerned with women's interests, the way it works in practice reflects both the defendant's interpretation of the sexual encounter (a view encapsulated in the recognition of a man's subjective mistake about the other person's consent as a defence) and a masculine view of the nature of female sexuality (for example in rules of evidence which construe the sexual history of the victim as potentially relevant to her credibility in alleging rape, and in the longevity of the marital rape exemption in many jurisdictions).[38] Other examples would include facially neutral immediacy of response requirements in criminal defences such as self-defence and provocation, which may serve to exclude the defences from people in vulnerable positions, of whom, in turn, women may make up a disproportionate number.[39] Once again, the issue here can be identified in terms of a critique of neutrality: in moving to a model based on the reasonable person rather than the reasonable man, have women's perspectives and interests really entered the law, or have they rather been yet more effectively buried from view?

B. The Constitution of the Legal Subject as Male

An important statement of this argument is to be found in the work of Naffine.[40] Naffine's is a complex argument which, like Olsen's, sets out from the power of binary, sexualized, and hierarchical oppositions such as male/ female, subject/object, and public/private in Western thought. To the extent that law's construction of its subjects is in terms of the characteristics of the first members of the pairs—in other words, as a rational individual, in control of its cognitive capacities, inhabiting the public sphere—the legal subject is implicitly a man, and women will find themselves subtly excluded, silenced.

We could draw an analogy here with the Enlightenment move in political and legal thinking from a world based on status to one based on contract. Naffine argues that the legal subject is quintessentially a contracting subject; a

---

[38] See Naffine, 'Possession: Erotic Love in the Law of Rape', 57 *Modern Law Review* (1994) 10; N. Naffine, *Feminism and Criminology* (1997). The honest mistake 'defence' is abolished in England and Wales by the Sexual Offences Act 2003.

[39] See e.g. O'Donovan, 'Defences for Battered Women who Kill', 18 *Journal of Law and Society* (1991) 219; McColgan, 'In Defence of Battered Women who Kill', 13 *Oxford Journal of Legal Studies* (1983) 508.

[40] Naffine, *supra* n. 11.

rational individual abstracted from his affective ties and emotional and bodily dependencies. Yet this subject is a fiction, for whilst these characteristics are culturally marked as masculine, they do not express the whole of men's lives: men have bodies, ties, emotions, private lives. These can be hidden, however, from legal view because they are being sustained by women in the private sphere. Hence Naffine speaks of woman as sustaining the 'impossible paradox of the man of law'.

C. Legal Methods as Masculine

Building on this argument about the legal subject, difference feminists have developed the idea that the very methods of law—its conceptual framework and reasoning processes—are gendered, and are gendered to the disadvantage of women. Prime targets here are the competitive system of arriving at/ constructing truth in adversarial legal orders in which legal processes are essentially a competition between individuals assumed to be equal, and abstracted from their social contexts and sexed bodies. There is an important link here with the influential work of psychologist Carol Gilligan,[41] which identified two distinctive methods of analysis in moral reasoning. The first, which Gilligan calls an 'ethic of rights', is remarkably law-like: it consists in the ranking of priorities; the formation of rules; and the application of rules to facts. By contrast, an 'ethic of care' analyses moral problems contextually, seeking negotiated or consensual solutions through an exploration of the social relationships involved. Gilligan's controversial claim was that these two ethics are gendered, in the sense that girls and women tend to adopt the ethic of care, while boys and men more often reason in terms of rights. To the extent that this can be shown, and that legal reasoning is rights-based, this has been argued to offer a framework for understanding the 'maleness' of legal methods (and, by implication, of rights-based reasoning).[42]

D. The Images of Women and Men, Femininity and Masculinity in Legal Discourse

Difference feminists have also been concerned to emphasize the dynamic role of law in the positive construction of sexual difference and of sexed social identities. When we look not just at legal doctrine but also at legal discourse— the structured language in which doctrine is formulated and discussed by

---

[41] C. Gilligan, *In a Different Voice* (1982).

[42] On the legal implications of Gilligan's argument, see M. J. Frug, *Postmodern Legal Feminism* (1992), at Chapter 3.

judges and other lawyers—we find powerful images of 'normal' women and men, of female and male sexuality, of femininity and masculinity. A spectacular example is the English law of incest, which explicitly construed the masculine sexual role as active and the feminine as passive.[43] The focus here is the subtle and dynamic role which law has not just in regulating/empowering women and men who arrive at the legal forum, but also in constituting us as sexed subjects.[44] In this context, new questions arise about feminist deployments of rights: does a rights framework help to convey a positive, empowered image of female legal subjecthood, or may it perpetuate a stereotype of women as victims or as in need of special protection?[45] And under what conditions might each of these discursive effects be expected to arise?

E. The Conceptual Framework of Legal Reasoning

Difference feminists have supplemented their critique of the substance of legal rules with a further analysis of the conceptual building blocks out of which those rules are, often implicitly, constructed (for example, in terms of the binaries already discussed). For difference feminism, the theoretical question is that of what moral and political assumptions are concealed by broad structures of legal regulation or non-regulation in particular areas. Key examples would include the implicit role of the public/private distinction in underpinning the difficulty of getting domestic violence or sexual harassment taken seriously as legal issues. Once again, we can see a link with the negative conception of freedom. The basis of the public/private distinction is a liberal argument about the threat which state power poses to individual freedom, understood negatively. Yet, as MacKinnon has argued in relation to pornography, the US First Amendment's blanket protection of speech leaves no space to ask whose speech or what kind of speech is effectively protected, nor to raise questions about whether certain positive conditions are needed to guarantee access to speech for certain groups on certain issues. MacKinnon's argument is that pornography silences and changes the meaning of women's speech by trapping them within a degraded and objectified image; but that because of its commitment to a predominantly negative conception of what constitutes freedom, this inequality cannot be comprehended by US law.[46] Once again,

---

[43] Sexual Offences Act 1956, 4 & 5 Eliz. 2, c. 69. The law is changed by the Sexual Offences Act 2003.
[44] See e.g. C. Smart, *Law, Crime and Sexuality* (1995). Much of the recent feminist legal theory in this genre is informed by the work of Judith Butler: see e.g. *Bodies that Matter* (1993); *Excitable Speech* (1997).
[45] See Kapur, 'Post-Colonial Economies of Desire', 78 *Denver University Law Review* (2001) 855.
[46] See e.g. MacKinnon, *supra* n. 23.

the effectiveness of rights—the positive as opposed to negative freedoms which rights can deliver—arises as a question of specific concern to feminists.

F. The Enforcement of Laws

Like other feminists, difference feminists insist that the key focus of legal scholarship should be not only legal doctrine and discourse, but also how law is interpreted and enforced by both legal and non-legal actors. Examples such as domestic violence, prosecution policy on marital rape, and non-enforcement of laws against racial hatred are deployed to illustrate the political disadvantages and intellectual indefensibility of a purely doctrinal approach. This issue of enforcement reminds us that instituting rights in legal doctrine, even if advantageous from a feminist point of view, is not necessarily to secure their implementation, and may even lead to a counter-productive 'centre-ing' of law in our political strategies.[47] This is of particular importance in the context of international conventions establishing human rights independently of any strong enforcement framework.

3. THEORIES OF RIGHTS

I shall now move on to consider the theoretical and historical basis of human rights, as a prelude to drawing out the implications of feminist legal theory for the analytic deployment of rights frameworks and for human rights-based strategies of legal and political reform.

What are rights? What does it mean to accord rights to human beings? What consequences does the according of rights have for rights-holders and others? What rights do or should human beings have? Do children, or insentient people, or foetuses, or animals, or plants, or the planet, or future generations have rights? These sorts of debates flourish[48] at a number of different levels—conceptual, legal, political, ethical—and these levels turn out to be very difficult to keep apart. For example, what position we take on the question of what rights 'are', conceptually, will inevitably affect who has rights and what kinds of rights they can have. Nonetheless, for expositional convenience, I shall try to separate out the different layers of the debate.

In this section, I am going to set out some theories of legal rights, starting with the most analytic/conceptual, and moving on to the theories which ask a broader set of questions about what it means to ascribe legal rights, and which

---

[47] See Smart, *supra* n. 16, at Chapter 8.

[48] Many of the most influential contributions are represented in J. Waldron (ed.), *Theories of Rights* (1984).

therefore blur the boundary between analytic/conceptual and moral/political arguments. I shall canvass the variety of rights usages in legal discourse, and then look at the various ways of theorizing that usage. I shall conclude by drawing out the differences between these theories in terms of their answers to three questions: first, what is the typical subject of legal rights—i.e. who can be legal rights-holders; secondly, what are the typical objects of legal rights—i.e. what do rights express or protect, what shape do they take; thirdly, what are the consequences of having legal rights, what—instrumentally and symbolically—is their force? Lastly, I shall move on to look at the place of rights in moral and political thought.

A. Theories of Legal Rights

It is worth beginning by reflecting on the vast range of appeals to rights in legal discourse: in the law of torts, in property law, in family law, in administrative law, as well as in constitutional law and international law. There have been four influential attempts to construct a coherent theory of what is implied by these contrasting deployments of the framework of rights.

At the most analytic level, we have Wesley Newcomb Hohfeld's famous classification of appeals to rights in terms of four distinct relations: claim rights, which are correlative to duties; privileges or liberties, which are correlative to 'no rights'; powers, which are correlative to liabilities; and immunities, which are correlative to disabilities.[49] The reciprocal rights and duties arising under a contract constitute a key example of Hohfeld's first pair: each contracting party has claim *rights* correlating to the *duties* of performance imposed on the other party. The 'right' of free speech represents, on the other hand, the liberty/no right correlation: in most legal systems, my *liberty* of expression correlates not to a duty on others to let me speak (let alone to provide resources such as education or access to the media which would facilitate my speech) but rather to others' *'no right'* that I not exercise my privilege of speech. The *powers* accorded to, thirdly, a trustee under a trust correlate to others' *liability* to having their legal position altered by the trustee's exercise of her power. And lastly, a person's *immunity* from prosecution under, for example, an amnesty correlates with a *disability* on the part of prosecuting authorities. These pairs also, according to Hohfeld, generate relations of opposition: I cannot have both a right and a no right, a liberty and a duty, a power and a disability, an immunity and a liability in relation to the same object. In Hohfeld's view, all legal relations could be accurately described in terms of some combination of these elements: he regarded the failure to distinguish between these different

---

[49] W. N. Hohfeld, *Fundamental Legal Conceptions as Applied in Judicial Reasoning*, ed. W. Wheeler Cook (1919).

senses of 'right' as one of the most common sources of confusion in legal
argument. While Hohfeld's argument operates at a highly analytic level, it is
clear that the scheme is essentially based on interpersonal rights rather than
rights *in rem*, and that the core notion of a claim right depends on a strong
conception of human agency.

More closely tied to a particular view of the subject, if not the object, of
rights is the 'will' or 'choice' theory of rights defended by H. L. A. Hart.[50]
Hart's argument proceeds from the liberal idea that the essence of a right is
choice or agency: a right is a specially protected choice to interfere with
another's freedom. This entails that private law rights, rather than inalienable
constitutional or human rights, are the paradigm of legal rights. Hart distinguishes, however, between general and special rights. Special rights, such as
contractual rights or a specific right to compensation for negligently caused
loss, flow from agreements such as promises, consent, a mutuality of political
restrictions, relationships. General rights, including 'human rights' such as
speech or non-discrimination, by contrast, proceed straightforwardly from the
overall value of human freedom. The structure of Hart's approach, not unlike
that of Hohfeld's claim rights, locates the conceptual specificity of rights in
their enforcement mechanism: rights create, in a sense, a sphere of mini-
sovereignty within which the rights-holder can exercise and impose his or her
choice upon certain others. At a normative level, Hart locates the basis of
rights in an equal right of freedom: if there are any rights, this is what they are
based upon, for if there is no right to freedom, there would be no need for
rights.[51] The model of the rights-holder as a freely choosing subject doubtless
connects with an important strand in the liberal tradition. As a theory of rights
it is subject, however, to the objection that it marginalizes what many would
see as the central case of rights—inalienable human rights. For their very
inalienability removes them from the sphere of sovereign choice which constitutes the essence of Hart's conception of a right. Another concern for some
commentators is the implication of the will theory that rights-holders must be
fully capable, choosing agents, and hence that children, animals, and those
with certain kinds of mental incapacities are by definition excluded.

A third image of rights is the interest conception, developed by Neil
MacCormick, building on Jeremy Bentham's conception of rights as specially
protected benefits. On this view, rights exist wherever someone benefits or
stands to benefit from the performance of a duty; or where an interest is
regarded as sufficiently important to justify the imposition of a duty.[52] For

---

[50] Hart, 'Legal Rights', in H. L. A. Hart (ed.), *Essays on Bentham* (1982) 162.

[51] Hart, 'Are there any natural rights?', 64 *Philosophical Review* (1955) 175.

[52] MacCormick, 'Rights in Legislation', in P. Hacker and J. Raz (eds), *Law, Morality and Society* (1977) 189. For another account of rights in terms of interests, see J. Raz, *The Morality of Freedom* (1986), at 165 ff; Raz, 'Legal Rights', in J. Raz (ed.), *Ethics in the Public Domain* (1994) 254.

example, the right of political participation or of free expression would be seen as based on the recognition that political participation or speech are such important human activities that they merit special institutional protection in the form of a periphery of correlative and non-correlative duties. On this more inclusive view, children and the mentally incapacitated can indeed be rights-holders. Furthermore, since rights can encompass many different kinds of interests, the interest conception sits easily with not only private law rights but also human rights: the interest theory can simply accommodate choice as one form of interest which—as in the case of contract—may in some circumstances be regarded as sufficiently important to merit special protection by means of a right. It is sometimes objected, however, that this conception downgrades rights by seeing them as mere reflections of duties. It has also been argued that, in its Benthamite form, the interest theory collapses rights into a general feature of utility: rights are simply 'rules of thumb' about what is most likely to maximize overall human happiness or preference satisfaction. And while its expansive conception of the subjects and objects of rights is an advantage, the interest theory does not give us a very clear view of the distinctive institutional consequences of having a legal right: on whom the rights-generating duties should be imposed, and whether and in what way they must be enforceable.

This institutional feature of rights is central to a fourth view of rights, defended by Ronald Dworkin, which builds on the interest theory and which is sometimes known as 'rights as trumps'. Dworkin[53] fixes on a familiar feature of rights talk in legal contexts. This is that when claims of right are made, they are thought of as having a special force: hence the idea of rights as 'trumping' background considerations. Dworkin's analysis of rights ties in with his analysis of legal reasoning. On his view, law does not just consist of rules which are applied deductively to cases, leaving ambiguities and gaps which have to be filled by judicial discretion. Rather, judges are also bound by legal principles. Principles are standards which have the characteristic of 'weight' or 'force': they express individual rights, which run through legal history, generating arguments which can apply and have weight even when they are not absolutely conclusive. What is distinctive about these right-based arguments of principle is that they are always capable of 'trumping' considerations of policy or general utility. Dworkin sees the background nature of political justification as utilitarian—as based on the maximization of preference satisfaction. But, he argues, utilitarianism is itself grounded in the deeper value of equality: the utilitarian maxim 'all should count for one and none for more than one' is an expression of the equal concern and respect due to all human beings. And since the unmitigated pursuit of utility might result in great

---

[53] R. M. Dworkin, *Taking Rights Seriously* (1977); see also R. M. Dworkin, *A Matter of Principle* (1981).

inequality—not least because resources would always be diverted to those who value them most—the utilitarian calculus needs to be refined or modified by respect for individual rights. Hence rights are not anti-democratic but rather the completion of the democratic ideal. In legal terms, arguing that judges must decide on the basis of rights or principles rather than of policy or utility entails that judges stay within their proper democratic role. They are not 'making law', according to undemocratic decisions about policy; rather, they are respecting the 'gravitational force' of arguments of rights. Rights, in other words, instantiate a stream of principle in legal systems which respect equality—hence underpinning Dworkin's ideal of 'law as integrity'.[54] It follows that, for Dworkin, conceptions of legal rights are irreducibly connected to wider precepts of political morality.

We are now in a position to summarize the key differences between these theories of legal rights in terms of the questions posed at the start of this section. In terms of the nature of the *subjects of legal rights* assumed by these theories, both the first two and, to a lesser extent, the fourth theories operate in terms of an image of the individual, sovereign, freely choosing agent capable of asserting claims and 'trumping' the claims of others, while the third can just as easily accommodate groups, children, and even non-human entities such as planets or corporations, in so far as their interests or benefits to them are particularly valued. In terms of the *objects of rights*, the second theory focuses exclusively on choices, and, at a more abstract level, individual freedom; the fourth focuses also on claim-making and, at an abstract level, on what is necessary to ensure that persons' fundamental interest in being accorded genuinely equal concern and respect can be met; the third can accommodate both of these abstract concerns, and conceptualizes the objects of rights in terms of values, benefits, or interests. As far as the *force of rights* is concerned, the interest theory has an underdeveloped account; the choice (and Hohfeldian) theory focuses on rights of enforcement; and Dworkin's theory fixes on the potential of rights to trump background considerations of general welfare and social policy, and elaborates a view of the institutional legal framework necessary to such a conception.

B. Rights and Political Morality

It is easy to recognize that law, morality, and politics are getting more and more intertwined as we proceed through these increasingly substantive legal theories of rights. The conceptual shape of rights is inevitably bound up with our views about who should have rights and what kinds of rights they should have. But are rights given or made, fixed or fluid, discovered or constructed? It

---

[54] R. M. Dworkin, *Law's Empire* (1986).

may be obvious to lawyers that legal rights are constructs: yet it is also clear that part of their rhetorical force comes from their links with 'natural' or 'human' rights. It is important, therefore, to know something about the genesis of rights in the history of political thought.

Rights may justly be seen as one of the defining features of moral, political, and legal discourse in modernity. The view of the individual as rights-holder and as legal subject, along with the famous declarations of rights in Europe and North America in the late eighteenth and early nineteenth centuries, unleashed a powerful immanent critique of the effective delivery of the democratic promise—a critique whose power continues to be represented in national constitutions and international conventions of human rights to the present day. Particularly since 1945, we have seen the inception of a 'human rights culture' across the globe: a culture in which, even when human rights abuses are endemic, oppressive regimes attempt to bring themselves within human rights discourse.[55] Conversely, actors often seek to justify abuses by removing their objects from the ambit of human rights discourse—as in the animalization of victims of war or torture. The contemporary human rights culture relates, in complex and interesting ways, to an older tradition of natural rights. This tradition viewed rights in terms of pre-social entitlements, given by God or nature, or flowing from human reason; pre-social entitlements which must be respected by 'artificial' political society.[56] Here we touch on a continuing source of controversy in the specification and interpretation of human rights: to what degree are rights specific and relative to particular cultures, and how far, conversely, are they determined by universal, transcultural human values?

This becomes a particularly pressing issue within contemporary human rights culture, in which we see radically competing conceptions of human rights. Is the primary bearer of rights the political subject, who has a reciprocal duty to respect the rights of others—a vision issuing in the classic codes of civil and political rights of free speech, association, conscience, equal protection? Or is the bearer of rights also a cultural, economic, social subject—a richer conception of rights-subjecthood which issues in more ambitious codes of economic, cultural, and social rights in fields such as work, education, social provision, or cultural practice? And can civil and political rights be clearly distinguished from economic and cultural rights once we take on board the importance of positive as much as negative freedom, and focus on the worth of rights to differently situated subjects?

These debates about the proper scope and content of codes of rights map in an intimate way onto different views of the values underlying rights: in other

---

[55] Rorty, 'Human Rights, Rationality and Sentimentality', in S. Shute and S. Hurley (eds), *On Human Rights* (1993) 111; C. Douzinas, *The End of Human Rights* (2000).
[56] See J. M. Finnis, *Natural Law and Natural Rights* (1980).

words, onto normative moral and political theories of rights. Here a broad divide—already encountered in our discussion of legal rights—may be drawn. On the one hand, we have those such as Hart, building on John Locke, who see rights as expressing the value of *liberty* and as providing exceptional justifications for interference with other human beings whose negative liberty must generally be respected. On the other, we have those like Dworkin who see rights as expressing the value of *equality*: what rights express is the equal claim to respect and concern shared by all human beings. On this view, assertions of rights express interests which are too precious to be left to the utilitarian calculus or which are likely to be corrupted within it, either because of prevailing prejudices or simply through the operation of a majoritarian system in which the discrete interests of minorities are liable to be ignored.

Lastly, it is instructive to note the rather different views among rights theorists about the relationship between rights and democracy. These differences cash out in terms of deep divisions about the ways in which rights should be institutionalized and rendered enforceable. At one end of the spectrum, we have Bentham.[57] Bentham inveighed against rights as anti-democratic and as anarchic in their tendency to restrict or question the democratic will. Towards the middle of the spectrum, in the hands of, for example, Hart,[58] rights are seen as potentially legitimate constraints on the democratic will, yet as distinct from it. At the other end of the spectrum, we have the Dworkinian view of rights as, at a deep level, expressing the same values as those underlying democracy, such that clashes between the two can be resolved without sacrificing democratic values. On this view, rights are not anti-utilitarian but rather correct the imperfections of a utilitarian calculus corrupted by 'external' other-regarding (prejudiced) preferences. Yet Dworkin's is also a view that restricts the operation of constitutional rights to the sphere of public action: the reconciliation of rights and democracy flows from an argument relevant to the power of political and legal decision-making, and not to relations between private individuals.

In the context of the international movement for human rights, one of the most important implications of these theoretical disagreements has to do with the role of the judiciary or other interpreting and enforcing institutions. How can judicial review of open-ended constitutional or convention provisions be reconciled with judges' constitutional position as interpreters and not makers of law? Can judicial review of state action be reconciled with democracy? And how can these issues, already complex at the national level, be resolved within an international legal order traditionally premised on the relations between

---

[57] Bentham, 'Anarchical Fallacies', reprinted in J. Waldron (ed.), *Nonsense upon Stilts* (1987) 46.

[58] Hart, 'Between Utility and Rights', in H. L. A. Hart (ed.), *Essays in Jurisprudence and Philosophy* (1983) 198.

sovereign states (a premise which is, of course, under serious pressure as a result of the increasing status of human rights within international law). Probably the most ambitious attempt to effect such a reconciliation remains Dworkin's elaborate theory of principles implicit within law which judges can find and develop. But the scope for conflict between judges interpreting rights and governmental freedom is amply illustrated by the history of human rights law in the international arena. Furthermore, differing views about the proper role of courts and judges may themselves impact upon the strength with which substantive rights are specified in codes, constitutions, and conventions. In this context, the varying strength of the articulation of, for example, the right of free expression, and the means whereby it can legitimately be derogated from, ranging from the absolutism of the US Constitution through to the capacious derogation conditions of the ECHR, is instructive.

It is important to see that, in the international arena, these questions of the relationship between different sources of political, legal, or moral authority are significantly more complex than at the national level. For they are not restricted to the classic constitutional questions about the relationship between judicial and legislative branches just rehearsed. Rather, questions arise about the relationship between human rights and sovereign states as complementary, but potentially competing, sources of authority in international law.[59] The emerging status of human rights standards as qualifying the autonomy and authority of sovereign states is thrown into sharp relief by the subtle mix of contract and legislation, negotiation and authority, represented by the frameworks for interpretation, development, and enforcement of international human rights conventions. For example, under the CEDAW, it is possible for states to ratify the Convention while entering declarations and reservations to that ratification, on condition that those reservations do not conflict with the fundamental purposes of the Convention. This is a framework which—like weak, procedurally based doctrines of judicial review in some national legal systems—accommodates the framework of rights to the politics of state sovereignty. The possibility of other states challenging reservations on the basis of their fundamental incompatibility with the Convention opens up the space for an international dialogue about human rights via the Committee on the Elimination of Discrimination against Women set up by Part V of CEDAW. This space for dialogue is potentially of great value. Yet, given the influence of power relations on the willingness of states to question the reservations of other states,[60] and given the contingency of the ultimate enforcement mechanism of reference to the International Court of Justice

---

[59] See Knop, 'Re/statements: Feminism and State Sovereignty in International Law', 3 *Transnational Law and Contemporary Problems* (1993) 293.

[60] Compare the absence of challenges to the US position on CEDAW. See Mayer, 'Reflections on the Proposed US Reservations to CEDAW: Should the Constitution be an Obstacle to Human Rights?', 23 *Hastings Constitutional Law Quarterly* (1996) 727.

upon the willingness of individual states to accept its jurisdiction (Article 29), this flexibility is arguably bought at the cost of risking the integrity of the rights framework itself.

4. RIGHTS AND FEMINIST THEORY

A. Feminist Critics of Rights

Given the strong association of feminism with the progressive ideas of Enlightenment thinking, and the key place of rights in both modern political theory and campaigns for women's equality, one would expect to find a substantial affinity between feminist legal theory and contemporary development of ideas of rights. Feminism and human rights grew, after all, out of remarkably similar and highly specific cultural histories. And indeed, in the contemporary international human rights movement, one does find an important strand of feminist activism and, increasingly, theorization.[61] However, if we return to the first section of this chapter to trace the relationship between feminist legal theory and theories of rights, we also find a substantial literature which applies the tools of feminist critique to rights theory itself, and which often finds theories and practices of rights deficient in ways which echo the problems which feminism has diagnosed in modern law more generally. Notwithstanding its connected political and intellectual history, therefore, feminist theory may provide a useful basis for critical appraisal of the contemporary culture of human rights. It is therefore worth rehearsing feminist critiques of rights in order to assess their relevance to current debates about the human rights of women in an international context.

Key aspects of the feminist critique of rights turn on the *individualism* of legal rights in the modern world. The holders of rights are the abstract individuals identified by Naffine and discussed above; similarly, the objects of rights are conceived as forms of individual property: collective goods or goods which move between groups or persons, which cannot be owned exclusively, tend to be marginalized. Particularly in the common law system, and perhaps in the weak enforcement context of the international legal order too, rights tend to be represented by residual liberties protected by negative freedom rather than the positive definition of interests and values. This criticism assumes particular salience, evidently enough, in the global context.

---

[61] See e.g. H. Charlesworth and C. Chinkin, *The Boundaries of International Law: A Feminist Analysis* (2000); Charlesworth, 'What are "Women's International Human Rights"?', in R. Cook (ed.), *Human Rights of Women* (1994) 58; Chinkin, 'International law and human rights', in T. Evans (ed.), *Human Rights Fifty Years On* (1998) 105; Nussbaum, *supra* n. 22.

What is more, the form of legal rights centres on the *competitive assertion of entitlements*: the legal and political world is constructed as a market of rights, competitively asserted as against other market actors. This has the extreme implication that, for example, the right to abortion can be seen as a claim for which a woman has to compete with her foetus. This market form of rights coheres, it is argued, with a certain cultural imperialism; rights express a particular, bourgeois liberal world-view, which they nonetheless construct as a neutral and universal order.

Even if these political objections to rights can be met, feminists have argued that there are practical objections to a political strategy founded on assertions of individual right. The resort to rights discourse for progressive political ends tends to engender a *multiplication of rights* which leads nowhere: as more and more rights are recognized, competition increases, political divisiveness ensues, and rights claims become less strong, less determinate. Rights may operate, in Dworkin's memorable phrase, as trumps: but trumps are of little use if there are many trumps in the pack. And this multiplicity of rights increasingly brings with it a reliance on a *coercive framework of enforcement* which, as Smart has argued, inevitably depends on legal power: rights are a creature of the state and hence a function of existing configurations of power.[62] This means, it is argued, that they are of limited use to the politically marginalized or for the construction of claims oppositional to prevailing power relations. These feminist critiques of rights as based in an opaque and falsely objective ontology; as assuming an implausible human atomism and independence; as encouraging egoistic and competitive social motivations; as presupposing an unrealistic equality between rights-holders; as indeterminate; as implying a coercive framework of enforcement; and as inviting an unhelpful rights inflation, find surprisingly close antecedents in the work of both Marx and Bentham.[63] Several aspects of these critiques, moreover, take on a particular urgency in the international context where, for example, questions about the universal validity of rights across different cultural and economic contexts; about the legitimacy and credibility of a statist model of enforcement; and about the unequal power relations between rights-holders are especially acute.[64]

These theoretical arguments about rights are probably best understood in relation to some specific examples. Let us turn first to the case of pornography. MacKinnon's and Dworkin's famous analysis of pornography identifies the genre as both means and symptom of the sexual objectification of women, of

---

[62] Smart, *supra* n. 16, at Chapter 8; Butler, *Excitable Speech, supra* n. 44.

[63] See extracts from Marx and Bentham in Waldron, *supra* n. 57; see also Lacey, 'Bentham as Proto-Feminist', 51 *Current Legal Problems* (1998) 441.

[64] For a perceptive meditation on some of the costs and benefits of human rights frameworks in the international context, see Kennedy, 'The International Human Rights Movement: Part of the Problem?' 3 *European Human Rights Law Review* (2001) 245.

the destruction of women's capacity for self-respect and, ultimately, of women's citizenship.[65] Their response was to draw on women's experiences of the damaging effects of pornography to draft an anti-pornography ordinance whose legal strategy was, essentially, to pitch the right to free speech against the right not to be discriminated against. This strategy ultimately forced the US courts to make explicit the legal 'facts' that American constitutional doctrine favours the former over the latter (speech wins over equal protection) and, moreover, defines the former in terms of negative freedom so that the question of the relative worth of freedom of speech to different groups—the effect of practices like pornography on the freedom not only to speak but to be heard and understood—is constitutionally irrelevant. There remains a question, however, about how well the framework of discrimination law captures the critical analysis of pornography which MacKinnon and Dworkin wanted to advance. In the light of the appeal to a comparative standard already discussed, what about male homosexual or child pornography? And where do race, ethnicity, or religion fit into the analysis? How can we accommodate, as Cornell, among others, has persuasively argued we must, the rights of workers in the pornography industry?[66] MacKinnon's and Dworkin's framework of rights to compensation in civil law and their legislative model, which set out from hearings with victims of pornography and which explicitly aimed at individual empowerment, exhibits all the strengths, and all the weaknesses, of an individual rights-based approach. Many of the difficulties illustrated by this campaign are exemplified yet more vividly in the international debate about the rights of sex-workers and the problem of 'trafficking' in women and children for sexual purposes: in the distinctive contexts of female poverty and harsh penalization of those violating immigration laws, it has been argued that a rights regime informed by a specific conception of rights against sexual exploitation which emerged from a very different context has importantly negative implications for the well-being of the very women and children whom the anti-trafficking movement sets out to protect.[67]

Another instructive example is that of abortion. One powerful discourse in the struggle for access to abortion has been that of the woman's right to choice and to control of her own body. Yet, powerful though this framework has been in mobilizing political support, the critique of rights reveals that it has some disadvantages. These include the decontextualization of the circumstances of choice; the choice is worth little if our circumstances are such that we can not make it with adequate information, or if we cannot implement it because of

[65] In addition to citations in earlier notes, see C. A. MacKinnon and A. Dworkin, *In Harm's Way* (1997).

[66] Cornell, *supra* n. 17, at Chapter 3; see also Nussbaum, *supra* n. 22, at Chapter 11.

[67] Chang, 'Redirecting the Debate over Trafficking in Women', 11 *Harvard Human Rights Journal* (1998) 65.

lack of access to medical or financial resources. This question of context is particularly acute in the international arena, in which the starkly varying economic, political, and cultural circumstances of rights-holders all too often threaten to convert international conventions of human rights from plausible frameworks for social and political progress to empty or even cynical rhetorical flourishes geared more to satisfying the consciences or political interests of nation states than to improving the material conditions of rights-holders. On a different level, there is an uncomfortable resonance between the assertion of rights and the characterization of women seeking abortions as 'unnatural', selfish, strident. Particularly in the context of the US constitutional conception of abortion as a privacy right, the right to abortion is associated with all the weaknesses of negative conceptions of freedom: it turns out that the right to abortion solves none of the problems of positive provision, and what is arguably the key question—whether availability of abortion is a precondition to women's personhood and citizenship—tends to drop out of the picture.

B. Critical Race Theory and the Critique of Rights Scepticism

In contrast to these familiar feminist arguments about the weaknesses of rights theory, critical race theorists—and along with them many international activists working in the fields of international human rights for women—have castigated feminism for its undue pessimism.[68] At one level, the argument is that feminists who reject rights frameworks are engaging in a form of *legal essentialism*: why should we accept that legal rights must always have their current, individualistic, decontextualized, and competitive form? Isn't this just as obtuse as the discredited Marxist argument that law is inherently bourgeois, and must wither away on radical social transformation rather than being transformed along with other social institutions? If the persuasive argument is that rights are competitive or individualistic because of underlying social and economic relations and if, politically, we are interested in changing those relations, we also need to think positively about how basic political and legal concepts such as rights can be rethought, reconstructed, and about how the circumstances of their institutionalization might be adapted.

A further objection to the feminist critique of rights is its implicit espousal of the *perspective of the relatively privileged*. Writers like Patricia Williams and Angela Harris remind us that white feminist scepticism about rights can be

---

[68] On the relevance of critical race theory to international human rights, see Andrews, 'Making Room for Critical Race Theory in International Law', 45 *Villanova Law Review* (2000) 855; Andrews, 'Globalization, Human Rights and Critical Race Feminism', 3 *Journal of Gender, Race and Justice* (2000) 373.

afforded only by the relatively privileged.[69] For the more deeply oppressed, the language of rights still represents an aspiration and ideal; it can be deconstructed only once a prior political battle has been won. Liberal feminism may have triumphed in at least some parts of the world, but can the same be said of the similarly modest aspirations of those committed to eradicating racial or ethnic oppression? In short, those who have been quick to develop critiques of rights have generally been those whose rights have not been seriously in issue. Particularly for African-Americans in the US and aboriginal groups in Australia or Canada, the recency of their accession to membership in the 'rights community' has generated a keen awareness of its power and of the political problems of a too ready dismissal. This explains why, at the national level in countries privileged enough to sustain a broad intellectual debate on these topics, it has often been those writing from a black feminist or critical race perspective who have argued most forcefully for a reconstruction rather than a refusal of rights.

Rights may on this view be seen not so much as transcendent, objective, or 'natural', but rather as an emergent critical force *within* modern societies; as the conscience or superego of modernity, and as a framework within which new political ideals can be articulated. This approach answers some of the critiques of the metaphysical aspect of rights voiced by Bentham and by Marxist, feminist, and postmodernist writers.[70] Its answer to the objection that 'you cannot destroy the master's house with the master's tools' is Audre Lorde's: if they are all that is available, there is no alternative but to seize them and do our best.[71] As a powerful social discourse—as evidenced by the civil rights movement in the USA, the land rights movement in Australia, and the post-War international movements for human rights—it is difficult and perhaps irresponsible for progressive social movements to ignore rights discourse.

C. Normative Reconstruction in Feminist and Critical Legal Theory

The feminist critique of rights proceeds from one of the main projects of feminist legal theory: the critical analysis of important aspects of the conceptual framework of modern law. But this is not the sole project of feminist theory, as these arguments from critical race theory suggest. In at least some of its guises, feminist legal theory has a strong normative, reconstructive, or even utopian voice: it engages not only in analysis and critique of current law, but also in reformist or imaginative argument about how law might be otherwise.

[69] Williams, *supra* n. 10; Harris, *supra* n. 25.
[70] For further discussion, see Nash, *supra* n. 32.
[71] A. Lorde, *Sister Outsider* (1984).

To engage in this reconstructive project, feminist and other critical legal theory itself needs a language, a set of concepts: there is therefore a close, albeit complex, relationship between critique, reformism, and utopianism. In this section, I shall look at the relationship between critique, reformism, and utopianism before returning to the particular questions of rights and of feminist reconstructions of rights. Critique, reformism, and normative reconstruction are each, I shall argue, important to the theoretical concerns underpinning feminist legal studies. I shall then go on to make some suggestions about how the projects relate to one another, and about the theoretical questions raised by an attempt to understand their relationship.

The first project I want to consider is that of *critique*. Here the enterprise may be understood as one of immanent or internal critique: the method is to scrutinize the discourses or practices in question in terms of their own realization of the values by which they profess to be informed.[72] Critique comes in more or less radical, searching forms. Liberal feminism might be regarded as a paradigm of a modest version—what I shall call internal critique: it held liberal legal systems up to scrutiny in terms of the standards which they professed to instantiate universally, by showing how aspects of legal and political practice systematically failed to accord rights or dispense justice even-handedly across different groups of citizens. Precisely the same might be said, currently, of the discussion of international human rights represented by conventions such as the International Covenant on Civil and Political Rights[73] and the CEDAW. The movement from liberal to 'difference' feminism exemplifies the ways in which an initially sympathetic internal critique can map a path towards a deeper, immanent critique which radically shifts understanding in ways which move beyond the normative framework with which the internal critique was sympathetic. For as feminist critique developed beyond an engagement with the surface level of practices or their impact, and began to scrutinize the conceptual framework on which liberal politics was based, self-contradictions and instabilities within that framework were gradually revealed. The classic example of this is probably the critique of the public–private distinction, which showed how a division fundamental to liberalism logically excluded the delivery of liberalism's own universalistic promise.[74]

As critique bit deeper and deeper into the conceptual framework, focusing on the various oppositions on which liberal and modern thought was premissed, the instability and fragility of that thought were progressively revealed. Values, ways of life, practices which were unacknowledged yet which were

---

[72] S. Benhabib and D. Cornell (eds), *Feminism as Critique* (1987); Lacey, *supra* n. 24, at Chapter 8.

[73] International Covenant on Civil and Political Rights, New York, 16 December 1966, in force 23 March 1976, 999 UNTS 171.

[74] See Lacey, *supra* n. 24, at Chapter 3; Olsen, *supra* n. 24; O'Donovan, *supra* n. 5.

central to the maintenance of liberal legal order—women's domestic work and
sexual subordination to take important examples—were revealed as hidden
underpinnings to the dominant understandings. The project of unearthing
these underpinnings revealed the contingency of current arrangements, and,
crucially, the role of various sorts of power in sustaining sets of arrangements
which were themselves being interpreted as highly problematic. And whilst
critique rather than reconstruction had a primacy in this work, evaluative,
moral questions were never far away.

It is the impulse further to develop this implicit normative project which
forms *utopianism*—the second of the theoretical tasks which I want to delineate. The 'utopian moment within deconstruction' has been most forcefully
articulated by Cornell. Like Derridean deconstruction, Cornell's critique is
premised on a particular (post-structuralist) view of the openness of language.[75] Language does not operate simply by reflecting objects in the world
in a directly representational way. Rather, it has an invariably performative or
constructive aspect. Hence language always in a sense operates at a metaphorical level. And because linguistic signs get their meaning not by any simple
correspondence with the world but also by reference to other signs, there is an
irreducible reference in all linguistic utterances to what was not, but might
have been, said. Meaning, in other words, is never closed. It is in discursive
opennesses and gaps that the possibility of other meanings, of other worlds,
may be discerned through a process which Cornell terms 'recollective imagination'. Implicit in this analysis is the idea that those worlds in some sense exist
in the very moment in which they are repressed (notwithstanding the fact that
their existence is also an affirmation of, because dependent upon, that which
represses).

Whilst Cornell is willing to use the word 'utopian' in relation to her project,
this is not so of all exponents of this second kind of imaginative ethical
thought. Irigaray, for example, has argued for the imagination of a distinctive
feminine law. She explicitly repudiates the idea of utopias, and speaks rather in
terms of the imagination of the impossible—wanting what is not yet as the
only possibility for the future.[76] Whilst this may appear mere semantic
quibbling, the disagreement about the propriety of the term 'utopia' touches
on a substantive issue about what it means to engage in this kind of imaginative thought. Far from engaging in the design of complete and idealized
blueprints—a project which arguably encounters democratic as well as intellectual objections—this form of utopianism is engaged in the task of thinking
beyond the conceptual limits of the present. The utopianism itself consists in
the ongoing project of (re)imagination—a process which would arguably be

---

[75] See Cornell, *supra* n. 13; D. Cornell, *The Philosophy of the Limit* (1992); D. Cornell,
Transformations (1993).
[76] Irigaray, *supra* n. 12, at 26.

killed in the very moment of its institutionalization. As I shall argue, however, it is a mistake to conclude that this imaginative and non-prescriptive utopianism has nothing to do with reconstructive politics.

What is distinctive about projects such as those of Cornell and Irigaray is that they operate first and foremost at an imaginative and rhetorical level. They build on the importance of critique's insight about contingency, by insisting that we can imagine the world differently, and that the normative concepts in terms of which we shape our world—rights, justice, equality—can be reimagined, reconstructed in radically different ways. Significantly, these kinds of projects are primarily interested in the shape and dynamics of the institution of language: they seek to break out of what might have appeared as a double bind for discourse-oriented critique in relation to radical politics. This is the fact that language is itself marked by socially predominant configurations of power, and therefore that our normative conceptual framework is, for example, marked by gendered and racialized exclusions. Hence it might be thought that there is no way forward from critique: the insights of critique seem to engender silence. The important message that critique is not so silenced is exemplified by these imaginative poststructuralist feminisms, which engage in the impossible project of speaking that which, according to their own analysis, cannot be spoken. So the reconstruction of ideas such as rights holds a central place in this kind of enterprise, and these writers open up a way of thinking about the international human rights movement as having a dimension beyond it status as a movement for institutional reform: a dimension consisting of an imaginative, rhetorical, consciousness-raising exercise.

Different again is the third and final task which I shall try to delineate. This is the *reformist* project of thinking, at a concrete and institutional level, how ideas generated at the level of critique or idealistic imagination might be approached or even realized in practice. This has evidently been an important project within feminist scholarship, much of which has argued directly for policy changes of one kind or another.

Policy-oriented reformist research encounters several practical and political problems which I shall not go into here. What I do want to focus on is an intellectual problem: the fact that the institutions which reformist interventions seek to change are themselves interwoven with and dependent upon a complex network of other institutions. Interventions within one set of practices often have unseen and sometimes adverse implications for others. And a concrete and specific attempt to redress, for example, an imbalance of power in one area of social practice is unlikely to be successful if the configurations of power which it tries to reshape in fact characterize all or most of the social institutions which go to make up the relevant environment. This is depressingly obviously true of configurations of power patterned around race, ethnicity, gender, to name just a few examples. This poses all reform-oriented feminist thought with a challenge. The challenge is to try to understand how social institutions interact with each other, which are the most open to change, and which means of changing them are likely, in particular contexts, to be least dangerous or most successful. For the institutional complexity of the world—the ways in which lives are lived across different practices, and move between different subjectivities—itself presents possibilities for, as much as barriers to, change. These possibilities can be approached only if feminist research is informed by adequate general social theoretic understandings. In the diverse global context of the human rights movement, this is a very serious challenge.

The relationship between the enterprises of critique, utopianism, and reformist policy prescription can be expressed schematically in a number of ways. We might say, for example, that the understanding of the power of contingent social arrangements to which critique works is generally motivated by a commitment to changing the world. This depends in turn upon the vision of a substantially different world imagined in utopian thought. And it has the ultimate (perhaps very distant) project of approaching that vision through the process of developing practices and institutions via reformism—the process and shape of reform itself in turn having rhetorical aspects and generating further ground for critique and reimagination. Two important features of this interdependence, however, make it far more complex and fragile than the schematic statement implies. First, the sort of rhetorical politics which is imagined in utopian thought may, if directly institutionalized, have effects very different from those ideally envisioned. This is simply because, by definition, they are realized within a very different kind of world. Utopias cannot be reached: rather they provide horizons towards which we attempt to move. Hence, secondly, the movement towards such utopias depends on a dynamic and general process of social transformation to which the consciousness of contingency and the discursive construction of difference are only *preconditions*. For the institutionalization of such imagined worlds without a more general change risks reproducing the very framework which it was trying to escape. It is evident that these two points raise particularly important questions for the international human rights movement.

In order to take utopian rhetorical strategies further, as well as to understand how the ethical visions emerging from critical legal theory relate to reformism, at least two other projects therefore also have to be advanced. First, rhetorical strategies beg a conception of what would constitute an adequate democratic practice—an understanding of how a genuine dialogue about visions of difference might be engendered. Secondly, they presuppose an understanding of how particular human societies and associations operate and develop, of how discursive and material practices and changes interact, of how power flows through the social body. In other words, the legitimacy as well as the power of rhetoric as politics depends upon the development of institutionally oriented social theoretic insights. Without this, the critique and the imaginative rhetoric of the first two projects, which themselves justifiably claim the status of distinctive political action or engagement, would not be capable of attaining any understanding of what their effects might be. Again, this question arises in vivid form for the human rights movement, which seeks to deploy campaigns for codes of rights to advance all three of the feminist projects delineated in this section.

D. Reconstructing Rights

I now want to illustrate the potential interaction of the projects of critique, utopianism, and reformism within arguments which engage from a feminist perspective in what I shall call the normative reconstruction of the concept of rights. As we have already seen, rather than engage in a swingeing critique of rights, critical race theorists among others have tended to argue for an *imaginative reconstruction of rights*, exploring concepts such as collective rights, practices of affirmative action, group rights, and procedures such as class actions. These arguments mesh with useful models within the more pragmatic wings of difference feminism: examples include Cornell's adaptation of Ronald Dworkin's right to equal concern and respect within the imaginary domain of sexed identities,[77] and Christine Littleton's thoughtful defence of a model of reconstructed equality based on the goal of equivalent worth of rights to members of different groups.[78] At the international level, the challenge for conceptual reconstruction equally concerns the distinctive subjects and objects of international law including, crucially, the implications of human rights for the reconceptualization of state sovereignty.[79] Let us therefore look in more detail at a number of models for reconstructing rights in ways which seek to escape the features of the critique outlined earlier, before moving finally to a summary of their potential implications for the movement for international human rights for women.

1. Rights of Equivalent Worth: Cornell, Littleton

The argument here depends on the distinction between negative and positive freedom. By analogy with our earlier discussion of the pornography debate: understood in terms of negative freedom, curbs on pornographic expression are certainly limits to free speech. But if we understand the value of the right to

---

[77] Cornell, *Transformations, supra* n. 75, at Chapters 5–7; Cornell, *supra* n. 22.

[78] Littleton, 'Reconstructing Sexual Equality', 75 *California Law Review* (1987) 1279.

[79] This is an issue to which Karen Knop has already made a substantial contribution in her sensitive deconstruction of the shifting images underlying appeals to and critiques of state sovereignty in both international legal discourse and feminist critique: see Knop, *supra* n. 59.

free speech in positive terms—not just in terms of being allowed to speak, but of living in an environment, free from discrimination, with adequate education, and so on, in which people actually can express themselves, and can do so in ways which can be heard—we can generate a conception of rights which escapes the false assumption of the equal situation of legal subjects identified by Bentham and Marx as well as by feminists. In other words, we should think of rights not just in formal but equally in substantial terms: if the underlying value of rights lies in human equality, we have to think about the content and enforcement of rights in terms of their equal value to differently situated subjects. This is reflected in the strategy of the CEDAW adopted by the UN General Assembly in 1979. The Convention seeks to address discrimination against women in other human rights declarations by calling on states '[t]o modify the social and cultural patterns of conduct of men and women, with a view to achieving the elimination of prejudices and customary and all other practices which are based on the idea of the inferiority or the superiority of either of the sexes or on stereotyped roles for men and women' (Article 5(a)).

This explicitly contextualized perspective also suggests a way of approaching some problems of competition between rights: if we are concerned with the relative value of rights to different subjects or groups, this may give us some guidelines as to how to deal with apparent conflicts between different people's rights. For example, it would militate against the idea that the right to property—a particularly unevenly distributed right—should be unrestricted in ways which affect other people's rights to a peaceful or safe environment.

2. Collective Remedial Rights: Affirmative Action

Perhaps the most obvious institutional example of a different sense of rights, the idea of collective remedial rights speaks mainly to the criticisms of the formalism and individualism of rights. The argument is that if the enjoyment of classic civil and political rights is systematically hampered for some groups because of the effects of past discrimination, then some collective remedial response is needed. Affirmative action in education and employment can then be seen as a way of bringing certain groups along to a social and economic position in which they can participate fully in the rights culture, where their rights can genuinely be of equivalent worth. At a political level, the effective assault on affirmative action in US constitutional law over the last 15 years is instructive in showing how firmly a more individualistic understanding of rights is embedded: in England, the very definition of sex (and race) discrimination defines affirmative action as discriminatory. More positively, however, the concept of indirect or effects-based discrimination, under which a facially neutral rule or practice which has a disproportionately excluding effect on members of a particular group provides a *prima facie* case of discrimination, may be seen as a weak form of collective remedial right in that it uses collective disadvantage as a jumping off point for claims of individual discrimination. At a procedural level, too, we can find aspects of both national and international law—class actions, generous standing rules for judicial review, and so on—which provide platforms for assertion of the needs and interests of groups.[80] In this respect, the approach taken by the CEDAW is once again instructive: Article 1 defines discrimination in terms of any 'distinction, exclusion or restriction made on the basis of sex which has the *effect or purpose* of impairing or nullifying the recognition, enjoyment or exercise by women, irrespective of their marital status, on a basis of equality of men and women, of human rights and fundamental freedoms' (emphasis added). Furthermore, Articles 3–6 anticipate the need for positive measures to ensure the 'full development and advancement of women', with Article 4 in particular specifying that 'temporary special measures aimed at accelerating de facto equality between men and women shall not be considered discrimination'.

3. Group Rights

A more thoroughgoing approach to normative reconstruction of rights would be to frame rights which had as their objects not only individual interests, and which constructed not only individuals as subjects of rights.

To start with groups as the subjects of rights, the recent recognition of the rights of an aboriginal population to the restoration of expropriated land in Australia provides a key example which illustrates that the accommodation of group rights, though still relatively rare, does not present serious conceptual problems for liberal legal orders. One might argue that both the rights (including property rights) of corporations and the identity and claims of nation states within international law also constitute prime examples of the incorporation of groups as rights-holding subjects in modern legal systems. Moreover, the elaborated framework of the CEDAW illustrates the possibility of recognizing that tackling the special needs or situation of a particular group—in this case, women—may be a *precondition* to the realization of the 'universal' human rights of that group. But if conceptual problems are less intractable than might have been feared, the same is not true for their political counterparts. The inglorious role of group 'rights' in the history of some of the more repressive of the world's political regimes—South African or Southern Rhodesian apartheid, Malaysian sectionalism, for example—serve as salient reminders that group rights can be used oppressively to fix members within identities which they may be keen to escape, and/or which are defined in a way which is inconsistent with basic civil, political, social, or economic rights.

In terms of feminist politics, moreover, there is also a question about whether key feminist demands can really be understood in terms of the cultural rights of a group in a way analogous to the claims to cultural

[80] For further discussion of this and related aspects of groups and rights, see Lacey, *supra* n. 24, at Chapters 1 and 5.

recognition of, for example, Native Americans or aboriginal Australians in relation to land claims. Once again, the question of whether women constitute a sufficiently unitary group for it to make sense to constitute them as a collective subject of special rights raises its head. To the extent that this can be justified, it would have to be argued out afresh in each specific context if the spectre of a damaging as opposed to a strategic essentialism—an essentialism based on assumptions about invariant sex differences as opposed to a prag-matic essentialism which builds on shared interests and positions to construct rights claims—is to be avoided. In relation to sexual violence, for example, continuities of risk and rights abuse may be easier to establish than, say, in relation to economic disadvantage. But even with sexual violence, local specificities and experiences pose a challenge to the constitution of any global women's interest group. The CEDAW's solution to this problem is to identify women as a group exclusively in relation to a guarantee of the realization of their universal human rights on a basis of equality with men. This is, arguably, the best compromise that can be reached on this issue, maintaining as it does a position which embraces strategies of both 'de-gendering' and 're-valuing the female', even if not 'the feminine'.

Moving to the object of rights, feminists have also explored the possibility of constructing collective interests as the objects of rights. The idea of collective rights-holders alone would be insufficient, for example, to accom-modate ecological issues such as the protection of a particular natural environ-ment or species. But it is possible to give either collective or individual legal subjects rights to enforce collective interests—a peaceful and undamaged environment, for example. This has in fact been the subject of legal develop-ment in the last 30 years, probably reflecting the activities of new social movements. The debate about the proper criteria for legal standing in muni-cipal legal systems arguably reflects, however, liberal legal orders' ambivalence about these kinds of rights.

4. Rights to Cultural Membership

A variation on the notion of rights to collective interests lies in the debate, particularly lively in Canada, about the need for legal subjects to be accorded an individual right to a collective good. Examples would include the right of French-Canadians to be educated in French; and a right to state support for diminishing cultural practices.[81] The correlative question arises again, how-ever, about fixing individuals within received identities. Furthermore, as we have seen, there is strong reason to doubt whether women's oppression is plausibly understood in terms of the denial of women's access to, or the under-valuation of, a distinctive culture. What weight should be accorded to the right to withdraw from the majority or minority culture—as, for example, has been

[81] W. Kymlicka, *Liberalism, Community and Culture* (1989).

a pressing concern for women brought up in cultural groups opposed to women's access to education or work in the public labour market? In this respect, the CEDAW pins its allegiance very firmly to liberal humanism rather than cultural rights: many of its provisions—notably those on education (Article 10), nationality (Article 9), and marital status (Article 16)—conflict directly with rights to membership of a range of cultures across the globe.[82]

5. 'Rights of Being'

In answer to the criticisms of rights as individualist and premissed on a false equality between subjects, Irigaray has proposed a model of rights which proceeds explicitly from the assumption that subjects are differently situated in relation to sex. Since rights must speak to people's specific human identities, the framework of rights must take this into account. As a feminist, Irigaray is particularly concerned with women: she argues that only men have been allowed to function culturally as full legal subjects, and that the way in which male subjectivity has operated has been on a proprietary model. Women and all other 'others' have been constructed as objects, and rights themselves have been construed as a commodity which only full subjects can 'have' or possess. By contrast, Irigaray argues that we should think in terms of rights which reflect a variety of identities and ways of life, and which would therefore function as rights 'of being' rather than 'of having'. This, she argues, entails recognizing irreducibly different human identities: male and female cultures which would be reflected in sexually specific rights. Rights to dignity and human identity would pertain to men and women, but would entail different entitlements: for example, rights to virginity and motherhood. Irigaray's is an imaginative approach, but it encounters some serious objections. Analogous to the difficulty of group rights, it appears to fix its subjects within particular sexed identities. Treating women as a group for all rights-ascribing purposes presupposes a damaging and implausibly unitary view of the 'essential' nature of women's social position; in attempting to recognize difference, how do we avoid fixing groups back within the identities which have been undervalued or despised, and from which they may well be seeking to escape?[83] As I have already suggested, the CEDAW framework, which embraces both universalism and particularism to some degree, is probably the best and perhaps the only available legal strategy for escaping this kind of rights-based essentialism.

---

[82] The provisions on marital and family status, in particular, underpin the reservations which many Islamic countries have made to the CEDAW: see Brandt and Kaplan, 'The Tension between Women's Rights and Religious Rights', 12 *Journal of Law and Religion* (1995–6) 105.

[83] For more detailed discussion of Irigaray's position, see Lacey, *supra* n. 24, at Chapter 8.

6. Relational Rights

Difficulties therefore remain to be resolved—notably in terms of how to avoid fixing group-based right-holders within particular identities and hence of replaying essentialism—in relation to most of the more radical proposals for the reconstruction of rights. However, the move in the work of writers like Jennifer Nedelsky to reconceptualize rights at a more fundamental level—to reconstruct them as relational and inter-subjective—probably represents one of the most promising developments in contemporary feminist and critical legal theory.[84] Nedelsky's argument has something in common with, but moves in important ways beyond, the relational ethic explored in different ways in the work of Gilligan and of Irigaray. Irigaray's argument is that one can only be a rights-holder if one already has access to an identity which is recognized and respected. This is precisely what women have lacked. But as soon as one recognizes that there are (at least?) two ways of being human—the male and the female—one opens up the possibility of rights which 'move between' the two genres. As we have seen, Irigaray conceives these as rights of being rather than property-type rights of having; and this conceptual idea of structurally relational rights that foster inter-subjectivity rather than covertly asserting the superiority of one genre, and which move beyond the masculine culture of competitive, proprietary rights, makes a distinctive contribution to feminist philosophy. There is an analogy here, too, with Cornell's argument for rights to social conditions under which one can imagine oneself as a whole person.

Instead of moving, however, to Irigaray's radical feminist conclusion in favour of special, sexuate rights, Nedelsky argues that we should emphasize recognition of the fact that rights inevitably construct, reflect, or express relationships. This simply means that the idea of an atomistic rights-holder makes no sense. And this implication, in turn, has radical implications for legal method. It brings with it, for example, a distinct caution about adversarial methods. On this view, rights may be viewed as instituting and fostering relationships of reciprocity and interdependence rather than of competition: the model of rights as relationship attempts to move beyond a subject–object conception of legal relations and its property model of rights. Nedelsky, answering Bentham's interdependence argument, claims that we can and should understand rights as collective decisions: they are not inimical to democracy because they in fact proceed from the democratic process, though they do not express purely democratic values but rather broader values such as equality and autonomy. All rights, she argues, express a certain view of relationships: all rights affect power relations, and create responsibilities as much as selfish claims. If we put this aspect of rights at the forefront of our

---

[84] Nedelsky, 'Reconceiving Rights as Relationship', 1 *Review of Constitutional Studies* (1993) 1.

thinking, and in particular if we abandon the idea that the paradigm rights are proprietary rights which consist in the power to *exclude* others, we can gradually reconstruct our rights culture towards a model of democratic dialogue and accountability.

Nedelsky suggests that this process be facilitated not just by a rethinking of what rights people should have, but of the institutions for their definition, enforcement, and reconsideration. She would like to see a special tribunal or court, with particular democratic credentials, which would operate as a distinctive part of the public sphere. In her view, the whole idea of rights as boundaries or constraints must be abandoned: it is equally possible, and much more helpful, to think of rights as threads linking subjects within particular kinds of relationships. A more egalitarian society would be a society of rights, but of rights rethought in particular ways, and through the operation of particular democratic processes. In this blend of conceptual and procedural argument, we find, I would argue, a rich source of insight for the future development of international human rights, and one in which not only legal institutions such as courts and legislatures but also the institutions of global and local civil society may be invoked.

5. CONCLUSION: CEDAW AND THE INTERNATIONAL HUMAN RIGHTS OF WOMEN

Given the centrality of rights discourse to progressive politics across the globe, and given the importance of rights-interpreting and enforcing institutions to the contemporary pursuit of justice for disadvantaged groups, the argument that feminists must 'take rights seriously' is compelling. However, as I hope to have shown in this chapter, the critical arguments developed within feminist legal and social theory about both the conceptual form and the substance of rights themselves deserve to be taken seriously.

In this respect, the CEDAW, which represents the most important framework specific to the realization of women's human rights in the international legal order, provides an interesting case study. On the one hand, the substance and institutional framework of the Convention speak directly and positively to many of the concerns voiced by feminist critics of rights. The Convention explicitly locates the realization of rights in its cultural context, and to some extent transcends gender essentialism by building in a recognition of certain important differences among women—for example, in its specific reference to the situation of women in rural areas in Article 14. The Convention also recognizes the importance of positive as distinct from negative freedom, not least in its prioritization of economic and social rights in fields such as education, employment, health, and economic and social benefits (Articles 10–13). Substantively, the Convention's location of women's human rights squarely within an overall commitment to the equality of men and women is also an advantage from a feminist point of view, and a distinct advance on rights frameworks (such as that of the US Constitution)[85] which stop short of recognizing such a right to equality. The Convention's communicative model of regular reporting, and challenges to reservations, by signatories to the Committee on the Elimination of Discrimination against Women potentially sets up an important space for transnational dialogue within which the potential of human rights to operate as a form of rhetorical utopianism, or of immanent critique of the socio-political arrangements within nation states, might to some extent be realized.[86]

However, several features of the CEDAW also exemplify some of the difficulties identified by feminist critics of rights. The problem of 'essentialism' may be somewhat diluted by the fact that the need for women to be identified as a distinctive group is realized at a very abstract level: in relation to discrimination in the fulfilment of purportedly universal human rights. But this level of abstraction has a cost, for it operates at such a high level of generality that its capacity to speak to the distinct concerns of groups of women whose sexed position intersects with cultural, ethnic, and religious affiliations and contexts, and its capacity to generate determinate conclusions about specific entitlements, may reasonably be doubted. Furthermore, the framework of possible reservations, while attempting to square the circles of international principle and power politics, of culturally imperialistic universalism and respect for cultural, economic, and political specificity, arguably achieves this at the cost of diluting the CEDAW framework to the vanishing point in many parts of the world. When we look at the main reasons advanced for reservations to CEDAW—economic circumstances, civil wars, cultural traditions—we glimpse the true difficulty of the project of institutionalizing a general regime of human rights across a diverse and culturally and politically divided globe. The critical dialogue potentially set up by CEDAW is, inevitably, distorted at every turn by the realities of political, cultural, and economic power. And while the CEDAW framework—like that of most of international law—adheres to a nation state model, we in fact live in a world in which, as we realize all too vividly in the wake of 11 September 2001, the powerful actors in

---

[85] On the limitations of the US constitutional framework for women's equality and on the status of the constitution as 'sacral text' in blocking US ratification of more extensive international conceptions of women's rights such as those inherent in CEDAW, see Mayer, *supra* n. 60.

[86] On the patterns of, and limitations on, this reporting, see Dormandy, 'Status of the Convention on the Elimination of All Forms of Discrimination against Women in 1998', 33 *International Lawyer* (1998) 637; Bustelo, 'Reproductive Health and CEDAW', 44 *American University Law Review* (1995) 1145. On the role of the discourse of human rights in legal reformism in the run-up to Hong Kong's return to Chinese authority, see Petersen, 'Equality as a Human Right: The Development of Anti-Discrimination Law in Hong Kong', 34 *Columbia Journal of Transnational Law* (1996) 335.

the international arena are not only 'sovereign' states. The greatest challenge for the future therefore remains the complementary development of institutions, interpretations, understandings, and strategies at the local level within the broad framework set up by international law.

If we want, as we surely do, to use the framework of rights to empower women and to dismantle sex-based disadvantage, we must therefore understand the limitations as well as the potential of rights. Clearly, this involves a great deal of context-specific empirical data-collection and institutional analysis. It simply cannot be assumed that the articulation and (attempted) enforcement of rights will be of similar efficacy in all situations, in all societies, in all parts of the world. The interaction between legal, political, economic, and cultural institutions is a key factor in shaping these differences, and a great deal of social science research needs to be done to enrich our understanding of these relationships.

However, distinct from these institutional questions—complex and crucially important though they are—there remain theoretical and normative questions which it is equally important to analyse and debate. Notwithstanding the tenet, central to feminist thought, that the relationship between theory and practice is an intimate one, in the real world, activism and analysis, politics and theory all too often glide in separate spaces. Campaigners are compelled by the urgency of the project at hand: theorists become intrigued by abstract debates all too often internal to the academy, or even to small spaces within it. Finding the time for dialogue, and finding a common language in which to conduct that dialogue, can be difficult. But it is much to be hoped that both time and language will be found. For, as I have tried to show, there remain key conceptual as well as political issues which need to be debated and resolved. The promise of both an effective international movement for women's rights and a politically relevant feminist analysis therefore depend upon the continuation of a dialogue between researchers and activists.

3

Take a Break from Feminism?

JANET HALLEY[*]

Here is a strong hypothesis about intellectual and activist work on the sex-affirmative left:

I want to challenge the assumption that feminism is or should be the privileged site of a theory of sexuality. Feminism is the theory of gender oppression. To automatically assume that this makes it the theory of sexual oppression is to fail to distinguish between gender, on the one hand, and erotic desire, on the other.[1]

Ever since Gayle Rubin offered that distinction—the date was 1984, the essay was 'Thinking Sex', the venue was the crucial intervention *within* Unitedstatesean feminism of *Pleasure and Danger*, Carole Vance's edited volume emerging from the tempestuous Barnard Conference of 1982—the critically-oriented, gay-positive, sex-positive feminist Unitedstatesean left has been wondering about whether it can and should have theory and practice on matters relating to sexuality, gender, and erotic life that is not specifically feminist. Here are just some of the liberal/left/progressive incursions that could be ranked under Rubin's rubric 'the politics of erotic desire': gay identity politics, gay *male* identity politics, transgendered and transsexual identity projects, anti-identitarian and postmodern remakes of all of those, 'sex-positive' and 'sex radical' feminism, a 'politics of acts' (that is, sex politics organized around an idea that sex is in some way 'all about' action, bodily locale, theatricality, or performance, that sexual liberation should turn in some decisive way on acts 'not identities'), genderfuck, the list goes on and on. Though the term 'queer theory' has remained a definitional trickster, it

[*] This chapter provided the basis for my contribution to a very clarifying exchange with Brenda Cossman, Dan Danielsen, and Tracy Higgins published in the *Columbia Journal of Gender and Law* Symposium issue on the question, 'Why a Feminist Law Journal?', held at Columbia Law School in April 2003, and published as B. Cossman *et al.*, 'Gender, Sexuality, and Power: Is Feminist Theory Enough?', 12 *Columbia Journal of Gender and Law* (2003) 601. My special thanks go to Cossman, Danielsen, Higgins, and the Columbia symposiasts for the opportunity to talk with them.

[1] G. Rubin, 'Thinking Sex: Notes for a Radical Theory of the Politics of Sexuality', in C. S. Vance (ed.), *Pleasure and Danger: Exploring Female Sexuality* (1984) 267, at 307.

hovers with delicious uncertainty over this rich congeries of theoretical and activist practical projects. And though much of the most interesting and powerful work that people see as 'queer theory' professes to be, and should also be seen as, feminist, some—much—of it is not. Rubin's hypothesis that a left sex radical could have an analysis or a political moment that engages the politics of erotic life without being feminist has come to have a significant descriptive validity, at least for now.

If any left sexual politics has a consensus position today, it is liberal feminism shot through with elements from more radical feminisms, many of which are precisely the aspects of feminism most at issue among the debates that I am arranging under the rubric of Rubin's hypothesis. The consensus posture enjoyed by liberal feminism is often belied when these aspects come up to the surface. Here would be an example. Feminists working in what I describe as a 'gender traits' model of gender—that is, feminists who find an important engine for women's subordination in the social and symbolic management of the 'traits' or 'performances' that are 'appropriate' to male and female persons—focus on the unjust inequality that is lodged in the stipulation that females must be feminine or perform feminine traits and that males must be masculine or perform masculine traits.[2] They see subversive, resistant, liberatory, or emancipatory possibilities when female persons become free to perform masculine traits and male persons to perform female traits. Gender trait feminism tends not to celebrate the idea of a female person performing feminine traits; the possibility is mostly ignored, and I suspect that's because exploring it would bring to the surface a range of paradoxes that have had significant 'play' in queer theory ('strength through obedience'; the campy quality of women's femininity; the multiple dimensions of masculinity and the idea that it can dominate itself, perhaps sometimes in good ways; etc.). I don't know why gender trait feminism fails to celebrate female femininity, but my guess is that it is rejecting these queer paradoxes in favour of its liberal feminist commitment to liberal norms of equality, dignity, and rationality. But the moment in gender trait feminism that I find most constitutive of its relationship to queer theory occurs when it refuses—as it does persistently and sometimes with indignation—to bestow any legitimacy *at all* on the subversive, resistant, or emancipatory possibilities of the masculinity *of men*. Here we get not merely elision but refusal. When I proposed this idea at a seminar at Tel Aviv University School of Law, some

---

[2] I am not thinking here of Judith Butler's *Gender Trouble*, which, perfectly internally consistently, rejects the idea that gender is a set of dimorphic traits backed up by a rule that male and female persons must adopt or perform the ones appropriate to them. J. Butler, *Gender Trouble: Feminism and the Subversion of Identity* (1990, rpt. 1999). For law reform examples of the feminist project I am describing, see e.g. K. Franke, 'What's Wrong with Sexual Harassment', 49 *Stanford Law Review* (1997) 691; and K. Yoshino, 'Covering', 111 *Yale Law Journal* (2002) 769.

feminists said: 'Why should we care about them?', and 'I don't need to stay to hear this.'

Again, it's not clear to me what is at stake here, but every plausible candidate sounds in cultural feminism. That is, a person committed to gender trait mobility might baulk at male masculinity because he or she holds it as a premiss that masculinity itself, unless it is laundered by female deviance from gender norms, carries with it dominance and/or moral wrongness; or perhaps the premiss is that there is something about the biological or social position of men that makes their masculinity worse than that of women. Surely, conceptually, this refusal must rely on a basic presupposition that male and female bodies exist and are the ground of our politics on these matters (rather than that they are powerful interstitial constructs, and rather than that they are the *effects* of our politics on these matters).[3] And queer theoretic work—both that emerging from the academy and that formulated on the street—contests these presuppositions; it frequently takes the form of a search for the redemptive, subversive, emancipatory possibilities of male masculinity, of the non-difference between male and female masculinity, of masculinity as a project or puzzle rather than reified human 'thing'; it celebrates the bottom and the top in male/male s/m undertakings; and it wonders what we are all doing to make men men. Gender trait feminism, which has been handily, if only partially, assimilated into liberal feminism,[4] is silently *not* queer theoretic at this point; and the disagreement is an important and probably unresolvable one which can best be understood as *sexual politics on the liberal/progressive left*.

So, in some of its important dimensions (by no means all) queer theory asks: Does feminism have an outside? Is there, or should we hypothesize that there is, something about the social world, something about justice, something about left ambitions, that need not be referred to feminism? Are there left aims, subordinated constituencies, as-yet undefined freedoms or shamed pleasures, that could become articulate, that we could measure our commitment to, only if we let ourselves 'Take a Break from Feminism'?

Very often these questions sound like a call for more *anti*feminist or *post*feminist neoconservative work of the kind offered (if that is the right term) to us by the likes of Katie Roiphe and Christina Hoff Sommers.[5] This misconstrual always seems to me to beg the question. The queer theoretic work I am describing asks whether 'our' engagement with erotic, sexual, and gender politics would be better off—whether *feminism* might be better off—if we left ourselves some room to imagine erotic, sexual, and gendered life under terms that some would think, or even that everyone would think, to 'Take a Break from Feminism'. To say that this is an anti- or post-feminist question is

[3] The latter would be the strong tendency of work drawing on Butler, *supra* n. 2.

[4] See e.g. *Price Waterhouse v Hopkins*, 490 U.S. 228 (1989).

[5] K. Roiphe, *The Morning After: Sex, Fear and Feminism on Campus* (1993); C. H. Sommers, *Who Stole Feminism?: How Women Betrayed Women* (1994).

to presuppose that 'we' are 'women'—a claim that would be untrue in a very trivial sense if 'we' are 'gay men and lesbians',[6] or 'black feminist women and progressive black men', or 'the working class'.[7] Many postmodernist feminist projects, moreover, wish to question the existential status of 'women'[8] and have utopian aims beyond 'women'.[9] To insist that Taking a Break from Feminism is anti- or post-feminist is to presuppose that feminism will always be the origin and destiny of left politics on sexuality. But that's exactly what Taking a Break from Feminism is *challenging*.

Feminism could still be alive and well without the utterly universal hegemony imagined by those who think Taking a Break from It is Against It. You can undertake the project while affirming—as I do—that there are many places in the US, and many places elsewhere, in other national locales and in international/global left politics, where feminism is indispensable. There are of course risks to Taking a Break from Feminism—it could be, in the long or short run, too dangerous, too willing to put feminism in competition with different demands on our time and energy, too demoralizing or demobilizing, too liable to cooptation. The risks will differ widely by the political situation in which the urge to Take a Break from Feminism arises. And so I offer this essay to the readers of this volume with some trepidation. I am urged on by two intuitions. First is my sense that feminist work on international human rights, both in its legal theoretical and in its activist modes, is no stranger to internal criticism, has an internal politics in which feminism itself is contested ground, and is mature, resilient, and institutionalized enough to bear some more. And second is the sense that Unitedstatesean feminism sometimes claims, sometimes is granted, an authority in global intellectual and political life that it perhaps doesn't deserve. 'If you're going to export American legal thought, then export the critique too!' Thus Lama Abu-Odeh.[10]

---

[6] See e.g. H. Abelove, M. A. Barale, and D. M. Halperin (eds), *The Gay and Lesbian Studies Reader* (1993).

[7] See e.g. H. Carby, 'White Women Listen! Black Feminism and the Boundaries of Sisterhood', in Centre for Contemporary Culture Studies (ed.), *The Empire Strikes Back: Race and Racism in '70's Britain* (1982) 212 (challenging white women: 'What do you mean when you say WE?'); Combahee River Collective, 'The Combahee River Collective Statement', in B. Smith (ed.), *Home Girls: A Black Feminist Anthology* (1983, rpt. 2000) 264.

[8] Butler, *supra* n. 2, *passim*.

[9] M. J. Frug, 'A Postmodern Legal Manifesto (An Unfinished Draft)', 105 *Harvard Law Review* (1992) 1045 (closing with: 'The closing lesson I want to draw from the anti-pornography campaign about feminist organization is the observation that exploring, pursuing, and accepting differences among women and differences among sexual practices is necessary to challenge the oppression of women by sex. Only when sex means more than male or female, only when the word "woman" cannot be coherently understood, will oppression by sex be fatally undermined.').

[10] L. Abu-Odeh, contribution to discussion at a European Law Research Center conference on 'The Globalization of Modern Legal Thought: Production and Reception, 1850–2000', Harvard Law School, 13–14 April 2002.

Unitedstatesean legal leftists can imagine that they are 'not exporting their thought' only in bad faith or in profound disaffiliation from leftists elsewhere. So here goes, a country report on the Unitedstatesean idea of Taking a Break from Feminism, as this participant in the critically oriented, gay-positive, sex-positive [feminist] Unitedstatesean left sees it.

***

The variety of feminisms in US political and intellectual life is quite stagger-ing. But some elements are virtually *essential* to feminism as it is practised and performed in the United States today. I could be wrong about these essential elements; and feminism could change so that these elements fade out and/or new ones become definitional. So in the spirit of offering an impressionistic description of current conditions, here are the essential elements of feminism in the US today, according to me.

First, to be feminism, a position must make a distinction between *m* and *f*. Different feminisms do this differently: some see men and women; some see male and female; some see masculine and feminine. While 'men' and 'women' will almost always be imagined as distinct human 'groups', the other paired terms can describe many different things: traits, narratives, introjects. How-ever a particular feminism manages these subsidiary questions, it is not 'a feminism' unless it turns in some central or core way on the distinction between *m* and *f*.

And secondly, to be a feminism in the US today, a position must posit some kind of subordination as between *m* and *f*, in which *f* is the disadvantaged or subordinated element. At this point feminism is both descriptive and norma-tive; it takes on the quality of a justice project while also becoming a subordi-nation hypothesis. Feminism is feminism because, as between *m* and *f*, it carries a brief for *f*.

If the essentials are this minimal, there are many, many features of contem-porary and historically important feminism that are optional, however much they appear to their proponents as indispensable. For instance, the register on which subordination should be noticed is seriously contested. For Catharine MacKinnon, the relationship is one of power, whereas for cultural feminism, it is one of ethical ranking. In MacKinnon's power theory, the eroticization of domination *produces* men and women, male and female, masculine and feminine, *as* domination and subordination, and this is bad because, however much the subordinated feminine might desire domination, she also longs for liberation from it. For cultural feminism, male, or men's, or masculine values have trumped those of femaleness, or women, or femininity, and this is bad because women's values are at least as good as—indeed are usually understood to be *better than*—men's.

There are also profound disagreements within feminism about how to describe subordination. On one side of the debate, feminists see reproduction, childbearing, care work, and related matters as central. In the US we have quite significant debates about how to approach this insight. There are equally powerful debates on the place of sexuality in subordination: as against MacKinnon's alliance with some cultural feminists to regulate heterosexual eroticism on the assumption that it is a key element in women's subordination and always, or almost always, or too often bad for women, there have been powerful sex liberationist, sex radical, and more recently 'sex positive' feminisms that understand sexuality to be a domain of 'Pleasure and Danger' to which women are entitled to untrammelled access. And there have been breakaway movements like the anti-identitarian 'politics of sexual acts' and 'queer theory' which seek alternative theoretical, social, and political modes of assessing the relationships between sex and power—modes in which m and f are not necessarily presupposed to have the salience that they have in feminism.

And feminisms differ a great deal in the degree to which they figure women's subordination as structural or episodic. A strictly structural theory would be one which posits the universal totality of male domination; MacKinnon's 'feminism unmodified' is strongly structural in this sense. Many feminists resist this aspect of MacKinnon's theory, and seek to understand male dominance as having an 'outside'. Now, that would be where they might also want to take a break from feminism; for if male dominance is not always already there, then we don't always need feminism.

I have noticed feminism resisting these moves in the direction of Taking a Break from Feminism in two chief ways.[11] One is what my colleague Duncan Kennedy, writing about something else, calls 'paranoid structuralism'.[12] Feminist paranoid structuralism either hypothesizes or presupposes (big difference) that, although things in the world *seem* to be organized in a way that does not invoke m/f or require us to carry a brief for f, this perception is probably a deep error and profoundly counterintuitive investigation will eventually reveal that, yep, it's $m > f$ all over again.

I am a huge fan of hypothetical paranoid structuralism, largely for its love of the covert, its need for highly astute interpretive practices, and its constant yearning for a radical transformation of consciousness. As my example I will offer Elizabeth Potter's recent *tour de force* study entitled *Gender and Boyle's Law of Gases*.[13] Yes, that was not a typo. Potter shows—I think persuasively to the point of near conclusiveness—that the first law of modern Western physics was no better at explaining the 'relevant facts' than another proposal that was,

---

[11] For what I expect are some new feminist responses to these moves that would be misdescribed by what follows, I very much look forward to the symposium responding to an essay, nominally by Ian Halley, entitled 'Queer Theory by Men', forthcoming in the *Duke Journal of Gender Law & Policy*. Those responses are in progress and, at the time this essay went to press, I had not the advantage of reading them.

[12] Duncan Kennedy, 'Semiotics of Critique', 22 *Cardozo Law Review* (2001) 1147.

[13] E. Potter, *Gender and Boyle's Law of Gases* (2001).

at the time, in equally wide circulation and which, until the contest between them was resolved in favour of Boyle's Law, had an equally valid claim for scientific legitimacy. Boyle presupposed a world made up of physical laws operating on dead matter; the alternative presupposed a world of animated matter involved in constant relational rearrangements. Both were equally good at explaining the seventeenth-century equivalent of the thermometer. When this happens in science (and it does, apparently, very often), we are (Potter argues) entitled to seek *social* reasons for the triumph of one rule over the other, the designation of one as 'true' and the other as 'magic and superstition'. And in this case those reasons can be found in the rich historical record, painstakingly assembled by Potter, showing that Boyle and his contemporaries saw that the 'dead matter' thesis presupposed a hierarchical and gendered physical order, a hierarchical and gendered social order, and a gendered experimental scientist in which and in whom m could $> f$—whereas the 'live matter' theory would have supposed a more contingent and indeterminate physical, social, and epistemological scheme (and was, not coincidentally, favoured by feminists, social and religious radicals, and antirationalists).

It takes a long, long time to work out a thesis as counterintuitive as Potter's; you have to stare at the record patiently waiting to see whether the pattern you've been taught will fade and be replaced by another that actually fits your hypothesis. And it's unequivocally thrilling when the work pays off. But will it always do so? Will we need (for instance) a feminist explanation for the timing with which asteroids have hit the Earth? Maybe, maybe not. *Presupposing* the covert importance of one's favourite paranoid idea—or claiming to see it precisely *because of* its seeming absence—can have the big downside of being—well—paranoid. It can lead you to not noticing other things that *are* going on, things that just can't and probably shouldn't be forced into the vocabulary of $m > f$.

The second mode in which feminism recuperates an ostensibly rejected structuralism is most noticeable in what I call the hybrid feminisms: socialist feminism, antiracist feminism, postcolonial feminism. These feminisms share the essential features of feminism as I have listed them; and they *also* posit that *some other system of social subordination*, operating according to *some other difference that defines the theory* and is essential to it in that sense, is also at work in the world. Class, race, empire: these are systematic social events that organize subordination in ways that are at least hypothetically distinct from m and f. There are two basic tendencies in these feminisms with respect to structuralism: a divergentist and a convergentist tendency. Divergentist hybrid feminism is ready to say that there are some things in, say, racism, that are simply not capable of being merged into the presupposition of $m > f$. There are tensions, splits, and sheer breakaway moments, in which an antiracist feminism would see things in terms of race *and not gender*; would be *for a man* and *against a woman,* and so on. Work like this ends up performing a firm rejection of the structuralist wish. These feminisms have learned how to Take a Break from Feminism, and I would argue that the strength of so much of this work (or perhaps simply my own admiration for it) is directly the result of a willingness to do so. Rejecting this approach, convergentist hybrid feminism posits that the theory is not good enough, the explanation not worked out enough, until everything in the socialist dimension, the antiracist dimension, or the postcolonial dimension of the project can be fully referred to and merged into its feminism. This is a jealously guarded moment in feminist thought. When it comes up, there is always a great deal of tension in the room. Oddly enough, it sometimes seems that feminism will stand accused of *racism* and *imperialism* (or *orientalism*) if it does not posit its ambition to 'top' both antiracism and anti-imperialism by emerging, when all is said and done, as their ultimate conceptual, normative, and political reference point. Structuralist ambitions figure in these gestures as an ultimate fealty to a transcendence, a utopia, or an harmonic convergence which, if we were only smart and good enough, we would be able to produce out of the terrible conflictual material we have to work with.

***

I think there are costs to all these recuperative strategies, as well as to the structuralism they covertly reintroduce; as well as to the definitional demands of feminism itself: its precommitment to *m/f* and to carrying a brief for *f.*

Before offering a few thoughts on that, allow me to insist that there are costs to Taking a Break from Feminism as well. They include: relaxing the epistemic vigilance that is needed to resist male epistemic hegemony; risking further splits among feminists at a higher conceptual location than most other splits, and thus risking new fissures in the intellectual, social, political, and legal endeavour; demobilizing and demoralizing feminists; laying oneself and one's arguments open to cooptation by the enemies of women's well-being; legitimating male dominance generally and specifically. If, for instance, feminism is our best weapon against the constant pressure of male sexual violence, weakening feminism in any of these ways could actually result in some guy's decision to rape a woman he would otherwise leave unmolested, or some prosecutor's willingness to see reasonable doubt in a rape case that would otherwise have seemed a clear prosecutorial priority. I see all that. Believe me, I do.

Still, I think it's also important for 'us' (that is, sex-affirmative, critically alert leftists, including sex-affirmative, critically alert, *feminist* leftists) to get clear about the costs of feminist structuralism, paranoid structuralism, and convergentism, and even the costs of maintaining a constant focus on the essentials of feminism as they exist today, the conceptual priority of *m/f* and the normative or political priority of carrying a brief for *f.* Some of those costs that we see in the US context are:

Brain drain. Everywhere I go as I travel around my country, women complain to me that academic feminism has lost its zing. Many key intellectual figures in feminism have decamped to other endeavours; Women's Studies Programs have undergone tumultuous transformations into Gender and/or Sexuality Studies Programs or disappeared altogether; feminist journals accept articles only on the proviso that the authors produce the effect of $m > f$, so that important new work gets submitted and published elsewhere. Faced with these trends, feminists say they have been betrayed and abandoned, and urge one another—the saving remnant—to a renewed commitment to feminist tenets. I think the feeling is misplaced and the remedy is probably counterproductive. That's because one motive force driving the brain drain is, surely, the sheer preclusion imposed on inquisitive minds and avid justice seekers by paranoid structuralist and convergentist presuppositions. Another is a widely held and powerful hunch that (as Kendall Thomas put it once when I presented an early version of this essay) 'women don't own gender': perhaps we need to examine m and f while suspending the stipulation that subordination is always their relation, and always takes the form of $m > f$. And another is the equally powerful hunch that many of the most devastating problems in the world might not be about m/f even a little.

Bad faith. If you look around the US, you see plenty of places where feminism—far from slinking about underground—is running things. Sex harassment, child sexual abuse, pornography, sexual violence: these feminist justice projects have moved off the street and into state and corporate bureaucracies. Schools and employers devote substantial resources now to extensive sexual harassment regulatory schemes. Child sexual abuse and rape enforcement have serious priority in many jurisdictions, and frequently tap into 'zero tolerance' enforcement modes much more readily than other kinds of child neglect and interpersonal violence. The Canadian Supreme Court has held that pornography that depicts the sexual subordination of women is an equality violation. In some important senses, *feminism rules*. Governance feminism.

Not only that, it *wants* to rule. It has a will to power.

Here its commitment to m/f and to carrying a brief for f has real world distributive consequences that feminism should not disavow: it wants to do, has done, and will do things on behalf of women *at the expense of men and other social interests*. This is not necessarily bad: justice in the real world sometimes means imposing costs. When it does this, feminism has effects. It gets blood on its hands. It needs—and I would suggest, is utterly without—a theory and practice of its own role in governance, of itself as responsible wielder of power.

Feminist convergentism and paranoid structuralism include their own special contributions to the denial of feminist power, the maintenance of the myth that feminism remains an utterly underdog movement needing complete and unbroken solicitude. But the possibility of a more nearly responsible attitude to the problem of 'feminism with blood on its hands' might also require Taking a Break from Feminism's definitional stakes of m/f and the subordination of f. I would suggest that these stakes not only make feminism what it is today, but also make it hard to for it to see around corners of its own construction. Unless it Takes a Break from itself, it can't see injury to men. It can't see injury to men by women. It can't see other interests, other forms of power, other justice projects. It insists that all justice projects will track a subordination model. And this refusal to see—sustained while feminism imposes costs on interests and projects outside its purview—gives us a text-book case of *bad faith*.

Power masquerading as servitude. At this point in my argument, I frequently hear that I don't care about women, have belittled the harm suffered by women, have denied the harm suffered by women, and have silenced women. These are fascinating charges—more than that, they sting.

These charges are brought to me on an assumption that they defend feminism. And they might well do just that; they certainly remind me of the importance of keeping one eye firmly fixed on the possibility that our real problem, the first thing we should be paying attention to, is $m > f$. But are there also some *costs to feminism* when it devolves to these charges.

First, nothing in what I've said *requires* me to concede that I don't care about women, have belittled the harm suffered by women, etc. Saying that women might harm men, for instance, is not the same as saying that women are not harmed. Saying something feminist women disagree with does not silence them. To be sure, saying that we should Take a Break from Feminism might have as a *downstream consequence* harm to women, a silencing of women; *I* might get blood on my hands. But I cannot help wondering whether feminists who imagine that my critique not only risks those consequences but *contains* and intrinsically *performs* them are attributing to me the only kind of power they can imagine for themselves. Their implicit vision of their opponents (and of themselves?)—as gods capable of performative utterances on the level of 'Fiat Lux', or 'I sentence you . . .'—is either very, very flattering or very, very scary.

Secondly, these accusations reassert precisely the presuppositions in feminism that I am calling into question. They redraw feminist disciplinary boundaries and implicitly require that feminists stay within them: a feminist will always describe everything in terms of m/f, and will always describe m/f as the domination of m and the subordination of f. That is, these charges are symptomatic of precisely the structuralism, with all the associated blind spots, which I am describing as costly *to* feminism.

Moral perfectionism and magic realism. Unitedstatesean feminists hearing my line at this point have responded, again and again, with a formulation something like this: if feminism had blood on its hands it would be because it had become a dominator; but feminism is definitionally *against* domination; and if it has dominated, if it has caused harm, it must chasten itself; but most likely feminism has not actually caused any harm; after all, feminism is powerless and in fact *suffers* harm. This argument, for all its moral modesty, is actually quite strict: feminism (to be feminism) must be morally immaculate; it is either subordinated (and harmless) or not-itself. A profound structural totalism—feminism is *the* subordination theory *par excellence*—subtends this formulation. And the willingness of feminism to undergo chastening in the name of its moral perfectionism is not necessarily meek all the way down. It stipulates for a binarized outcome: feminism can either assume guilt *or* deny harm. At moments when guilt has been the preferred stance, feminism has been notoriously not-fun; memories of these episodes have probably done a lot to fuel the brain drain. The fact that denial is framed as the chief alternative has produced a certain magic realist tendency in feminism; and of course it has produced a lot of distrust in allied projects—antiracist projects, pro-gay projects, etc.—where the constituency that arguably ends up bearing the costs of feminist governance decisions resides. Lastly, it has discouraged the investigation of internal ambivalence among self-identified feminists. Feminism in this mode does not particularly want to hear me say, 'As a gay man, I . . .'. And I might well decide to Take a Break from Feminism rather than give up on the hope of finding out what it might mean to say it.

Constituting women, heterosexuality, and women's suffering. One of the most crucial moments in the genealogy of US feminism, as I see it, was the nearly simultaneous publication in 1990 of Judith Butler's *Gender Trouble* and Eve Kosofsky Sedgwick's *Epistemology of the Closet*.[14] In different ways, and opening onto different consequences, both of them argued that what I have called here the definitional stake tying feminism to *m/f also* ties it, at the most fundamental level, to *the heterosexual*. To the extent that feminism defines itself as the -ism of this distinction, it *is* heterosexual; it *requires* heterosexuality, and is basically not friendly to the homo-affirmative aim. Sedgwick responded by seeking a suspension of feminism; to articulate a 'gay affirmative' agenda she felt the need to Take a Break from Feminism; she asked instead whether the homoerotic could be understood with richness and nuance in an account that did not turn substantially on *m* and *f*; and proposed that study of same-sex eroticism might well return to feminism, but at an uncertain future date. Butler responded to the very same dilemma by turning feminism *against* the *m/f* distinction itself; a feminism that did not question its own role in producing the discursive strictures that require there to be women, and the feminine, and femininity, could not escape the charge of heteronormativity and thus could hardly merit the name of feminism.

A similar critical move can be performed on the definitional stake tying feminism to the subordination of *f.* What if, as well as *describing* and *opposing* this social and psychic event, feminism *helps to produce it?* What if the politics

---

[14] E. K. Sedgwick, *Epistemology of the Closet* (1990).

of injury and of traumatized sensibility which have almost completely occupied the space cleared by MacKinnon's politics of domination and subordination are helping to authorize and capacitate women as *sufferers*? If indeed feminism is a powerfully constitutive discourse, it might well have a shaping contribution to make *to women's suffering* when, for instance, it insists that a raped woman has suffered an injury from which she is unlikely ever to recover. What if real raped women, believing this feminist line, proceed never to recover? What if some men are 'guided' by this bull's-eye to target women for rape rather than fomenting other aggressions, perhaps more manageable, perhaps directed elsewhere? When feminism insists that any effort to trace the causes of particular rapes in the woman's conduct blames the victim, revictimizes her, is a second rape, it might make rape seem more magical and random than it is, might make women more risk-averse about it than they need to be, and might induce women to concede more social power to the threat of rape than they otherwise would. So much feminist rape discourse insists on women's object-like status in the rape situation: man fucks woman, subject verb object. Could feminism be contributing to, rather than (only) describing and resisting, the alienation of women from their own agency in narratives and events of sexual violence?

These questions pose a very profound problem about the nature of power and resistance. If a social subordination exists, and an anti-subordination discourse ratifies it, fixes it, creates the discursive capacity for its experiential uptake by the subordinated, all the while hanging a bull's-eye on it—where does one intervene to attack it? It has fascinated me, as I have begun to learn how to ask this question, to notice the strong feminist impulse to refuse it as unfeminist. The reaction has fuelled my intuition that we might need to Take a Break from Feminism precisely to be *for women* and *against this increment of injury.*

***

So what might we get out of Taking a Break from Feminism? I'm going to read the 'facts' and 'law' of an amazing case in US (actually, because we do most of our family law at the state level, I should say *Texas*) family law: *Twyman v Twyman.*[15] Reading this extraordinary case will allow me to provide a short, very graphic display of what might be possible if we try Taking a Break from Feminism sheerly as a conceptual, analytic project. I'm going to read the facts reported in the published opinions against the elements of the cause of action for intentional infliction of emotional distress—and then re-read them as if they were our best examples of *nonfeminist* theories about morals, power, and sex that I derive from Friedrich Nietzsche's *On the Genealogy of Morals: A Polemic* and Michel Foucault's *The History of Sexuality, Volume One*—to set out some possibilities.[16]

[15] *Twyman v Twyman*, 855 S.W.2d 619 (Tex. 1993).
[16] F. Nietzsche, *On the Genealogy of Morals: A Polemic*, trans. D. Smith (1996); M. Foucault, *The History of Sexuality, Volume I: An Introduction*, trans. R. Hurley (1980).

Allow me to reiterate that by 'facts' I mean the narrative bites that we get from the various Texas Supreme Court Justices: I disavow any suggestion that the resulting formulations describe the real human beings, Sheila and William Twyman.

The Texas Supreme Court remanded the case on what amounts to a ruling that the facts in the record were sufficient to sustain findings: (1) that William's conduct was outrageous, beyond all possible bounds of decency, atrocious, and utterly intolerable in a civilized society; (2) (at this point there is some legal uncertainty so I include all the options considered important by various Justices) that, when he engaged in that conduct, he *intended* to cause Sheila severe emotional distress and/or he *knew* he might cause her severe emotional distress and *recklessly* ran the risk, and/or he *recklessly ignored the risk* of emotional distress;[17] (3) and that his conduct did cause (4) her to suffer severe emotional distress. No one disputed that Sheila was 'devastated', etc.: the dicey questions seem to be: what was the outrageous conduct, exactly; and what causally linked it to Sheila's distress.

All the Justices who give us any facts agree that William first introduced 'bondage' into their sexual relationship. We learn from Justice Hecht that both Sheila and William tied each other up in those early encounters; her willing participation in those scenes, and the mobility of 'top' and 'bottom' roles in them, fall out of the narrative for all the remanding Justices. Sheila then told William that she had been raped before they married, and told him that she did not want to engage in sadomasochistic sex with him any more; the Justices represent this moment, which I will call the 'rape disclosure', very differently, as we will soon see. There is no inconsistency between the Justices on the basic facts of the rape, however. Sheila testified that she had been raped before her marriage, at knifepoint; and had been cut with the knife; and had feared for her life.[18]

Some years later Sheila discovered that William was in psychotherapy, and, confronting him to find out why, was told that he was having an affair with a woman who was willing to engage in bondage. At this point he introduced

---

[17] The Restatement rule does not include any requirement that the defendant knew of the risk, or even that he recklessly ignored the risk, of emotional distress. Restatement (Second) of Torts § 46 (1965), quoted by Justice Cornyn, *supra* n. 15, at 621. Justice Cornyn nevertheless supposes that the factfinder on remand would have to find that William had such knowledge, or was reckless when he failed to think about it, *supra* n. 15, at 623–4. As Justice Hecht points out, the idea that the liability requires *intentional* conduct is significantly eroded by the 'recklessness' proviso; *supra* n. 15, at 630. The same view of the underlying conduct that classifies it as 'outrageous' could well supply all a factfinder needed to conclude that the defendant recklessly ignored the likelihood that it would produce distress. Indeed, 'outrage' *is* 'distress'.

[18] Justice Cornyn tells us that she was raped at knifepoint (*supra* n. 15, at 620, n. 1); Justice Hecht tells us the same thing (*supra* n. 15, at 636); Justice Spector adds that Sheila was actually cut with the knife and placed in fear for her life (*supra* n. 15, at 641).

what I will call the 'divorce threat': as Justice Hecht put it, he told Sheila that 'if she could only have done bondage, nothing else would have mattered'.[19] As Justice Spector put it, 'he told Sheila that if she would not satisfy his desires by engaging in bondage, there would be no future to their marriage'.[20] Justice Hecht further tells us that:

For the remainder of the year the couple sought counseling. On their counselor's advice, William and Sheila discussed William's bondage fantasies, and Sheila again tried to participate in bondage activities with William. But she found the activity so painful and humiliating that she could not continue it. Their last encounter, which did not include bondage activities, was so rough that she was injured to the point of bleeding.[21]

Like Justice Hecht, Justice Spector understands that it was these last bondage encounters, and not the final sexual event in which Sheila sustained gynaecological injuries, that are at the heart of Sheila's claim to actionable mental distress:

Sheila experienced 'utter despair' and 'devastation,' as well as physical problems— weight loss and, after one encounter, prolonged bleeding that necessitated gynecological treatment. The *pain and humiliation of the bondage activities* caused her to seek help from three professional counsellors.[22]

It is the bondage, not the last night of rough sex, that the Justices continually return to as the crux of William's conduct. We are left, then, with this basic narrative configuration: faced with the divorce threat, Sheila reluctantly but willingly engaged in them, decided during or after them that they were intolerable to her, also had some very rough sex which the Justices seem to agree she did not claim was humiliating, and suffered intense anguish.

So there are three causal elements. One is William's desire for and solicitation of sadomasochistic sex. A second is Sheila's narrative to William of a rape that occurred before the marriage and her refusal (apparently rescinded near the end of their life together) to engage in bondage for that reason. And the third is William's inability/refusal to relinquish his kink, his pursuit of it with a lover, and his telling Sheila, when she discovered that he was seeing a psychotherapist, that the marriage would fail if she could not participate in bondage with him.

For one Justice, the divorce threat and the sadomasochistic solicitations are crucial and the rape seemingly irrelevant. Justice Gonzales indicates that the element of 'outrageousness' was fully met by William's solicitation of and participation in bondage activities with her, 'under the rationale that such activities were necessary to the future of their marriage'. He makes no reference to the claims that these solicitations, episodes, or arguments had a

---

[19] *Twyman v Twyman, supra* n.15, at 636.
[20] Ibid., at 641.   [21] Ibid., at 636.   [22] Ibid., at 641 (emphasis added).

severe emotional impact on her because of the rape, or that William should incur liability for them because she had warned him that they would.[23] He almost suggests that the solicitation of mild sadomasochistic sex with a spouse, especially if you really need it and she later finds this out, is itself outrageous, and can be presumed to cause any emotional distress that follows. It's a draconian anti-kink stance, and not intrinsically feminist (though some feminists would no doubt endorse it, for feminist reasons that do not appear to have motivated Justice Gonzales).

For the other Justices who reflect substantially on the facts, all three elements—the bondage solicitations, the rape disclosure, and the divorce threat—matter, and there are indelible marks of feminism in their under-standing of their interrelation in a causal progress leading to Sheila's distress. To Justice Cornyn (writing the plurality opinion, and concluding that the action for intentional infliction should be allowed, and the case remanded) 'Sheila testified that William pursued sadomasochistic bondage activities with her, even though he knew that she feared such activities *because she had been raped at knife-point before their marriage*'.[24] (This logic must exclude the bondage scenes that happened before William knew about the rape.) Justice Hecht (who would have rejected all infliction actions as indeterminate and thus not capable of being brought within the rule of law) narrates the moment of disclosure thus: 'She revealed to him that she *associated the activities with the horrible experience of having been raped* at knife-point earlier in her life.'[25] And Justice Spector (who would have endorsed a rule allowing negligent infliction actions because of the disproportionate harm insensitive men cause more emotionally alert women, and who would have affirmed the judgment for Sheila even on an intentional infliction rule) basically repeats Justice Hecht's narrative here: after William 'introduced bondage activities into their rela-tionship after their marriage[,] Sheila told William that *she could not endure these activities because of the trauma of having been raped* several years earlier'.[26]

Justices Cornyn, Hecht, and Spector (though they agree about little else) agree that Sheila's special sexual history was crucial to her claim, and the last two (though they agree about almost *nothing* else) agree that it made her particularly vulnerable to harm in sexual exchange with her husband. They use a strange temporal locution—'the experience of having been raped'; 'the trauma of having been raped'—that locates the moment of injury in a perpetual present. Sheila is *always* undergoing the experience of having been raped, *always* suffering the trauma of having been raped. In much feminist rape discourse, this is exactly right. Once raped, always raped. Contemporary feminist rape discourse repeatedly insists that the pain of rape extends into every future moment of a woman's life; it is a note played not on a piano but on

---

[23] *Ibid.*, at 626.   [24] Ibid., at 620, n. 1 (emphasis added).
[25] Ibid., at 636 (emphasis added).   [26] Ibid., at 641 (emphasis added).

an organ. Justice Spector's cultural feminism probably supplies this under-standing; Justice Hecht, who, as we will see, attempts to reconstitute Sheila as a responsible agent with considerable powers, resorts to it in a gesture that seems almost compensatory.

At this point Justices Spector and Hecht part company, and as the latter departs from Justice Spector's cultural feminist line I feel strongly tempted to follow him. On the question 'what did William know about Sheila's likely emotional reaction to a bondage solicitation', Justice Hecht tells us that, after the first experiments with neckties, 'Sheila told William she did not like this activity and did not want to participate in it further'.[27] Strong, decisive, self-knowing. An agent. But not a person with a plausible claim that her husband's desire for what she did not desire constituted 'intentional infliction of emo-tional distress'. Justice Spector, however, understands the disclosure quite differently: after the rape disclosure 'William understood that Sheila *equated* bondage with her prior experience of being raped'; 'Sheila told William that she *could not endure* these activities.'[28] Once again Justice Spector deals in standard cultural feminist rape tropes: the deathlike pall of sexual injury, and the literal equation of every rape-*like* event with *rape itself.* If bondage reminded Sheila of her rape, it was the rape all over again; and because the rape was death, being reminded of it was also death: she *could not endure it.*

And what about the divorce threat? Justice Hecht gives it a somewhat pathetic cast: 'William told Sheila that if she could only have done bondage, nothing else would have mattered.'[29] None of the other renditions of this fact have anything like this wistful sound. Justice Spector quotes the trial court, which found that William had engaged in 'a continuing course of conduct of attempting to coerce [Sheila] to join in his practices of "bondage" by continu-ally asserting that their marriage could be saved' only if she participated in them.[30] Justice Cornyn also quoted the trial court's finding that William 'attempted to emotionally coerce [Sheila] in "bondage" on an on-going basis'.[31] Perhaps this is where the rape-likeness of the last bondage scenes finally emerges: the threat of divorce is like the threat of a knife. Under threats like this, a woman loses her agency, and if she consents to sex, it is nevertheless coerced. This, too, is a completely familiar element of feminist rape discourse. Why so many feminisms want women to experience them-selves as completely devoid of choice when they bargain their way past a knife by having sex they really really don't want, I don't know. But wait! Justice Spector has just extended this agency-less construction of women to situations involving the threat not of physical mutilation or death, but of *divorce. Divorce* is represented as so life-threatening that, faced with the possibility of it, women cannot be regarded as agents.

---

[27] *Twyman v Twyman, supra* n.15, at 636.   [28] Ibid., at 641 (emphasis added).
[29] Ibid., at 636.   [30] Ibid., at 641.   [31] Ibid., at 620, n. 1.

This image of male power and female subordination—the utter pathos of Sheila, submitting to sex with her husband that he wants but that they both know will humiliate and anguish her, all to save her marriage precisely to the author of her suffering—is of course not at all required by any particular strand of feminism. Nor, as Brenda Cossman and Dan Danielsen have shown, need feminism endorse or seek the remedy granted by the Texas Supreme Court in this case.[32] But can feminism accommodate a completely reversed image of the Twymans' marriage? Imagine it: the utter pathos of William, begging for sex he can't get from his wife, guiltily sneaking off to have it with another woman, whipped through round after round of psychotherapy to figure out why he is such a pervert, and finally submitted to the public humiliation of testifying about his hopeless intimacies and suffering a published opinion deciding that his marital conduct is very likely outrageous, beyond all possible bounds of decency, atrocious, and utterly intolerable in a civilized society. As against that, imagine: the astonishing powers of Sheila, laying down the moral law of the couple's sex life, pursuing William like a Fury for breaking it, and extracting not only a fault-based divorce but possibly also money damages specifically premissed on her alliance with the state against him. Imagine further: *Twyman* as background family law rule that husbands with enduring ineradicable desires for sex that their wives find humiliating must either stay married to those wives, or, if they seek a divorce (which they might well want to do simply to remarry and have non-adulterous sex with women who do not find their desires humiliating), pay a heavy tax in shame, blame, and cash. Can feminism acknowledge that women emerge from the court's decision with new bargaining power in marriage and a new role as enforcers of marital propriety? And can feminism see how costly this 'bargaining endowment' might be *to women*, who can tap into it only if they find the sex in question painful and humiliating? Can feminism read the case as male subordination and female domination—and still as bad for women?

Very possibly. There might well be a place for feminism that carries a brief for *f*, but without presupposing *m* > *f*. I think this is largely where Cossman and Tracy Higgins[33] see the possibility of substantial gains for feminism. But my project here is to expose some of the distinctive attractions of Taking a Break from Feminism. To do that, I'm going to reduce *On the Genealogy of Morals* and *The History of Sexuality, Volume One*, in that order, to a set of counterhypotheses, and offer brief re-readings of *Twyman v Twyman* designed to exploit the explanatory power of the resulting hypotheses. Again I hope it will be understood that I am not making any claims about the real human

---

[32] See the contributions of Brenda Cossman and Dan Danielsen to B. Cossman *et al.*, 'Gender, Sexuality, and Power: Is Feminist Theory Enough?', 12 *Columbia Journal of Gender and Law* (2003) 601.

[33] Again, see the contributions of Cossman and Tracy Higgins to Cossman *et al.*, *supra* n. 32.

beings, Sheila and William Twyman; instead, working from the obviously highly artful constructions of them that we receive from the Justices of the Texas Supreme Court, I'm going to bracket feminism and reconnnect all the dots à la Nietzsche and à la Foucault.

First, let's consider the moralistic character of Sheila's project with William. Note that she was not content to seek a fault-based divorce, and apparently did not seek damages or pursue criminal charges against him for that last night of sex between them that left her bleeding. Instead, she seeks a judge's finding that—through the sadomasochistic solicitations, the rape disclosure, and the divorce threat—William has engaged in conduct that is outrageous, beyond all possible bounds of decency, atrocious, and utterly intolerable in a civilized society. What can we say about her decision if we take Nietzsche's *Genealogy of Morals* as our theoretical ground? In the following extractions, I rewrite the 'slave revolt in morals' as if it were achieved not over the broad sweep of human history but by an individual:

1. The historical starting point of slave morality is the slave's perception of himself as dominated and as suffering under the will of the master. He sees his as a *passive* location in the world: the master is *active*; and in his passivity the slave suffers.
2. Though originally the slave could have understood his suffering as bad and the master's activity as good (and could have sought to be active too), this is not what happens. Instead, he translates the power relation into a moral one: he is good and the master is evil. It is now a relationship of dominated virtue and dominating vice. Morality is born as a covert mechanism of power, a sublimated form of domination.
3. This translation removes any reason for the slave to experience himself as having *a will*. Will is now evil. The rage of the slave against his suffering—his own will to power—is now denied.
4. His will, his activity, don't go away though. Instead, translated yet again into *ressentiment*, they are rerouted both *out*, against the master, in gestures of meek but biting vengeance; and *in*, against the slave himself, in a new form of suffering, under the whip of his own morality, the new innerness of a *guilty conscience*.
5. Slave morality wreaks itself with splendid sadism on the master, and with stupefying intensity it also punishes the slave himself for his own active impulses—impulses without which the whole terrible cycle would never have started. It establishes a third human class, the priestly class, with powers that are made more uncanny because they are waged under the sign of weakness and use not the pathetic devices of physical coercion but the intimate stringencies of conscience and inner pain. 'Bad air! Bad air!'

It's not hard at all to re-read Sheila Twyman as the intense sufferer and wielder of slave morality. Her rapist, that blond beast, could have been her enemy, but (possibly with the assistance of feminism) became her master. His power to rape her at knifepoint became *a* if not *the* central fact of her life. Experiencing herself as utterly dominated, she determined to oppose him with the power of the weak: he was bad not in the sense that he acted inimically to her will, but in the sense that he was evil. And her moral project of punishing him, in its ferocious will for revenge, failed to notice that William was— well a different guy. Wielding the moral code of good sex, Sheila made William grovel; but she also suffered intensely herself. Justice Spector (of course) provides us with the gruesome details: Sheila 'experienced "utter despair" and "devastation"', lost weight, accepted sex with William that left her bleeding; 'the pain and humiliation of the bondage activities caused her to seek help from three professional counsellors'. (It is an amazing detail that Justice Spector's *and* Justice Hecht's Sheila seems to find sex with neckties, but not sex that produces gynaecological injuries, to be painful and humiliating. A Nietzschean reading of this discrepancy would propose that this Sheila was devoid of a self-preservative impulse, could not attend to the well-being of the body, so devoted was she to quickening of her wounded soul.) She experienced her self as utterly powerless, utterly broken, and the more intensely she sought and obtained vengeance on William, the more deeply she became embedded in the stringencies of the suffering that justified it.

I can think of many reasons why Taking a Break from Feminism so as to be able to read the case in this way is a good idea. It brings strongly to my attention the possibility that Sheila Twyman is no ally of mine. *If* this reading of her is right—and the reading itself is no empirical warrant—I have several important political insights I would not have without it. First, it warns me to think of her as no weakling, but rather as a formidable enemy who will pursue her goals with fierce drive. Secondly, it suggests that she nevertheless suffers terribly with every new access of subordinated sensibility. And, thirdly, it helps me to see that *feminism* might be responsible not only for her power, but also for the terrible suffering that grounds it.

But maybe my *ressentiment* of Sheila's *ressentiment* is torquing my reading too much. Let's look for something milder, something that suspends completely the idea that power must take the form of domination and subordination, and something that lifts us out of moralism and the temptation to fall into a moralistic rage against it. As I read Volume One of Foucault's *A History of Sexuality*, it offers some theoretic hypotheses that differ very strikingly from those I have attributed to US feminism[34] and to Nietzsche. In what follows I proceed as though Foucault's hypotheses about power were simple and

[34] Of course I know that there have been many efforts, some quite successful, to converge Volume One into feminism. I nevertheless offer this divergentist reading, trusting that pushing feminism and Foucault as far apart as I can will also be productive, albeit in a different way.

straightforward rather than contradicted, ambivalent, and in tension throughout this text.[35] Four key points:

1. For the Foucault of Volume One, the task was to imagine power not as the
   relation of dominance and subordination, but as a highly fragmented and
   temporally mobile 'field of force *relations*'. Power could be *micropouvoir*: it
   could achieve vast social and consciousness effects not by dropping
   down on people from on high, but by being constantly moved about
   among them; and not only through physical violence, but also through
   formations and reformations of the possibilities for organized experience.
   Discourses.
2. For the Foucault of Volume One, power was not necessarily bad. It might
   be *pouvoir*—the capacity to create effects—rather than *puissance*—the
   capacity to dominate or coerce.
3. For the Foucault of Volume One, sexuality emerged historically as a
   discourse and produced as its effect the people we are—people who
   think their lives crucially involved knowledge of their deepest sexual
   selves. There is something excruciating and 'stuck' about this; a more
   mobile relationship to sexuality not as a truth but as a practice might
   be better. Foucault did not imagine liberation, but rather a perpetual
   search for the *rearrangement* of powers in the social and experiential
   fields.
4. Very few of the chief discourses of sexuality in the modern era turn in any
   sustained way on *m/f*. None of them bears the mark of sustained male
   dominance. Instead, the organization of knowledge and knowledge practices are far more likely to be the way in which power constitutes sexuality.
   These will not oppress particular persons or groups, so much as produce
   differentiations within the population, spread it out in mobile but patterned arrays. Biopower.

These hypotheses would allow us to Take a Break from Feminism in both of its
essential points: they analyse sexuality, *m/f*, and power in quite different terms.

So let's read the *Twyman* facts as if these hypotheses were the only ones
available. The first thing that 'goes' is the presumption, silently carried along
in all the opinions of the court, that Sheila Twyman has a meaningful moral
claim that William's conduct was wrong. The question addressed by the
Justices is whether that claim is *legally cognizable*; Justice Hecht comes closest
to the claim that the power relationships between husband and wife are

---

[35] Thus Foucault describes power as *both* sovereign and fragmented; liberation as *both*
desirable and a ruse; historical forms of power and social life as *both* superseded and enduring.
For a brilliant reflection on the nonpropositional quality of Volume One, see A. Parker,
'Foucault's Tongues', *Mediations* 182 (Fall 1994). For some perhaps adequate reflections on
Foucault's ambivalent periodizations, see J. Halley, '*Bowers v Hardwick* in the Renaissance', in
J. Goldberg (ed.), *Queering the Renaissance* (1994) 15.

indeterminate, but even he fell for the 'trauma of having been raped' line. Reading the case as if it were an example of how right Foucault's hypotheses in Volume One could be, however, requires us to give that presumption up.

One of the things that then immediately emerges is the intense, and formally almost identical, sexual pathos of both Shiela *and* William. Both are committed to the idea that they have deep, inner, injured sexual selves beyond which they cannot move one micron, and which must they must enact with near-fatal completeness. William *must* live out the affliction of a perverse implantation, a deeply resisted fetishistic desire. He is a classic subject of the psychiatrization of perversions. Sheila *must* live out the affliction of rape trauma. Rape trauma is her deep inner truth, and her experiential life must make it manifest. In a terrible way, William and Sheila are perfectly matched to provoke the complete manifestation of their diametrically opposite desires; but oddly, this is because they are basically the same.

Moreover, Foucault always seems to think that this experience of deep inner truth is introduced into modern consciousness by a discourse—a power/knowledge—that imposes it on us while distracting us from the real action, the real place where power connects with sexual life. The suffering of the shamed fetishist is pathetic—indeed, it is cruel, and quite one of the terrible wrongs inflicted on the tremulous human spirit by the psychiatric discourse of sexual truth; and the suffering of the rape survivor is similarly pathetic—indeed, it is cruel, and quite one of the terrible wrongs inflicted on the tremulous human spirit by the feminist discourse of sexual truth; but both are distractions from the real game, the real place where power meets the population. (This is *Foucault's* paranoid structuralism.)

And where might we look in the *Twyman* facts for a warrant of the hypotheses of Volume One? We are looking for something broadly regulatory, not *m/f*, and capable of complex biopoweristic and micropoweristic deployments. I propose marital monogamy. Marriage provides spouses with an amazing power over each other: the power to perform (and inflict), and to prohibit (and punish), infidelity. The monogamy rule and all the possible ways of breaking it provide rich social scripts, carefully elaborated at every level of cultural detail. Those scripts provide many ways of seeing a relationship of 'power over' in the *Twyman* facts. It is very easy to say that William has breached his promise of sexual continence, indulged in gratifications inconsistent with adult self-discipline and decent regard for Sheila's dignity, and cracked one of the building blocks of civilization. Also easy to articulate an idea that he has unleashed the brute force of sexual yearning against the fragility of civilization. But we could see the subordination as running the other way: William enacts that immemorial figure, the Hapless Adulterer; he is the helpless bumbling dupe of a dozen trite tropes in the adultery script; the deep purpose of his affair was realized only when Sheila discovered it and gained the upper hand; Sheila as the wronged wife, the enforcer of marriage vows, fiercely restores the fidelity rule to its proper place, with the avid assistance of almost every judge involved in the case.

But let's try one more time, for a third reading without a victim and a victimizer, without dominance and submission, but *with* power. What if the struggle between the two over William's infidelity—their divorce had been pending for eight years by the time the Texas Supreme Court remanded the case *for a new trial!*—was for both of them a paroxysm of intimacy, a sustained crescendo of erotic interrelatedness, which, if it should ever end, would leave both of them aimless and lonely to the last degree?

***

It might be that these alternative readings of the facts recorded in *Twyman* just don't have any real world plausibility. Maybe Sheila is never the fomenter of slave morality; maybe Sheila and William never seek love in power without domination, suffering without subordination, in the cruel coils of divorce. There is both strength and danger in framing the possibilities described by these readings. Only if we articulate and explore them, will we ever look into the world and see if it matches them. Our political desires and projects could be significantly rerouted, in very good ways, if we found a match: noticing that slave moralistic Sheila Twymans are not my allies has meant a profound reorientation of my feminism and my stance towards feminism, one I think has been very helpful to me. I admit there is danger here too, in the form of a spiral: if our axiom is 'I'll see it when I believe it', theory can change reality by changing what we can notice in it; and maybe feminism is right to close its eyes. As I've suggested, I'm strongly inclined to think otherwise.

And maybe there is something terrifying about losing one's grip on a 'moral compass' or in admiring a cruel marriage rule *because* people can use it for intense, crazy, masochistic love. Very possibly, critical disorientation is an unaffordable luxury, especially in times, like these, of acute consolidation of conservative power. Again, I'm strongly inclined to think otherwise; and hope my hunch turns out to be right.

***

Over the past decade or more, international human rights projects working in a wide range of legal disciplines, and the debates surrounding them, have 'received'—not without controversy of course—a cluster of ideas from Unitedstatesean feminism. At the core of this cluster is the idea that sexuality is a distinct domain of women's subordination. This idea has appeared in debates about rape as a violation of human rights in war settings; in efforts to regulate sex work, especially by women and children; in controversies over the international diffusion of 'pornography'; in national feminist struggles to instantiate regulatory schemes resembling Unitedstatesean sexual harassment and domestic battery law; and, more generally, in efforts to figure as international and public rather than local and private various practices affecting women, from genital cutting to arranged marriage, and to subsume women's distinctive suffering in globalization and in 'culture' under the rubric 'violence against women', where rape, not market exchange, is the paradigm violent act. More generally, it has been important in the way in which Unitedstatesean feminist thought and Unitedstatesean civil rights and rights thinking and practice intervene in a number of conceptual problems that are important in international human rights work: the tension between individual and group rights, the tension between cultural preservation and personal agency in setting the normative goals of justice work, the place of knowingness, certainty, and their opposites in decisional debates, and so on.

I don't pretend to know what it should mean, inside these international human rights projects, or inside national contexts where these projects have become an element of left/liberal/progressive work, that the core idea—that sexuality is a distinct domain of women's subordination, and that feminism provides the 'proper' justice discourse for addressing it—has been elaborated, modified, and contested in the Unitedstatesean intellectually and politically engaged left. I offer this essay in the hope that it will be productive for people directly engaged in those projects to have direct access to the resulting debates and a clear and sympathetic statement, in legally inflected terms, of some the conceptual stakes. A brief annotated bibliography for those who wish to explore them further appears in the Appendix.

APPENDIX

Teaching a short course at the European University Institute was a crucial moment for me in coming to grips with the debates from which this essay emerged. I am very grateful to the Institute, to the students, to the other teachers participating, and to Karen Knop for a series of engagements that have made a huge impact on my understanding of feminism. What follows is what I now wish had been the syllabus for my lectures, with very slight annotations. This list concentrates on, but is not exclusively limited to, work produced in the US. It is highly selective and tilts strongly towards the elaboration of differences *within* queer theoretic work, especially relating to law and law reform; for attacks on and criticisms of this general project from 'outside' it, readers will want to look elsewhere. I include only four items that have already been cited—the first four—so that I can insist on their preeminent place in my own genealogy of the debates. In sum, this is an 'interested', not an 'objective'—a 'genealogical', not a 'historically accurate'—list.

1. C. A. MacKinnon, 'Feminism, Marxism, Method and the State: An Agenda for Theory', 7:3 *Signs* (1982) 515; C. A. MacKinnon, 'Feminism, Marxism,

Method and the State: Toward Feminist Jurisprudence', 8:4 *Signs* (1983) 635. These provide an early, 'unmodified' statement of MacKinnon's radical feminism. In my view, many positions (or perhaps better said, analytic methods) that she now rejects, and which have migrated into queer theory, appear *within* radical feminism in these important articles.

2. M. Foucault, *The History of Sexuality, Volume I*, trans. R. Hurley (1980). Just as radical as MacKinnon's articles, and widely read as an equally crucial but entirely alternative analysis of sexuality and power. Actually, they share a surprising number of positions and analytic practices. Widely regarded as crucial to the emergence of queer theory in the US.

3. F. Nietzsche, *On the Genealogy of Morals: A Polemic*, trans. D. Smith (1996). Not as important as it ought to be in left legal theory and practice.

4. C. Gilligan, *In a Different Voice: Psychological Theory and Women's Development* (1982); R. West, 'The Difference in Women's Hedonic Lives: A Phenomenological Critique of Feminist Legal Theory', 3 *Wisconsin Women's Law Journal* (1987) 81; R. West, *Caring for Justice* (1997). The first is a classic in cultural feminist thought; West brings cultural feminism as fully into the liberal feminist project as anyone.

5. E.K. Sedgwick, *Epistemology of the Closet* (1990); J. Butler, *Gender Trouble: Feminism and the Subordination of Identity* (1990; rpt. 1999). Together, almost graphically a crossroads for feminsm, pro-gay, and queer understandings of sex, sexuality, and gender.

6. A. Snitow and C. Stansell, *Powers of Desire: The Politics of Sexuality* (1983); L. Duggan and N. Hunter (eds), *The Sex Wars: Sexual Dissent and Legal Culture* (1995); B. Cossman *et al.*, *Bad Attitudes on Trial: Pornography, Feminism, and the* Butler *Decision* (1997). Feminists directly contesting the law reform projects undertaken by MacKinnon-style feminists and cultural feminists (see also of course *Pleasure and Danger*, cited in n. 1 *supra*).

7. L. Bersani, 'Is the Rectum a Grave', in D. Crimp (ed.), *AIDS: Cultural Analysis, Cultural Activism* (1988) 197; R. Rambuss, 'Christ's Ganymede', 7 *Yale Journal of Law and the Humanities* (1995) 77; B. Martin, 'Sexualities without Genders and Other Queer Utopias', 24:2–3 *diacritics* (1994) 104. Gender takes a queer turn: gay male and lesbian feminist interventions in the early days of queer theory.

8. Duncan Kennedy, 'Sexual Abuse, Sexy Dressing, and the Eroticization of Domination', in Duncan Kennedy (ed.), *Sexy Dressing Etc.* (1993) 126. The only major intervention in legal theory that I regard as equally critical *and* queer.

9. J. Butler, 'Against Proper Objects', in E. Weed and N. Schor (eds), *feminism meets queer theory* (1997) 1. Critical reflections on the taxonomy of sexuality studies.

10. M. Warner, *The Trouble with Normal: Sex, Politics and the Ethics of Queer Life* (1999); David Kennedy, 'The Spectacle and the Libertine',

in L. V. Kaplan and B. I. Moran (eds), *Aftermath* (2001) 279. Reflections on the place of normativity in queer thought and practice: the first seeks a specifically ethical queer life; the second sets out a libertine project.

11. V. Bell, 'Beyond the "Thorny Question": Feminism, Foucault and the Desexualization of Rape', 19 *International Journal of the Sociology of Law* (1991) 83; P. Haag, '"Putting Your Body on the Line": The Question of Violence, Victims, and the Legacy of Second-Wave Feminism', 8:2 *differences* (1996) 23; S. Marcus, 'Fighting Bodies, Fighting Words: A Theory and Politics of Rape Prevention', in J. Butler and J. W. Scott (eds), *Feminists Theorize the Political* (1992) 385. Feminists reframing rape; the first two are primarily genealogical; the third argues for a reshaping of the project going forward. All historicize and contest the paradigmatic place that some feminists grant to rape in defining women's subordination.

12. L. Berlant, 'The Subject of True Feeling: Pain, Privacy and Politics', in W. Brown and J. Halley (eds), *Left Legalism/Left Critique* (2002) 105; W. Brown, 'Wounded Attachments', in W. Brown (ed.), *States of Injury: Power and Freedom in Late Modernity* (1995) 52. Left reconsiderations of the place of injury, trauma, and painful sensibility in rights claiming.

13. W. Brown, 'The Impossibility of Women's Studies', 9:3 *differences* (1997) 79; R. Wiegman, *Women's Studies on its Own* (2002). If feminism is a governance project, one thing it governs in the US is Women's Studies. These titles provide an entry into the internal critique that has sprung up in recent years.

14. W. Brown and J. Halley, 'Introduction', in W. Brown and J. Halley (eds), *Left Legalism/Left Critique* (2002) 1. An argument that left internal critique, though admittedly dangerous, can be fun and very good for left justice projects.

4

Citizenship in Europe and the Construction of Gender by Law in the European Charter of Fundamental Rights

SUSANNE BAER

Citizenship, in a broad sense,[1] was an issue of visible interest to political thinkers in the 1990s.[2] It became interesting to European law experts in 1997, when the Maastricht Treaty of the European Union (TEU) established European citizenship by way of legal recognition. Article 8 of the Treaty provides that (1) 'Citizenship of the Union is hereby established. Every person holding the nationality of a Member State shall be a citizen of the Union', and that (2) 'Citizens of the Union shall enjoy the rights conferred by this Treaty and shall be subject to the duties imposed thereby'.[3]

It was clear from the start that European citizenship is special, as it does not directly refer to a state but relies on nation state membership and transfers it to

---

[1] In German, 'Staatsangehörigkeit' is the status of belonging to a state, while 'Staatsbür-gerschaft' is the status of those who belong. On the distinction, see Baer, 'Citizenship, Loyalty, and the Ordering of Gender', in A. Sev'er (ed.), *Frontiers in Women's Studies. Canadian and German Perspectives* (1998) 57, at 58–9.

[2] Kymlicka and Norman explain the rise of interest in citizenship by its conceptual conjunction of democracy and justice, and by some political phenomena that highlight the state of citizenship, like voter apathy as an indicator of political crisis, people's poverty as an indicator of run-down welfare states, and socio-cultural conflicts as indicators of unresolved questions of pluralism and tolerance in democratic societies. Kymlicka and Norman, 'Return of the Citizen: A Survey of Recent Work on Citizenship Theory', 104 *Ethics* (1994) 352. Cf. the much earlier Dahrendorf, 'Citizenship and Beyond: The Social Dynamics of an Idea', 41 *Social Research* (1974) 673. See also V. Ferreira, T. Tavares, and S. Portugal (eds), *Shifting Bonds, Shifting Bounds. Women, Mobility and Citizenship in Europe* (1998); J. Shaw, *Citizenship of the Union: Towards Post-National Membership?*, Harvard Jean Monnet Working Paper 6/97 (1997); A. Ward and J. Gregory, *Women and Citizenship in Europe: Borders, Rights, Duties* (1992); E. Meehan, *Citizenship and the European Community* (1993); R. Voet, *Feminism and Citizen-ship* (1998).

[3] See Koslowski, 'EU citizenship: implications for identity and legitimacy', in T. Banchoff and M. P. Smith (eds), *Legitimacy and the European Union: a contested polity* (1999) 155.

a transnational phenomenon. Thus, European citizenship cannot be reduced to a mere status of belonging to a state in a legal sense. This necessitated the question what exactly should be understood as distinctly European about being a legal subject in a member state. For example, Advocate General Jacobs, when he delivered an expert opinion on a case in front of the European Court of Justice (ECJ), argued that:

[t]he notion of citizenship of the Union implies a commonality of rights and obligations uniting Union citizens by a common bond transcending Member State nationality. The introduction of that notion was largely inspired by the concern to bring the Union closer to its citizens and to give expression to its character as more than a purely economic union.

He adds that:

[f]reedom from discrimination on grounds of nationality is the most fundamental right conferred by the Treaty and must be seen as a basic ingredient of Union citizenship.[4]

But is freedom from sex discrimination included, too?

Only a few years later, the proclamation of the European Charter of Fundamental Rights (hereinafter the 'Charter')[5] in 2000 seemed to be a significant step in the evolution of a 'Europe of Citizens'.[6] The Charter, it seems, does indicate a social dimension of Europe, rather than a pure multi-level government structure, or a union of constitutions, a *Verfassungsverbund*, or some other primarily organizational transnational configuration. In this context, European Commissioner E. António Vitorino, as a member of the leading executive organ of the EU comparable to a minister of state, envisioned a European 'civic citizenship' as a postnational model.[7] But what exactly does that mean? This chapter will discuss the citizen behind the Charter, with special attention paid to how gender is constructed by inventing this person as well to how gendered that person is.

The Charter is particularly interesting for various reasons. As a catalogue of individual rights, the Charter is evidence of the rise of the individual subject in

[4] Case C-274/96, *Bickel*, Opinion of AG Jacobs, judgment of 9 March 1998.

[5] European Charter of Fundamental Rights, OJ 2000 C 364, at 1. On its genesis, see Baer, 'La Carta europea dei diritti fondamentali o dell'ambivalenza', *Diritto Pubblico* (2001) 901.

[6] Cf. d'Oliveira, 'European Citizenship: Its Meaning, Its Potential', in R. Dehousse (ed.), *Europe after Maastricht. An Even Closer Union?* (1994) 126; see also P. Alston (ed.), *The EU and Human Rights* (1999); A. Clapham, *Human Rights and the European Community: A Critical Overview* (1991).

[7] A. Vitorino in agreement with M. Diamantopolou, Communication from the Commission to the Council and the EP on a Community Integration Policy, 22 October 2000, Brussels 2000, 20. See also K. Eder and B. Giesen (eds), *European Citizenship between National Legacies and Postnational Projects* (2001); A. Ong, *Flexible Citizenship: The Cultural Logics of Transnationality* (1999); R. Bauböck, *Transnational Citizenship: Membership and Rights in International Migration* (1994).

international law, which challenges a formerly state-based legal order. More important, for our purposes, the Charter poses and answers the question who is currently the paradigmatic actor within a scheme of human rights in the world, at least according to Western and some Eastern Europeans consulted in the process. And the Charter may be seen as the most contemporary legal construction of what at least people in the Western world consider fundamental to humans today. It tells us what concepts inform human rights today.

The individual, the human at the centre of any idea of human rights law, is a socially constructed subject, rather than an *a priori* starting point for law. We may debate the status and nature of the human being to be considered as a subject of rights, as in the extreme cases of reproductive rights. But the citizen as the individual subject of human rights law is an entity created by that very law, thus, as any subject which appears in law, an entirely constructed yet lived *persona* in itself. And while citizenship as a concept is at the crossroads of various perspectives and theoretical undertakings, and subject to fervent debate, the citizen as a legal subject and actor can be detected in law and jurisprudence, including in the ways that law develops over periods of time. This chapter attempts to detect that very being: the legally constructed citizen. While it may add to the debate on citizenship, it will not use one of the many normative concepts of the citizen and test whether the law fits this philosophical dress. Rather, the legal outfit of the citizen will be detected within the law, in order to illustrate what political and philosophical concepts result in when they are forced to melt down to a catalogue of legal rights, as in the Charter. This advanced understanding of the legal construction of the subject in European law may then be informative of other areas of human rights law as well.

The chapter thus aims to set an example. It attempts to provide tools for a specific type of analysis of legal texts. Such tools will enable us to find the implicit as well as the explicit constructions of the subject as the citizen anywhere. In particular, such tools will enable us to analyse law and jurisprudence with gender competence, that is, a profound knowledge of the complexities of gender in culture, society, politics, and thus law, an ability in demand when the process of 'gender mainstreaming' gains hold in the world of law-making and legal analysis.[8] In so far as it recognizes that laws construct the very social phenomena they regulate, this type of analysis is part of a constructivist approach to law. In so far as it goes beyond the usual explanation and rationalization of legal texts and excavates the deeper political, historical, or philosophical logics that structure them (or some such explanation of deconstruction), the attitude is deconstructive. It is inevitable that topics of an already canonical nature in feminist, and more recently, in queer legal

[8] Article 2 of the European Community Treaty establishes gender equality as a general goal of all Union politics. Cf., for the history before it was passed, C. Hoskyns, *Integrating Gender. Women, Law and the Politics of the European Union* (1996).

theory will come to the forefront of this still distinctively legal, but not exclusively doctrinal reasoning. We shall see that the citizen in law is not fully understood without having an eye on the implied masculinity of legal subjects, without having an eye on the public/private dichotomies which inform law, and without having an eye on the gendered structure and setup of rights.

An analysis of the legal construction of citizens sheds new light on issues relevant to human rights law all over the world. For example, the tension between universalism and cultural relativism, which involves how different peoples or people may act under a legal regime, can be more adequately understood when looking at the underlying assumptions of who peoples and people *are* according to a given legal order. As another example, understanding legal constructs of the citizen may inform our understanding of the occurrence and effects of more and more human rights throughout the world. The rise of human rights, at least on paper, may be seen as part of constitutionalizing nation states in transition, or as part of globalization when states join international trade and become international markets, or, if we believe in the grand stories, as an effect of the ratio of modernity. In the last case, however, it entails the dilemmas that Max Horkheimer and Theodor Adorno so aptly identified. Modernity itself may counter its very endeavours. Thus, we need to understand what happens to *people* with such new sets of rights.

The chapter is organized as follows. Since the Charter to date is only a nonbinding proclamation, we have to start with a brief comment on proclaiming human rights, rather than ratifying a binding document. We proceed next to summarize the current understandings of citizenship. As preparation for a better reading of the Charter, we then collect the tools to analyse the gendered construction of subjects in a body of law. Feminist legal theory is useful to this enterprise because it engages history, in looking at traditions of exclusion of women particularly in the public sphere, and because it pays attention to the specificities of law and of rights, which contributed to that very exclusion but may also serve as liberators, and because it focuses on the dynamics of law's effects in the world. Constructivism as employed here is thus not just another approach inspired by the linguistic or pictorial turns we encounter in many disciplines; feminist legal theory as it is presented in this chapter analyses the distinctly legal ways to construct a deeply and specifically gendered world. More generally, such an approach is particularly helpful in an attempt to understand the fundamentals of human rights law today. The gains will become visible when we apply the tools to a body of law. This application will not only produce the European citizen, as legally constructed. It will also highlight some fundamental aspects of law-making today, among them the issues of implicit exclusion and tolerance of difference that we often find debated in terms of law's approach to multiculturalism.

1. PROCLAIMING HUMAN RIGHTS: SYMBOLS AND THE LAW

The moment of proclaiming new human rights for the world or one of its regions is a moment of historical as well as cultural significance, and thus a moment of symbolic significance. As O'Donovan points out in a discussion of the British constitution, 'Words on a piece of paper do not have a life of their own'[9] but need interpretation and implementation. However, they also need an aura, to be symbols, in order to create the willingness to take them seriously. To look at such symbols may thus give us a first impression of the potential of a legal text.

When the Charter was signed in Nice in 2000, we saw a picture that tells us a story prior to the law (see Figure 4.1). First, the moment of proclamation reified the nature of Europe as a governmental structure. Despite the fact that the Charter was drafted by a convention that consisted of representatives from the European Parliament and from parliaments of member states,[10] as well as representatives of governments—a revolutionary step in European law-making—it was government executives who signed the Charter and thus a very selective set of citizens of the Union. An alternative image of proclaiming human rights would have had to capture the peoples of Europe.[11] This image can therefore be interpreted as yet further evidence of the democratic deficit of the Union.

A closer look reveals more. Secondly, those present at the moment of proclaiming the Charter were, predominantly, men. Thirdly, everyone present in the picture was 'white'. Again, we see a very selective, and not purely coincidental and meaningless, set of citizens. Fourthly, the people in the picture sign a piece of paper, not more, not less. By now, this 'piece' exists in 15 languages, which may even differ in some regards. It also, as any other legal text, develops a life of its own. It is just a piece of paper, but its words are directed at varying audiences, and their meaning will be shaped by various agents of interpretation, as well as by a heterogeneous public.

It is thus only a text, and its proclamation only a gesture, and the picture only symbolic, but we shall see that all this informs the law, and the subject the law envisions, which is the European citizen.

---

[9] O'Donovan, 'A New Settlement between the Sexes? Constitutional Law and the Citizenship of Women', in A. Bottomley (ed.), *Feminist Perspectives on Foundational Subjects of Law* (1996) 243, at 244.

[10] In federal states like Germany, the delegates were representatives of the people, as members of the national parliament, as well as members of the second chamber representing the states within a state. Thus, the percentage of representatives who are elected directly is lower than it seems.

[11] The procedure which has been discussed and remains an option for the enactment of a European constitution is the referendum. It is well known that this version of direct democracy does not necessarily benefit minorities or citizens who lack access to the tools which form political opinions.

Figure 4.1. Helmut Friche, *Feierliche Verkündung der EU-Grundrechtecharta in Nizza* © Helmut Friche/Frankfurter Allgemeine Zeitung (8 December 2000).

2. THEORIES: DIFFERING APPROACHES TO CITIZENSHIP

There are many ways to understand and analyse constructions of citizenship.[12] Not all are attached to the same terminology. Throughout history, we encounter the 'human being', the 'person', the 'subject', and at times also the 'individual' in law. The 'human being' serves as the anthropological starting point of many national constitutions as well as human rights documents. It is a contested entity in the age of biopolitics, genetic engeneering, and legalized euthanasia.[13] The 'person', as the human recognized by other humans, where, according to Georg Hegel, acknowledgement produces personhood, is also a well-known figure in legal documents. In legal and political theory, we furthermore meet a 'subject', who Thomas Marshall in 1949 defined as a

---

[12] See, in addition to work already cited, Y. N. Soysal, *Limits of Citizenship: Migrants and Postnational Membership in Europe* (1994); B. Turner and P. Hamilton (eds), *Citizenship: Critical Concepts*, 2 vols (1994); J. Barbalet, *Citizenship Rights, Struggle and Class Inequality* (1988).

[13] Anthropology even informs imagery of the state as a 'body politic' with political 'organs', as well as the law of corporations which is based on anthropological foundations of artificial constructs.

citizen with a specific set of rights.[14] But only the relationship between human beings and a state turns them into citizens. It is the moment we may remember in Jean-Jacques Rousseau's work, who establishes the Social Contract not only as the moment of the creation of law, but also as a moment of distinct rationality, in which nature becomes a society, and human beings become persons, as citizens under law. A citizen, then, is, as Aristotle would have put it, a genuine *zoon politikon*. This theoretical understanding of citizenship informs the background of what we will see in the law. Theory is therefore different from images and symbols, not a tool and definitely not a normative starting point, but rather one additional source of information in the search for the citizen in law.

A. Beginnings: From Subject to Citizen

In what is seen as the beginning of legal history of the West, citizenship was status. As legal subjects, citizens were already present in Roman law. But Roman law also already created three kinds of status for human beings, not all of them vested with citizenship rights. Just as Greek philosophy conceptualized a second-class status for women, slaves, and other dependants, the classic notion of citizenship is therefore based on a patriarchal understanding of social order. As status, citizenship is also seen as stable rather than as a developing concept over time.

Then, as is particularly well known in the British legal tradition, subjects moved from status to contract. This formula is meant to describe the invention of an image of the agency or autonomy of the contracting citizen. Contracts were not only the paradigm of market-type interaction, but served as the legitimating device for nation states as well.[15] With the contract, the *other* enters the picture. While status implies a certain loneliness of the subject, a being on his own, contract implies inter-subjectivity, a being with another. Such inter-subjectivity can be radicalized in a concept of rights as relationships, as Jennifer Nedelsky exemplifies in her work.[16] However, inter-subjectivity has predominantly been reduced to autonomy with obligations. Legally speaking, rights are now supplemented with duties, a move revived in conservative attempts to weaken 'rights talk', modify rights-based welfare systems, and reinstall the virtues so many consider to be missing in modern societies today. From a gender-sensitive perspective, duties and obligations at least

---

[14] T. H. Marshall, *Citizenship, Social Class, and Other Essays* (1950); see also M. Bulmer and A. M. Rees, *Citizenship Today: The Contemporary Relevance of T.H. Marshall* (1996).

[15] Cf. N. Yuval-Davis, *Gender & Nation* (1997).

[16] Nedelsky, 'Citizenship and Relational Feminism', in R. Beiner and W. Norman (eds), *Canadian Political Philosophy: Contemporary Reflections* (2001) 131.

historically carry the odour of inequality, since the duty of care has not been imposed on men and has limited the choice of women to do anything else.[17]

B. Similar Citizens: Commonality Approaches

Status-based and contract-based concepts of citizenship both employ a common citizenship strategy. The emphasis is on sameness rather than difference and pluralism, on homogeneity rather than heterogeneity. Here, citizenship is about all of us who belong, rather than I and you and they who meet. With this emphasis on common features, citizenship forms the basis of community as such. The contract version of this commonality approach to citizenship informs most nation states today. They live off the notion of subjects on common ground, and that ground is citizenship.

A commonality approach to citizenship as the basis of a contracted nation state, Günter Frankenberg argues,[18] informs the concept of the European transnational configuration and the newly developed notion of European citizenship. As such, it does not give us any criteria for deciding which characteristics the commonality is based on. The common citizenship strategy rather allows for ethnically defined, culturally selective, or religious states, as well as for secularized visions of a commonality of mankind. In this context, human rights may be understood as an attempt to install that secular vision of commonality of all.

However, the common citizenship approach entails various problematic features. For example, the focus is on fully developed human beings. It presupposes an independent adult. The question how you become a citizen and how you live as one is neither posed nor answered. This implicit ignorance of people growing up is then based on a quite explicit focus on the public sphere, ignoring the 'private'. This excludes the family, women, and many aspects of the coming about of a person. It coincides with the tradition of theories of the state, where, as Susan Moller Okin has demonstrated, private matters were arbitrarily and often inconsistently placed outside the realm of law, politics, and theory.[19] Birth, growing up, and the life of citizens are excluded. As Carole Pateman has added, a sexual contract informs the formation of the liberal state,[20] or, as Anne Phillips has argued about the republican tradition, a male norm underlies it.[21]

---

[17] Cf. Fraser and Gordon, 'Reclaiming social citizenship: Beyond the ideology of contract versus charity', in P. James (ed.), *Critical Politics* (1994) 59.

[18] Frankenberg, 'The Return of the Contract. Problems and Pitfalls of European Constitutionalism', 6 *European Law Journal* (2000) 257.

[19] S. Moller Okin, *Justice, Gender, and the Family* (1989).

[20] C. Pateman, *The Sexual Contract* (1988).

[21] A. Phillips, *Engendering Democracy* (1992); A. Phillips, *Democracy and Difference* (1993).

This move to hide the private sphere from closer scrutiny and analysis, and thus from criticism or reform, implies a very specific understanding of politics. It is a vision of politics as an enterprise to serve the common good in quite selective ways. To use some recent examples, the work done in charity organizations, and even the catering service at a Global Leader Summit, are not seen as political activities, while the work done in administering charity organizations, or even the talk over lunch at the Summit, are defined as political. Sociological data inform us that activities mostly performed by men tend to enter the public sphere, while things done by women remain private. The gendered history of the professions is a line of evidence to this point.

The common citizenship approach based on autonomy and contract, and based on a focus on rights and obligations rather than bonds and responsibilities, is thus ignorant of gender and hence incomplete. As Carol Gilligan showed in her critique of Lawrence Kohlberg's scheme of moral development, rights and obligations are not all there is to human interest and activity. Nor, as Austrian philosopher Herta Nagl has shown, are they all there is to a Kantian tradition of notions of subjectivity, a point that also appears from, for example, Berns' critique of the sense of justice at the heart of John Rawls' philosophy, or Benhabib's critique of the generalized other informing modern philosophy up to Jürgen Habermas.[22] Therefore, newer approaches to understanding citizenship tend to blur or redraw the boundaries between the public and the private, between rights and responsibilities, and between autonomy and relations.[23]

C. Different Citizens—Multiplicity Approaches

Rather than emphasizing common ground, other theories of citizenship emphasize multiplicities as the basis of citizenship.[24] The most prominent concepts that theorists draw upon are identity and, as opposed to difference, differences.

The first option for conceptualizing citizenship based on multiplicities is to think of identity.[25] The concept of identity that informs such political and

---

[22] See Berns, 'Tolerance and Substantive Equality in Rawls: Incompatible Ideals', 8 *Law in Context* (1990) 112; Benhabib, 'Der verallgemeinerte und der konkrete Andere. Ansätze zu einer feministischen Moraltheorie', in E. List and H. Studer (eds), *Denkverhältnisse—Feminismus und Kritik* (1989) 454; Nagl-Docekal, 'Gleichbehandlung und Anerkennung von Differenz: Kontroversielle Themen feministischer Philosophie', in H. Nagl-Docekal and H. Pauer-Studer (eds), *Politische Theorie, Differenz und Lebensqualität* (1996) 3.

[23] Ferreira, Tavares, and Portugal (eds), *supra* n. 2.

[24] Meehan, 'Political Pluralism and European Citizenship', in P. Lehning and A. Weale (eds), *Citizenship, Democracy and Justice in the New Europe* (1997) 69; A. Phillips (ed.), *Feminism and Politics* (1998).

[25] For thoughts on national identity see L. Holmes and P. Murray (eds), *Citizenship and Identity in Europe* (1999).

legal theories of citizenship is originally sociological. Defined as the individual's successful arrangement with her role and external expectations, this concept envisions that we internalize a specific subjectivity. In Germany, identity was an important part of the theory of community already at the beginning of the twentieth century.[26] In North America, the communitarian vision of citizens in their group or community context recently revived such approaches.[27] And identity as an option for framing citizenship is also attractive to many who neither identified with nor were accepted by the common approach dominating nation states. Identity politics thus formed a starting point for many social movements, from Black Power to Gay Liberation.[28] When nation states are too big, and a neighbourhood is too small, such communities look like the entities needed for social cohesion.

On the other hand, identity has been the driving force in wars and social conflict from the Balkans to Ireland. In addition, such small communities shatter the far wider sense of solidarity on which modern welfare systems are based. And lastly, imagined communities of any sort are based on static stereotypes which inform exclusion as much as inclusion of the other.[29]

As an alternative to identity-based concepts of citizenship, other theorists offer a vision of citizenship as manifested difference. For example, Iris Marion Young has developed a theory of differentiated citizenship,[30] which forms the basis of representational rights for subordinated groups but risks essentializing such collectives. Pateman draws upon 'sexually differentiated citizenship'[31] and risks regressing into polarized and essentialist visions of gender.[32] Will Kymlicka has designed a multicultural citizenship which forms the basis of different sets of rights for different types of groups, and faces conflicts

---

[26] The sociologist who elaborated on the distinction between society and community is F. Tönnies, *Community and Civil Society*, ed. J. Harris, trans. M. Hollis (2001).

[27] Most prominently M. Walzer, *Spheres of Justice* (1983), whose work gives rise, among others, to critique from a feminist perspective by E. Frazer and N. Lacey, *The Politics of Community* (1993).

[28] For critical discussion, see S. Hark, *deviante subjekte. Die paradoxe Politik der Identität* (1996); D. Herman, *Rights of Passage. Struggles for Lesbian & Gay Liberation* (1994); N. Beger, *Que(e)rying Political Practices in Europe. Tensions in the Struggles for Sexual Minority Rights* (2001). On the intersection of sexual orientation, sexuality, and gender, see C. A. MacKinnon, *Sex Equality* (2001).

[29] B. Anderson, *Imagined Communities* (1983).

[30] I. M. Young, *Justice and the Politics of Difference* (1990).

[31] C. Pateman, *Women and Democratic Citizenship* (1985).

[32] This is true for 'maternal thinkers', who base gender difference on women's capacity for childbirth and motherhood. The most prominent theorist here is Elshtain, 'Antigone's Daughters. Reflections on Female Identity and the State', in I. Diamond (ed.), *Families, Politics and Public Policy* (1983) 300. See also West, 'The Difference in Women's Hedonic Lives: A Phenomenological Critique of Feminist Legal Theory', 3 *Wisc. Women's LJ* (1987) 81.

if people belong to more than one collective.[33] All of these theorists reject the common citizenship approach, but they replace it with a notion of citizenship based on smaller collectives. Thus, they encounter the same criticism which can be levelled against communitarian visions. In particular, the relatively static vision of such collectives, as well as the separation of them based on criteria of identity, leave individuals with multiple attachments to various groups outside. This is extremely problematic from a gender-sensitive point of view, which attempts to avoid such 'boxing' of people in the face of ever-contingent and varying facts of personality and selfhood.

D. Active Citizens: Participatory Approaches

Those who want to avoid the gender gaps of status- or commonality-based approaches, and who resist the temptation to form the better community, based on a shared difference, start thinking about a citizenship of different, yet constantly changing individuals who still form a community.[34] The question then is whether there is an approach to citizenship which combines the commonality needed for any claim to universal and inalienable human rights with respect for individuality, particular experience, and belonging as important assets of modern selves. In the search for answers, feminist scholars particularly contribute to our understanding of citizenship in very specific ways. A focus on gender not just as difference, but as an interplay of sex, sexuality, and sexualities in a context of power, not only opens a way to analyse law and the construction of the sex/gender difference,[35] it also paves the way to deal with pluralism or particularities as such.

Such approaches to citizenship may more generally be summarized as participatory approaches. Among them, we find a search for the communicative

---

[33] W. Kymlicka, *Multicultural Citizenship* (1995) and the discussion with S. Moller Okin in S. Moller Okin with Respondents, *Is Multiculturalism Bad for Women?*, J. Cohen, M. Howard, and M. C. Nussbaum (eds) (1999).

[34] Among them, in different versions, are C. Mouffe, *Dimensions of Radical Democracy. Pluralism, Citizenship and Community* (1992); Siim, 'Engendering Democracy—the interplay between Citizenship and Political Participation', 1 *Social Politics. International Studies in Gender, State and Society* (1994) 286; R. Braidotti, *Nomadic Subjects* (1994); Baer, 'Verfassung und Geschlecht. Anmerkungen zu einem geschlechtssensiblen deliberativen Konstitutionalismus', in B. Christensen (ed.), *Demokratie und Geschlecht* (1999) 101. Fiona Williams uses the image of a polyhedron which reflects different and changing experiences, cited in Lister, 'Tracing the Contours of Women's Citizenship', 21 *Politics & Polity* (1993) 3.

[35] On this point, see Richardson, 'Sexuality and citizenship', 32 *Sociology* (1998) 83; Stychin, 'Sexual Citizenship and European Union', 5 *Citizenship Studies* (2001) 285; D. Evans, *Sexual Citizenship: The Material Construction of Sexualities* (1993).

elements of citizenship,[36] while the focus may also be on more traditional forms of political participation along with a consideration of the social underpinnings and the resources key to the ability to participate. Gender sensitivity, which is at its core a sensitivity to sexualized hierarchies transgressing time, class, and space, enables us to look at the participation of different citizens, but to also distinguish difference from dominance. This is the issue we are confronted with in discussions of multiculturalism, in which prominent authors took pains to reach the point that feminist legal theory has already been debating for quite a while. The focus on dominance, and on the mechanisms which inform, manifest, and reproduce it, is the perspective from which to approach differences, if they amount to conflict and thus to issues of law. This focus on dominance, in the context of citizenship, is a focus on who belongs and who does not, on inclusion and exclusion. While the common story of the development of modern states has been one of gradual inclusion, the feminist story is one with moments of inclusion as well as shifting and changing patterns and devices of exclusion.[37]

For example, a particularly long-lasting vision of citizenship was based on the conjunction of citizenship and defence of one's mother country. The formula of citizenship and participation was fight and vote. The mother country is, until today, not only embroidered with female allegories for nation states—like Marianne for France and Germania for Germany—it is also loaded with a particular image of home as the site of the family and the feminine as the foundation of all. In addition, the nation works with an image of soldiers as men who fight, expressing masculinity as the ability to create, lead, and defend the nation/family/feminine. Political citizenship, defined as the ability to vote, derived from such masculine abilities. A non-citizen was thus defined as a female state of dependency with the sole right to be defended. Today's feminization of poverty and the creation of the female client of the welfare state replicate these images. In addition, the law on the military defines even today that being a soldier is about being male.[38]

It is only masculine human beings who are needed in warfare today, and therefore, courts all over Europe exclude gay men (non-males, according to the heterosexual norm of gender) from the ranks just as they justify the

---

[36] At the University of Bielefeld, Germany, Alfons Bora and other scholars are working on a project on Participation and the Dynamics of Social Positioning (PARADYS), which seeks to understand 'communicating citizenship' in a field of environmental law in seven European countries.

[37] Compare J. Shklar, *American Citizenship: The Quest for Inclusion* (1991); K. Karst, *Belonging to America: Equal Citizenship and the Constitution* (1989); G. Procacci, *Poor Citizens: Social Citizenship and the Crisis of Welfare States*, EUF Working Paper, 96/5 (1996).

[38] E.g. Case 285/98, *Kreil* (2000) 21 *HRLJ* 88 (general exclusion of women from military posts involving the use of arms contrary to the principle of equal treatment for men and women as regards access to employment).

exclusion of women from core units despite a general move to integration. Although today, biological women in uniform can make it to the front lines, the construction of the citizen-soldier still re-enforces a specific vision of manhood. And feminist analyses reveal that there is more to history of citizenship than gaining political rights based on a willingness to die for one's country. Around the time when the vote was given to men based on their willingness to die, the vote was not extended to women who died for the country as well, because femininity as entrenched in motherhood required the willingness to sacrifice oneself for the nation in bearing a child. At that time, thousands of women faced death in childbirth, but the empirical analogy did not lead to legal change. The recognition of the family as the foundational unit of nation and state, still to be found in human rights documents, is thus not paralleled by an extension of rights to those who bear responsibilities.

A focus on inclusion in and exclusion from participation has thus to take complex social and cultural phenomena into account. This complexity is part of the attempts to define exclusion adequately, namely, to understand discrimination as the violation of a right to equality.[39] This understanding of citizenship as in/exclusion is particularly relevant to new formations like a 'Fortress Europe'. The central question then is not only who is allowed to enter, which many citizenship debates tend to focus on exclusively and which organizes analysis of the law of immigration, refugees, and asylum. The central question is also one of who really belongs. This concept of discrimination as in/exclusion thus moves beyond a formal drawing of lines and into a substantive analysis of the complexities of social integration.

What is interesting about moments of in/exclusion is their contingency, and the role of law in creating and undoing them. Laws can reconcile a loss particularly by re-establishing citizenship in a specific sense. If we define in/exclusion as not letting someone in—Fortress Europe and migration—and if we see this as discrimination rather than national self-defence (defence of what exactly?), we will design certain immigration laws. If we understand the loss of nationality rights as a result of marriage or of divorce not as a constitutive element of nation-building but as discrimination, we will design a prohibition of such losses in law. If we see the relegation of someone to second-class status by means of disrespect as a problem, laws may enable people to claim respect as

---

[39] Discrimination, then, is exclusion by stereotyping, degrading treatment, a violation of dignity, and it is group-related, but with individual targets, and with substantive effects. See Lacey in this volume (at Chapter 2), and S. Baer, *Würde oder Gleichheit?* (1995). One of the interesting decisions by the ECJ has been handed down in Case 158/97, *Georg Badeck and Others, (interveners: Hessischer Ministerpräsident and Landesanwalt beim Staatsgerichtshof des Landes Hessen)* [2000] ECR I-1875, on a German state sex equality law which provides strict quotas for educational purposes as well as quotas based on personnel planning decisions. On the more problematic decisions see Bell, 'Shifting Conceptions of Sexual Discrimination at the Court of Justice: from P v S to Grant v ST', 5 *ELJ* (1999) 1.

compensation. If we analyse politics as means to see or ignore the wants and needs of some but not of others, we will design laws to have such others heard, or to open access to resources, be it a voice or other means of living. And if law defines someone as sick or not normal, and thus excludes, law can undo that if it protects gay men and women who do not fit the heterosexual gender paradigm, or if it gives transsexuals an existence of choice documented in a passport and by a name.

To add a complicated question, the focus on exclusion is not easy to maintain. On the one hand, exclusion is the discrimination described in the examples above. On the other hand, it is a necessary ingredient of social organization. Legal theory which makes use of psychological understandings of the world will highlight that any group,[40] and, actually, any self, constitutes itself around categories of who is not like them or me. The focus on in/exclusion is thus based on a distinction between what is necessary to constitute a self, and what is problematic as a rejection of others.

E. Critical Positioning—Citizenship as Activity

Lastly, from participatory concepts of citizenship, we also see that citizenship is not just a status but also an activity. While Will Kymlicka and Wayne Norman refer to citizenship as an 'identity, an expression of one's membership in a community',[41] a feminist perspective would avoid relying on identity. Feminist—and even more radically, queer—theories have undermined the idea that individuals live or have an identity, because it is too tempting to associate wholeness, commonality, essence, and status with it. Rather than equating citizenship as an expression of membership with identity, I would argue that it can be seen as critical positioning. The idea of critical positioning allows for expressions of belonging and exclusion, trust and distrust, as experience and action. Because it allows us to capture social hierarchies, and ambiguities as well, it captures more than classic civic republicanism. It also differs from approaches which focus on civil societies as places of belonging, not of dissent. Citizenship as critical positioning, most importantly, indicates a willingness to be a part of some bigger unit, like a society, or a state, or humankind and the world. Then, exclusion and inclusion can be seen as things done to people, with effects on their status as citizens, or as outsiders, 'the stranger'. With this approach, things that form experience are part of what citizenship means, and this gives those included or excluded a voice in defining what it is about.

[40] See the work of R. Salecl, *Politik des Phantasmas* (1993) (using Freud and Lacan). Note that Carl Schmitt defined exclusion as a necessary ingredient of politics in the sense of we/you.
[41] Kymlicka and Norman, *supra* n. 2, at 368.

F. Resources and Citizenship

To have a voice is not a natural asset. If we look at participation from another angle, citizenship must also be understood as access to resources, mediated via passports which allow access to nation states (or transnational entities like Europe), and thus access to welfare systems which provide for the material conditions of living and access to rights which are preconditions for cultural conditions of life.[42] Passports are entry tickets into states, signs of belonging, and vouchers for rights to protection. Thus, if citizenship is the sign the passport signifies, citizenship is a resource in itself. This follows a line of thought from political theorist Hannah Arendt. Standing against the statelessness of Jews expelled from Germany between 1939 and 1945, Arendt viewed citizenship as the right to have rights.[43] However, Arendt's position highlights that such a concept of citizenship is a positivist concept relying on the resources a state deploys, rather than an analytic or philosophical concept to understand modern human beings living under conditions defined by law. At the same time, this concept allows us to ask the question of what exactly it is we are looking for when we look for citizens as rights-bearing individuals (or parts of collectives). To answer the question of who a citizen is in a given situation, we have to analyse what rights a subject has in a given legal context. Thus, we come to the point in which rights constitute the citizen, which is the point where we leave theory and concepts and turn to doctrine and law. The focus on citizenship as a resource builds the bridge from theory to legal practice. There, we can find the legal construction of citizenship.

3. TOOLS OF DE/CONSTRUCTING CITIZENS IN LAW

We have to read the law. 'Reading', to lawyers as to many other professionals, is just the activity by which to gain access to a text and reveal its meaning. Mostly, jurists emphasize a difference between reading and interpretation. As part of the technique of legal method, reading means to find the relevant norm, while interpretation means to apply the norm to the text. However, a search for the citizen in law is neither simple reading nor simple application,[44] if that exists at all. It is a reconstructive analysis of a body of law, in this case, European human rights law. Reading then means to apprehend the given and hidden

---

[42] Balibar, 'Propositions on Citizenship', 98 *Ethics* (1988) 729.

[43] This view was taken up by the US Supreme Court in *Trop v Dulles*, 356 U.S. 86, 102 (1958). See also Stratton, 'The Right to Have Rights: Gender Discrimination in Nationality Laws', 77 *Minnesota Law Review* (1992) 195.

[44] A mixed approach is utilized by O'Leary, 'Putting Flesh on the Bones of European Union Citizenship', 24 *ELR* (1999) 68.

meanings of a text, to reconstruct what is said and what is left out, to—in legal terms—build a case from law only.[45]

Citizens, then, are the paradigmatic bearers of rights, European citizens the actors in a case which we could call a European society. To find a European citizen, we have to read European law and reconstruct which image, or case, inspired its regulations. This type of legal analysis is thus not based on the idea of law as a system or set of norms ideally beyond social or cultural understanding, where life follows law, but on the idea that life forms law and law forms life, as interdependent dynamics. It is a constructivist approach based on an understanding of law as culture and law as social fact, and it is a feminist approach which pays particular attention to the dynamics of sexualizing and constructions of gender.

Such a search for the citizen, in a gender-sensitive, critical, and reconstructive fashion, may be part of what Phillips calls 'gendered substitution'.[46] In 'gendered substitution', the undertaking is to reshape, rather than reject, a term. Regarding 'citizens', gendered substitution calls for a gender-sensitive reconstruction of legally created and socially experienced status, based on a critical analysis of the laws which are relevant to that process. Then, by reconstructing who that is—a citizen—we can work in the area of law to open not only the linguistic space of meaning, but also, by way of changing laws, to open the political space of action.

A. Histories and Realities

First, such an analysis of European law has to take the histories and the realities of seemingly neutral norms into account.

Part of the history of a norm is always the history of who defined its wording and meaning. And since citizenship relies on participation, the histories of political participation rights explicitly excluding women and others for long periods of time have to be acknowledged.

In addition, there are always certain realities which inform what is part of human rights. Human rights are reactions to paradigmatic violations which individuals experience, and thus can be interpreted as a form of recognition of who and what counts in the world. Rights manifest a particular acknowledgement that something matters, which is why American scholar Patricia Williams

[45] This idea is obviously taken from cultural studies. Among those who apply such techniques to legal texts are James Boyd White, Stanley Fish, Sanford Levinson, Drucilla Cornell, Alan Norrie, and Peter Goodrich.
[46] Phillips, 'Citizenship and Feminist Theory', in G. Andrews (ed.), *Citizenship* (1991) 76. The same is true for the term 'individual', which Pateman calls a patriarchal category, but which much feminist work reshapes as more inclusive.

defends 'rights talk' with the remark that 'it is still so deliciously empowering to say' that one has them, coming from a situation of rightlessness.[47]

When we thus read the European (or any other) body of law, we are confronted with tips of, among other, historically gendered icebergs, and have to melt down the layers grown in time and space which still inform such regulations.

B. Sexual Citizens

A second tool of analysis in our search for the citizen in European law is based on the foundational assumption of all feminist, gender, and queer theories, which is that gender and sexuality play a decisive role in all areas of life. As simple as that, this statement is a fundamental challenge to the assumption that sex and gender are private or natural matters without much significance in the rationalized world of politics and markets. In addition, the emphasis on the relevance of gender and sex everywhere challenges the related assumption that there is something like a subject which is *not* sexed or gendered. To assert the importance of gender is to assert the gendered and sexed nature of the subject, including the subject of law.[48]

However, it is important to pay attention to what exactly is meant when we talk about a gendered or sexed nature of the subject. In feminist theory, sex has for a long time been distinguished from gender to underline the distinction between biological definitions and social constructions of who men and women are. In languages other than English, the term 'gender' has been used to refer to such social constructions as well. More recently, however, sex, sexuality, and gender have been seen as interrelated phenomena, to be understood neither as essentially natural nor as virtually social or cultural alone. Nature is as much a product of culture, as culture depends on nature. The history of sexuality is thus as much a story of bodies and chemicals as it is a story of activity and culture. Lastly, sex, sexuality, and gender live off specific configurations and norms. Most importantly, men and women are determined within a system of, as Adrienne Rich called it, compulsory heterosexuality, which later theorists discussed as a heterosexual matrix or heteronormativity.[49]

---

[47] Williams, 'Alchemical Notes: Reconstructed Ideals from Deconstructed Rights', 22 *Harvard Civil Rights—Civil Liberties Review* (1987) 401, at 404.

[48] N. Naffine (ed.), *Sexing the Subject of Law* (1995); Baer, 'Komplizierte Subjekte zwischen Recht und Geschlecht. Eine Einführung in feministische Ansätze in der Rechtswissenschaft', in C. Kreuzer (ed.), *Frauen im Recht—Entwicklung und Perspektiven* (2001) 9; N. Lacey, *Unspeakable Subjects* (1998).

[49] Rich, 'Compulsory Heterosexuality and Lesbian Existence', 5 *Signs: Journal of Women in Culture and Society* (1980) 631; M. Wittig, *The Straight Mind and Other Essays* (1983); J. Butler,

Furthermore, there are histories which inspire the legal construction of citizenship which reveal stories of sexualizing subjects.[50] In most criminal law, either on the books or via application, the assumption has been (and sometimes still is, based on powerful messages of what heterosexual normalities look like in pornographic iconography) that all men have a sex drive they cannot control, and that all women want sex, defined as intercourse, whatever they say. This has the tragic effect that rape laws and laws of sexual abuse tend to privilege a perpetrator's perspective in that they define his socially constructed perception of a situation as decisive. Further effects can be seen in more recent laws against sexual harassment in the workplace, where sexuality is seen as interruption of a capitalist dynamic of production, but at the same time is played down as a private matter of no significance in public spaces, turned into a fault of those who suffer from it.

With this is mind, we can now assort the tools used to analyse how sexual a subject or citizen is within a body of law. According to Margaret Davies, there are various ways of sexing the subject of law.[51] She distinguishes between explicit sexing and implicit sexing, the use of concept and metaphor which imply sexualized meaning, and the intersection of law with other modes of attributing meaning.

Explicit sexing is what lawyers know as direct discrimination: the verbal reference in a body of law to men or to women. What most lawyers do not know yet is that much law—most prominently, family law—refers to heterosexual subjects as well. Based on newer guarantees of equality, which explicitly protect against discrimination on the basis of sexual orientation or sexualities, explicit references to heterosexuality should gradually gain the status of doubt that explicit references to only men or only women are confronted with today.

Implicit sexing consists of references to neutral situations or subjects in law which in fact constitute a reference to men or women, and to be added, or heterosexuals, or homosexuals, or transsexuals only. Lawyers tend to know this as indirect or disparate impact discrimination,[52] but there is still much work to do to eliminate all such seemingly neutral rules which harmfully affect people of different genders and sexualities.

Gender Trouble (1990); and J. Butler, *Bodies that matter. On the discursive limits of 'sex'* (1993). For elaboration and discussion, see Davies, 'taking the inside out: sex and gender in the legal subject', in N. Naffine and R. Owens (eds), *sexing the subject of law* (1997) 25, at 33–4.

[50] On the legal implications of such an approach, see MacKinnon, *supra* n. 28. For a different perspective, see Halley, in this volume (at Chapter 3).

[51] I note that Davies rejects the distinction between gender and sex. I follow this line of thought, based on the work of Catharine MacKinnon, who emphasizes the interdependency of sexual construction of gendered worlds, in that gender as the construction of man/masculinity and women/femininity is a product of sexualizing individuals. MacKinnon, *supra* n. 28.

[52] These are misleading terms since direct discrimination is detrimental only if and because it has disparate impact on men or women too.

For example, in most legal systems, labour law does not cover housework, and family law does not provide for meaningful lives with families and activities beyond the home. Such law is based on the stereotype that all women are mothers just as all men are wage-earners; thus women do not work and men do not parent. Even more specifically, most labour law is based on the stereotyped assumption that all women are short, weak, and good at working on small objects with their fingers, while all men are tall, strong, and good at working in leadership positions. Without being a linear cause, this has the effect that women are in law—in labour law, in tax law, in insurance regulations, in unemployment benefit laws, and schemes of integration in the labour market from immigration to welfare—and in fact positioned in the home or relegated to industries that they fit, like the textile industry with elements of knitting, sewing, washing, and ironing. Vice versa, men tend to work outside the home in high positions. Work division is, then, a way of doing gender.[53]

Similarly, legal systems tend to assume that all men are born to fight, and therefore drafted to military service, and all women are born to bear life and be protected, which has the tragic effect that until recently, violence against women was not recognized in international law as one of the age-old means of war and as a war crime.

The use of concept and metaphors is another aspect to look for in the search for the citizen or subject in law. This is the tool to dig deeper into the cultural and epistemological history of what law refers to. For example, if dignity is the starting point of a European Charter of Rights, the Charter uses a term which has gendered meaning: male honour and female virtue. To render the Charter more inclusive, the term 'dignity'—just as the term 'citizen'—may thus also be a candidate for gendered substitution. Here, the architecture of rights—what comes first? what last? why is liberty protected earlier than equality in the Charter?—is also of importance. And, as another example, most law not only refers to specific individuals, but also singles out the specific forms of collectivity it refers to, while not acknowledging others.

In addition, and as an elaboration of Davies, an analysis of law does not only have to pay attention to concepts and metaphors in a social or cultural sense. In addition, fundamental legal concepts that inspire the law may also have a gendered meaning. To give just one example: if the Charter provides rights against European actors only, it may rely on protection against national actors based on national constitutions still in place. However, it continues to ignore

[53] See Ackers, 'Women, Citizenship and European Community Law: The Gender Implications of the Free Movement Provisions', 17 *Journal of Social Welfare and Family Law* (1994) 391 (discussing whether the evolution of European citizenship rights, derived from employment status, effectively institutionalizes a dependent and inferior status for women of the European Union). See also T. Boje and L. Arnlaugu (eds), *Gender, Welfare State and the Market—Towards a New Division of Labour?* (2000).

the threats of private actors to individual rights, be they private European or private national entities or individuals. We thus find in European law the problem of a focus on state action already known from international law, which is only gradually moving to protect people against the dangers of private forms of violence, particularly those forms targeting women.

Lastly, in an analysis of the construction of gendered/sexed subjects in law, one may pay attention to the last element Davies defined as important: the intersection of law with other modes of attributing meaning. For example, the subject in law is not just a rational male, but may also be an intrinsically capitalist economic actor. But if that is true, what do the rights of solidarity in the Charter mean? With this kind of critical analysis in mind, intersections of law with other fields of meaning have to be taken into account.

C. Resourceful Citizens

After a look at histories and the ways of sexing the subject, a third tool for analysing a body of law in search of the citizen is to consider what is needed to make use of the rights provided for. This not only allows for a gender-sensitive analysis, since women more often than men lack the resources to mobilize the law on their behalf. It also allows for considerations of people's different physical, mental, social, material, and cultural abilities, and of legal assumptions about how able one has to be in order to move into the realm of a rights-bearing entity. For example, human rights law often presupposes the ability to use law in case a violation occurs. For many people, however, this is not the case. Lack of resources and access, lack of support and knowledge contribute to a hidden rightlessness of individuals. In a transnational setting, this always implies the question of who cares for whom. In the case of *Grzelczyk*,[54] in which a student sued for public assistance, two European member state governments submitted that:

[c]itizenship of the Union does not mean that Union citizens obtain rights that are new and more extensive than those already deriving from the EC Treaty and secondary legislation. The principle of citizenship of the Union has no autonomous content, but is merely linked to the other provisions of the Treaty.

But the European Court of Justice responded that:

Union citizenship is destined to be the fundamental status of nationals of the Member States, enabling those who find themselves in the same situation to enjoy the same treatment in law irrespective of their nationality, subject to such exceptions as are expressly provided for.[55]

---

[54] Case C-184/99, *Grzelczyk v Centre public d'aide sociale d'Ottignies-Louvain-la-Neuve* [2001] ECR I-6193.
[55] Ibid., at Rec. 31.

According to the Court, citizenship is thus a right of its own, and extends to resources, yet rests on the basis of national membership.[56] Thus, inspired by theories of citizenship as a resource, an analysis of the law must pay attention to the assumptions behind the norm regarding its use.

4. APPLICATIONS: CITIZENSHIP BY LAW

As just seen, the law's role in constructing subjects is played by means of explicit or implicit (hetero-) sexing, by use of gendered metaphors and concepts, and by building on specific intersections with other systems of meaning. The search for the citizen—as a gendered and sexed subject—then rests on deconstructing such hidden agendas of the law, and may result in reconstructing more gender-sensitive—which implies more just—norms. To apply theory to legal practice, I will first *read* the European Convention on Human Rights and Fundamental Freedoms (hereinafter the 'Convention') to find the gendered subject. Not only is the Convention a well-known charter of human rights, it has also been a point of reference for the new European Charter of Fundamental Rights. I will then *re-read* that very Charter, and attempt to demonstrate the constructive potential of feminist critique.

A. Reading the European Convention on Human Rights and Fundamental Freedoms

European human rights, until now, derive from various sources. Since the Charter, unlike the Convention, is not legally binding, the human rights regime in Europe consists of the international treaties that European states have ratified, with whatever reservations individual states have entered to them. In particular, Europeans drafted for their own region the European Convention on Human Rights and Fundamental Freedoms, which has been supplemented by various protocols. The Convention has been used as a dynamic document by the (former) Commission and Court in charge of implementing it, and has recently been incorporated into the domestic law of the United Kingdom.[57]

---

[56] As Advocate General Geelhoed has argued in Case 413/99, *Baumbast and R v Secretary of State for the Home Department* [2002] ECR I-7091, it extends to rights, e.g., of residence, for family members of migrants, too. The first case to be listed under the heading of 'citizenship' is Case 192/99 *The Queen v Secretary of State for the Home Department, ex parte Manjit Kaur* [2001] ECR I-1237, in which the ECJ decided that it is a European status derived from the nationality laws of member states.

[57] From a feminist perspective, see Palmer, 'Critical Perspectives on Women's Rights: The European Convention on Human Rights and Fundamental Freedoms', in Bottomley, *supra* n. 9, 231; for other perspectives, see Waldron, 'A Rights Based Critique of Constitutional Rights', 13 *Oxford Journal of Legal Studies* (1993) 18; R. Dworkin, *A Bill of Rights for Britain* (1990).

Because of its impressive history, until the moment that Europeans proclaimed the new, non-binding Charter, many argued that the Union should join and ratify the Convention rather than creating another level of rights. From a gender-sensitive perspective, was that a good idea? And who then would be the European citizen, partly constructed by the rights attributed in the Convention?

1. Histories and Realities

When we look at the history of the Convention from the perspective of participation, we see, simply put, the male-dominated state of affairs which is part of almost all grand documents in history until today. As most national constitutions, such documents were—and most are still—drafted and proclaimed by men. Individuals like Eleanor Roosevelt, who played an important role in drafting the United Nations Charter, are the exception, not the rule.

The Convention regards injustices as the realities which must be recognized adequately and thus form the foundations of human rights. In doing so, the Convention is oriented toward the traditional liberal set of ideas. It prioritizes freedom over equality ('rights and freedoms'). It lists rights of physical integrity and freedom (Articles 2, 4), including their procedural safeguards (Articles 3, 5, 6, 7), first, which implies the prominent function of a public sphere, and the danger to the individual from public actors. The private is not protected as a right to privacy directly, but as a right to respect for private and family life (Article 8). The private is thus of a seemingly derivative and less important nature. There is no sense of injustice within the family, a concern of utmost importance from a gender-sensitive perspective.

What follows in the architecture of the Convention are freedoms of the rational individual to think and believe (Article 9), and to speak and get information (Article 10). The paradigmatic injustice is censorship, again, by public actors, rather than the cultural silencing so often part of discrimination.

Furthermore, Article 12, with the right to marry and form a family, may be a reaction to the injustice of forced marriage commonly practised as part of sex discrimination, as much as the paradigmatic injustice which informs this right may be the prohibition on marriage between different faiths that was part of anti-Semitism throughout Europe.

Lastly, the injustice which informs the right to equality in the Convention is treating differently what is seen as similar, rather than hurting someone because of gender, sexual orientation, ethnic origin, or the like. Therefore, Article 14 of the Convention protects against unequal distribution and enjoyment of guaranteed freedoms, but does not establish an independent right to equality.[58]

---

[58] For discussion and further references, see Palmer, *supra* n. 57.

The injustices which inspire the Convention are thus partial elements of specific experiences particular people sometimes have, rather than things all humans, or even all Europeans, care for equally.

2. The Sexed Subject

The next step in our reading of the Convention is to take a look at the sexed subject living in the document.

Depending on the language version, there are more or fewer elements of explicit sexing. The German version is, as most legal texts up until the late 1990s, fully masculine. It is a he and never a she who bears the rights of the Convention, or it is a human, then referred to as 'he'. The only exception is Article 12, which guarantees the right to marry to men and women. Despite the fact that recognition of the female sex may be hailed as a step towards gender sensitivity, the context renders this a peculiar victory. It enshrines a narrow definition of heteronormativity rather than contributing to more liberating understandings of gender and sexualities.

There is much more implicit sexing in the Convention. As already mentioned, the Convention prioritizes the public over the private, and thus renders the realm of the female irrelevant, thus also ignoring most forms of sexual hierarchy which is played out in the family and the home.[59] In addition, the Convention implicitly relates to a subject with functioning rational capacities, able to read (which implies knowledge of language) and willing to speak or assemble. There is nothing said about affection and emotions, or any other side of individual expression and formation of self. Rather, the paradigmatic rights-bearer is, in the modern sense, a fully capable adult, and, taking the dualistic understanding of culture/nature, ratio/emotion, male/female into account, a male. If we look at citizenship as resource, the Convention does not establish access to it, but rather relies upon the resourceful individual, socially, again, a male of the sexual, ethnic, and cultural majority.

This could also be seen as a reference to specific concepts and metaphors. Here, less gendered but still relevant, we also find references to very specific forms of social activity. The next right guaranteed in the Convention, in order to participate in the workings of society, is to act as an orderly collective (Article 11). It is not the associational ad hoc formation of civil societies, and even less the spontaneous and fluctuating groups which are the basis of dissident movements of women, gays, lesbians, or queer people for example, that inform the right to assembly. Rather, it is collectives that serve the state's needs ('external and internal security') and 'morals', historically charged and exclusionary as these are, that inform the Convention.

Regarding concepts and metaphors, it is not surprising that the Convention guarantees the right to choose marriage and found a family in Article 12.

---

[59] See S. Walby, *Gender Transformations* (1997), at 175.

Within a liberal philosophical tradition, the family served as the foundational unit of that orderly society we see around Article 11 as well. It therefore makes sense that families, according to Article 12, depend on what states allow a family to be, thus again excluding dissident sexualities and associational forms of living.

The Convention itself finally refers to one intersection with a non-legal phenomenon. In Article 15, it provides for special rules in cases of war, implicitly drawing upon an understanding of war as 'just war' between nations, rather than civil wars or other forms of pervasive violence.

As a whole, the Convention displays most features of a Western liberal human rights document. Compared to the United Nations Universal Declaration of Human Rights[60] of 1948, the European Convention is a document much less explicit in many of its assumptions. However, in the historically informed search for explicit as well as implicit sexing, and for charged concepts and metaphors, it is still possible to sketch the citizen behind it: male, resourceful, orderly, behaved, and serving the general good. It is definitely not all there is to us.

B. Re-reading the European Charter of Fundamental Rights

The European Council in Cologne and later in Tampere decided to have a document of fundamental rights protection drafted for the European Union. This resulted from a moment of convergence of a German social democratic drive to constitutionalize Europe and a German Green Party willing and dedicated to guaranteeing basic rights and furthering an idea of Europe of the citizens, and a change of goverment that brought these parties to power at the very moment of the German presidency of the Council. An amazingly few months later, in December 2000, the Charter of Fundamental Rights in Europe became part of the global collection of legal curiosa. Despite its formal character—it is, according to the proclamation in Nice, a decidedly political, not legally binding, proclamation—it was made, received, and is now used as a document of full legal force. Therefore, re-reading it to conceive its potential for constructing European citizenship seems like a justifiable effort.

1. Histories and Realities

Regarding participation, the way the Charter was made exemplifies a distinctly new form of law-making for the Union.[61] The use of the Internet allowed for greater transparency, and there was widespread involvement via mailed input and national as well as European hearings in addition to lobbying. However,

---

[60] Universal Declaration of Human Rights, GA Res. 217A (III), 10 December 1948.
[61] See Baer, 'Grundrechtscharta ante portas', *Zeitschrift für Rechtspolitik* (2000) 151.

this process of transparency and participation was not well organized or structured to integrate weaker voices. It thus failed to activate and integrate people's concerns on an equal basis, but rather replicated the unequal structure of policy formation within Europe even on the virtual level.[62] This is also what we saw at the symbolic starting point of the Charter, the moment of its proclamation which we discussed as a symbol giving meaning at the beginning of this chapter. The Convention that drafted the Charter consisted of 62 persons. Nine of them were women: parliamentarians from Finland, Italy, and Luxemburg, as well as from the European Parliament,[63] and four who were only replacements for others with no rights of their own. However, many feminist law organizations were a more or less dissenting part of that process, and it is their work and the work of many other non-governmental organizations (NGOs) I partly rely on in the following analyses.[64] The European Women's Lobby (EWL)[65] commented on the process:

The EWL deeply regrets the present situation: not only because it is distressing to see that women's position is still undervalued within EU institutions, national parliaments and governments, but also because the lack of women in the Convention will certainly affect the outcome of its work.[66]

There is definitely not a straight line between the biological sex of members of the Convention and the work it produces. However, there are strong arguments to the effect that the presence of more than the exceptional women in such a setting makes a difference, particularly regarding the attention a body pays to gender and gender-specific injustice.

The Charter itself is a reaction to injustices, and in the drafting processes it was emphasized again and again that the Charter is the attempt to react to the dangers of our times rather than simply restate the rights that safeguard against dangers of the past. Therefore, we find a right against genetic engineering at the very beginning of the Charter (Article 3), and explicit protections against abuse of personal data in Article 8 as well as a right to market activity (rather than just property) in Article 16.

At the centre of the Charter, we find a triad of dignity, self-determination, and equality. However, other features of human rights were prominent topics of the discussion at the Convention. The question of social rights—or goals?—

---

[62] Schwenken, 'Citizenship in der Europäischen Grundrechtecharta', *femina politica* (2001) 38, at 41. More generally, see C. Harlow, *Voices of Difference in a Plural Community*, Harvard Jean Monnet Working Paper 3/00 (2000).
[63] Compare the regrets by Leutheusser-Schnarrenberger, 'Rede zum Jahresempfang djb 2001', in Ausschuss für die Angelegenheiten der EU, *Beiträge zur Verfassungsdiskussion der EU* (2001) 25, at 79.
[64] 'The Quality Test 2000' was purported by 30 NGOs to test the Charter regarding gender and ethnicity.
[65] See European Women's Lobby, *Overcoming Discrimination* (2000).
[66] CHARTE 4132/00, Contrib 27, 18 February 2000.

was as important to the delegates as the question of inclusion and exclusion, while the question of who belongs to the citizenry created by the Charter[67] was raised yet neither sufficiently discussed nor convincingly answered. Migrant communities are thus effectively excluded from citizenship.[68] Citizenship, in the Charter, does not go global, since it is not philosopher Immanuel Kant's *Weltbürgerschaft* or global citizenship. Yet transnationalism remains the new facet of a formerly nationalistic phenomenon, because the Charter prohibits discrimination against different nationals in Article 21, section 2. It thus envisions only European, not global citizens.

As in the European Convention, the Charter, by its very architecture, states which injustices count, at least symbolically, and which do so with greater priority than others. If we think of an alternative architecture of rights in such a document, we see which choices inform this new set of human rights. The Charter chose dignity first, and not the body, or relationships, but an individual notion of oneself. Then there are freedoms—rather than equalities, or associations. Next, the Charter names equality—rather than equalities; next, solidarity—thus not a precondition of all rights, but a mix of spheres like labour and safeguards like health care. After that, the Charter recognizes citizens—defined as members of states which are part of the Union, the only ones with political rights with an impact. And lastly, the Charter cares for justice, as the right to legal protection.

2. The Sexed Subject

More specifically, the Charter is part of legal sexing of the subject. There is, notably, very little explicit sexing in the text. In the early days of the Convention, the Association of Women of Southern Europe (AFEM) appealed in an extremely friendly manner to the delegates: 'AFEM kindly asks the Convention to kindly note that the expressions used in the provisions should be sex neutral or should refer to both sexes.'[69] Gradually, the Convention responded. Most articles refer to men and women alike, and some references can be understood as particularly gender-sensitive.

---

[67] On the construction of citizenship by law see Baer, 'Ist Ruhe erste Bürgerpflicht?, oder: Zur Konstruktion des Bürgers durch Verfassungsrecht', 82 *Kritische Vierteljahresschrift für Gesetzgebung und Rechtswissenschaft* (1999) 5; Bauböck, 'Recombinant Citizenship', in M. Kohli and A. Woodward (eds), *Inclusions/Exclusions* (2000); Koslowski, 'EU citizenship: implications for identity and legitimacy', in T. Banchoff and M. P. Smith (eds), *Legitimacy and the European Union* (1999) 155; Ward and Gregory, *supra* n. 2. Joseph Weiler argues differently when he criticizes the conflation of rights with citizenship and offers a concept of socio-pyschological belonging and loyalty instead. Cf. J. Weiler, *The Constitution of Europe* (2000).

[68] See D. Cesarani and M. Fulbrook (eds), *Citizenhip, Nationality and Migration in Europe* (1996).

[69] AFEM CHARTE 4157/00, Contrib 42, 13 March 2000.

For example, we find a right of protection of pregnancy as a social right in Article 34. But on the other hand, this right is guaranteed next to protection in cases of illness, accidents, or old age. This renders it problematic that attention is paid to a gender-specific problem as a gender-neutral phenomenon. Pregnancy is not an illness, but the law here constructs it as an abnormalcy. The potential of the Charter is thus to be more gender-sensitive but, at the same time, a critical reading still reveals problematic assumptions which underlie this move.

The extinction of explicit sexing thus does not solve the problem of implicit sexing, or of references to gendered or sexually and ethnically charged concepts and metaphors. For example, the Charter mentions various forms of violence as fundamental violations of human rights, but is oblivious to gender-based and sexual violence, despite the fact that recognition has been lobbied for in the interest of those affected by it deeply on a daily basis.

Reading through the whole document reveals the person behind the Charter—the 'citizen', according to the text—as a much more gendered person than the person which is the subject of the European Convention on Human Rights. In the Charter, the subject is still only a coherent (dignified) market actor,[70] with a shed-off private life (Article 7), taking part in modern activities including data transactions (Article 8), then maybe married (Article 9), almost certainly religious (Article 10), interested in a variety of information (Article 11) and orderly association (Article 12), and using administrative procedures (Articles 34–6, 41 *et al.*). It may be a child, a woman, an old person, or disabled, but moved to the back in Articles 22–6, these are exceptions to a rule of normalcy implied everywhere else.

We find a far-reaching equality provision in Article 21, section 1, but also ambivalence, since Article 22 ensures the right to diversity. This is the human rights analogy to the tension visible in Article 6 of the TEU, which restates the common principles of Europe in section 1 and the diverging national identities in Europe in section 3, and in the preamble to the TEU, which confirms the desire 'to deepen the solidarity between their peoples while respecting their history, their culture and their traditions'. Also, the Treaty of Amsterdam refers to diversity when it requires 'care [to] be taken to respect well established national arrangements and the organization and working of Member States' legal systems'.[71] Again, multiculturalism, multinationalism, or, more generally, the tension between difference and equality, to be solved with a focus on dominance, are part of the task the Charter puts upon those who will use it.[72]

---

[70] For an analysis of the European treaty law, see Biondi, 'The Flexible Citizen: Individual Protection after the Treaty of Amsterdam', 5 *EPL* (1999) 245; more generally Conover, 'Citizen Identities and Conceptions of the Self', 3 *J. of Pol. Phil.* (1995) 133; J. Flax, *Disputed Subjects. Essays on Psychoanalysis, Politics and Philosophy* (1993).

[71] Treaty of Amsterdam, Protocol on the Application of the Principle of Subsidiarity and Proportionality, at para. 7.

[72] See S. Baier-Allen and L. Cucic (eds), *The Challenges of Pluriculturality in Europe* (2000).

Rather than setting up a task, the Charter acknowledges the general idea of constructing rather than assuming a resourceful citizen. This is manifested in the chapter entitled 'Solidarity', which is an interesting invention as such. There, the Charter lists rights of workers to information and assistance in seeking a job, to fair working conditions or health care, to social security or the ability to combine care for children with a career, and to the protection of the environment as well as the interests of consumers.[73] It is a mix rather than a concept, and ample evidence of the fact that the drafters were willing to go further than those who empowered them to draft.[74] But what is more important here, the emphasis on 'solidarity' states the need to activate rather than address citizens, and to position individuals in a social collective, which is a significant move beyond traditional liberalism. It is a reaction to the injustice of social exclusion.[75]

Thus, the Charter is a big step forward towards inclusiveness of human rights, and their potential to protect those formerly marginalized, but it is not all that can be done to bring human rights to all humans.

5. EUROPEAN CITIZENSHIP?

American legal scholar Joseph Weiler denounces the European citizenship established by the TEU as utterly impotent, contradictory, and undecided.[76] Article 8 of the TEU, which creates European citizens, is, according to Weiler,

---

[73] In addition, other chapters contain social rights as well: the chapter on liberties includes the right to education (Article 14); the chapter on equality includes the right to integration of persons with disabilities (Article 26).

[74] Jürgen Meyer, the German delegate to the Convention, called solidarity the 'first column' of the Charter, meant to imply an 'additional value-oriented decision' common to all member states. Meyer drafted proposals with the French delegate Braibant in June 2000. The willingness of the Convention to include social rights is partly based on its willingness to draft a conclusive Charter, rather than parts of a growing Charter.

[75] The European Commission reacts to this with support programmes directed at 'active citizenship', e.g., DGXXII, *Education and active citizenship in the European Union* (1998), based on the 1997 Commission Communication 'Towards a Europe of Knowledge'. Edith Cresson wrote in the introduction: 'Traditions and approaches to citizenship vary across Europe, but the basic idea of democratic citizenship in modern society is that active participation and commitment to one's chosen community support the creation of knowledge, responsibility, common identity and shared culture. ... The concept of active citizenship ultimately speaks to the extent to which individuals and groups feel a sense of attachment to the societies and communities to which they theoretically belong, and is therefore closely related to the promotion of social inclusion and cohesion as well as to matters of identity and values.' Thus, the Commission endorses a concept of more than theoretical inclusion via membership in a European state; compare Article 8, TEU.

[76] Weiler, *supra* n. 67, at 324, 332 ('failure of Europe is colossal') *et seq.*

an 'embarrassment', a 'failure'.[77] Beyond the TEU, the Charter spells out what citizenship means in Europe. If we concentrate on the fact that the Charter is not binding but only declaratory in nature, impotence looks like a strong criticism. But we can already watch the gradual infiltration of the Charter into European human rights law as soft law, which might be at points as decisive as norms which are stronger in a formal sense. In Luxemburg in February 2001, Advocate General Tizzano used the Charter to make a legal argument, despite its formally non-legal character. He stated that 'I consider the Charter provides us with the most reliable and definitive confirmation' of the existence of the right in question, and argued that 'we cannot ignore its clear purpose of ... serving as a substantive point of reference for all those involved'.[78] He acted just like NGOs learned to do in many countries of the world where governments ratify human rights but never observe them, since NGOs use such rights as arguments, implying the integrity of a state to adhere to a document it signed. And Tizzano is not alone, in that Advocate General Mischo argued in September 2001[79] that 'I know that the Charter is not legally binding, but it is worthwhile referring to it given that it constitutes the expression, at the highest level, of a democratically established political consensus on what must today be considered as the catalogue of fundamental rights guaranteed by the Community legal order'. He went on to interpret the law accordingly. A little bit shyer, Advocate General Stix-Hackel referred to the Charter in a footnote.[80] But with this in mind, and in the spirit of recognizing the plurality of forms law takes on in the world today, one may rightfully see the Charter as a step towards constitutionalizing Europe.[81] This process was intensified at the

---

[77] Ibid., at 332.

[78] Case C-173/99, *The Queen v Secretary of State for Trade and Industry, ex parte Broadcasting, Entertainment, Cinematographic and Theatre Union* [2001] ECR I-4881.

[79] Opinion delivered on 20 September 2001 in Joined Cases C-20/00 and C-64/00, *Booker Aquaculture Ltd, Hydro Seafood GSP Ltd v The Scottish Ministers*, judgment of 10 July 2003.

[80] Opinion delivered on 13 September 2001, Case C-459/99, *Mouvement contre le racisme, l'antisémitisme et la xénophobie ASBL (MRAX) v The Belgian State* [2002] ECR I-6591, fn. 26.

[81] It was not the first step. The Institutional Committee of the European Parliament drafted a constitution in 1994; see Cromme, 'Der Verfassungsentwurf des Institutionellen Ausschusses des Europ. Parlaments von 1994', *Zeitschrift für Gesetzgebung* (1995) 256. See also Preuß, 'Grundrechte in der Europäischen Union', 31 *Kritische Justiz* (1998) 1; Weber, 'Die Europäische Grundrechtscharta—auf dem Weg zu einer europäischen Verfassung', *Neue Juristische Wochenschrift* (2000) 537; Oeter, 'Europäische Integration als Konstitutionalisierungsprozess', 59 *Zeitschrift für ausländisches öffentliches Recht und Rechtsvergleichung* (1999) 901. On a republican vision of European constitutionalism see Frankenberg, *supra* n. 18. The German liberal party FDP called the Charter a cornerstone of a European constitution; see BT-Drs. 14/4253 v. 11.10.2000; while the conservative parties CDU/CSU emphasize the Charter as an ordering of values; BT-Drs. 14/4246, 10.10.2000. The Green Party calls it a contribution to the creation of a European identity; BT-Drs. 14/4269, 11.10.2000.

Laeken summit which called for another Convention to draft the rest of a European constitution.

In contrast to Weiler's charge that the idea of European citizenship is undecided, the Charter moves beyond the simple reference to concepts of citizenship which focus on belonging to nations. Rather, it reacts to injustices of social exclusion by establishing rights of solidarity, and it reacts to modern threats to physical integrity as well as informational privacy. It avoids explicit sexing of subjects and opens space for the inclusion of sexual minorities. Thus, from a gender-sensitive perspective, re-reading the Charter offers the potential to construct a more inclusive citizenship. Next to the prohibition of discrimination based on nationality, the idea of Europe carries a vision of not discriminating based on gender and sexualities. This is one of the rather typical small victories in the fight for human rights. Rather than condemnation, a new legal text of this kind deserves creative use.[82] This would be part of an understanding of citizenship as critical positioning, an activity between determination and choice, and something the Charter, as any other human rights document, allows for.

---

[82] This active dimension has been emphasized as well in the report by H. Köchler, *Decision-Making Procedures of the European Institutions and Democratic Legitimacy: How can democratic citizenship be exercised on the transnational level?*, Report prepared for the Council of Europe—Research Project 'European Studies for Democratic Citizenship' (1999). On this approach, see my discussion with Beger and da Silva, 'Recht und Rechte: Zwischen legaler Anerkennung und kulturell-politischer "Revolution"', in questio (ed.), *Queering Demokratie—sexuelle politiken* (2001) 182.

5

Constitutional Domestication of International Gender Norms: Categorizations, Illustrations, and Reflections from the Nearside of the Bridge

RUTH RUBIO-MARÍN AND
MARTHA I. MORGAN

1. INTRODUCTION

The relationship between national and world citizenship is increasingly complex but women remain subject to the interrelated consequences of each of these statuses, as well as to those flowing from their membership in more local forms of government and in non-geographically defined communities. The challenge facing advocates for gender justice is more clearly to identify and understand the ever-changing relationships between these statuses and to develop complementary nuanced and mutable strategies for enriching gender rights by transporting or incorporating positive developments among these arenas, giving appropriate deference to differences and to the need for contextualization while guarding against erosion or dilution of core rights that more fluid boundaries may also portend. The task is daunting and requires that the corresponding boundaries between specialists in international law and domestic and comparative constitutional law become more porous than is now commonly the case, and that the scholarship and practice of both constitutional and international law become more integrated.

Our role as participants in this project on gender and human rights is to examine one of the areas where such boundary-stretching 'enrichment' strategies have been pursued—that of the incorporation of international and regional human rights norms protecting gender rights into the domestic constitutional law of various countries. As scholars of domestic constitutional law, we present observations from our side (the 'nearside') of the bridge that spans the traditional divide between the 'here' of domestic constitutional law and the 'there' of international law.[1] Aware of the potential for myopia inherent in such perspectives, we invite conversation about, and critique of, our views, especially from those whose expertise differs.

After decades of activity directed to promoting the domestic incorporation of international human rights law regarding gender discrimination and other women's rights issues,[2] it is time to step back and assess what has occurred and what lessons we can draw from the experiences thus far. We present categoriza-

---

[1] Karen Knop, in Knop, 'Here and There: International Law in Domestic Courts', 32 *New York University Journal of International Law and Politics* (2000) 501, addresses the domestic interpretation of international law as a problem of translation where different meanings interact with one another to produce new meanings. She prefers this metaphor to both current models of the use of international law in domestic courts—the traditional model, where international law is understood as binding transcendent authority that domestic judges apply in an all-or-nothing fashion, and transjudicialism's alternative understanding of its merely persuasive uses—because it recognizes the creativity and thus uncertainty involved in domestic interpretation. The general literature on uses of international law by domestic courts includes T. M. Franck and G. H. Fox (eds), *International Law Decisions in National Courts* (1996); B. Conforti and F. Francioni (eds), *Enforcing International Human Rights in Domestic Courts* (1997); Koh, 'How is International Human Rights Law Enforced?', 74 *Indiana Law Journal* (1997) 1397; Koh, 'The 1998 Frankel Lecture: Bringing International Law Home', 35 *Houston Law Review* (1998) 623; L'Heureux-Dubé, 'The Importance of Dialogue: Globalization and the International Impact of the Rehnquist Court', 34 *Tulsa Law Journal* (1998) 15; Slaughter, 'Judicial Globalization', 40 *Virginia Journal of International Law* (2000) 1103; 'Developments in the Law—International Criminal Law: VI. The International Judicial Dialogue: When Domestic Constitutional Courts Join the Conversation', 114 *Harvard Law Review* (2001) 2049.

[2] A website providing valuable citations and links on the domestic incorporation of regional and international gender rights is maintained by the Women's Human Rights Resources Project (WHRR), at http://www.law-lib.utoronto.ca/diana/mainpage.htm. A description of many of the principal gender protections provided in regional and international human rights documents, and a survey of much of the early jurisprudence incorporating these rights, is presented in A. Byrnes, *Human Rights Instruments Relating Specifically to Women, With Particular Emphasis on the Convention on the Elimination of All Forms of Discrimination Against Women, Advancing the Human Rights of Women: Using International Human Rights Standards in Domestic Litigation*, Papers and Statements from the Asia/South Pacific Regional Judicial Colloquium (1996) (available online at WHRR). Spanish translation in A. Facio and L. Fries (eds), *Genero y Derecho* (1999). See also J. Connors, *General Human Rights Instruments and Their Relevance to Women, Advancing the Human Rights of Women: Using International Human Rights Standards in Domestic Litigation*, Papers and Statements from the Asia/South Pacific Regional Judicial Colloquium (1996) (available online at WHRR). For strategies to use international human rights law to defend women's human rights, see Women, Law and Development International, *Women, Law and Development & Human Rights Watch Women's Rights Project, Women's Human Rights Step by Step: A Practical Guide to Using International Human Rights Law and Mechanisms to Defend Women's Human Rights* (1997). For citations to over 20 treaties devoted specifically to women and issues related to sexual discrimination, see Bayefsky, 'General Approaches to the Domestic Application of Women's International Human Rights Law', in R. J. Cook (ed.), *Human Rights of Women: National and International Perspectives* (1994) 351, at 369–70, n. 1. See also, United Nations Publications, *International Legal Instruments Relevant to Women* (1995); González Martínez, 'Human Rights of Women', 5 *Washington University Journal of Law and Policy* (2001) 157.

tions and illustrations that we hope will be useful for understanding, connecting, and building upon this early experience to strengthen protection for gender rights at all levels.

In '2. Categorizing Domestic Incorporation: A Suggested Typology' (at pp. 117–29 below), we begin by presenting a typology for identifying and describing primary processes through which international human rights law and domestic constitutional law interact in the domestic realm. We describe three major forms of incorporation or domestication of international human rights law that result from such interaction: *assimilation, supplementation*, and *adaptation. Assimilation* occurs when international human rights norms influence the drafting of fundamental rights provisions of domestic constitutions during periods of constitution-making or amendment. With *supplementation*, international human rights norms come to be treated as a supplementary part of a country's domestic law by explicit or implicit constitutional directive. However, the international law retains its separate status, whether that status is as part of one legal system spanning international and domestic law, or as part of a separate legal system. This is distinct from the question of rank or position it enjoys hierarchically. Lastly, *adaptation* involves a blending or hybridizing of international with domestic law through the process of interpretation, whether this process is required by the domestic legal system (for example, through use of a presumption of conformity in so far as possible) or is a matter of judicial discretion (a persuasive use akin to the use of comparative law). Although international lawyers have dealt with adaptation matters, such as the presumption of conformity and increasingly the comparative law-style uses, their main focus has been on theorizing the dynamic of what we refer to as supplementation. These three forms of incorporation are non-exclusive and may operate simultaneously within the same domestic system. Variations and sub-categories within each of the paradigms will be examined.

In '3. Examining Primary Effects and Potential: Illustrations from the Homefronts' (at pp. 129–51 below), we categorize and examine some of the primary effects that these various forms of incorporation have had upon gender jurisprudence in the realm of domestic constitutional law. For analytical purposes, we group these domestic effects as substantive and structural. We examine jurisprudence illustrating how international gender norms and jurisprudence have helped shape domestic constitutionalism by either *expanding, complementing*, or *concretizing* substantive constitutional parameters. Lastly, we explore the actual and potential *structural* uses of international law to redefine structural allocations of power by filling gaps or forging new frontiers of authority to act with respect to gender issues.

The web of vertical and horizontal interactions or dialogues between and among national and supranational and governmental and non-governmental actors involved in these processes of domestic incorporation has corresponding effects on the shaping of international human rights law.[3] Indeed, much of the extensive commentary to date has focused on the actual or potential 'upwards' or 'farside' effects of domestication of international norms. For example, much of the general literature is concerned with the intrinsic effects of domestic incorporation on international law—such as what effects it will have on the scorecard in the universality versus relativity debate, and whether domestic lawyers and judges are up to the job.[4] Particularly in the literature dealing with incorporation of regional or international human right norms, the focus is often more instrumental—promoting domestic incorporation as providing enforcement and implementation mechanisms that are often absent or weak at the international level.[5] Our primary interest differs and we emphasize the 'nearside' intrinsic effects of such incorporation on the development of domestic constitutional law itself.[6]

The illustrations we present include cases from both civil law systems and common law systems. Given our areas of special interest and experience, we draw our primary examples of civil law cases from Latin America and Spain, and our primary examples of common law cases from Australia and India,

[3] International and regional human rights tribunals have also employed various processes through which domestic law has influenced their interpretation or application of human rights documents. For a critique of how the European Court of Human Rights has used domestic law in interpreting and applying the European Convention on Human Rights, including its use of the margin of appreciation concept, see Carozza, 'Propter Honoris Respectum: Uses and Misuses of Comparative Law in International Human Rights: Some Reflections on the Jurisprudence of the European Court of Human Rights', 73 *Notre Dame Law Review* (1998) 1217. Also see Gross and Ní Aoláin, 'From Discretion to Scrutiny: Revisiting the Application of the Margin of Appreciation Doctrine in the Context of Article 15 of the European Convention on Human Rights', 23 *Human Rights Law Quarterly* (2001) 650; Neuman, 'Human Rights and Constitutional Rights: Harmony and Dissonance', 55 *Stanford Law Review* (2003) 1863.

[4] See e.g. Bayefsky, *supra* n. 2; Byrnes, *supra* n. 2.

[5] See e.g. Byrnes, *supra* n. 2. Knop, *supra* n. 1, at 516, makes this point and provides additional citations. The new Optional Protocol to the Convention on the Elimination of All Forms of Discrimination against Women (CEDAW), which authorizes individuals to file petitions alleging Convention violations with the Committee, promises to strengthen enforcement at the international level. See generally, United Nations Publications, *Optional Protocol: Text and Materials—The Convention on the Elimination of All Forms of Discrimination against Women* (2000). The resulting decisions have the potential for enriching interchanges between supra-national and national decision-making forums considering CEDAW. Of course, as elsewhere in the web of what might be described as 'trans-tribunal communication', the quality of this dialogue will depend upon the willingness and ability of national and international decision-makers and advocates to stay abreast of relevant decisions. For a categorization and discussion of 'transjudicial' communications, see Slaughter, 'A Typology of Transjudicial Communication', in Franck and Fox, *supra* n. 1, at 37–69.

[6] For other considerations of nearside effects, see Heyns and Viljoen, 'The Impact of the United Nations Human Rights Treaties on the Domestic Level', 23 *Human Rights Law Quarterly* (2001) 483 (findings and recommendations of study initiated in 1999 of six UN human rights treaties, including CEDAW, in 20 different countries); Beer, 'Book Review, International Law, Human Rights, and Japanese Law: The Impact of International Law on Japanese Law by Yugi Iwasawa', 23 *Human Rights Law Quarterly* (2001) 464.

though some references to other national systems will be made in passing. Cases from Spain and Latin American countries are particularly interesting because they reflect domestic influences from both regional and United Nations human rights documents and accompanying jurisprudence. Our illustrations are drawn from cases where the decisions of supreme or constitutional courts have been affected by international norms apart from cases where these courts have acted directly to comply with a judgment of an international tribunal.

We consider domestic constitutional incorporation of gender rights flowing from regional human rights conventions of the European and Inter-American systems, as well as universal instruments, including but not limited to the Convention on the Elimination of All Forms of Discrimination against Women (CEDAW).[7]

Issues concerning the domestic application of customary international law,[8] and those related to how international gender law influences realms of domestic law and practice other than constitutional law,[9] are addressed only peripherally.

2. CATEGORIZING DOMESTIC INCORPORATION: A SUGGESTED TYPOLOGY

Women, as well as other traditionally marginalized groups to which many of them also belong, often have won broader formal recognition of their gender-specific fundamental human rights within international and regional human rights documents than within national or subnational constitutions. Yet supranational enforcement mechanisms remain weak and distant.[10] The national or subnational levels of constitutional and statutory law retain their

---

[7] Convention on the Elimination of All Forms of Discrimination Against Women, New York, adopted 18 December 1979, in force 3 September 1981, 1249 UNTS 13.

[8] For a recent exploration of these broader issues generally, see Koh, 'Bringing International Law Home', *supra* n. 1.

[9] For a survey of the domestic impact of CEDAW that includes discussion of its impact beyond constitutions and courts, see I. Landsberg-Lewis (ed.), *Bringing Equality Home: Implementing the Convention on the Elimination of All Forms of Discrimination Against Women (CEDAW)* (1998).

[10] For example, Penelope Andrews has pointed out the difficulties the arcane world of international law presents for aboriginal women in Australia, for whom 'the symbolism and substance of human rights provide a useful backdrop for buttressing these issues locally', but using international forums of legal redress 'necessitates overcoming formidable obstacles; cumbersome enforcement mechanisms locked in a truly distant world'. Andrews, 'Violence against Aboriginal Women in Australia: Possibilities for Redress within the International Human Rights Framework', in A. K. Wing (ed.), *Global Critical Race Feminism: An International Reader* (2001) 303, at 311–12.

primacy as the strategic focus of many women's rights activists. The most accessible forums for seeking protection of women's rights and legal redress for their violations remain those closest to home. This state of affairs has fuelled international, regional, national, and local campaigns, orchestrated by women's rights activists, non-governmental organizations, and supportive governmental officials and organizations, to promote the domestic incorporation of international and regional human rights law protections for women.[11] As is commonly the case in the twilight zone of interactions between international and domestic law, the result of these efforts is a growing body of 'messy' or 'blurry' yet important developments in domestic constitutional law. These legal developments may appear confused, uncertain, and even contradictory, and thus lie at the opposite end of the spectrum from the mythical black letter law, which exhibits only certainty and clarity.

The ways in which international law is 'domesticated' are complex and the resulting effects on both international and domestic law are often difficult to assess. This is no less true with respect to gender rights than other areas of law. Any readily understandable scheme of models or paradigms for describing how the various forms of domestication occur carries risks of over-simplification. Nevertheless, the typology that follows offers a broad organizational framework for understanding this particular area of law.

Broadly speaking, the domestic incorporation of gender norms contained in regional and international human rights documents occurs in one or more of three ways, which we refer to as internal assimilation, hierarchical supplementation, and interpretive adaptation. The terms governing the legitimacy and availability of these methods may be expressly provided for in a particular nation's constitution and governing statutes, or these terms may be determined to be implicitly so provided for by judicial interpretations.

Assimilation refers to the processes through which international human rights law has, at times of the adoption or amendment of national constitutions, provided a direct or indirect blueprint for reshaping the contours of domestic constitutional rights or for the recognition of new ones. Assimilation can be difficult to spot by simply reading constitutional text because, unless it directly parrots the textual provisions assimilated, the international or regional pedigree of the newly-minted domestic constitutional law may be obscured. Similarly, its effects on domestic constitutional jurisprudence may escape notice.

Supplementation refers to the process through which domestic systems of constitutional law adopt various forms of hierarchical ordering of international and national law as component parts of an integrated system of internally applicable law. This category encompasses a wide assortment of

---

[11] See e.g. Byrnes, *supra* n. 2, at 220, for a description of some of the efforts to introduce Commonwealth judges to international human rights law standards and jurisprudence.

express and implied arrangements resulting in varying degrees of receptivity (or resistance) to incorporation.

Adaptation refers to those processes through which the interpretation and application of existing domestic constitutional law is influenced by international law. The variations here are particularly pronounced, ranging from express constitutional directives of various sorts, to judicially recognized presumptions of consistency, to more subtle persuasive influences.

As international law increasingly becomes not just one competing source within hierarchies of positive law but is taken to express a universal community of conscience or universal human rights ethos, this very quality allows it to sneak into constitutive national narratives in much more subtle ways. In the text that follows, we will describe further variations and sub-groupings within each of these three categories and illustrate each with examples from contemporary systems of domestic constitutional law.

A. Assimilation

As we use the term, assimilation can occur at different stages of constitution-making and revision. In recently published findings from their study of the impact of UN treaties at the domestic level, Christof Heyns and Frans Viljoen[12] emphasize the importance of this type of constitutional recognition of treaty norms, especially where the constitutional human rights provisions are justiciable, as one of the most powerful ways in which treaty norms can be enforced at a local level.[13]

1. Constitution-making

Countries generally are most receptive to international human rights norms during periods of transition to democracy, in which they are likely to incorporate such norms into their new constitutions.[14] Colombia provides a vivid illustration of this method being utilized at the stage of framing a new constitution. The delegates to the constitutional convention that drafted the 1991 Colombian Constitution relied upon principles from a number of international human rights documents, including the International Covenant on Civil and Political Rights (ICCPR)[15] and the International Covenant on Economic, Social, and Cultural Rights (ICESCR).[16]

[12] Heyns and Viljoen, *supra* n. 6.
[13] Ibid., at 500.
[14] Ibid., at 530.
[15] International Covenant on Civil and Political Rights, adopted 16 December 1966, entered into force 23 March 1976, 999 UNTS 171.
[16] Heyns and Viljoen, *supra* n. 6, at 500; International Covenant on Economic, Social, and Cultural Rights, adopted 16 December 1966, entered into force 3 January 1976, 993 UNTS 3.

120   *Ruth Rubio-Marín and Martha I. Morgan*

Less obvious perhaps, but of particular importance in the gender jurispru-
dence of the Colombian Constitutional Court that we will refer to at
pp. 139–42 below, is the influence that CEDAW had upon this new charter.
As a result of the efforts of women's organizations, and of the parallel efforts of
supportive men and women within the constitutional assembly, the 1991
Constitution contains several explicit guarantees related to women's rights.
One of the primary demands of Colombian women's groups was that the
Constitution incorporate the principles of CEDAW, including its concept
of substantive equality.[17] Although not incorporated word-for-word, key
CEDAW principles are embodied in several provisions of the new Consti-
tution.[18] Article 1 of CEDAW broadly defines discrimination against women:

For the purposes of the present Convention, the term 'discrimination against women'
shall mean any distinction, exclusion or restriction made on the basis of sex which has
the effect or purpose of impairing or nullifying the recognition, enjoyment or exercise
by women, irrespective of their marital status, on a basis of equality of men and
women, of human rights and fundamental freedoms in the political, economic, social,
cultural, civil or any other field.

Article 4 embraces the concept of positive discrimination or affirmative action
by providing that temporary special measures to accelerate de facto equality of
opportunities and treatment shall not be considered discrimination as defined
by the Convention. In addition, Article 3 expressly charges states parties to
pursue all appropriate steps, including legislative measures, to ensure women's
full development and progress, and Article 7 obligates states to take all
appropriate measures to eliminate discrimination against women in political
and public life.

The 1991 Constitution expressly reflects CEDAW principles in its embrace
of the dual strategy of prohibition of discrimination against women and
approval of special positive measures as a means of assuring substantive
rather than merely formal equality as incorporated in Article 13 of the new
Constitution:

[17] *Propuestas de Mujeres a La Asamblea Nacional Constituyente* (January 1991), described in
Morgan with the collaboration of Alzate Buitrago, 'Constitution-Making in a Time of Cholera:
Women and the 1991 Colombian Constitution', 4 *Yale Journal of Law and Feminism* (1992)
353, 375–6, n. 91 (describing the role of women and women's rights activists in the adoption of
the 1991 Constitution). Also see Plata, 'Reproductive Rights as Human Rights: The Colombian Case', in Cook, *supra* n. 2, at 518–19.
[18] Other examples of assimilation of CEDAW principles include Article 40, which provides
that 'the authorities will guarantee the adequate and effective participation of women in the
decision-making levels of Public Administration'; Article 42, which recognizes equal rights and
responsibilities between spouses; and Article 43, which prohibits discrimination against women
and guarantees equal rights and opportunities between women and men. Also, Article 53
includes equality of opportunity and special protection for women, maternity, and minors
among the fundamental principles to be considered by Congress in enacting a labour law.

All persons are born free and equal before the law, shall receive the same protection and treatment from the authorities, and shall enjoy the same rights, liberties and opportunities without any discrimination for reasons of sex, race, national or family origin, language, religion, or political or philosophical opinion.

The State shall promote conditions so that equality will be real and effective and shall adopt measures in favor of groups discriminated against or marginalized.

The State shall specially protect those persons who because of their economic, physical or mental condition find themselves in circumstances of manifest weakness and shall punish abuses and mistreatment that are committed against them.

Women's rights activists also led successful campaigns to ensure that CEDAW norms be reflected in the 1988 Brazilian Constitution,[19] the 1995 Ugandan Constitution,[20] and the 1998 South African Constitution.[21]

2. *Constitutional Amendment*

Assimilation of norms can also take place during the amendment or partial reform of an existing constitution. For example, international human rights documents were influential bases for the 1982 *Canadian Charter of Rights and Freedoms.* Justice L'Heureux-Dubé has written that 'the drafters of the *Canadian Charter of Rights and Freedoms* drew extensively on international human rights treaties'.[22] The ICCPR was especially influential.[23] Former Chief Justice Lamer has also remarked upon this influence: '[T]he *Charter* can be understood to give effect to Canada's international legal obligations and should therefore be interpreted in a way that conforms to those obligations.'[24]

---

[19] Landsberg-Lewis, *supra* n. 9, at 14–16 (pointing to the Brazilian Constitution's provisions on gender equality, gender-based violence, state responsibility for the prevention of domestic violence, equality of rights within marriage, family planning, and equality in employment as gender equality provisions that parallel CEDAW provisions). See generally, S. E. Alvarez, *Engendering Democracy in Brazil: Women's Movements in Transition Politics* (1990).

[20] Landsberg-Lewis, *supra* n. 9, at 13–14. (Members of the Women's Caucus of the 1995 Ugandan Constituent Assembly referred to CEDAW as establishing a minimum acceptable standard and the Convention is reflected in provisions on gender balance and fair representation, prohibitions on sex discrimination, and reservation of a minimum number of elected parliamentary seats for women.) See generally, A. M. Tripp, *Women and Politics in Uganda* (1999).

[21] Landsberg-Lewis, *supra* n. 9, at 17. (The coalition presenting women's demands in the form of a women's charter of rights drew on CEDAW principles and CEDAW provided a useful framework for specific rights.)

[22] L'Heureux-Dubé, *supra* n. 1, at 24.

[23] Heyns and Viljoen, *supra* n. 6, at 500.

[24] Knop, *supra* n. 1, at 518, includes this quote from a 1997 address by Chief Justice Antonio Lamer. As his remarks underscore, assimilation of international human rights law is closely related to our third category of interpretive incorporation, often serving as the justification for such uses. Lamer, 'Enforcing Human Rights Law: The Treaty System in the 21st Century', in A. F. Bayefsky (ed.), *The UN Human Rights Treaty System in the 21st Century* (2000).

A more recent general illustration is the United Kingdom's domestication of the European Convention on Human Rights (ECHR) in its Human Rights Act of 1998, which became effective on 2 October 2000, thus finally giving some domestic constitutional[25] effect to the ECHR in UK law.[26]

Argentina offers a clear example of the assimilation of international gender norms through partial constitutional reform. Provisions adopted as part of the 1994 Constitutional Reform assimilated the concept of substantive gender equality of Articles 4 and 7 of CEDAW.[27] The French Constitution provides a more recent, if less obvious, example of assimilation through constitutional reform. The French Constitutional Chamber's earlier invalidation of electoral quotas for women candidates precipitated a 1999 reform of the French Constitution's Article 3 (national sovereignty), which added a new paragraph providing that 'Statutes shall promote equal access by women and men to elective offices and positions'. Pursuant to this amendment, the Constitutional Council upheld a June 2000 law requiring parity (50:50) between

[25] Although the United Kingdom does not have a single written constitution and previously had no bill of rights, the Human Rights Act 1998 is generally regarded as a major constitutional change in UK law that is analogous in some respects to the inclusion of an unentrenched bill of rights.

[26] For discussion of practices of English courts prior to the 1998 Act, see Clements, 'Bringing it all back home: Rights in English law before the Human Rights Act of 1998', 21 *HRLJ* (2000) 134. Clements notes that although the incorporation has been characterized as a 'revolutionary' change in English law, prior judicial practices make it less of a revolutionary change.

[27] Article 75(23) of the Constitution of Argentina includes among the functions of Congress:

> Legislating and promoting measures of affirmative action that guarantee the real equality of opportunities and treatment, and the full enjoyment and exercise of the rights recognized by this Constitution and by applicable international human rights treaties, in particular with respect to children, women, the elderly, and persons with disabilities.
>
> Dictating a special and comprehensive social security regime for protection of unprotected or abandoned children, from pregnancy until the end of the period of basic education, and for women during pregnancy and nursing.

The text of this provision was proposed by the Committee on Integration and International Treaties in response to proposals from women members of the 1994 Constitutional Assembly. The first paragraph reflects the principle of affirmative action of the first paragraph of Article 4 of CEDAW, and the second paragraph is based on the second paragraph of Article 4 which clarifies that special protections to protect maternity are not considered discriminatory. See J. P. Cafiero *et al.*, *Jerarquía constitucional de los tratados internacionales* (1996), at 75–85. The 1994 Reforms also included a specific affirmative action provision in the second paragraph to Article 37, which states that 'real equality of opportunities between men and women in access to elected and party positions will be guaranteed through positive actions in the regulations of political parties and in the electoral regime'. An accompanying transitory provision states that 'the positive actions referred to in the last paragraph of art. 37 shall not be less than those existing at the time this Constitution becomes effective and their duration shall be that determined by law'. In 1991, Argentina had become the first Latin American country to adopt legislation requiring that a minimum percentage (30 per cent) of certain electoral candidates be women. In the following decade, a dozen countries in the region adopted some version of a 'quota' law for women's participation in elected or appointed public positions.

women and men candidates for elective office, which Council member Noëlle Lenoir has described as meeting the concern in other European Constitutional Councils and of the European Courts (at Strasbourg and Luxembourg) that fundamental rights, including non-discrimination on the basis of gender, be concrete and effective, and as following the remedial spirit of international instruments such as CEDAW, which was ratified by France in 1984.[28]

In contrast to the French example, where constitutional amendment was required to undo a prior interpretation by the Constitutional Council, amendments to the Costa Rican Constitution in 1999 afford an example of the amendment process being used to assimilate into the Constitution's fundamental rights provisions the results of previous judicial incorporations of supranational norms. The 1999 amendments replaced gender-specific language with gender-neutral terms in several provisions. The general equality guarantee in Article 33, which the Constitutional Chamber of the Supreme Court earlier had interpreted as protecting persons of both sexes, when read alongside international gender norms, was amended by replacing the phrase 'every man is equal before the law' with 'every person is equal before the law'.[29] Similarly, Article 20 was amended to read 'every person is free'. At the same time, Article 14(5) was reformed expressly to extend eligibility for naturalization to foreign persons of both sexes who marry Costa Ricans, and thus incorporate the Constitutional Chamber's earlier interpretation of the supra-constitutional effects of international treaties ratified by Costa Rica on the prior version of this Article, which is discussed at pp. 129–31 below.

B. Supplementation

A second major method for the incorporation of international human rights treaty norms is to treat them as a supplementary part of a country's domestic law. In this regard, distinctions have been drawn between so-called monist versus dualist systems,[30] depending on whether international and domestic law are seen as separate legal orders, existing independently of each other. A further distinction between treaty provisions that are self-executing versus non-self-executing is drawn in some systems to differentiate international human rights norms that are deemed automatically to form part of the country's internal legal order once duly ratified or adopted from those that instead require further direct legislative action to become so incorporated.

---

[28] Lenoir, 'The Representation of Women in Politics: From Quotas to Parity in Elections', 50 *International and Comparative Law Quarterly* (2001) 217, at 242–6.

[29] Ley No. 7880, 27 May, 1999.

[30] Countries adopting the monist approach to incorporation of treaty norms include Brazil, Colombia, Japan, and Spain. Among those characterized as dualist are Australia, Canada, India, South Africa, and Zambia.

Elsewhere a distinction between adoption versus transformation theory has been used.[31] In any event, not all sources of international law are internally received in the same way, nor do national constitutions always play the same role in determining the form of incorporation.[32] Our research suggests tendencies towards a monistic approach in civil law systems and towards dualism in common law systems.

Apart from the issue of how international norms become seen as supplementary parts of the domestic order, and the role that national constitutions play in defining such supplementation, it is particularly important (though sometimes difficult) to understand many constitutions' role in establishing the position or rank these incorporated norms occupy within a particular country's hierarchy of domestic law. A distinction can be drawn between those that grant international law a 'pre-eminent' status, be it over the constitution itself or over national statutory norms,[33] and those constitutions that grant international law the same status as national statutes or state that it forms part of the supreme law of the nation.[34]

C. Interpretive Adaptations

As previously noted, this third category is somewhat of a catch-all and may be used either independently or in conjunction with the other forms of incorporation discussed above. Often, the justification for interpretive use is express in

[31] Bayefsky, *supra* n. 2, at 360.

[32] For example, under Germany's Basic Law, customary international law is self-executing (Article 25) but treaty law is not (Article 59).

[33] Some constitutions refer to international human rights treaties and conventions as having pre-eminence over internal law, without any further specification (see Article 93 of the Political Constitution of Colombia, Article 7 of the Costa Rican Constitution, and Article 46 of the Guatemalan Constitution). This type of language lends itself to the interpretation of international human rights law as having supraconstitutional status. In Costa Rica, for example, the Constitutional Chamber of the Supreme Court has expressly sanctioned such supremacy (see Voto No. 5759–93). In Colombia, the Constitutional Court first reached a similar conclusion, but later changed course and interpreted Article 93 as according constitutional status to international human rights law. In some cases, there is a direct or indirect recognition of international law as having an intermediate status between the national constitution and national statutes. Thus, Article 96 of the Spanish Constitution recognizes that international treaties validly adopted by Spain, once officially published in that country, form part of the internal order, and that their provisions can be derogated from, modified, or suspended only in the manners previously provided for in the treaties themselves, or in accord with the general norms of international law. Article 95, however, provides a mechanism for pre-ratification review which enables the constitutional court to decide, *a priori*, on the compatibility between a treaty and the Constitution so as to determine whether or not ratification would require prior and explicit constitutional amendment.

[34] For examples of provisions providing that the constitution, national laws, and treaties are the supreme law of the nation, see Article 31 of the Constitution of Argentina or Article VI of

constitutions, which sometimes single out human rights treaties as valid sources for the interpretation of relevant constitutional rights. This is, for instance, the case with the Spanish Constitution which, in its Article 10.2, provides that 'the norms related to the fundamental rights and liberties which the Constitution recognizes shall be interpreted in conformity with the Universal Declaration of Human Rights and the treaties and international agreements on these matters ratified by Spain'.[35] It is not surprising that some of the countries with such express interpretive provisions are among those whose courts have been more prone to rely on international instruments when interpreting their national constitutions.[36]

Sometimes the reference to international law explicitly contained in the constitution is a more generic one, which the courts then use to develop an interpretive rule. For instance, this has been the case in India, where Article 51c of the Constitution (among the Directive Principles of State Policy) provides that 'the State shall endeavor to ... foster respect for international law and treaty obligations in the dealings of organized people with one another', a mandate upon which the Constitutional Court has grounded the duty of courts 'to give due regard to International Conventions and Norms for construing domestic laws, especially when there is no inconsistency between them and there is a void in domestic law'.[37]

the United States Constitution. Article VI of the US Constitution is interpreted as according treaties the same status as federal laws. Following the 1994 amendments to the Argentine Constitution, Article 75(22) generally accords treaties and conventions supra-statutory status and lists ten specific human rights documents (including CEDAW) that are accorded constitutional status. Other human rights treaties and conventions approved by the Congress require a separate vote of two-thirds of the members of each legislative chamber to enjoy constitutional status. For further discussion of the 1994 reforms and of their effect upon the hierarchy of norms in Argentina's legal system, see Cafiero *et al.*, *supra* n. 27.

[35] See also Article 93 of the Colombian Constitution, Article 13(2) of the Ethiopian Constitution, and Article 39.1 of the South African Constitution.

[36] Heynes and Viljoen found that the Colombian Constitutional Court has an exceptional record of reference to the treaties (in 129 cases between 1992 and 1998 it has based its decisions on the ICCPR). Heynes and Viljoen, *supra* n. 6, at 502. Spain is listed among other countries where domestic courts make frequent interpretive references to international human rights treaties (28), as is South Africa (28). Canada's *Charter of Rights and Freedoms* contains no express interpretive provision, and yet Canada is also one of the countries with courts making frequent use of international law as an interpretive tool (169 references were identified in the study). Presumably, the influence of existing international law at the time of constitution-making or amending also has an influence on the interpretive dimension. See Slaughter, *supra* n. 1. Finland was the other country which was included in the 'frequent use' category.

[37] See *Apparel Export Promotion Council v AK Chopra* [1999] All India Rep (S.C.) 625, [2000] 1 Law Reports of the Commonwealth 563, para. 28; *Githa Hariharan v Reserve Bank of India* [1999] 1 Law Reports of India 151; prior to that, *Vishaka v State of Rajasthan* 1997 SOL Case No. 177, para. 13: 'It is now an accepted rule of judicial construction that regard must be had to international conventions and norms for construing domestic law when there is no inconsistency between them and there is a void in the domestic law.'

Lastly, there are countries where the interpretive value of international instruments is not explicitly sanctioned in the constitution and relies, instead, on jurisprudential construction of what we could call interpretive presumptions, or on judicial resort to international norms or jurisprudence as of persuasive or contextual value. Canadian jurisprudence contains numerous interpretive references to international human rights norms that are, perhaps predictably, somewhat more difficult to classify.[38] Sometimes there seems to be implicit the thesis that the *Charter of Rights and Freedoms* should be interpreted to provide at least as much protection as is provided in the international human rights documents Canada has ratified.[39] In the more recent decisions, the Canadian Supreme Court has referred more generically to 'values reflected in international human rights law' as 'able to inform the contextual approach to statutory interpretation and judicial review', even if such instruments could not be applied directly domestically because they had not been implemented by Parliament.[40] The idea is that in determining the meaning of the *Charter* provisions, the Court has to look to the external context at the time the *Charter* was drafted. Because the legislature is presumed to have knowledge of the relevant law, international sources are presumed to have been an inspiration and therefore are used to inform the interpretation of the provisions.[41] The fact that a human rights tribunal has considered a clause similar to the constitutional provision in need of interpretation is sometimes considered an additional reason for relying on international sources.[42] In other national settings the interpretive use of

[38] See e.g. WHRR, *supra* n. 2; Bayefsky, *supra* n. 2.
[39] See e.g. *Slaight Communications Inc. v Davidson* [1989] 1 SCR 1038, 1056–7, where the Court looked to Canada's international human rights obligations in interpreting both the content of *Charter* rights and the sufficiency of any justifications for restrictions upon such rights. See also *Ephrahim v Pastory and Another*, Decision of the High Court of Tanzania, [1990] Law Reports of the Commonwealth (Const) 757, where the Court treated principles expressed in the Universal Declaration of Human Rights, CEDAW, and the African Charter on Human and Peoples' Rights as expressing 'a standard below which any civilised nation will be ashamed to fall'. The Court relied upon the constitutional interpretive value of these principles to strike down customary law that discriminated against female members of a clan by denying them the right to sell land.
[40] See *Baker v Canada (Minister of Citizenship and Immigration)* [1999] 2 SCR 817. For further discussion of this case, see Knop, *supra* n. 1, at 507–12. See also *Reference re: Firearms Act (Can.)*, 1998 ABCA 306, aff'd [2000] 1 SCR 783, where the Alberta Court of Appeal decided that the new gun control legislation did not violate the Canadian Constitution, noting that Parliament's efforts were motivated in part by the desire to reduce the incidence of firearms-related domestic violence consistent with the philosophy of CEDAW. The Court explicitly declared that 'where legislation is open to two interpretations, one of which is more consistent with international human rights norms, then that interpretation is to be preferred', even if it has not been expressly incorporated into domestic law.
[41] See *2747–3174 Québec Inc. v Québec (Régie des permis d'alcool)* [1996] 3 SCR 919.
[42] See *R v Demers* [1999] BCJ No. 1818 (SC), aff'd [2003] BCJ No. 75, 2003 BCCA 28.

international human rights law is strengthened in those cases in which there is explicit recognition of the fact that constitutional rights were modelled on existing international instruments, as it is then assumed that such constitutional rights 'give expression' to the relevant international instruments.[43] Sometimes the fact that there was international involvement in the drafting of the Constitution is taken to reinforce the need to interpret it in the light of then existing international human rights agreements, whether or not they have become part of domestic law.[44]

The growing consensus towards recognition of the interpretive value of international instruments and jurisprudence for constitutional adjudication, whether or not expressly sanctioned, is unfortunately contradicted by the stubborn practice of some states, such as the United States. The paucity of illustrations of interpretive influence in US jurisprudence is lamentable but not surprising. The United States has ratified few human rights treaties (CEDAW remains unratified) and has made reservations severely limiting the practical effect of those that have been ratified.[45] The constitutional text recognizes treaties as part of the supreme law of the land. But the US Supreme Court distinguishes between self-executing and non-self-executing treaties, and the US Congress frequently has declared specific treaties to be non-self-executing.[46] Of course further explanation is needed to understand why US courts have also been so resistant to using norms of international human rights documents more subtly as sources of persuasive authority. The growing conservatism of the federal judiciary in recent years and the continuing parochialism of all branches are key factors.[47] The current US Supreme

---

[43] See, for instance, *Chairman, Railway Board v Mrs Chladrima Das* AIR 2000 S. Ct 988, where the Indian Supreme Court held that rape is a violation of the fundamental right to life with dignity guaranteed under Article 21 of the Indian Constitution. The Court placed reliance on the broad construction that the term 'life' had to be given in reference to the Universal Declaration of Human Rights upon which this section of the Indian Constitution was modelled.

[44] See, for instance, *Kauesa v Minister of Home Affairs and Others,* Decision of the High Court of Namibia [1995] 1 South Africa Law Reports 51.

[45] See e.g. Roth, 'The Charade of US Ratification of International Human Rights Treaties', 1 *Chicago Journal of International Law* (2000) 347.

[46] Scholars have generally viewed the distinction as constitutionally questionable, but there is a new conservative movement in favour of the concept of non-self-executing treaties. See e.g. Yoo, 'Globalism and the Constitution: Treaties, Non-Self-Execution, and the Original Understanding', 99 *Columbia Law Review* (1999) 1955.

[47] Kenneth Roth, Executive Director of Human Rights Watch, describes the view in Washington that the US should not embrace international human rights law except in so far as it parallels existing US practice as informed by 'the assumption that the United States has nothing to learn from the rest of the world when it comes to human rights—that US human rights protections are already state-of-the-art—and that improvement upon them is either inconceivable or undesirable'. Accordingly, 'the ratification process is treated not as an opportunity to bring US conduct up to the level of international standards, but as a legal exercise in "dumbing down" international standards to equate them with US practice'. Roth, *supra* n. 45, at 351.

Court seems unlikely to make any rapid changes in this regard. However, gradual change is occurring as advocates and individual judges become more knowledgeable about the existence and use of international and comparative human rights norms and their use in other systems.[48] The broader change process is underway[49]—and ripple effects can be seen with respect to gender rights.[50] Importantly, references moved from footnotes to text in the recent

---

[48] In Breyer, 'Constitutionalism, Privatization, and Globalization: Changing Relationships Among European Constitutional Courts', 21 *Cardozo Law Review* (2000) 1045, Associate Justice Stephen Breyer reflects on what he learned during a 1988 visit that he and three other US Supreme Court justices and others made to several European courts with constitutional responsibilities, and on the relationship between EC and ECHR decisions and domestic courts. Moreover, Justice Breyer's dissenting opinion in *Knight v Florida*, 528 U.S. 990, 996–7 (1999) cites foreign authority, including opinions of the Privy Council, India, Zimbabwe, Canada, the European Court of Human Rights, and the United Nations Human Rights Committee, in considering whether execution of prisoners who have spent nearly 20 years or more on death row violates the US Constitution's prohibition of cruel and unusual punishment. He argues that authority from national and supranational courts is useful though not binding, and cites cases demonstrating that 'this Court has long considered as relevant and informative the way in which foreign courts have applied standards roughly comparable to our own constitutional standards in roughly comparable circumstances'.

[49] For an important case by the US Court of Appeals for the Second Circuit that relies on international human rights law as demonstrating that torture by state officials violates customary international law, see *Filartiga v Pena-Irala*, 630 F. 2d 876 (2d Cir. 1980). Also see *Beharry v Reno*, 183 F. Supp. 2d 584 (E.D. N.Y. 2002), in which Judge Weinstein recently held that because of treaty and international law requirements (including the ICCPR, the Universal Declaration of Human Rights, and the unratified Convention on the Rights of the Child) immigration statutes should be interpreted to require pre-deportation hearings on the effect deportation would have on family. Otherwise, he found that treaties and international law override the statutes and require such a hearing. In discussing the policy reasons for honouring international human rights obligations, he wrote: 'This nation's credibility would be weakened by non-compliance with treaty obligations or with international norms. The United States seeks to impose international law norms—including, notably, those on terrorism—upon other nations. It would seem strange, then, if the government would seek to avoid enforcement of such norms within its own borders.'

[50] Advocates have urged the US Supreme Court to be more attentive to international human rights law. An example in a case raising gender discrimination issues can be found in the following argument from an amici brief filed with the United States Supreme Court in *United States v Morrison*, 120 S.Ct. 1740 (2000) by international legal scholars and human rights experts, which is discussed further at pp. 150–1 below: ' "Courts in the United States have increasingly looked to international human rights standards as law in the United States or as a guide to United States law." RESTATEMENT (THIRD) OF FOREIGN RELATIONS LAW OF THE UNITED STATES at 701, Reporter's Note at P.7 (1987). The reasoning underlying the principle stated by this Court in The Charming Betsy, 6 U.S. (2 Cranch) U.S. 64, 118 (1804) that "an act of Congress ought never be construed to violate the law of nations, if any other possible construction remains," also supports constitutional interpretations that are consistent with international law and allow Congress to meet international obligations.' Amici Brief, at 18.

case of *Lawrence v Texas*.[51] The majority opinion, which invalidated a Texan sodomy law, included references to the jurisprudence of the European Court of Human Rights at two separate points.

3. EXAMINING PRIMARY EFFECTS AND POTENTIAL: ILLUSTRATIONS FROM THE HOMEFRONTS

The malleability and inexactitude of the typology presented above suggests the difficulty of tracing and quantifying the direct causal effects or the specific forms of impact on domestic constitutional law that flow from such oft-time nebulous forms of domestication of international human rights norms. Nevertheless, domestic constitutional law has been influenced, and some general observations may be helpful in better understanding the specific ways in which this has happened with respect to gender rights. Accordingly, in this section we examine some of the effects of the interplay between international human rights and constitutional law on the protection of women. To do so, we classify some illustrative cases where international norms and jurisprudence with respect to gender or gender-related issues play, or have the potential to play, mutually non-exclusive 'constitutional functions' in either substantive or structural terms.

A. International Gender Norms and Jurisprudence as Expanding Constitutional Parameters

Sometimes, the *constitutional* validity of a certain state conduct or norm is made dependent on its compliance with international norms or obligations. When this is so, international law actually becomes the *ratio decidendi* of the constitutional question, so that the constitutional parameters are actually expanded. For obvious reasons this may well be the case when the constitution specifically embraces *supplementation* and sanctions the supremacy of international law over constitutional law. It also happens when this rule of supremacy is not explicit in the constitution but results from a respective supreme or constitutional court's reading of it. In such cases international norms and jurisprudence constitute a higher source of authority that functions to confer power to review or amend the constitution. In this respect Costa Rica offers an interesting example of a constitutional provision being deemed invalid

[51] 123 S. Ct. 2472 (2003). *Atkins v Virginia*, 122 S. Ct. 2242 (2002), invalidating application of death penalty to the mentally retarded, included a footnote reference to the opinion of the world community and to an earlier brief of the European Union. 122 S. Ct. 2249 n. 21. Also see Justice Ginsburg's reference to CEDAW and the Convention on the Elimination of All Forms of Racial Discrimination in her concurring opinion in *Grutter v Bollinger*, 123 S. Ct. 2325, 2347 (2003).

because of its incompatibility with an international norm.[52] Section I, Article 7 of the Costa Rican Constitution expressly incorporates international human rights treaties and conventions ratified by Costa Rica and declares them to have authority 'superior to the laws'.[53] The Constitutional Chamber of the Supreme Court has interpreted Article 7 as incorporating and according supra-constitutional status to international human rights conventions ratified by Costa Rica and as making them self-executing, or of immediate application.[54] A 1993 opinion explained the hierarchy in these terms: 'human rights instruments applicable in Costa Rica have not only a value similar to the Constitution, but to the extent that they grant greater rights or guarantees to the people, they prevail over the Constitution'.[55]

In 1992, the same Constitutional Chamber was presented with a petition challenging an application of Article 14(5) of the Constitution, which provided that foreign women who had been married to a Costa Rican for two years and had resided in the country during this period were eligible to obtain Costa Rican citizenship by naturalization.[56] The justices declared that this provision discriminated against a foreign man who married a Costa Rican woman, and was invalid because it was contrary to fundamental equality

---

[52] For a broader discussion of Costa Rican gender jurisprudence which we draw upon here, see Facio, Jiménez, and Morgan, 'Gender Equality and International Human Rights in Costa Rican Constitutional Jurisprudence', in B. Baines and R. Rubio-Marín (eds), *Constituting Women: The Gender of Constitutional Jurisprudence* (forthcoming).

[53] Article 48 of the Costa Rican Constitution provides that all persons have the right to file an *amparo* action in the Constitutional Chamber of the Supreme Court to maintain or re-establish the enjoyment of rights granted in the Constitution, as well as those fundamental rights established in international human rights instruments applicable in the country.

[54] The Constitutional Chamber has also recognized that interpretations of the Inter-American Court of Human Rights, whether in contentious cases or consultative opinions, have the same value as the norm interpreted. Voto No. 2313–95.

[55] Voto No. 5759–93. Thus, Article 7 opens the door to the recognition of broad concepts of gender equality under several important international documents that Costa Rica has ratified, including the Inter-American Convention on the Granting of Civil Rights to Women and the Inter-American Convention on the Granting of Political Rights to Women (both ratified by Law No. 1273 of 13 March, 1951), the Convention on the Political Rights of Women (ratified by Law No. 3877 of 3 June, 1967), the Convention on the Elimination of All Forms of Discrimination Against Women (ratified by Law No. 6969 of 2 October, 1984), and the Belém do Pará Inter-American Convention on the Prevention, Punishment, and Eradication of Violence Against Women (ratified by Law No. 7499 of 2 May, 1995).

[56] In 1999, Article 14(5) was amended to extend potential eligibility for naturalization to any person who marries any Costa Rican. Ley No. 7879, 27 May, 1999. It now provides: 'Foreign persons who upon marrying a Costa Rican lose their nationality or who after having been married to a Costa Rican for two years and having resided in the country during this same period, manifest their desire to acquire Costa Rican citizenship.' Although the effect of this change is to make the eligibility criteria gender-neutral, Article 14(4) was not deleted. It reads: 'The foreign woman who upon contracting marriage with a Costa Rican loses her citizenship.'

principles of constitutional and international human rights law. The opinion expressly relied upon international instruments, including Articles 2 and 7 of the Universal Declaration of Human Rights (UDHR),[57] Article 2 of the ICCPR, and Articles 1 and 24 of the American Convention on Human Rights.[58] The Constitutional Chamber further declared that wherever legislation uses the terms 'man' or 'woman', the terms must be interpreted as synonymous with 'person'.[59]

More often, international law functions to expand the parameters against which to judge the constitutionality of infraconstitutional norms or state conduct, and does so in more subtle ways resulting from a dialogue between national and supranational law. In those cases in which the constitution expressly embraces *interpretive adaptation*, say by referring to the interpretive force of international human rights norms in construing constitutional rights, the constitutional *expansion* is also constitutionally sanctioned. Where judicial or quasi-judicial supranational bodies exist and are given pre-eminence in the interpretation of the supranational or international norm, the dialogue is necessary, as often such bodies come to function as de facto instances of appeal which may interpret a given treaty provision in a different, more or less expansive way than that used by national courts to interpret analogous constitutional provisions. Given the duty of *interpretive adaptation*, such more expansive or restrictive readings will be incorporated into the interpretation of the constitution. Thus, we see that international or supranational law in fact has the potential to become indirectly constitutionalized, *expanding* the constitutional parameters of review. Although the increase in number of international or supranational instruments of protection for women is likely to have an expansive impact on women's rights, in theory we cannot say that expanding the scope of women's rights and expanding the parameters upon which to judge the constitutionality of a treatment given to women are the same thing. The international or supranational doctrine read into the national constitution may imply a restriction with regards to the status of women's

---

[57] Universal Declaration of Human Rights, GA Res. 217A (III), 10 December 1948.

[58] This opinion quotes the full text of the relevant provisions. However, it makes no mention of the earlier advisory opinion of the Inter-American Court of Human Rights on proposals to amend the prior similarly discriminatory naturalization provisions of the Costa Rican Constitution. Advisory Opinion OC-4/84 of 19 January, 1984, Inter-Am. Ct. H.R. (Ser. A) No. 4 (1984). In a later opinion, the Costa Rican Constitutional Chamber afforded the Inter-American Court of Human Rights' interpretations of relevant human rights documents the same value as the norm interpreted. Voto No. 2313–95.

[59] The opinion ignored CEDAW, however, presumably because the justices did not see Article 14(5) as discriminating against women. Thus they failed to note that the naturalization rule discriminated against Costa Rican women by not permitting them to confer eligibility for citizenship on their spouses, and failed to recognize that uses of the term 'woman' might be necessary or appropriate in the context of measures adopted for the purpose of ensuring or promoting substantive, as opposed to merely formal, equality.

rights if domestic law is ambiguous and the relevant international legal norm supports the most restrictive interpretive option. What is decisive in identifying this operation of international law as an *expanding* function is the shift that takes place when the parameters upon which to judge the very constitutionality of a given norm or conduct are expressly or implicitly changed by international or supranational law. Let us look at two relevant examples.

One is offered by Spain[60] where, as said, and according to Article 10.2 of the Spanish Constitution, the UDHR and the international treaties on human rights validly ratified by Spain have to be taken into account in interpreting equivalent constitutional rights. The Spanish Constitutional Court has read this interpretative directive as also encompassing the doctrine set by international or supranational bodies which apply those instruments. Because Spain is a member of the European Union and has also ratified the ECHR, through this provision the doctrines set by both the European Court of Justice (ECJ) when interpreting both primary and secondary European law and the European Court of Human Rights when interpreting the Convention have been taken into account in interpreting the rights and freedoms recognized in the Spanish Constitution.

The range of options for women's constitutional litigation that are thus opened are clear enough, though the results will always depend on whether, as interpreted, the supranational provisions offer greater protection than the equivalent constitutional clauses, which is not always the case. Of course, this also means that the interpretation of domestic constitutional provisions may change as these supranational norms or their interpretation change. The following case illustrates the potential of this type of *expansion* of domestic constitutional law. In 1997, the Spanish Constitutional Court upheld the constitutional validity of a set of rules dating back to medieval times whereby the inheritance of nobility titles follows an established order according to which the male takes precedence over the female, overruling the prior doctrine of the Supreme Court which, since 1989, had started to declare the old rule of transmission unconstitutional because of sex discrimination.[61]

In synthesis, the Court argued that, unlike in the past, nobility titles nowadays do not assign people a privileged citizenship status. They are only a 'prerogative of honour' and have only the meaning and significance that society decides to grant them. Thus, above all, nobility titles have a strictly symbolic meaning. Moreover, they have a very limited social reach, as they affect a very restricted number of people, namely, those belonging to the lineage of the original title-holder. To the extent that they have survived after

[60] For a comprehensive summary of women's constitutional status in Spain under the 1978 Spanish Constitution and the relevant constitutional jurisprudence of the Constitutional Court see Rubio-Marín, 'Engendering the Constitution: the Spanish Experience', in Baines and Rubio-Marín (eds), *supra* n. 52.

[61] See STC 126/1997 of 3 July.

the Constitution, and hence, that they are not unconstitutional in and of themselves, as the Constitution contemplates among the prerogatives of the King of Spain that of allocating honours and distinctions, it is futile to try to assimilate nobility titles to a constitutional logic. Rather, they have their own preconstitutional logic that needs to be respected, an inherent element of which is the legally pre-established order of succession. Amending the rules governing the transmission of the titles so as to comply with the principle of the equality of the sexes would entail introducing anachronistic requirements into a practice moulded by history. Thus, deep down the majority decision actually reflects an attitude of general contempt for nobility titles that the Court sees doomed to natural extinction because of their practical meaning-lessness, hence the futility of any attempt to 'modernize' them.

Interesting for us is the fact that the case was subsequently brought to the European Court of Human Rights on claims of breach both of the non-discrimination principle of Article 14 of the ECHR in relation to Article 8 of the Convention, which sanctions the protection of family life, and also of Article 1 of Protocol No. 1 to the Convention, which refers to the protection of possessions, given the alleged economic advantages that can be derived from nobility titles. In a decision of 28 October 1999, the Court declared that the appeal was inadmissible *ratione materiae*. Unlike surnames and forenames, the Court held that noble titles do not fall within the scope of protection that the Convention grants to family life. Neither can a noble title be considered a possession within the meaning of Article 1 of Protocol No. 1. The possibility that a title could be commercially exploited is not sufficient for that purpose. Resting the claim on a breach of the anti-discrimination principle was clearly insufficient, as under Article 14 of the European Convention the discriminatory treatment necessarily has to be in relation to some other right or freedom recognized in the Convention.

In this respect it is interesting to notice that the new Protocol 12 to the Convention contemplates an independent mandate of non-discrimination which does not require the denounced discriminatory treatment to be framed in connection with the breach of any of the other rights of the Convention. Had it been ratified by Spain and in effect at the time, the result might have been very different. Granted, even in that event, we might still have ended up with a Spanish judgment based on constitutional reasoning whereby the differential treatment is not discriminatory and a judgment by the European Court saying that it was discriminatory according to the Convention. But the chances are that the Constitutional Court, bound as it is to interpret the Constitution in the light of prior doctrine of the European Court of Human Rights, would have had to change its doctrine *pro futuro*. Also, had the Constitutional Court been aware in the first place of the possibility that the European Court might decide otherwise in view of other related case law, the chances are that it would have then interpreted the sufficiently broad prohibition of sex discrimination as encompassing the inheritance of nobility titles. Aware of this, we see plaintiffs framing their constitutional claims always in relation to supra- or international instruments or jurisprudence favourable to their demands. And this shows how the latter thereby become, indirectly, parameters of constitutional control.

Moving beyond interpretive constitutional clauses that expressly incorporate supra- or international law and jurisprudence into the 'relevant reading' of the constitution, the next example shows that a similar shift of constitutional parameters with expansive or restrictive results can be achieved when supranational law affirms its primacy over domestic law and such claim is constitutionally respected. This is the case with European law in those fields that it validly occupies according to the limited range of competencies of the European institutions. If the matter at stake is within the European jurisdiction, European law, rather than constitutional law, is likely to become the ultimate source of control of the validity of a given measure. But because contradictions cannot be accepted in the legal order, and the constitutional courts will find the need to harmonize their claim to the superior hierarchy of the constitution with that of primacy of European law within its field, unless there is a clear breach of constitutional provisions, those courts will, most likely, absorb the parameters of European law and doctrine into the constitution even when the latter lacks an explicit interpretive provision. Aware of this, it is not unlikely that plaintiffs will simply assume European instances to be their last resorts. Let us look at an example taken from Germany.[62]

Several affirmative action programmes are in effect in Germany. Since the 1980s, there have been both federal and state laws to further equality between men and women, including those designed to promote the number of women in higher positions. Among the most common statutory measures are those that require the development of affirmative action measures, including some form of quotas for women in the public sector. The constitutionality of such measures as a means of furthering gender equality has been widely discussed. The most controversial type of quotas have been the so-called 'decision quotas', which require that where a male and a female candidate for a position are equally qualified, preference should be given to the woman if women are under-represented in the sector. Often there is the additional qualification that the preference will prevail unless the male candidate displays extraordinary qualities that outweigh it.

The constitutional debate has been framed by taking into account Article 3 of the German Basic Law, which provides for equality before the law, equality of rights between men and women, and the prohibition of discrimination on the grounds of sex. Since a 1994 amendment, this provision also provides that

---

[62] The next paragraphs draw extensively from Rodríguez and Sacksofsky, 'Gender in the German Constitution', in Baines and Rubio-Marín (eds), *supra* n. 52.

the state shall promote the actual implementation of equal rights for women and men and take steps to remove those disadvantages that now exist. Because Article 33.2 of the German Constitution also refers to the fact that every German shall be equally eligible for any public office according to his aptitude, qualifications, and professional achievements, the question is whether decision quotas, which seem compatible with Article 3, are allowed in view of Article 33.2. The general consensus is that the latter would not allow quotas that give preference to women if they are not equally qualified as their competitors, but when the decision quotas sanction the equal qualification requirement things are less clear. The issue has never reached the Federal Constitutional Court and, so far, lower court decisions do not express a consensus. While the Federal Constitutional Court has not yet ruled on this matter directly, an increasing commitment to substantive notions of equality, which can be seen in the above-mentioned constitutional reform and which the doctrine has detected in the Court's most recent case law, would indicate a favourable stance towards the constitutionality of such quotas.

Relevant for our considerations is that, thus far, the dispute has basically been shifted to the arena of European law, allowing the ECJ, instead of the Federal Constitutional Court, to have the last word. The question that was presented on three occasions by German courts to the ECJ was whether certain quotas were compatible with European Directive 76/207/EC of 9 February 1976 on the implementation of the principle of equal treatment between men and women as regards access to employment, vocational training and promotion, and working conditions. It is interesting that such directive also includes a provision that, like the German constitutional provision after the reform, sanctions the validity of measures taken to remove existing obstacles which affect women in particular so as to ensure equal opportunities for men and women.[63]

The two cases in which the European Court applied the Directive to decide on the validity of decision quotas were the *Kalanke*[64] and the *Marschall* cases.[65] In *Kalanke,* the ECJ invalidated a statutory provision according to which women had to be given priority over male candidates with equal qualifications in the event of promotion, in a sector where women are underrepresented, on the grounds that the provision granted absolute and unconditional priority to women over men. On the contrary in *Marschall,* the Court validated a statutory provision which was rather similar to the one at issue in *Kalanke,* with the exception that it included a clause recognizing the possible existence of

---

[63] See Article 2(4).

[64] *Eckhard Kalanke v Freie Hansestadt Bremen,* 17 October 1995—Case C-450/93, concerned Article 4 of the State of Bremen Law on the equality of men and women in the civil service (*Landesgleichstellungsgesetz*).

[65] *Helmut Marschall v Land Nordrhein-Westfalen,* 11 November 1997—Case C-409/95, concerned a provision of the Law of Civil Servants of the *Land* of Nordrhein-Westfalen.

'reasons specific to an individual [male] candidate [that may] tilt the balance in his favour'.

Despite doubts about the significance that such clauses should be granted, for our purposes the interesting point is that these European decisions have had the effect of silencing the debate about the constitutionality of quotas in the general awareness that, even if the questioned quotas were held to be constitutional by the Federal Constitutional Court, the more restrictive European Community limitations are binding for Germany.[66] Here again, then, when thinking about the Constitution in its role of setting limits to the range of legitimate political options for the national legislator, we see European law as partly competing for that constitutional function. Again, the consequences for women's constitutional status, as shown in the German example, depend on the levels of protection that both the constitutional and the European legal order sanction for women.

Lastly, some courts have also *expanded* their constitutions by in effect turning international obligations of the state to adopt certain measures to enforce instruments, treaties, or conventions and achieve the goals proclaimed in them into constitutionally enforceable rights of citizens. Once again, Costa Rica offers a telling case. In 1998 the Constitutional Chamber of the Supreme Court ruled in favour of Legislative Assembly Deputy Marlene Gómez Calderón, who filed an *amparo* against the President of the Republic and the President of the Legislative Assembly challenging as unconstitutional omissions their failure to include any women as candidates for political appointment to the Board of Directors of the Public Services Regulatory Authority.[67] In Costa Rica *amparo* actions generally can be brought to challenge the constitutionality of either actions or omissions. Here the Court explicitly based its decision on Article 33 of the Constitution's principle of equality, but also on Articles 1, 2, 3, 6, and 7 of CEDAW, and on Costa Rica's 1990 Law for the Promotion of the Social Equality of Women, which was designed to implement CEDAW principles. Because the legislation was enacted to fulfil Article 7 of CEDAW, which requires state authorities to take appropriate measures to eliminate discrimination and promote women's participation in

---

[66] Granted, the German Federal Constitutional Court has affirmed that it will recognize the supremacy of European law as interpreted by the European Court of Justice only as long as those fundamental rights contained in the German Basic Law are respected. But even if decision quotas, including those without qualification, were declared compatible with the German Basic Law in view of the commitment of Article 3 to substantive equality, they cannot be interpreted as being mandatory under the Constitution. It is not the case that the Constitution grounds an individual claim to such measures which the European institutions could not violate. An example of how this European law can be used to shape constitutional law is offered by Ireland, where the Constitution Review Group relied on the *Kalanke* judgment to argue against allowing affirmative measures in the Constitution; see C. Hoskyns, *Integrating Gender: Women, Law and Politics in the European Union* (1996), at 121.

[67] Voto No. 716–98.

public positions, as well as corresponding legislative provisions, the state's omission to enforce its international and legal obligations by appointing only men was interpreted as a constitutional infraction under the equality provision of the Constitution, which is understood to embody a commitment to a democratic form of government.[68]

In 2003, the Constitutional Chamber of the Costa Rican Supreme Court issued a similarly far-reaching opinion in a suit brought by five members of the Legislative Assembly (four women and one man) against the President of the Assembly challenging the constitutionality of their President's omission or failure to name female and male legislators to 2002–3 permanent committees on housing, agricultural, and social affairs in proportion to their membership in the Assembly as a whole.[69] The challengers argued that failure to name proportional numbers of women and men to each of these committees meant that their respective perspectives on the reality of Costa Rican society were missing from decision-making. The Constitutional Chamber unanimously ruled that the President's omissions were inconsistent with Article 33 of the Constitution, as well as CEDAW and the American Convention on Human Rights.

B. International Law and Jurisprudence as Complementing Constitutional Parameters

Probably the most common though less dramatic function of international law in the constitutional adjudication of women's rights is that of *complementing* constitutional claims. In this function international instruments or jurisprudence are called upon to strengthen claims that could in principle be sustained on constitutional grounds alone. This use is common, for obvious reasons, when *adaptation* is embraced as a form of incorporation and the interpretive function of international instruments ratified by the state is expressly sanctioned in the constitution or in constitutional case law. It also happens when international law is incorporated through *assimilation* and the drafting or amendment of the constitutional text has relied on existing international norms which are then more likely to be interpreted with

---

[68] For another decision in which an international obligation formed an essential ingredient in the relevant constitutional interpretation see *Muojekwu v Ejikeme*, Decision of the Court of Appeal, Enugu Division, Nigeria [2000] 5 Nigerian Weekly Law Reports 402, where the Court found that the custom of allowing a man to keep one of his daughters unmarried perpetually in his home to raise children for him violated the right to marry and the freedom of association, making reference to CEDAW and in particular to its provisions calling on states to eliminate discriminatory customary practices.

[69] A record-breaking twenty of the fifty-seven members of the 2002 assembly (or 35%) were women, yet the membership of these committees was as follows: Housing Affairs—8 men (73%) and 3 women (27%); Agricultural Affairs—8 men (89%) and 1 woman (11%); and Social Affairs—3 men (35%) and 6 women (65%).

reference to the decisions of those international bodies which are in charge of generating their authentic interpretation.

Occasionally courts have affirmed the interpretive function of international instruments even when they have not been ratified by the state.[70] This may suggest that constitutional rights are gaining ground as expressions of a universalizable international ethos of human rights of which constitutional rights are only local expressions that facilitate their enforcement. With or without ratification and with or without express constitutional sanction, the interpretive use of international instruments is frequent in countries with weak democracies which are more likely to look to the international community, rather than to their own democratic traditions, to support the legitimacy of their new constitutional regimes, which often epitomize their transition to democracy.[71] Given the growing importance of the protection of women on the international agenda, this shift has a great potential for strengthening women's constitutional status especially vis-à-vis the resistance of discriminatory cultural practices which may be more or less tolerated in the national ethos. Let us look at some examples of various forms of *complementary* uses of international human rights norms.

An early example of the Costa Rican Supreme Court's reliance on international conventions in gender-related cases illustrates this *complementing* function. In this 1992 case, several members of the Costa Rican women's movement had filed an action against the Human Reproduction Committee of the Costa Rican College of Physicians and Surgeons challenging the Committee's interpretation and application of an executive decree governing sterilizations. They alleged that the Committee was using the regulation to require that married women have the consent of their spouses to obtain a therapeutic sterilization.[72] With two dissenting justices, the majority of the

---

[70] See *Makwanyane*, 1995 (3) SA 391(CC), in which the South Africa Constitutional Court stated that in using international law, it would not limit itself to conventions to which South Africa is a party but would consider 'non-binding as well as binding law'. Thus far neither litigants nor the courts have made much use of international law, though they refer extensively to comparative case law. See also *Wajid Shama-ul-Hassan v Federation of Pakistan*, All Pakistan Legal Decisions 1997 Lahore 617, where the Court expressly asserted that the mere non-ratification of the UDHR and the ICCPR by Pakistan did not undermine the interpretive value of the internationally recognized rights included in them.

[71] Sometimes this is even done expressly. See, for instance, *Unity Dow v Attorney General of Botswana*, Decisions of the High Court and Court of Appeal, [1991] Law Reports of the Commonwealth (Const) 574 (High Court), affirmed [1992] Law Reports of the Commonwealth 623 (Court of Appeal), where the Court struck down a provision of the Citizenship Act that denied citizenship to children born in wedlock to women citizens of Botswana while granting it to children born to male citizens, using international human rights instruments as an aid to constitutional interpretation on the grounds that they contained the aspirations and values upon which the Constitution of Botswana was drafted, and noting also that Botswana was one of the few liberal democracies in Africa and could not insulate itself from the progressive movements going on around it.

[72] Voto No. 2196–92.

Chamber issued a 'conforming interpretation', ruling that while the regulation did not expressly require such consent, if it were interpreted as the petitioners claimed, it would be unconstitutional because contrary to the equality and liberty principles of the Constitution, as well as to the principles of equality, non-discrimination, and equality within marriage guaranteed in international human rights instruments ratified by Costa Rica, including CEDAW, the American Convention on Human Rights (hereinafter, the 'Pact of San José'),[73] the ICCPR, and the ICESCR.[74]

Another Costa Rican example of use of international human rights law to *complement* constitutional parameters is a 1999 case in which the Constitutional Chamber of the Supreme Court rejected a challenge brought by male employees of the National Bank of Costa Rica against the bank's regulations, which established different retirement ages of 55 for women and 57 for men.[75] After setting out the text of CEDAW Articles 1, 2, 3, 4, 5, and 11.1, and of Article 1(a) of Convention No. 111 of the International Labour Organization (ILO), the Chamber upheld the validity of the challenged regulation noting that its clear purpose was to implement this international law. The opinion concluded that the regulation was consistent with concepts of substantive equality as embodied in constitutional principles, international law, and the doctrine the Chamber had developed in its jurisprudence.

The Colombian Constitutional Court created under the 1991 Colombian Constitution has also frequently relied upon international human rights conventions and treaties in its mission to nurture the domestic human rights culture envisioned by the drafters of the new Constitution. Detecting the overall domestic effects of international human rights documents is more difficult here because much of the incorporation was through *assimilation* of key principles of documents such as CEDAW (for example, substantive equality, political participation) into the expressly enumerated fundamental rights provisions of the Constitution. But Article 93 also expressly incorporates international human rights documents and provides an interpretive

---

[73] American Convention on Human Rights (Pact of San José), signed 22 November 1969, entered into force 18 July 1978, OASTS 36, O.A.S. Off. Rec. OEA/Ser.L/ V/II.23, doc.21, rev.6 (1979).

[74] The opinion noted that the challengers had relied upon Articles 1, 2, 3, 5, 12, 14, and 16 of CEDAW (as well as Articles 7, 10, 33, 52, and 129 of the Constitution) and that the Attorney General had argued that if the regulation were interpreted as the challengers alleged, it would violate Articles 1, 2, 3, 5, and 12 of CEDAW as well as Articles 3, 16, and 26 of the ICCPR, Articles 3 and 12 of the ICESCR, and Articles 3, 11, and 24 of the American Convention on Human Rights. The Court concluded that such an interpretation would violate the foundational principles of CEDAW as well as the articles relative to the rights of women in the American Convention, the ICCPR, and the ICESCR.

[75] Voto No. 6472–99.

directive to the courts.[76] Some examples will demonstrate the effects of this combination of incorporationist approaches with respect to Colombian gender jurisprudence.[77]

In a 1993 reproductive rights case, the Colombian Constitutional Court expressly relied in part on CEDAW and other international human rights conventions to protect the rights of women prisoners.[78] Attorney Blanca Amelia Medina Torres, who was a pre-trial detainee in The Good Shepherd Women's Detention Center in Bogotá, filed an action challenging regulations and practices requiring that women inmates who desire conjugal visits take sex education courses and either show they were incapable of conceiving, or be fitted with an IUD, or take contraceptives. Male prisoners were not subject to any similar requirements. The warden of the prison defended the regulations, arguing that Medina Torres would try to get pregnant to escape punishment. The Court said that this assumption violated Article 83 of the Colombian Constitution, which requires public authorities to presume the good faith of individuals in *all* actions that come before them. According to the Court, the unequal treatment of women prisoners constituted sex discrimination in violation of Article 13 (prohibiting discrimination on the grounds of sex and mandating the duty of states to take measures to ensure the substantive equality of discriminated groups), and violated reproductive and family rights provisions of Articles 42 ('[t]he couple has the right to decide freely and responsibly the number of their children') and 43 ('[d]uring pregnancy and after birth, women will enjoy special assistance and protection of the state') of the Constitution as well as similar provisions in international human rights

[76] Article 93 provides: 'International treaties and conventions ratified by Congress, that recognize human rights and prohibit their limitation in states of emergency, prevail in the internal order. The rights and duties consecrated in this Charter will be interpreted in conformity with the international treaties on human rights ratified by Colombia.'

[77] For fuller discussions of the early gender jurisprudence of the Colombian Constitutional Court, which we draw upon here, see Morgan, 'Taking Machismo to Court', 30 *University of Miami Inter-American Law Review* (1999) 253; Morgan with the collaboration of Alzate Buitrago, 'Founding Mothers in Contemporary Latin American Constitutions: Colombian Women, Constitution Making, and the New Constitutional Court', in A. K. Wing (ed.), *Global Critical Race Feminism: An International Reader* (2000) 204; and Morgan, 'Emancipatory Equality: Gender and the Colombian Constitution', in Baines and Rubio-Marín (eds), *supra* n. 52.

[78] Sentencia No. T-273/93. The Court had earlier concluded that incarcerated persons' right to conjugal visits was a limited fundamental right, dependent upon the capacity of the facility to accommodate such visits: Sentencia No. T-222/93. The Court also charged the state to equip all detention facilities to permit conjugal visits. A case raising related issues that has yet to be ruled on by the Constitutional Court also serves to illustrate the previously discussed interactions between domestic and supranational gender litigation. In this case the Colombian Supreme Court ruled in favour of a lesbian prisoner who challenged the denial to her of conjugal visits. The Court ruled that she must be permitted such visits monthly: *Hechos Judicial—Visitas de homosexuales*, El Tiempo, 14 October 2001. Similar claims had been rejected in earlier cases, prompting the filing of a challenge with the Inter-American Commission on Human Rights (IAHRC).

documents incorporated in the Constitution, including CEDAW. The opinion cited the text of the Convention's preamble to the effect that 'women's role in procreation must not be a reason for discrimination', and its Article 16 which embraces the same right as Article 43 of the Colombian Constitution. It also found violations of Article 11 of the Pact of San José ('No one may be the object of arbitrary or abusive interference with his private life, his family, his home, or his correspondence, or of unlawful attacks on his honor or reputation.') and the similar provision in Article 17 of the ICCPR.

As mentioned before, the assimilative nature of the Colombian Constitution's embrace of the principles of CEDAW's concepts of substantive equality (in Article 13, Colombian Constitution) and of the imperative of promoting the political participation of women (in Article 40, Colombian Constitution) seems to have influenced the Court's practice of relying not only on international treaties, but also on international documents which are not strictly binding, including even guidelines set by the international bodies in whose framework the treaty was adopted, when interpreting the Constitution. One striking example is the 29 March 2000 unanimous opinion of the Constitutional Court reviewing a quota law that had passed both Houses of the Colombian Congress in June 1999.[79] Among other things, the law established a 30 per cent quota for women in high-level decision-making positions in the public sector. The Court's opinion noted that positive actions, including inverse discrimination, are expressly authorized by the Constitution, which not only guarantees the principle of non-discrimination but also alludes to a substantive dimension of equality that the Court described as having 'a remedial, compensatory, emancipatory character, corrective and defensive of persons and groups situated in conditions of inferiority'. Consequently, 'authorities can appeal to race or sex, or other *suspect* category, not to marginalize certain persons or groups or to perpetuate inequalities, but to lessen the harmful effect of social practices that have placed these same people or groups in unfavorable positions'.

Accordingly, while the Court did not expressly rely on CEDAW, it declared certain provisions of the quota law to be consistent with the Constitution's express commitment to ensuring women's adequate and effective participation in decision-making positions within the public sector (Article 40) and its explicit embrace of substantive equality in Article 13. It approved of, for example, the 30 per cent quotas for top, and other high-level, appointed decision-making posts established in Article 4, so long as the quotas are understood to be temporary measures and are applied gradually, as new positions become vacant. The quotas were obligatory and 'rigid', but the Court found they were justified under the proportionality framework it has used to determine whether a difference in treatment is constitutional.

---

[79] Sentencia No. C-371/ 2000.

Dismissing arguments against the law's failure to establish a quota of 50 per cent, it noted that the law imposed a quota of 'at least' 30 per cent and did not close the doors to women's occupying a higher percentage of the positions. The percentage chosen was not gratuitous or unfounded but is the figure the United Nations considers a 'critical mass', and is the percentage that Colombia accepted in the Beijing Platform for Action and that several other countries (including Argentina, Bolivia, Brazil, Panama, and Venezuela) have adopted in legislation designed to stimulate women's participation in popular elections.[80]

Guatemala offers another interesting example.[81] Following an unsuccessful attempt in 1993 to rely on constitutional and international human rights protections against gender discrimination to challenge several provisions in the Guatemalan Civil Code—including a requirement that a married woman have her husband's consent (or a judge's permission) to work outside the home,[82] in 1996, the Guatemalan Constitutional Court accepted the arguments presented by several women's rights activists against the penal code's gender-discriminatory definitions and punishments for the conduct of marital infidelity, or adultery.[83] The challengers relied expressly both on constitutional guarantees of equality and on the Guatemalan Constitution's Article 46 incorporation of international human rights treaties and conventions as having pre-eminence over internal law. They argued that Guatemala had ratified CEDAW, the Inter-American Convention on the Prevention, Punishment and Eradication of Violence against Women,[84] and the Pact of San José, and thus under Article 46 the Court had a duty to strike down any laws discriminating against women. The Constitutional Court agreed, likewise basing its decision both on the Constitution's equality guarantees[85] and on the incorporative effects of Article 46. The Court concluded that the continued existence of the challenged provisions would not only be nugatory of

[80] The Colombian Court, however, rejected the imposition of electoral or other quotas on political parties as inconsistent with other constitutional norms.

[81] The 1985 Guatemalan Constitution establishes in its Article 46 the general principle that with respect to human rights, treaties and conventions adopted and ratified by Guatemala have pre-eminence over internal law. This provision lends itself to an interpretation that accords such international norms supraconstitutional status, but the gender cases we will discuss have presented challenges to national codes and do not address this issue.

[82] Expediente 84–92, 24 June 1993. Following the Constitutional Court's rejection of this case, a challenge was filed with the IAHRC. The pressure of this litigation helped bring about amendments to the Civil Code.

[83] Expediente No. 936–95, 7 March 1996.

[84] Inter-American Convention on the Prevention, Punishment, and Eradication of Violence against Women, signed 9 June 1994, entered into force 3 March 1995, reprinted in 33 *ILM* (1994) 1534.

[85] Article 4: 'In Guatemala all human beings are free and equal in dignity and rights. Men and women, whatever their civil status, have equal opportunities and responsibilities.'

the constitutional mandate to eliminate inequality, but would also 'leave virtually empty of content the international treaties ratified by Guatemala in this material, those that according to article 46 of the Constitution have pre-eminence over the Penal Code'.

Although the examples mentioned show how this constitutional function of international law can have a positive impact on women's constitutional status, there are also cases where the effects achieved have been the opposite. International law is still used as a *complement* in constitutional reasoning but to achieve a result which restricts women's rights. In this respect, as Andrew Byrnes cautions, it would be a mistake to assume that all effects of domestic incorporation of human rights laws covering gender-related issues will be positive or women's rights-enhancing ones.[86] Indeed, when the resolution of the constitutional conflict depends on the consideration of several fundamental rights in tension and there are different human rights instruments, calling on human rights to *complement* constitutional rights will not by itself predetermine the result, as the court is in principle free to choose which of the international instruments it will rely upon in deciding how to interpret the relevant constitutional provision.

Thus, notwithstanding its positive use of international human rights law related to gender mentioned above, the Constitutional Chamber of the Costa Rican Supreme Court released an opinion in 2000 that seems strikingly out of line with earlier cases. The case involved an action of unconstitutionality brought against an executive decree regulating the use of 'In Vitro Fertilization and Transfer of Embryos'.[87] The decree authorized use of the technique but only under very strict regulations, including an absolute prohibition on fertilizing more than six ova per period of treatment and a requirement that all fertilized ova be transferred to the patient's uterus (with absolute prohibitions on discarding or preserving ova for later use in either the same patient or other patients). It absolutely prohibited any genetic manipulation, experimentation, or commercialization. The challenger claimed that the decree violated not only Article 21 of the Costa Rican Constitution's guarantee that 'human life is inviolable', but also provisions of the American Convention on Human Rights and the Convention on the Rights of the Child,[88] because the technique regulated by this decree involved a high loss of embryos. The Chamber's opinion focused on these provisions without referring to other

---

[86] Byrnes, 'Toward More Effective Enforcement of Women's Rights Through the Use of International Human Rights Law and Procedures', in Cook, *supra* n. 2, at 227, n. 68, citing Iwasawa, 'The Impact of International Human Rights Law on Japanese Law—The Third Reformation for Japanese Women', 21 *Japanese Ann. Int'l. L.* (1991) 56.

[87] Voto No. 2000–02306.

[88] Convention on the Rights of the Child, adopted 20 November 1989, entered into force 2 September 1990, GA Res. 44/25, 44 UN GAOR, Supp. (No. 49), UN Doc. A/44/49, at 166 (1989).

constitutional or international norms. Thus the question as posed by the majority was: 'When does human life begin?'

The Constitutional Chamber recognized that specialists disagreed on the answer to this question, but the majority sided with those contending that life begins at the very moment of conception. The opinion acknowledged that the decree imposed much stricter limitations on the use of the technique than other countries, using text from Article 11 of Spain's Law on the Techniques of Assisted Reproduction[89] as an example of a more permissive approach. Nevertheless, it proceeded to declare the challenged decree unconstitutional, relying primarily on Article 21 of the Constitution's recognition of the inviolability of life and on Article 4.1 of the American Convention on Human Rights, which provides: 'Every person has the right to have his life respected. This right shall be protected by law and, in general, from the moment of conception. No one shall be arbitrarily deprived of his life.'[90]

The Supreme Court of Argentina's decision upholding an administrative regulation of the National University of Córdoba which required the university-affiliated college preparatory high school, Colegio Monserrat, to admit females, provides another, more positive, illustration of judicial resolution of tension between potentially conflicting provisions of international human rights law which is called upon to *complement* constitutional law. In this case, a group of parents of students then enrolled in the high school filed suit challenging the administrative order and arguing that it violated their rights under various international and constitutional provisions related to parental rights.[91] The judge in the first instance ruled for the parents, but the federal appellate court and the Supreme Court disagreed. The members of the Supreme Court unanimously affirmed the university's authority to issue the order. Five of the nine wrote separate opinions expressing their views on the extent to which the university's decision was constitutionally mandated. These separate opinions relied extensively on constitutional equality guarantees and on international human rights norms expressly accorded constitutional status as part of the 1994 revisions mentioned earlier, and looked as well to comparative constitutional and human rights jurisprudence.

C. International Law as Concretizing Constitutional Parameters

A function which is midway between the *expansion* and the *complementation* of constitutional parameters is that played by international instruments and

---

[89] Ley No. 35/1988.

[90] The opinion also found the decree was invalid because the matter regulated was beyond the authority of the executive power to regulate through an executive decree.

[91] G. 653. XXXIII. *Recurso de Hecho, Gonzalez de Delgado, Cristina y otros c/Universidad Nacional de Córdoba*, 19 September 2000.

jurisprudence when domestic courts rely on them to fill out the content of relatively generic constitutional provisions. Although formally there are specific constitutional provisions on which the argumentation rests, substantively we see domestic courts incorporating international law, as well as non-binding international instruments, to fill out the generic constitutional provisions. It is interesting in these cases how domestic courts are able to spare the energies that would be required to reason according to traditional constitutional hermeneutics (which in civil law systems, for instance, typically rest on historical, systematic, grammatical, and teleological criteria for interpretation). Clearly this function is facilitated again when the constitution contains interpretive clauses sanctioning the interpretation of constitutional rights and freedoms in the light of human rights conventions. The function is also encouraged when a consolidated body of international law and doctrine has already been developed at the time that the domestic court starts functioning.

Here again, Spain offers an interesting example. The equality provision in Article 14 of the 1978 Spanish Constitution, like so many, embraces the principle of equality before the law and the prohibition of discrimination on the grounds of sex. The Constitution also contains a provision which embodies a commitment to minimal notions of substantive equality. Although not strictly related to Article 14's equality principle, Article 9.2 makes it the function of public authorities to take positive measures to ensure that the rights and freedoms constitutionally recognized can be effectively enjoyed by citizens and the groups to which they belong. Lastly, the Constitution contains an interpretive clause, Article 10.2, which sanctions the need to interpret constitutional rights and freedoms in the light of human rights treaties.

By the time the Spanish Constitutional Court started operating in 1981, there were already many international instruments relevant for women's equality, some of which Spain had ratified or was about to ratify.[92] More importantly when it joined the European Communities in 1985, several important European directives on equality had been approved,[93] and the ECJ had already started developing rich case law on gender discrimination in the workplace. Since the beginning, then, the Spanish Constitutional Court has concretized Article 14's generic mandate of non-discrimination with well-articulated European law, and there is hardly any significant decision on the matter that does not rely on European law and judicial doctrine. The Court's embrace of impact-based discrimination; the doctrine of equal pay for equal work or work of equal worth, and the criteria for determining what equal worth means; the inversion of the burden of proof in employment

---

[92] Some of the most commonly relied upon in the Court's case law are CEDAW and ILO Conventions 100, 111, and 103. See, for instance, SSTC 128/1987; 145/1991; 173/1994; 317/1994; 136/1996.

[93] The most frequently relied upon by the Constitutional Court include EC Directives 117/1975; 207/1976; 117/1975; 7/1979; 92/1985; and 378/1986.

discrimination; the consideration of discrimination on the basis of pregnancy; the *a priori* conformity with affirmative action measures, have all been incorporated primarily by calling on pre-existing European law and under the vague constitutional umbrella of a generic prohibition of discrimination on the basis of sex.[94]

India offers another interesting example of how courts have called on international instruments to fill out with very specific regulation what are, in principle, rather vague constitutional provisions. The decision that best illustrates this is *Vishaka v State of Rajasthan*.[95] The case was a class action petition filed by several social activists and NGOs seeking enforcement of fundamental constitutional rights of working women, including the right to 'gender equality', 'right to life and liberty', and right 'to practice any occupation or carry out any occupation, trade, or business', in the prevailing climate in which alleged violation of these rights through the sexual harassment of working women was 'not uncommon'. The Supreme Court opinion points out that the immediate cause for filing the petition was the alleged brutal rape of a social worker in a village in Rajasthan, but notes that the incident was the subject of separate criminal proceedings and considers no further mention of it necessary in these class action proceedings.

The Court concluded that each incident of sexual harassment of working women results in a violation of the fundamental constitutional rights relied upon by the petitioners, and thus found that they were entitled to an effective remedy under Article 32 of the Indian Constitution. In the absence of legislative or executive enforcement of these rights, the Court declared that 'an effective redressal requires that some guidelines should be laid down for the protection of these rights to fill the legislative vacuum'.

Before announcing guidelines, which had been developed through a series of hearings and with the consent of the Union of India given through the Solicitor General, the Court explained the relevance of international conventions and norms to its interpretation of the fundamental constitutional rights and its determination of the guidelines necessary for their protection.[96] The

---

[94] See, for instance, SSTC 241/1988; 145/1991; 5/1992; 58/1994; 317/1994; 147/1995; 136/1996; 198/1996; 240/1999.

[95] 1997 SOL Case No. 177.

[96] As support for its views on the relevancy of international conventions and norms to the case, the opinion cites provisions of the Constitution, including the provision stating that the state shall endeavour to 'foster respect for international law and treaty obligations in the dealings of organized people with one another' (Article 51) and the provision authorizing Parliament to make laws enforcing international agreements (Article 253), as well as the provision that the executive power shall extend to matters over which Parliament has the power to make law (Article 73). As mentioned at p. 125 above, it also relied on the 'accepted rule of judicial construction that regard must be had to international conventions and norms for construing domestic law when there is no inconsistency between them and there is a void in the domestic law'.

opinion quoted from CEDAW Articles 11 (obligating states parties to take all appropriate measures to eliminate discrimination against women in employment) and 24 ('States parties undertake to adopt all necessary measures at the national level aimed at achieving the full realization of the rights recognized in the present Convention'), as well as the CEDAW General Recommendations under Article 11 with respect to violence and equality in employment, and the Indian government's official commitments at the Fourth World Conference on Women in Beijing. The opinion then stated: 'We have, therefore, no hesitation in placing reliance on the above for the purpose of construing the nature and ambit of constitutional guarantee[s] of gender equality in our Constitution.' After setting out guidelines and norms for the prevention of sexual harassment (covering both public and private employers, with certain differences in treatment) which were based largely on the CEDAW General Recommendation, the Court declared:

Accordingly, we direct that the above guidelines and norms would be strictly observed in all work places for the preservation and enforcement of the right to gender equality of the working women. These directions would be binding and enforceable in law until suitable legislation is enacted to occupy the field. These Writ Petitions are disposed of, accordingly.

In other words, the Court drew on rather generic constitutional provisions, 'gender equality', 'right to life and liberty', and right 'to practice any occupation or carry out any occupation, trade, or business', to decide not only that sexual harassment violates such rights but to develop further a constitutional definition of sexual harassment. In doing so, it basically relied on CEDAW and its General Recommendation. Even though the decision mandates that public authorities enact the suitable legislation, presumably such legislation will have to follow the guidelines expressed in CEDAW and its General Recommendation and incorporated into the Constitution through the Court's decision.

D. International Law as Redefining the Constitution's Structure of Powers

International law can have an impact not only on substantive constitutional issues, but also on the constitutional structure of power, and this can be relevant for our purposes when what is at stake are the rules on the allocation of public authority over women's issues. By structure of power we mean the allocation of powers between branches of a government, and here particularly between state and national powers in federalist systems, as opposed to the recognition of rights and duties in a constitutional bill of rights. Depending on the process through which international law comes to affect the constitutional structure of power we could also talk here about international law *complementing*, *expanding*, or *concretizing* constitutional law. However, because this is a rarer interplay between international law and constitutional law we address substantive and structural questions separately and dedicate this section to the latter. Some examples, two drawn from the Australian experience and one from the US practice, will shed light on this.

Australia presents a particularly interesting situation because its Constitution contains no bill of rights. Australian jurisprudence demonstrates that international treaties can be used not only to help shape the interpretation of existing constitutional gender-related provisions in constitutional bills of rights, but also to help 'fill power gaps' that may limit women's ability to obtain national legislative protection for many of their rights.

In *Aldridge v Booth*,[97] the Federal Court considered an application filed by Lynette Jane Aldridge seeking an order giving effect to the Human Rights Commission's determination that she was entitled to $7,000 damages from Grant Rodney Booth on her complaint of violations of the federal sex discrimination legislation. Section 28 of the Commonwealth Sex Discrimination Act of 1984 prohibits discrimination involving sexual harassment in the workplace. Aldridge alleged that Booth had repeatedly sexually harassed her during her prior employment in the 'Tasty Morsel' cake shop that was owned by Booth and his wife and parents.

In the Federal Court, Booth challenged the validity of section 28 of the Act, arguing that it was not a valid exercise of section 51 of the Constitution's foreign affairs power because it did not 'give effect' to CEDAW. Section 51(xxix) of the Australian Constitution empowers the Federal Parliament to make laws for the 'peace, order and good government of the Commonwealth' with respect to 'external affairs'. Since the *Tasmanian Dam Case*, Australian courts have held that legislation passed by Parliament in fulfilment of treaty obligations is legislation with respect to 'external affairs'.[98] Booth contended that section 28 could not be interpreted as 'giving effect' to CEDAW so as to satisfy the requirements of section 9(10) of the Act: (a) because sexual harassment does not involve discrimination 'against women' or 'on the basis of sex'; and (b) because the section confers protection on women but not men, and thus it fails to ensure women the same rights 'on the basis of equality with men'. Because the federal government does not have explicit power to pass 'equality rights' legislation, the turning point in the constitutional adjudication then became to what extent the Act was a valid exercise of federal powers, and that was made dependent upon whether it could be said to give effect to CEDAW or not.

In the end, the Court rejected Booth's arguments and upheld section 28 as a proper exercise of the federal legislative foreign affairs power. The Court first emphasized that 'the Convention requires appropriate legislative measures to be adopted, including sanctions, where appropriate'. Accepting that by its terms the applicability of section 28 was limited to sexual harassment against women, the opinion nevertheless rejected Booth's assumption that 'one cannot promote the exercise and enjoyment of rights "on the basis of equality with men" by prohibiting discrimination against women'. The implicit argument of the necessity for a legislative prohibition of sexual harassment of men to be in existence could not be accepted as it would 'seriously restrict the operation of the Convention, and its implementation ... [by putting] an unwarranted premium on the existence of legislation, which may or may not reflect the true position in fact'.[99]

A more recent Australian case is *McBain v State of Victoria*.[100] This 2000 case involved not only what is to be understood as a measure that gives effect to a certain international treaty, but also how such doctrine should affect the judicially consolidated interpretive rule whereby the Acts of Parliament are supposed to be interpreted as being in accordance with international human rights obligations. The case was filed by Dr John McBain, who wished to provide infertility treatment (in vitro fertilization) to Lisa Meldrum, a single woman not living in a de facto union. He challenged the constitutionality of Victoria's Infertility Treatment Act, arguing that it was inconsistent with the Commonwealth Sex Discrimination Act and thus invalid under section 109 of the Commonwealth Constitution, which provides that where a state Act is inconsistent with a Commonwealth Act, the state Act is invalid to the extent of the inconsistency. Under Victoria's state law, to be eligible to undergo infertility treatments a woman either had to be married and living with her husband, or be living with a man in a de facto relationship. Among its provisions, the Commonwealth Sex Discrimination Act prohibits the refusal of services on the grounds of a person's marital status. The Federal Court of Australia held that fertility treatment was a 'service' under the federal Act, and thus the state Act was invalid to the extent it required women to be married or living in a de facto relationship to receive such treatments.

In *McBain*, the Catholic Church filed a submission that raised the 'incorporation issue'. It argued that the state law was not inconsistent with the Sex Discrimination Act, citing the Court's earlier jurisprudence establishing a presumption that Parliament intends to legislate in accordance with its international human rights obligations. The Catholic Church argued that international documents, including the Convention on the Rights of the Child, ICCPR, and ICESCR, recognize 'the right of a child to be born into a family,

---

[99] The Court also noticed that the Act is entitled 'An Act relating to discrimination on the ground of sex, marital status or pregnancy or involving sexual harassment', and that its objects, as set out in section 3, included '[giving] effect to certain provisions of the Convention on the Elimination of All Forms of Discrimination Against Women', and '[eliminating], so far as possible, discrimination against persons on the ground of sex in the area of work and education'.

[100] [2000] FCA 1009.

to be raised by its mother and father, and to know its parents', and that the word 'services' in the federal law must be read consistently with these treaty rights. The Court rejected this argument, accepting instead that the purpose of the Commonwealth Act was to give effect to a specific treaty, namely CEDAW. The Catholic Church's argument would give primacy to implications from other treaties over the words of the very treaty to which the Commonwealth Act gives effect.[101]

Although not addressed by the US Supreme Court's decision in the case, arguments made in a recent US case suggest the potential impact of international instruments on structural constitutional norms and the possible effects of this on the adjudication of women's rights. It speaks volumes about US jurisprudence that it is an amici brief rather than the Court's actual opinion that we point to here. However, given the US judiciary's current resistance to incorporation of international human rights law, we believe that the recent amici brief filed in the United States Supreme Court in a case challenging the constitutionality of certain provisions of the Federal Violence Against Women Act of 1994 (VAWA) merits discussion for what its arguments might portend for future changes in the prevailing isolationists' attitudes. The amici brief was filed in 1999, by several international legal scholars and human rights experts, in the case of *United States v Morrison*, decided by the Court in 2000.[102]

The *Morrison* case arose out of a civil rights damages action filed by Christy Brzonkala, a college student, against Antonio Morrison and another member of the football team at the state university they all attended, for allegedly raping her in a dormitory room. She sued under a provision of the VAWA that authorized the filing of civil damages actions against private individuals for acts of gender-based violence. The defendants challenged the constitutionality

---

[101] Notice that the expansion of the protection of women is contingent on the federal statute being more progressive than state legislation and this may not always be the case. However, in practice federal legislation implementing international treaties will often be more progressive because it imports aspirational standards from the international human rights system.

[102] 120 S. Ct. 1740 (2000). The brief identified those filing this brief as follows: 'Amici curiae are 36 international legal scholars and human rights experts. Amici include law professors and scholars who have studied and contributed as jurists to the development of the international law respecting human rights and the recognition of violence against women as a violation of human rights. Some of the amici currently hold positions as independent experts elected to human rights treaty bodies of the United Nations and the Inter-American system that are charged with implementing human rights, and one has recently completed a report on violence against women as a United Nations Special Rapporteur. The amici also include human rights experts and advocates, who have dedicated their lives to building the legal foundations of universal human rights protections, and have participated in various ways in the drafting and adoption of major UN and Inter-American instruments recognizing violence against women, inflicted by private persons as well as by officials as one of the paramount violations of international human rights today. Finally, there are among the amici international law scholars who have focused on the relation between the constitutional powers of the federal government and the international commitments of the United States.' Amici Brief, at 3.

of this provision of the VAWA, arguing that it was neither within Congress's power over interstate commerce nor within its power under section 5 of the Fourteenth Amendment to enforce the protection against state actions denying equal protection.

The case was closely watched and hotly contested, with numerous amici briefs filed supporting each side. The amici brief filed by the international legal scholars and human rights experts differed from others in that it raised arguments in support of the challenged provision based upon Congress's power to enforce treaties and customary international law, and on an interpretive canon dictating a presumption of consistency with international obligations. For our purposes we paraphrase here the relevant arguments that Congress had unquestionable authority to enact legislation to meet both international treaty and customary law obligations. It was argued that the US ratification of the ICCPR, among other international documents, empowered Congress to enact legislation implementing the treaty. The text of the treaty, in conjunction with subsequent unanimous and binding interpretations by the international community, made clear that the ICCPR requires the US to provide protection from gender-based violence from both private persons and public officials. In addition, the emergence in customary international law of a clear norm recognizing women's right to live free of gender-based violence, provided additional constitutional authority for the enactment of the federal civil rights cause of action at issue in this case. Lastly, it was also well settled and fundamental to the US constitutional system that, whenever possible, domestic law should be interpreted so as to enable the US to fulfil its international obligations, a principle which strongly supported interpretations of both the Commerce Clause and section 5 of the Fourteenth Amendment that would confirm Congressional authority to enact the VAWA and similar implementing legislation.[103]

In a five to four decision, the US Supreme Court agreed with the arguments of the respondents and their supporters and held that the challenged provision of the VAWA was unconstitutional. No mention was made of the arguments raised in the amici brief of the international legal scholars and human rights experts. Nevertheless, the brief itself is evidence of the growing awareness of how far out of step the US judiciary is in this area, and of the increasing determination by human rights activists to seek new avenues for changing this situation.

4. CONCLUSION

As domestic constitutionalists, we began this project with the aim of providing a 'nearside' view of one sector of the rapidly evolving legal terrain that spans

---

[103] Amici Brief, *supra* n. 102, at 3–4.

the traditional divide between international human rights law and domestic constitutional law. From the start, we were cognizant of the complexity of the boundaries and relationships we were exploring and of their correspondingly nuanced possibilities for advancing gender equality. We close with some brief reflections on the character and potential of this truly interstitial body of law.

Admittedly, a more straightforward account of the binding influence of international human rights law in domestic constitutional interpretation would have the advantage of clarity. Broader acceptance of this approach also might seem the most direct avenue for advancing women's legal status. But the developments we have traced defy description as embracing, or even tending towards, any direct or unitary approach, and we see little to suggest that this situation will change in the near future.

On the positive side, however, the complexity and even strangeness of the interplay between international human rights law and domestic constitutional law may provide some advantages from the standpoint of the development of progressive constitutional gender jurisprudence. Strategically, the possibilities for using international human rights law are not exhausted when particular provisions are deemed not binding on domestic judges. While assimilative and persuasive uses may pose greater threats of dilution of core norms, they may also facilitate more contextualized and particularized applications of these norms.

The diversity in approaches to the incorporation of international human rights law may also provide advantages from the perspective of legitimacy. The different modes of domestication of international gender norms offer different possibilities for legitimating international law from below or inside. International human rights that are assimilated through constitution-making or revision may be seen as procedurally legitimated in ways that lessen concerns about their hegemonic or imperialistic character. Similarly, express constitutional recognition of the supplementary status of international gender norms may be interpreted as consent of a different nature than that perceived from treaty ratification. Express interpretive imperatives share this advantage. Additionally, interpretive approaches that blend international and constitutional provisions and jurisprudence in various manners are particularized in ways that may further legitimate the resulting interpretations.

6

Individual(s') Liability for Collective Sexual Violence

PATRICIA VISEUR SELLERS [*]

War, systematic attacks against civilians, or the eruption of genocide entail and breed collective criminal conduct. Collective conduct denotes crimes dependent upon the coordinated or simultaneous acts of multiple perpetrators and crimes that often ensnare multiple victims, notably massacres, large-scale deportations, or prolonged civilian detention. Whether by sexual threats or actual sexual assaults, the susceptibility of sexual violence to collective conduct seems predictable. The individuals eventually charged and tried for these crimes, in truth, only hint at the number of perpetrators.

For accused who appear before the International Criminal Tribunal for the Former Yugoslavia (ICTY),[1] the Statute[2] obliges the Prosecutor to prove, regardless of the collective nature of the acts, the underlying crime. Accordingly, Tribunal judgments and decisions have defined and interpreted the elements of crimes accepted as serious violations of international humanitarian law. The Trial Chambers and the Appeals Chamber have germinated a similar, yet less acknowledged examination of an accused's form of participation in a crime, otherwise known as the individual mode of liability.

Security Council Resolution 808[3] recalled that persons who commit or order the commission of grave breaches of the Geneva

---

[*] Ms Sellers is the Legal Advisor for Gender-related Crimes in the Office of the Prosecutor for the ICTY. The opinions expressed in this article are solely those of the author and are not intended to represent the official views or policies of the Office of the Prosecutor of the ICTY, nor those of the United Nations.

[1] SC Res. 827, 25 May 1993 (establishing the International Criminal Tribunal for the Former Yugoslavia).

[2] Statute of the ICTY, attached to the Report of the Secretary General Pursuant to Paragraph 2 of the Security Council Resolution 808, UN Doc. S/25704, Annex (1993), reprinted in 32 *ILM* 1159 (1993).

[3] SC Res. 808, 22 February 1993.

Conventions[4] are individually responsible or liable in respect of such breaches. Flowing from the international law principle of individual responsibility for international crimes, Article 6 of the ICTY Statute sets forth the Tribunal's competence *ratione personae* or personal jurisdiction. The ICTY Appeals Chamber has consequently ruled that no one who participates in a serious violation of humanitarian law escapes the Tribunal's jurisdiction.[5]

The Tribunal limits attribution of personal culpability to natural persons, and does not confer competence *ratione personae* on juridical entities, political parties, associations, or groups.[6] Nevertheless, personal jurisdiction is triggered for individual accused who, by means of formal or informal groups, participate in collective criminal conduct.[7]

An accused's participation or liability must satisfy the specificities of Article 7(1) or (3) of the ICTY Statute. Two broad types of individual liability exist: direct criminal responsibility, and indirect or superior responsibility. Direct responsibility implicates any accused who has planned, instigated, committed, ordered, or aided or abetted the execution of crimes within the jurisdiction of the Statute. Indirect criminal responsibility attributes liability to a person in a position of superior authority, whether military, political, business, or any hierarchical status, for acts directly committed by his or her subordinates. The traditional military doctrine of command responsibility is the most commonly used mode of indirect liability.

Proof of the form of liability fulfils a crucial part in constructing an accused's individual criminal responsibility. Direct and indirect liability apply to all crimes within the competence *ratione materiae* or subject matter jurisdiction listed in the provisions of Articles 2–5 of the ICTY Statute. Either form of liability amply covers justiciable sexual assault conduct.

---

[4] The four Geneva Conventions, signed 12 August 1949, in force 21 October 1950, are the Geneva Convention (I) for the Amelioration of the Condition of the Wounded and Sick in Armed Forces in the Field, 75 UNTS 31; Geneva Convention (II) for the Amelioration of the Condition of the Wounded, Sick and Shipwrecked Members of Armed Forces at Sea, 75 UNTS 85; Geneva Convention (III) Relative to the Treatment of Prisoners of War, 75 UNTS 135; and Geneva Convention (IV) Relative to the Protection of Civilian Persons in Time of War, 75 UNTS 287.

[5] *Prosecutor v Duško Tadić*, Decision on the Defence Motion for Interlocutory Appeal on Jurisdiction, 2 October 1995, Case No. IT-94-AR72, para. 92 (hereinafter '*Tadić Jurisdiction Decision*').

[6] Report of the Secretary-General Pursuant to Paragraph 2 of Security Council Resolution 808, UN Doc. S/25704 (1993), reprinted in 32 *ILM* 1159 (1993) (hereinafter 'Report'). Paragraph 50 of the Report states, in part: '[T]he ordinary meaning of the term "persons responsible for serious violations of international humanitarian law" would be natural persons to the exclusion of juridical persons.'

[7] Ibid., at para. 51. Paragraph 51 concludes by stating that: '[T]he criminal acts set out in this statute are carried out by natural persons; such persons would be subject to the jurisdiction of the International Tribunal irrespective of membership in groups.'

The issuance of sound, reasoned sexual assault jurisprudence is an acknowledged achievement of the ICTY.[8] In the 'early days' of the 1990s, reservations persisted as to whether the prohibition of rape, strikingly absent from the grave breach provisions of each Geneva Convention, constituted a *serious* violation of the laws and customs of war, that compelled prosecution. Upon deliberation of sexual assault evidence, the ICTY Trial and Appeals Chambers have repeatedly confirmed that several acts of sexual violence, not just the enumeration of rape as a crime against humanity, were serious violations of international humanitarian law and, thus, within the subject matter jurisdiction of the Statute.

In a like fashion, the Trial Chambers and Appeals Chamber have confirmed direct liability to encompass a form of criminal liability not expressed in Article 7(1). Co-perpetration or joint criminal enterprise is a form of direct liability based upon a perpetrator undertaking to participate in criminal conduct with a plurality of actors. In regard to sexual assault evidence, this implied form of liability emerged starting with the cryptic language of common purpose in the first ICTY judgment, *Prosecutor v Tadić*,[9] and with the subsequent differentiation of a co-perpetrator from an aider and abettor in the *Prosecutor v Furundžija* decision.[10] It progressed through the defining *Tadić*[11] and *Furundžija*[12] appeal judgments and then received noteworthy application in the *Krstić*[13] and *Kvočka*[14] trial judgments.

In this 'midlife' stage of the Tribunal's existence,[15] the Prosecutor has increasingly indicted superiors in positions of military or political leadership for collective criminal conduct. The indictments against former Serbian President, Slobodan Milošević, and the former members of the Bosnian-Serb Presidency, Momćilo Krajišnik and Ms Biljana Plavsić, allege they were co-perpetrators who, with other participants, ethnically cleansed the former Yugoslavia. The primary mode of liability is joint criminal enterprise, governed by Article 7(1) of the ICTY Statute.

[8] J. G. Gardam and M. J. Jarvis, *Women, Armed Conflict and International Law* (2001), at 208–18.

[9] *Prosecutor v Tadić*, Judgment, Case No. IT-94-1-T, 7 May 1997, 536 (hereinafter '*Tadić Judgment*').

[10] *Prosecutor v Anto Furundžija*, Judgment, Case No. IT-95-17/1-T, 10 December 1998 (hereinafter '*Furundžija Judgment*').

[11] *Prosecutor v Tadić*, Judgment, Case No. IT-94-1-A, 15 July 1999 (hereinafter '*Tadić Appeals Judgment*').

[12] *Prosecutor v Furundžija*, Judgment, Case No. IT-95-17/-A, 21 July 2000 (hereinafter '*Furundžija Appeals Judgment*').

[13] *Prosecutor v Krstić*, Judgment, Case No. IT-98-33-T, 2 August 2001, para. 2 (hereinafter '*Krstić Judgment*').

[14] *Prosecutor v Kvočka et al.*, Judgment, Case No. IT-98-30/&-T, 2 November 2001 (hereinafter '*Kvočka Judgment*').

[15] See the minutes from the SC, 4429th Meeting, 27 November 2001, S\PV.4429 (discussing the Prosecutor's 'exit strategy' for the ICTY and the ICTR).

This chapter traces the important, parallel steps between the emergence of common purpose or joint criminal enterprise under the ICTY Statute and its use in determining personal liability for collective sexual assaults. The chapter is divided into three major sections and a conclusion. The first section will identify and briefly highlight provisions of the Secretary-General's Report that express an intention to prosecute perpetrators of sexual assaults under the ICTY Statute within the context of the principle of individual criminal responsibility. The second section will review substantive sexual assault jurisprudence, focusing on selected judgments that detail the development of the common purpose or joint criminal enterprise doctrine as applied to collective sexual assault conduct. The third section offers some midlife or *intermezzo* reflections on the legal demystification of sexual assault prosecution, as assisted by the common purpose doctrine. The conclusion underscores the prospects for the common purpose doctrine to be an engine of liability for sexual violence in the *Milošević* cases.

This chapter does not presume to predict, only speculate upon the munificent effect the common purpose or joint criminal enterprise doctrine might have on the development of sexual assault jurisprudence.

1. SECRETARY-GENERAL'S INTENT TO PUNISH PERSONS LIABLE FOR SEXUAL ASSAULTS

The Secretary-General's Report,[16] in assessing numerous humanitarian law violations, proposed a Statute for the establishment of an ad hoc International Criminal Tribunal for the former Yugoslavia that left little doubt that gender crimes, or more precisely sexual assaults, would feature in the institution's mandate. Governmental, non-governmental, and international organizations,[17] members of civil society, and the United Nations-authorized Report of the Commission of Experts[18] consciously documented allegations of sexual violence uncovered on all sides of the armed conflict, principally against women and female children, and to a lesser extent, against men. As requested,[19] the Secretary-General informed the Security Council of the gravity of crimes committed, citing:

[16] Report, *supra* n. 6, at para. 2.

[17] Ibid., at para. 14.

[18] Ibid., at para. 9.

[19] In para. 2 of SC Res. 808, the Security Council '... Requests the Secretary General to submit for consideration by the Council at the earliest possible date, and if possible no later than 60 days after the adoption of the present resolution, a report on all aspects of this matter, including specific proposals and where appropriate options for the effective and expeditious implementation of the decision contained in paragraph 1 above [to establish an ad hoc Tribunal], taking into account suggestions put forward in this regard by Member States.'

[An] interim report of the Commission of Experts (S/25274), [which] concluded that grave breaches and other violations of international humanitarian law had been committed in the territory of the former Yugoslavia, including 'ethnic cleansing, mass killings, torture, rape, pillage and destruction of civilian property, destruction of cultural and religious property and arbitrary arrest'.[20]

The Secretary-General's Report reference to conclusions in the interim report of the Commission of Experts seemingly confirms that its recommendation to the Security Council to create the Tribunal stemmed from accepting that, *inter alia*, evidence of physical and mental abuses such as rape could be afforded the legal characterization of grave breaches and other violations of international humanitarian law. The Secretary-General's perception that rape, together with other crimes, required legal redress was further underscored in paragraph 11 of the Report, recalling Security Council Resolution 820,[21] which condemned:

[A]ll violations of international humanitarian law, including in particular, the practice of 'ethnic cleansing' and the massive, organized and systematic detention and rape of women, and confirmed that those who committed or who have committed or order or ordered the commission of such acts will be held individually responsible in respect of such acts.[22]

Resolution 820 presages the important duty to prove the substantive crime *and* the mode of liability. The Report's insightful emphasis on Resolution 820 moreover acknowledges that the uncontested principle of individual criminal responsibility for international crimes would be appropriately applied to the systematic detention and rape of women in Yugoslavia.

The Secretary-General elected to incorporate into selected articles of the proposed Statute, as explained by pertinent introductory comments, the dual realization: (1) that serious violations of humanitarian law committed in the region, including sexual violence, constitute the subject matter or *materiae ratione* jurisdiction of the Tribunal; and (2) that those persons who perpetrated such crimes are individually bound by the *in personam* jurisdiction of the Tribunal.

The *materiae ratione* or subject matter jurisdiction over acts of sexual violence under the ICTY Statute, appears, on its face, restricted to one express provision on rape found in Article 5(g) of the Statute.[23] However, use of the phrase 'rape and sexual assaults' in the Report, presages that the enumeration of rape as a crime against humanity would not exclude or exempt the

[20] Report, *supra* n. 6, at para. 9.

[21] SC Res. 820 and the famous reference to systematic detention and rape often caused scholars and lawyers to mistake the adjective 'systematic' for a legal requirement in order to prosecute rape. Under crimes against humanity, the attack against the civilian population must be systematic, or widespread. The underlying acts must form part of the attack, but they need not be widespread or systematic. See discussion at pp. 192–3 below on 'systematic' rapes.

[22] Report, *supra* n. 6, at para. 11, citing SC Res. 820, 17 April 1993.

[23] Article 5 of the ICTY Statute, entitled 'Crimes Against Humanity', reads: 'The International Tribunal shall have the power to prosecute persons responsible for the following crimes

prosecution of other sexual assaults. In the predicate paragraph to Article 5 of
the Statute, the Secretary-General said that, 'inhumane acts have taken the
form of widespread and systematic rape *and other forms of sexual assault
including enforced prostitution*'.[24]

Beyond Article 5(g), the Statute's subsequent interpretation removes any
ambiguity apropos the sex-based criminal conduct covered by the Tribunal's
mandate. The Appeals Chamber, in its first important decision that examines
the breadth of the Tribunal's subject matter jurisdiction, opined that prohibitions of sexual violence encompassed in common in Article 3 to the Geneva
Conventions,[25] came within the implicit scope of Article 3 of the Statute.
Subsequently, Trial Chambers have held and the Appeals Chamber affirmed
that sexually violent conduct can result in convictions under several criminal
provisions under the Statute, other than rape as a crime against humanity.[26]

Given the legal hindsight of the International Criminal Tribunal for
Rwanda (ICTR) Statute,[27] the early jurisprudence[28] of the ad hoc Tribunals,
and indeed the International Criminal Court (ICC) Statute,[29] the Secretary-
General's limited enumeration of sexual assault offences strikes one as amazingly conservative if not blushingly timid.

A rigorous reading of the Report and proposed Statute, however, contra-
dicts any restricted approach to the intended jurisdiction over sex-based
crimes. The Report's predicate paragraph 88 to Article 16 of the Statute, in
particular, outlined the tasks of the Prosecutor to investigate and prosecute
crimes, and declared that because of 'the nature of the crimes committed and
the sensitivities of *victims of rape and sexual assault,* due consideration should
be given in the appointment of staff to the employment of qualified women'.[30]

when committed in armed conflict, whether international or internal in character, and directed
against any civilian population: (a) murder; (b) extermination; (c) enslavement; (d) deportation; (e) imprisonment; (f) torture; (g) rape; (h) persecutions on political, racial and religious
grounds; (i) other inhumane acts.'

[24] Report, *supra* n. 6, at para. 48 (emphasis added).
[25] *Tadić Jurisdiction Decision, supra* n. 5, paras 89, 98.
[26] See '2. Collective Liability and Substantive Sexual Assault Jurisdiction', at pp. 162–89.
[27] Statute of the International Criminal Tribunal for Rwanda, *attached to* Prosecution of
Persons Responsible for Genocide and Other Serious Violations of International Humanitarian
Law Committed in the Territory of Rwanda and Rwandan citizens responsible for genocide and
other such violations committed in the territory of neighbouring States, between 1 January
1994 and 31 December 1994, SC Res. 955, Annex, 8 November 1994 (hereinafter 'Statute of
the ICTR'), *reprinted in* 33 *ILM* 1598 (1994), Articles 3 and 4.
[28] For example, in *Prosecutor v Radovan Karadžić and Mladić,* Review of the Indictments
Pursuant to Rule 61 of the Rules of Evidence and Procedure, Case No. IT-95-S/T-95-18-R61,
11 July 1996, at paras 13, 93, the Chamber already opined that rape and other sexual violence
could constitute acts of genocide.
[29] Rome Statute of the International Criminal Court, UN Doc. A/CONE.183/9, 17 July
1998 (hereinafter 'ICC Statute').
[30] Report, *supra* n. 6, at para. 88 (emphasis added).

A plausible interpretation of Article 16, paragraph 3, which asserts 'the Office of the Prosecutor shall be composed of a Prosecutor and such other staff as may be required', would strongly suggest that the Prosecutor's recruitment of staff *shall* take into consideration sexual assault crimes, in addition to the rapes highlighted in paragraphs 9 and 11 of the Report.[31]

In Article 15,[32] the Secretary-General directed the judges to adopt measures for the conduct of trial and appellate proceedings, the admission of evidence, witness protection, and any other appropriate matter. Significantly, the understanding that the Tribunal's jurisdiction did cover multiple types of *sexual assaults*, was evidenced in the initial adoption of the Rules of Procedure and Evidence.[33]

The first appointed Tribunal judges drafted the intriguing Rule 96.[34] This specialized evidentiary rule[35] pronounced, simultaneously, procedural requirements, such as modalities for the admission or exclusion of evidence, and substantive determinations, notably evidence that vitiates a victim's consent.[36] The present rule reads:

In cases of sexual assault:

   (i) no corroboration of the victim's testimony shall be required;
  (ii) consent shall not be allowed as a defence if the victim
     (a) has been subjected to or threatened with or has had reason to fear violence, duress, detention or psychological oppression, or
     (b) reasonably believed that if the victim did not submit, another might be so subjected, threatened or put in fear;
 (iii) before evidence of the victim's consent is admitted, the accused shall satisfy the Trial Chamber in camera that the evidence is relevant and credible;
 (iv) prior sexual conduct of the victim shall not be admitted in evidence.[37]

---

[31] A similar interpretation extends to the staffing of the Victim and Witness Unit. The Registrar supervises the services of the Victim and Witness Unit as regards both defence and prosecution victims and witnesses. As discussed below, measures to protect witnesses must take into consideration the victims and witnesses of sexual assaults. Rule 34 of the Rules of Procedure and Evidence, in response to the types of victims and witnesses and the nature of the crimes, requires the Unit to: '34(A) provide counselling. ... 34(B) consideration shall be given to the appointment of qualified women.'

[32] Article 15 of the ICTY Statute reads: 'The judges of the International Tribunal shall adopt rules of procedure and evidence for the conduct of the pre-trial phase of the proceedings, trials and appeals, the admission of evidence, the protection of victims and witnesses and other appropriate matters.'

[33] Rules of Procedure and Evidence, UN Doc. IT/32, 1 February 1994 (hereinafter 'Rules').

[34] Entitled 'Evidence in Cases of Sexual Assault'.

[35] Sellers, 'Rule 89(C) and (D): At Odds or Overlapping with Rule 96 and Rule 95', in R. May *et al.* (eds), *Essays on ICTY Procedure and Evidence in Honour of Gabrielle Kirk McDonald* (2001) 279.

[36] Ibid., at 280–1.

[37] Rule 96. See *infra* n.38.

Its fascination is well deserved. Rule 96 has been amended three times, the first time ostensibly due to a male-generated outcry because consent appeared to be eliminated, not qualified, as a defence to wartime rape.[38] Rule 96 is cited for embodying a general rule regarding victim corroboration, applicable to all, not just sexual assault, witnesses.[39] Contrary to the plain language of sub-sentence (ii), it has most recently been interpreted as not regulating sexual assaults defences.[40] Nevertheless, Rule 96 indisputably focuses the judiciary, the defence, and the prosecution on the anticipated submission of sexual assault evidence within the Tribunal's procedural framework.

The Secretary-General also foresaw that protective provisions must be elaborated in view of sexual assault witnesses. Article 22 of the Statute complies with the Report's instruction to the International Tribunal to ensure that the '[n]ecessary protection measures should therefore be provided in the rules of procedure and evidence for victims and witnesses, especially in the cases of rape or sexual assault'.[41] In response, the Tribunal judges adopted Rule 75 and provided for the grant of multiple protective measures for witnesses and victims at the discretion of the Trial Chamber.[42] Although the text of Rule 75 is devoid of any mention of sexual assault witnesses, the patent concerns voiced in paragraph 88 of the Report certainly compelled the comprehensive coverage of Rule 75.

The subject matter jurisdiction is completed by the *in personam* jurisdiction. The Secretary-General's incorporation of *in personam* jurisdiction in the Statute, the origin of individual criminal responsibility, is tersely stated in

[38] To review the amendments of Rule 96, see UN Doc. IT/32, 1 February 1994; UN Doc. IT/32/Rev. 3 (1994); and UN Doc. IT/32/Rev.3/Corr. 3 (1995).

[39] *Tadić Judgment, supra* n. 9, at para. 536.

[40] *Prosecutor v Kunarac et al.*, Case No. IT-96-23-T & IT-96-23/1-T, 22 February 2001, para. 463, (hereinafter '*Kunarac Judgment*').

[41] Report, *supra* n. 6, at para. 108.

[42] Rule 75 reads, in part:

(A) A Judge or Chamber may, *proprio motu* or at the request of either party, or of the victim or witness concerned, or of the Victim and Witnesses Section, order appropriate measures for the privacy and protection of victims and witnesses, provided that the measures are consistent with the rights of the accused.

(B) A Chamber may hold an in camera proceeding to determine whether to order:
   (i) measures to prevent disclosure to the public or the media of the identity or whereabouts of a victim or a witness, or of persons related to or associated with a victim or witness by such means as:
      (a) expunging names and identifying information from the Tribunal's public records;
      (b) non-disclosure to the public of any records identifying the victim;
      (c) giving testimony through image- or voice-altering devices or closed circuit television; and
      (d) assignment of a pseudonym;
   (ii) closed sessions, in accordance with Rule 79;
   (iii) appropriate measures to facilitate the testimony of vulnerable victims and witnesses, such as one-way closed circuit television.

Article 6: 'The International Criminal Tribunal for ex-Yugoslavia shall have jurisdiction over natural persons pursuant to the provisions of the present Statute.'

Articles 2–5, the substantive criminal provisions, commence in turn with the phrase that the 'International Tribunal shall have the power to prosecute *persons*'.[43] Emphasis on the individual criminal is linked to proving how and to what degree a person participated in a substantive offence. This principle contrasts sharply with the hitherto accepted attribution of guilt based upon membership in a criminal group, political party, or organization that, together with individual criminal liability, was the basis of convictions in the International Military Tribunals after World War II.[44]

The predicate paragraphs to Article 6 drew upon Security Council Resolution 808's use of the term 'persons responsible for serious violations of international humanitarian law' to emphasize that competence *ratione personae* covered only natural persons and that such persons were subject to the Tribunal's jurisdiction irrespective of their affiliation with a group.[45]

However, it is Security Council Resolution 820, as cited above, that foresaw the Tribunal's recognition of multiple forms of participation and criminal liability. Conscious of the on-going nature of the armed conflict in 1993, Resolution 820 exhaustively condemns those individuals who *presently* commit or order crimes, or individuals who *will* commit or order crimes in the future, or those who *already* have committed or ordered crimes in the past. The text of Article 7 of the ICTY Statute that the Secretary-General eventually proposed to the Security Council differs from yet, while broadening the language, captures the spirit of Resolution 820.

Article 7 reads, in part:

1. A person who planned, instigated, ordered, committed or otherwise aided and abetted in the planning, preparation or execution of a crime referred to in articles 2 to 5 of the present Statute, shall be individually responsible for the crime.

. . .

3. The fact that any of the acts referred to in articles 2 to 5 of the present Statute was committed by a subordinate does not relieve his superior of criminal responsibility if he knew or had reason to know that the subordinate was about to commit such acts or

---

[43] Emphasis added. Under Article 2 of the ICTY Statute, it is stated that 'the International Tribunal shall have the power to prosecute persons committing or ordering to be committed grave breaches'; Article 3 gives the Tribunal powers to 'prosecute persons violating the laws and customs of war'; Article 4 addresses 'persons committing genocide'; while Article 5 speaks of 'persons responsible for the following crimes when committed in armed conflict . . . and directed against a civilian population'.

[44] See Article II, 2 of Control Council Law No. 10, which states: 'Any person without regard to nationality or the capacity in which he acted, is deemed to have committed a crime . . . if he was . . . (e) a member of any organization or group connected with the commission of any such crime.'

[45] Report, *supra* n. 6, at paras 50, 51.

had done so and the superior failed to take the necessary and reasonable measures to prevent such acts or to punish the perpetrators thereof.[46]

Article 7 sets forth forms of express liability for persons who participate in crimes. Liability is generated not only by ordering and committing, but also by planning, instigating, and aiding and abetting in planning, preparation, and execution of crimes, thus exceeding the forms previewed in Resolution 820. Even though the texts of Articles 2–5 of the Statute refer only to persons who either commit or order crimes, the Tribunal's jurisprudence has not read these predicate sentences as placing restrictions on Article 7.[47] On the contrary, the Trial and Appeals Chambers have developed a broad interpretation of Article 7 that encompasses an explicit and, as will be discussed in the following sections, an implicit form of criminal liability for collective criminal activity. Suffice it to say that the implicit form of personal liability, known as common purpose or joint criminal enterprise, has advanced to the forefront of the Prosecutor's allegations against the top military and political leadership.

The author asserts that Secretary-General's dual prerequisites that joined the intended subject matter jurisdiction, whether expressed or implied, to the forms of personal liability, both explicit and implicit, functioned as useful legal tools in the prosecution of sexual assaults.

Having glanced at the Secretary-General's proposal to the Security Council to incorporate sexual assault crimes under the subject matter jurisdiction of the Tribunal, coupled with the intent to reach all persons who might be guilty of serious violations of humanitarian law, including sex-based crimes, we can now undertake an examination of the intertwining evolution of collective forms of individual liability and its relevance to collective sexual assaults.[48]

2. COLLECTIVE LIABILITY AND SUBSTANTIVE SEXUAL ASSAULT JURISPRUDENCE

The ad hoc Tribunals have delivered landmark jurisprudence on international criminal law. Most notably, the Tribunals' interpretation of the crime of

[46] Article 7 of the ICTY Statute.

[47] In addition to the forms of individual liability expressed in Article 7, it is important to note that in Article 4 of the ICTY Statute and in Article 3 of the ICTR Statute, the genocide provision, liability exists for persons who conspire to commit, are complicit in, or incite genocide, as well as for persons who commit acts of genocide. This double layer of liability is not the focus of the present chapter.

[48] The author suggests that the evolving doctrines of individual liability, in particular command or superior responsibility, exist to provide further protection to victims of the core crimes recognized under international humanitarian and criminal law, including rape and other sexual assaults. See Sellers, 'The Context of Sexual Violence: Sexual Violence as Violations of International Humanitarian Law', in G. McDonald and O. Swak-Goldman (eds), *Substantive and Procedural Aspects of International Criminal Law* (2000) 286, at 291.

genocide[49] and the ICTY's procedural application of individual responsibility to the prohibitions of common Article 3 to the Geneva Conventions are significant achievements.[50] The Tribunals' concerted investigation, prosecution, and adjudication of sexual assault conduct under international law stand as equally singular judicial accomplishments. The judgments and opinions of several Trial Chambers and the Appeals Chamber have deliberated upon evidence of sexual violence and examined its varied legal characterization in light of the Statutes.

The Nuremberg Tribunal, but more particularly the Tokyo Tribunal and several subsequent national trials, produced judgments that held sexually violent conduct during armed conflict to constitute war crimes or crimes against humanity. Unfortunately, little strenuous legal analysis has been produced about these judicial pronouncements,[51] engendering the mistaken belief among many scholars and practitioners that sex crimes were omitted, almost entirely, from previously rendered humanitarian law jurisprudence. By resolutely labouring under their mandate, the Tribunals have broken the impasse that presumed either the unavailability of legal instruments to redress sex-based crimes, or the inevitability of massive sexual violence that could not be prosecuted. The ad hoc Tribunals, by trying and convicting perpetrators, fomented a legal climate beyond their jurisdiction that led to the inclusion of several sex-based crimes in the Rome Statute of the ICC.

A cursory view of the jurisprudence confirms that the Tribunals have recognized acts of sexual violence as encompassing, *inter alia*, acts of genocide,[52] sexual mutilation,[53] rape,[54] enslavement,[55] torture,[56] persecution,[57] or inhumane acts such as crimes against humanity and war crimes,[58] in both international and, importantly, internal armed conflicts. A closer, chronological assessment of the case law reveals the reasoning behind and evolution of many of the substantive aspects of this unique jurisprudence.

---

[49] See generally *Prosecutor v Kayeshima*, Judgment, Case No. ICTR-95-1-T, 21 May 1999; *Prosecutor v Musema*, Judgment, Case No. ICTR-96-13-T, 27 January 2000; and *Krstić Judgment, supra* n. 13.

[50] *Tadić Jurisdiction Decision, supra* n. 5, at para. 137.

[51] For a discussion on the World War II jurisprudence, see K. D. Askin, *War Crimes against Women: Prosecution in International War Crimes Tribunals* (1997); P. V. Sellers, *The Context of Sexual Violence: Sexual Violence as Violations of International Humanitarian Law* (2000).

[52] *Prosecutor v Akayesu*, Judgment, ICTR-96-4-T, 2 September 1998, at para. 731 (hereinafter 'Akayesu Judgment').

[53] *Tadić Judgment, supra* n. 9, at para. 729.

[54] See *Akayesu Judgment, supra* n. 52, at para. 686; *Kunarac Judgment, supra* n. 40, at para. 655.

[55] *Kunarac Judgment, supra* n. 40, at paras 738, 739, 742.

[56] *Kvočka Judgment, supra* n. 14.

[57] *Krstić Judgment, supra* n. 13, at paras 517, 537.

[58] *Prosecutor v Delalić et al.*, Judgment, Case No. IT-96-21-T, 16 November 1998, at para. 1066 (hereinafter 'Čelebići'); *Furundžija Judgment, supra* n. 10, at paras 210, 272. Two brief

This chapter focuses on a more narrow range of the Tribunals' sexual assault jurisprudence, namely, those cases that shaped the emergence or application of common purpose or joint criminal liability as interpreted in Article 7 of the Statute. Accordingly, the *Tadić* and *Furundžija* trial and appellate judgments and the *Kvočka* and *Krstić* trial judgments will be examined in detail below.

A. *Prosecutor v Tadić*

Tadić,[59] the first completed trial at either ad hoc Tribunal, is cited more often for the withdrawal of two sexual assault witnesses, rather than for its significant sexual assault jurisprudence.[60] The Prosecutor submitted two types of sex-based evidence: the first category went to proof of the jurisdictional or common elements needed to trigger Article 5's crimes against humanity, while the second category established the elements of the underlying act or provision of Article 5.

Witness Suada Ramić, a Bosnian Muslim woman,[61] testified to having been subject to multiple rapes and sexual abuse during the takeover and detention of Muslims in the Prijedor region. Her testimony, along with evidence of other witnesses, substantiated the general context of discrimination that existed

examples are *Furundžija* (para. 267—Croat soldier who was sexually tortured by being forced to witness sexual violence); and *Čelibići* (para. 471) and *Kvočka* (para. 154) (the Trial Chamber's acceptance of gender as a prohibited purpose under the elements of torture).

[59] *Tadić Judgment, supra* n. 9.

[60] The Prosecutor announced the withdrawal of Witness F, who, according to the indictment, was to have testified that the accused, Tadić, raped her in the Separacija building of Omarska camp. The Prosecutor, therefore, moved to withdraw Counts 2, 3, and 4 of the indictment. The Trial Chamber granted the motion. See *Tadić*, Prosecution Motion to Withdraw Counts 2 to 4 of the Indictment Without Prejudice, Case No. IT-94-1, T. Ch. II, 25 June 1996, in *Tadić Judgment, supra* n. 9, at para. 27. However, in *Kvočka*, the Trial Chamber noted that Witness F appeared and testified that she was taken to the Separacija building where she was forced to have sexual intercourse with Mirko Babić and Tadić: *Kvočka Judgment, supra* n. 14, at para. 100. In addition, during the *Tadić* trial, the Prosecutor invited the Trial Chamber to disregard the testimony of Witness L in regard to allegations of gang rapes committed by the accused and set out in para. 4.3 of the indictment, when the credibility of the witness was damaged on cross-examination. See *Tadić*, Order for the Prosecution to Investigate the False Testimony of Dragan Opacić, Case No. IT-94-1, T. Ch. II, 10 December 1996; *Tadić Judgment, supra* n. 9, at para. 33.

[61] Ramić testified that she had been subjected to rapes at the Prijedor military barracks, after which she was required to abort a four-month pregnancy. Upon returning home from the hospital, Ramić was raped by a Serb colleague, who searched her home. On the following day, she was arrested and taken to the police station by a Serb officer, where again she was raped. From the police station, she was transferred to the Keraterm camp and finally the Omarska camp. There, Ramić testified that she was raped on five occasions. *Tadić Judgment, supra* n. 9, at para. 470.

against non-Serbs.[62] The Appeals Chamber overturned the Trial Chamber's ruling that crimes against humanity required an element of discriminatory intent.[63] However, Ramić's testimony, minus its relevancy to discriminatory intent,[64] illustrated the nature of the attacks against the civilian population.

Indeed, Ramić's evidence did not allege an underlying crime, directly or indirectly, committed by the accused; instead, it described a facet of the attack against the civilian population—a context that the accused was aware existed and into which his specific crimes fitted. The Trial Chamber and Appeals Chamber accepted her evidence because it proved, in part, the jurisdictional elements, and thereby the applicability of the crimes against humanity provision of Article 5 of the ICTY Statute.[65]

Counts 8 to 11 of the *Tadić* indictment comprised the second category of sexual assaults—those alleged to have been the direct responsibility of the accused. It is the collective criminal conduct of the perpetrators of this second category of sexual assault evidence that drives our attention. In the *Tadić* case, where there was evidence of multiple beatings and sexual violence described in paragraph 6 of the indictment, the Trial Chamber opined that the collective criminal conduct was undertaken for a *common purpose*.

Paragraph 6 of the indictment reads, in part, that 'During the period between 1 June and 31 July 1992, a group of Serbs, including Duško Tadić, ... forced two other prisoners, G and H, to commit oral sexual acts on Harambasić and forced G to sexually mutilate him.'[66] The charges relating to these acts consisted of inhumane acts under Article 5(i), crimes against humanity; cruel treatment, as a violation of common Article 3(a), under Article 3; and torture and inhumane treatment under Article 2(b).

To prove the charges, the Prosecutor called Witness H, an anonymous witness.[67] Witness H recounted that he and Witness G, both male detainees in

---

[62] Ibid., at paras 473–7.

[63] *Tadić Appeals Judgment, supra* n. 11, at para. 305.

[64] The Trial Chamber legal findings concluded that 'an aspect of this conflict was a policy to commit inhumane acts against the civilian population of the territory, in particular the non-Serb population, in the attempt to create a Greater Serbia. In furtherance of this policy these inhumane acts were committed against numerous victims and pursuant to a recognisable plan. As such, the conditions of applicability for Article 5 are satisfied'. *Tadić Judgment, supra* n. 9, at para. 660. However, the Appeals Chamber understood the Prosecutor's argument appealing the imposition of a discriminatory element as not seeking 'to overturn the Trial Chamber's verdict or findings of fact in this regard', nor to invalidate the decision or claim a miscarriage of justice within the meaning of Article 25(1) of the Statute. *Tadić Appeals Judgment, supra* n. 11, at para. 281.

[65] *Tadić Judgment, supra* n. 9, at para. 660.

[66] *Tadić*, Second Amended Indictment, at para. 6.

[67] Witness anonymity, a witness protection measure granted under Rule 75 of the Rules of Procedure and Evidence, was granted to four witnesses, including Witness H. Anonymity as a protective measure allowed H to testify in closed session, shielded from the view of the accused, but in plain sight of defence counsel. Of the four witnesses granted anonymity, only two

the Omarska camp, were ordered to jump into an inspection pit, along with Fikret Harambasić, who was in a state of forced nudity and who was bleeding from having been beaten. The Trial Chamber observed that:

[W]itness H was ordered to lick his [Fikret Harambasić] naked bottom and G to suck his penis and then to bite his testicles. Meanwhile, a group of men in uniform stood around the inspection pit watching and shouting to bite harder. All three were then made to get out of the pit onto the hangar floor and Witness H was threatened with a knife that both his eyes would be cut out if he did not hold Fikret Harambasić's mouth closed to prevent him from screaming; G was then made to lie between the naked Fikret Harambasić's legs and, while the latter struggled, hit and bit his genitals. G then bit off one of Fikret Harambasić's testicles and spat it out and was told that he was free to leave.[68]

The sexual assaults culminating in mutilation were collective in that they were driven on by the group of men in uniform and the accused, Tadić, who demanded and encouraged the sexual violence. The victims were Harambasić, witnesses H and G, as well as the other detainees who had no choice but to watch. The *Tadić* trial offered the first view of collective sexually violent conduct wherein individual liability must be assessed.

The Trial Chamber, based upon the evidence, concluded that witnesses H and G were 'compelled to and did take part' in the sexual assault against detainee Harambasić as the prosecution alleged. Furthermore, it found that Witness G was 'compelled' to sexually mutilate Harambasić.[69] The Trial Chamber found that the witness testimony established the sexual assault conduct beyond a reasonable doubt. Whether the accused participated, or played any role in the sexual assaults, would depend upon further evaluation of Witness H and another detainee's testimony about the appalling incident.

As to Tadić's physical presence, Witness H frankly told the Trial Chamber that he did not see the accused that day and, moreover, that during the beating and sexual attack on Harambasić, he had 'kept his gaze mostly downwards because of fear'.[70] Another detainee, Halid Mujkanović, however, recounted that he saw the accused on the hangar floor when Harambasić was attacked and sexually assaulted.[71] The accused pleaded the defence of alibi, maintaining that he was not at the Omarska camp that day. The Trial Chamber found that the alibi lacked credibility.[72]

---

testified. Witness H was the only one who availed himself of anonymity as a protective measure. See Decision on the Prosecutor's Motion on Requesting Protective Measures for Victims and Witnesses; *Tadić*, Case No. IT-94-1, T.Ch. II, 10 August 1995.

[68] *Tadić Judgment, supra* n. 9, at para. 206.
[69] Ibid., at para. 198.
[70] Ibid., at para. 227.
[71] Ibid., at para. 222.
[72] Ibid., at para. 229.

The Trial Chamber then considered whether these acts, even if proved, could be attributed to Tadić utilizing Article 7(1) criteria.[73] It commenced the discussion of liability by recalling the Secretary-General's admonishment that 'all persons who participate in the planning, preparation or execution of serious violations of international humanitarian law... contribute to the violation and are, therefore, individually responsible'.[74] What neither the Secretary-General nor Article 7 specified, and thus left to the Trial Chamber, was the degree of participation necessary to trigger individual liability under customary international law.

A review of individual liability decisions in the post-World War II cases, supported a customary law recognition of personal culpability for principals, accessories to the commission of crimes,[75] those who are complicit,[76] or those who in pursuit of a common design to commit acts did wilfully, deliberately, and wrongfully aid, abet, and participate[77] in war crimes or crimes against humanity. Moreover, the Trial Chamber concluded that the Convention against Torture and Other Cruel, Inhuman or Degrading Treatment or Punishment[78] condemns persons who are complicit or who participate in torture,[79] and that the International Convention on the Suppression and Punishment of the Crime of Apartheid[80] condemns those who 'participate in, directly incite, or conspire in, or directly abet, encourage or cooperate in the commission' of apartheid.[81] These two international criminal instruments illustrate personal liability and forms of participation that reside in customary international law. The Trial Chamber then resolved that under the authority granted by the Security Council it could find Tadić guilty as a principal, or as an accessory to a crime.

The Trial Chamber opined that where an accused did not directly commit the offences but was 'present at the time of, or otherwise involved in their commission', in order to hold such an accused personally liable it would have

---

[73] According to the indictment, the prosecution did not allege that Dusko Tadić was a superior, either military or civilian. Thus, his liability never contemplated Article 7(3) responsibility (see pp. 161–2).

[74] *Tadić Judgment, supra* n. 9, at para. 661.

[75] Article II, 2 of Control Council No. 10, cited in *Tadić Judgment, supra* n. 9, at para. 665.

[76] *Trial of Wagner and Six Others*, Vol. III Law Reports 24, 40–2, 94–5, cited in *Tadić Judgment, supra* n. 9, at para. 667.

[77] *Trial of Martin Gottfried Weiss and 39 Others (Dachau* case*)*, Vol. XI Law Reports 5, cited in *Tadić Judgment, supra* n. 9, at para. 668.

[78] Convention against Torture and Other Cruel, Inhuman or Degrading Treatment or Punishment, adopted 10 December 1984, entered into force 26 June 1987, GA Res. 39/46, 39 UN GAOR, Supp. (No. 51) UN Doc. A/39/51, at 197 (1984).

[79] Ibid., at Article 4(1).

[80] International Convention on the Suppression and Punishment of the Crime of Apartheid, adopted 30 November 1973, entered into force 18 July 1976, GA Res. 3068 (XXVIII), 1015 UNTS 243.

[81] Ibid., at Article III.

to be satisfied that his conduct sufficiently connected him to the crime. Again, the Trial Chamber sought guidance from the World War II trials[82] and observed that the International Law Commission Draft Code had distilled the customary basis of personal liability derived from those post-war trials by attributing culpability, *inter alia*, to one who 'knowingly aids, abets or otherwise assists, directly or substantially in the commission of such a crime'.[83] The Trial Chamber thus determined that the appropriate form of liability under Article 7(1) was aiding and abetting. It held that:

[A]iding and abetting includes all acts of assistance by words or acts that lend encouragement or support, as long as the requisite intent is present. Under this theory, presence alone is not sufficient if it is ignorant or unwilling presence. However, if the presence can be shown or inferred, by circumstantial or other evidence, to be knowing and to have a direct and substantial effect on the commission of the illegal act, then it is sufficient on which to base a finding of participation and assign the criminal culpability that accompanies it.

Moreover, when an accused is present and participates in the beating of one person and remains with the group when it moves on to beat another person, his presence would have an encouraging effect, even it he does not physically take part in this second beating, and he should be viewed as participating in this second beating as well. This is assuming that the accused has not actively withdrawn from the group or spoken out against the conduct of the group.[84]

Returning to the legal findings, the *Tadić* Trial Chamber determined the subject matter jurisdiction or legal characterization of the acts and individual criminal responsibility of Tadić. It held that the acts of sexual violence charged under Count 10 conformed to the subject matter jurisdiction of Article 3, the violations of the laws and customs of war, as recognized by common Article 3(1) of the Geneva Conventions, namely, cruel treatment. It further held that under Count 11, mutilation typified 'inhumane acts' within the meaning of Article 5(i) crimes against humanity. In regard to the second prong of the dual duty, individual responsibility, the Trial Chamber stated:

The Trial Chamber finds beyond a reasonable doubt that those beating and other acts of [*inter alia*] sexual violence were suffered by the six victims . . . [and] further finds that the accused in some instances was himself the perpetrator and in others intentionally assisted directly and substantially in the *common purpose of inflicting physical*

---

[82] The Trial Chamber examined cases that dealt with the participation of various accused who were not the principal agents of death, but who contributed to the death of camp inmates or prisoners of war: these included the *Trial of Werner Rohde and Eight Others*, Vol. XV Law Reports 51; the *Trial of Joseph Altstotter and Others (Justice case)*, Vol. VI Law Reports 88; the *Trial of Bruno Tesch and Two Others (Zyklon B case)*, Vol. I Law Reports 93; the *Trial of Max Wielen and 17 Others*, Vol. XI Law Reports, 43–4, 46.

[83] ILC Draft Code Article 2(3)(a) and (d), cited in *Tadić Judgment, supra* n. 9, at para. 688.

[84] *Tadić Judgment, supra* n. 9, at paras 689–90.

suffering upon them and thereby aided and abetted in the commission of the crimes and is therefore individually responsible for each of them as provided by Article 7, paragraph 1, of the Statute.[85]

Although the Trial Chamber does not voice the need to identify the principal perpetrator of the sexual violence, it is convinced that Tadić did aid and abet the commission of the crimes of cruel treatment and inhumane act. As such, the Trial Chamber's ultimate Article 7 determination of Tadić's liability falls squarely within 'aided or abetted in the preparation, planning, or execution of a crime', an express mode of liability. Having satisfied proof of the subject matter jurisdiction and the personal jurisdiction through examination of Article 7 liability, the Trial Chamber can pronounce Tadić guilty of the charges.[86]

However, it is the Trial Chamber's description of the accused's criminal conduct that furthered the group's common purpose—inflicting physical suffering on the detainees—that is pertinent. Notably, in the Tribunal's first judgment, a Trial Chamber recognized that a group of perpetrators can unite in a common criminal purpose to inflict sexual violence, and that other perpetrators can aid and abet this common purpose. Ironically, in July 1999, when the *Tadić* Appeals Chamber crystallized common purpose participation as an Article 7 form of liability, the incidents of the indictment's paragraph 6, replete with sexual violence, are not revisited. The first direct outgrowth of the *Tadić* Trial Chamber's holdings on common purpose liability is taken up in the *Furundžija* Judgment, rendered in December 1998.

B. *Prosecutor v Furundžija*

The *Furundžija* case concerned events that transpired outside Vitez, a town in the Lasva Valley region of Bosna Herzog.[87] Atrocities in the Lasva Valley have generated five Tribunal prosecutions to date.[88] The *Furundžija* case is the only

[85] Ibid., at para. 730 (emphasis added).
[86] Tadić was found guilty of Counts 10 and 11, in regard to the sexual assaults. Tadić was acquitted on Counts 8 and 9 because the Prosecutor had not proved beyond a reasonable doubt that the victims were protected persons, as required by Article 2 of the Statute. *Tadić Judgment*, *supra* n. 9, at paras 720, 726, 730.
[87] Bosna Herzog is the name for the Bosnian-Croat territory of the former territory of Bosnia and Herzegovina.
[88] Allegations of crimes committed in the Lasva Valley during the armed conflict between Bosnian-Croats and Bosnian Muslims were the subject of the following cases: *Prosecutor v Blaškić*, Judgment, Case No. IT-95-14-T, 3 March 2000 (hereinafter '*Blaškić Judgment*'); *Prosecutor v Kupreškić et al.*, Judgment, Case No. IT-95-16-T, 14 January 2000; *Prosecutor v Dario Kordić and Mario Čerkez*, Judgment, Case No. IT-95-14/2-T, 26 February 2001 (hereinafter '*Kordić Judgment*'); *Prosecutor v Aleksovski*, Judgment, Case No. IT-95-14/T, 25 June 1999; and *Furundžija Judgment*, *supra* n. 10.

Lasva Valley case expressly to allege sexual violence[89] and, moreover, sex-based crimes perpetrated by the collective conduct of an accused and an unnamed accused.

By April 1992, the complete Bosnian-Croat political control of Vitez was enforced by the HVO military. Bosnian Muslims who lived in Vitez and the surrounding area suffered arbitrary arrests, detention, and were subjected to other forms of cruel treatment by HVO soldiers. In mid-April 1992, the HVO military police, commonly known as the 'Jokers', arrested Witness A, a Bosnian Muslim woman who lived in Vitez. She was transported to the Jokers' headquarters, 'the Bungalow', for questioning. Upon arrival at the Bungalow, Witness A was taken to the Jokers' sleeping quarters and instructed to wait for Furundžija, the 'Boss'.

Witness A testified that Furundžija interrogated her while Accused B physically assaulted her. Later into the interrogation, Furundžija would confront Witness A with Witness D, a Bosnian-Croat soldier who was suspected of being a traitor by the Jokers. The amended indictment charged Furundžija with violations of the laws and customs of war, namely, the war crimes of torture and outrages upon personal dignity, including rape.

The Trial Chamber summarized its factual finding, as follows:

Witness A was interrogated by the accused. She was forced by Accused B to undress and remain naked before a substantial number of soldiers. She was subjected to cruel, inhuman and degrading treatment and to threats of serious physical assault by Accused B in the course of her interrogation by the accused. The purpose of this abuse was to extract information from Witness A about her family, her connection with the ABiH and her relationship with certain Croatian soldiers, and also to degrade and humiliate her. The interrogation by the accused and the abuse by the Accused B were parallel to each other.

Witness A was left by the accused in the custody of Accused B, who proceeded to rape her, sexually assault her, and to physically abuse and degrade her . . .

The interrogation of Witness A continued in the pantry, once more before an audience of soldiers. Whilst naked, but covered by a small blanket, she was interrogated by the accused. She was subjected to rape, sexual assaults, and cruel, inhuman and degrading treatment by Accused B. Witness D was also interrogated by the accused and subjected to serious physical assaults by Accused B. He was made to watch rape and sexual assaults perpetrated upon a women whom he knew, in order to force him to admit allegations made against her. In this regard, both witnesses were humiliated.

Accused B beat Witness D and repeatedly raped Witness A. The accused was present in the room as he carried out the interrogations. When not in the room, he was present in the near vicinity, just outside an open door, and he knew that crimes including rape were being committed. In fact, the acts by Accused B were performed in pursuance of the accused's interrogation.[90]

[89] The Trial Chamber in *Blaškić*, however, held the accused liable for the sexual violence committed by HVO forces against civilians who were detained under his control in the Dubravica School. *Blaškić Judgment, supra* n. 88, at para. 732.

[90] *Furundžija Judgment, supra* n. 10, at paras 124–8.

After deliberation upon Witness A's and Witness D's testimony, the Trial Chamber was satisfied that she, as well as Witness D, had been tortured.[91] Furthermore, the Trial Chamber found that Witness A had been raped and thus upheld the charge of outrages upon personal dignity, including rape as alleged in Count 14:

[M]embers of the Jokers were watching. . . . They laughed at what was going on. The Trial Chamber finds that Witness A suffered severe physical and mental pain, along with public humiliation, at the hands of the accused in what amounted to outrages upon her personal dignity.[92]

To arrive at a finding of guilt, the Trial Chamber examined the acts or omissions of the accused and his individual responsibility. Succinctly stated, Furundžija was held responsible under Article 7(1) as a co-perpetrator of torture and, also under Article 7(1), as an aider and abettor of rape. How the Trial Chamber examined the accused's participation in the torture and rape, both in cooperation with and in contrast to the participation of Accused B, leads us to a major theme of this article—examining liability for collective criminal conduct.

The conduct of participants in modern torture systems varies, intentionally. Ironically, to shield them, not the victims, from the onerous moral and psychological burden of torture, different individuals often perform distinct duties in a torture system. The Trial Chamber painstakingly described the operative, collective criminality that torturers exercise:

Thus, one person orders that torture be carried out, another organises the whole process at the administrative level, another asks the question while the detainee is being tortured, a fourth one provides or prepares the tools for executing torture, another physically inflicts torture or causes mental suffering, another furnishes medical assistance so as to prevent the detainee from dying as a consequence of torture or from subsequently showing traces of the sufferings he has undergone, another processes the results of interrogation known to be obtained under torture, and another procures the information gained as a result in exchange for granting the torturer immunity from prosecution.[93]

Cognizant of torture's modern manifestation, the Trial Chamber opined that a teleological interpretation of the customary rules governing torture and of

---

[91] The Trial Chamber, after a lengthy examination of international customary law, held that the elements of torture (i) consist of the infliction, by act or omission, of severe pain or suffering, whether physical or mental; in addition (ii) this act must be intentional; (iii) it must aim at obtaining information or a confession, or at punishing, intimidating, humiliating, or coercing the victim or a third person, or at discriminating, on any ground, against the victim or a third person; (iv) it must be linked to an armed conflict; (v) at least one of the persons involved in the torture must be a public official, or must at any rate act in a non-private capacity, e.g. as a *de facto* organ of a state or any other authority-wielding entity.

[92] *Furundžija Judgment, supra* n. 10, at para. 272.

[93] Ibid., at para. 253.

international law was necessary to 'cope with this despicable practice'.[94] Neither the administrative or psychological dilution, nor compartmentalization of a torturer's role could absolve one of liability. The least implicated, when participation is established, should benefit only from imprisonment commensurate with the degree of culpable participation.

The Trial Chamber stated that, when participation rises to the level of co-perpetration, 'it is crucial to ascertain whether the individual who takes part in the torture process also *partakes of the purpose behind the torture*'.[95] Axiomatically, if one does not partake of the torture purpose, there is no individual liability under the rubric of co-perpetrator. Earlier in the judgment,[96] the Trial Chamber set forth the elements of torture, including the prohibited purposes of torture, that distinguish torture from other forms of ill-treatment.[97] To ascribe to the torture purpose meant that the perpetrator 'acts with the intention of obtaining information or a confession, of punishing, intimidating, humiliating or coercing the victim or a third person, or discriminating on any ground, against a victim or a third person'.[98]

In the Trial Chamber's view, Furundžija acted collectively with Accused B, yet each accused performed a different task:

The Trial Chamber is satisfied that the accused was present in the large room and interrogated Witness A, whilst she was in a state of forced nudity. As she was being interrogated, Accused B rubbed his knife on the inner thighs of Witness A and threatened to cut out her private parts if she did not tell the truth in answer to the interrogation by the accused. The accused did not stop his interrogation, which eventually culminated in his threatening to confront Witness A with another person, meaning Witness D and that she would then confess to the allegations against her. To this extent, the interrogation by the accused and the activities of Accused B became *one process*.

... Both Witness A and D were interrogated by the accused and hit on the feet with a baton by Accused B in the course of this questioning. Accused B again assaulted Witness A who was still naked, before an audience of soldiers.... The accused continued to interrogate Witness A in the same manner as he had done earlier in the large room. *As the interrogation intensified, so did the sexual assaults and the rape.*[99]

Furundžija's participation embodied the 'other' who asks questions while the detainee is being tortured. As stated in the factual summary, '[t]here is no doubt that the accused and Accused B, as commanders, divided the process of interrogation by performing different functions. The role of the accused was to question, while Accused B's role was to assault and threaten'.[100]

Although torture purposes such as humiliation, intimidation, coercion, as well as discrimination, punishment, or confession were recognized, the Trial Chamber stressed the purpose of obtaining information. It stated, repeatedly,

[94] *Furundžija Judgment, supra* n. 10, at para. 254.   [95] Ibid., at para. 252.
[96] Ibid., at paras 134–64.   [97] Ibid., at para. 162.   [98] Ibid., at para. 252.
[99] Ibid., at paras 264–6 (emphasis added).   [100] Ibid., at para. 130.

that the intention of Furundžija as well as Accused B 'was to obtain information which they believed would benefit the HVO'[101] from Witness A, on Bosnian Muslim military affairs, and from Witness D for his purported betrayal of the HVO. In sum, co-perpetration liability under Article 7(1) was attributed to Furundžija because his interrogation was an 'integral part of the torture' and both accused participated in the torture to obtain information.

However, the Trial Chamber's expressed judgment that co-perpetration depended upon partaking in the (torture) purpose generated short-lived confusion. The *Furundžija* judges readily surmised that shared purpose is necessary for co-perpetration of torture. Torture, a crime the very elements of which require proof of a prohibited purpose, easily fits, and probably spurred the prerequisite language of 'partaking in the purpose'. Why did the *Furundžija* judges enunciate the purpose requirement in such a narrow sense? If Accused B acted to discriminate against Witness A because of ethnicity and punish Witness D as a traitor, while Furundžija acted to obtain information from them, would they have been viewed as co-perpetrators? Moreover, how would judges and the parties decipher a shared purpose, if an underlying purpose were not a distinct element of the crime?

Tadić had addressed collective criminal conduct for sexual violence and underlined that the perpetrators exhibited, by their acts, the *common purpose of inflicting physical suffering.*[102] The *Tadić* common purpose appears broader, more descriptive of the harm inflicted, and not explicitly pegged to an element of the alleged crimes. Although it is arguable that the war crime, cruel treatment, and inhumane acts as a crime against humanity require infliction of serious injury, it is not evident that the *Tadić* Trial Chamber bore in mind this legal construct of common purpose.[103] Nevertheless, could not *Furundžija* have required either a partaking in the intentional infliction of physical or mental harm, *or* the torture purposes?

Furundžija's conviction for rape, while illustrative of the legal demarcation between aiding and abetting and co-perpetration as forms of liability, sheds little light on these inquiries. In a lengthy discussion bolstered by the case law from the trials subsequent to World War II,[104] the Trial Chamber determined

---

[101] Ibid., at para. 265.

[102] *Tadić Judgment, supra* n. 9, at n. 75.

[103] The *Tadić* Trial Chamber opined that 'cruel treatment such as torture, mutilation, or any form of corporal punishment was prohibited': *Tadić Judgment, supra* n. 9, at para. 725. More recent jurisprudence has held that cruel treatment is 'an intentional act or omission, that is an act which, judged objectively, is deliberate and not accidental, which causes serious mental or physical suffering or injury or constitutes a serious attack on human dignity': *Krstić Judgment, supra* n. 13, at para. 516.

[104] The Trial Chamber relied in part upon the *Trial of Otto Ohlendorf and others (Einsatzgruppen)*, in *Trial of War Criminals Before the Nuremberg Military Tribunals under Control Council Law No. 10, Vol. IV,* and the *Zyklon B* case, *supra* n. 82, p. 93.

that Furundžija's physical presence during the sexual violence, similar to Tadić's, offered encouragement or moral support that had a substantial effect on the perpetration of the rapes committed by Accused B. Furthermore, Furundžija possessed the requisite *mens rea* for aiding and abetting, because he knew that Accused B was committing rapes while he offered support. Indeed he was present. The Trial Chamber stated, obliquely, that the accused 'did not personally rape Witness A, nor can he be considered, under the circumstances of this case, to be a co-perpetrator'.[105] Thus the Trial Chamber concluded that:

[T]he presence of the accused and his continued interrogation aided and abetted the crimes committed by Accused B. He is individually responsible for outrages upon personal dignity including rape, a violation of the laws or customs of war under Article 3 of the Statute.[106]

The Trial Chamber did not examine Furundžija's actions beyond the scope of facilitation, recalling the rationale of the accused's conviction in *Tadić* for aiding and abetting sexual violence. In *Tadić*, whilst the physical perpetrators were Muslim detainees, those whom Tadić aided and abetted were the non-physical (co-)perpetrators or principals. The *Furundžija* Trial Chamber did not attribute a common purpose to Accused B, nor did it suggest a purpose behind the rapes.[107] Was that because only Accused B physically committed the rapes and rape must have a physical co-perpetrator, or because the crime of rape does not require proof of a purpose?

Co-perpetration, as designated in *Furundžija*, is the first time the ICTY 'named' this aspect of Article 7(1) responsibility, even though its existence ostensibly flows from 'committed', an express form of Article 7(1) liability. Common purpose under *Tadić* and co-perpetration under *Furundžija* were

---

[105] *Furundžija Judgment, supra* n. 10, at para. 273.

[106] Ibid., at para. 274.

[107] According to the *Furundžija* Trial Chamber, the elements of rape comprise: (1) the sexual penetration, however slight, (a) of the vagina or anus of the victim by the penis of the perpetrator or any other object used by the perpetrator; or (b) of the mouth of the victim by the penis of the perpetrator; (2) coercion or force against the victim or a third person. The *Furundžija* definition represented a departure from the *Akayesu* and *Čelebići* Trial Chamber definitions, which held rape to be 'a physical invasion of a sexual nature committed on a person under circumstances which are coercive'. Subsequent Trial Chambers, most notably in *Kunarac*, have modified the *Furundžija* definition and interpreted the element of coercion and force to necessitate the addition of a *mens rea* requirement, namely, that the perpetrator had the 'intention to effect this sexual penetration, and the knowledge that it occurs without the consent of the victim': *Kunarac Judgment, supra* n. 40, at para. 460. In the Appeals Chamber Judgment of the *Prosecutor v Kunarac*, Judgment, Case Nos IT-96-23 & IT-96-23/A, 12 July 2002, at paras 127–33 (hereinafter '*Kunarac Appeals Judgment*'), the definition of rape pronounced by the Trial Chamber was upheld, with the proviso that non-consensual and non-voluntary must be understood to be examined in light of the facts demonstrating any type of coercive circumstances.

the embryonic stages of what would evolve into joint criminal enterprise or common purpose tenets, and that would resolve more complex factual settings about collective sexual assault conduct. That growth is found in the *Tadić* Appeals judgment.

C. Common Purpose in the *Tadić* Appeals Judgment

Tadić lodged several grounds of appeal,[108] but did not directly appeal his conviction for cruel treatment or inhumane acts for the male sexual violence. The prosecution cross-appealed the accused's acquittal of the murder of five villagers from Jaskici. The Prosecutor accepted the findings of fact, but asserted that the Trial Chamber erred because it misdirected application of the common purpose doctrine when it held that:

This Trial Chamber is satisfied beyond a reasonable doubt that the accused was a member of the group of armed men that entered the village of Jaskici, searched it for men, seized them, beat them, and then departed with them and that after their departure the five dead men named in the indictment were found lying in the village . . . However, this Trial Chamber cannot, on the evidence before it, be satisfied beyond reasonable doubt that the accused had any part in the killing of the five men or any of them. Save that four of them were shot in the head, nothing is known as to who shot them or in what circumstances. . . . The fact that there was no killing at Sivici could suggest that the killing of villagers was not a planned part of this particular episode of ethnic cleansing of the two villages, in which the accused took part; it is accordingly a distinct possibility that it may have been the act of a distinct group of armed men, or the unauthorized and unforeseen act of one of the forces that entered Sivici, for which the accused cannot be held responsible, that caused their death.[109]

Interestingly, at the trial level, the common purpose doctrine was not articulated in the legal findings in regard to the Jaskici murders. The Appeals Chamber, however, used the Prosecutor's appellate ground to examine the common purpose doctrine under international law and to chisel its parameters within Article 7(1) of the Statute.

First the Appeals Chamber asked whether an accused can be liable for acts arising from the 'criminal culpability of another where both participate in a criminal plan'.[110] The inquiry aimed to delimit the *in personam* reach of the ICTY Statute, in light of the Secretary-General's view that '*all* persons who participate . . . in serious violations of international humanitarian law . . . are

---

[108] The Appellant raised inequality of arms, resulting in a denial of a fair trial, and error of fact leading to a miscarriage of justice.

[109] *Tadić Judgment, supra* n. 9, at para. 373.

[110] *Tadić Appeals Judgment, supra* n. 11, at para. 185.

individually responsible'.[111] Article 7(1) extends personal jurisdiction over a person who planned, instigated, ordered, committed, or otherwise aided and abetted in the planning, preparation, or execution, who shall be individually responsible for the crime. There is no explicit form of liability for, say, conspiracy that necessitates more than one perpetrator; however, neither is there an express restriction on exercising jurisdiction over persons who act jointly.[112] The Appeals Chamber, mindful of the gap between the Secretary-General's intent and the plain language of Article 7(1), sought to discern the customary law basis of the common purpose doctrine that could implement the Statute's purpose and objective.

Secondly, the Appeals Chamber's query begged for a coherent description of this wartime conduct, not born from the propensity of single individuals but that constituted manifestations of collective criminality.[113]

The carefully crafted response incorporated international, post-World War II cases[114] and domestic legal experiences, and concluded that common purpose[115] derived from customary law and resided, albeit implicitly, in Article 7(1). The common purpose doctrine can be divided into three distinct categories of co-perpetration that differ not only because of the factual nature of the crime, but, more importantly, because of the accused's possession of specific *mens rea*. First, cases of co-perpetration, where all participants in the common design possess the same criminal intent to commit a crime (and one or more of them actually perpetrate the crime, with intent). Secondly, the so-called 'concentration camp' cases, where the requisite *mens rea* comprises knowledge of the nature of the system of ill-treatment and intent to further the common design of ill-treatment. Such intent may be proved directly, or as a matter of inference from the nature of the accused's authority within the camp or organizational hierarchy.

With regard to the third category of cases, it is appropriate to apply the notion of 'common purpose' only where the following requirements concerning *mens rea* are fulfilled: (i) the intention to take part in a joint criminal enterprise and to further—individually and jointly—the criminal purpose of

---

[111] Report, *supra* n. 6, at para. 54 (emphasis added).

[112] ICTY Statute, *supra* n. 2, at Article 7.

[113] *Tadić Appeals Judgment*, *supra* n. 11, at para. 191.

[114] With regard to category one, the Appeals Chamber reviewed the reasoning in *Trial of Otto Sandrock and three others*, British Military Court for the Trial of War Criminals, held at the Court House, Amelo, Holland, on 24–6 November 1945, UNWCC, vol. I (*Amelo* Case); *Hoelzer et al.*, Canadian Military Court, Aurich, Germany, Record of the Proceedings 25 March–6 April 1946, vol. I (RCAF Binder 181, 009) (D2474). With regard to category three, the Appeals Chamber examined *Trial of Erich Heyer and six others*, British Military Court for the Trial of War Criminals, Essen, 18–19 and 21–22 December, 1945, UNWCC, vol. 1 (*Essen Lynching* case).

[115] In this instance the Appeals Chamber uses, interchangeably, the terms 'common design', 'common purpose', 'joint criminal enterprise'; *Tadić Appeals Judgment*, *supra* n. 11, at para. 220.

that enterprise; and (ii) the foreseeability of the possible commission by other members of the group of offences that do not constitute the objects of the common criminal purpose. Hence, the participants must have had in mind the intentention, for instance, to ill-treat prisoners of war (even if the plan arose extemporaneously), and one or some members of the group must have actually killed them. In order for responsibility for the deaths to be imputable to the others, however, everyone in the group must have been able to *predict* this result. What is required is a state of mind in which a person, although he did not intend to bring about a certain result, was aware that the actions of the group were most likely to lead to that result but nevertheless willingly took the risk.[116]

The first category is a straightforward instance of group criminality wherein all actors intend to commit a crime and participate in an aspect of the crime, such as Furundžija's co-perpetration of torture. The second category, given the historical background of 'concentration camp jurisprudence', considers the typical actions of accused in an operative system of collective criminality.[117]

The *actus reus* of the common purpose doctrine is satisfied when there exist: plurality of persons; a plan, design, or purpose that may have been previously arranged or that may materialize extemporaneously; and participation of the accused in the common purpose by commission, or assistance in, or contribution to a specific crime under the Statute.[118]

When the Appeals Chamber applied its common purpose doctrine to the case at hand, it turned to the third category of common purpose. Tadić was deemed to have actively taken part in the common purpose that consisted of 'inflicting inhumane acts to get rid of the non-Serbs population of Prijedor'.[119] Even though the Appeals Chamber held that the criminal purpose was not to kill all non-Serb men,[120] it found beyond doubt that the appellant was aware of the killings accompanying the commission of inhumane acts against the non-Serb population.[121] The Appeals Chamber then observed, 'that non-Serb might be killed in effecting of this common aim was, in the circumstances of the present case, foreseeable. The Appellant was aware that the actions of the group of which he was a member were likely to lead to such killings, but he nevertheless willingly took the risk.'[122] Tadić was convicted for

---

[116] Ibid., at para. 222.
[117] The camp cases examined included the *Trial of Martin Gottfried Weiss and 39 Others*, General Military Court of the United States Zone, Dachau, Germany, 15 November–13 December, 1945, UNWCC, vol. XI (*Dachau* case); *Trial of Josef Kramer and 44 Others*, British Military Court, Luneberg, 17 September–17 December 1945, UNWCC, vol. II. P.1 (*Belsen* case).
[118] *Tadić Appeals Judgment, supra* n. 11, at para. 227.
[119] Ibid., at para. 231.
[120] Ibid.
[121] Ibid.
[122] Ibid., at para. 232.

the Jaskici murders under the common purpose doctrine implicitly contained in Article 7(1). Upon remand to the Trial Chamber for sentencing, Tadić eventually received 20 years for the murders.[123]

The Appeals Chamber revisited the application of the common purpose doctrine in the *Furundžija* appeals judgment.

D. Common Purpose in the *Furundžija* Appeals Judgment

Furundžija likewise lodged several grounds of appeal, including one that questioned whether the conduct charged substantively rose to the level of torture. The Appeals Chamber tersely ruled that it

[F]inds this element of the ground to be unmeritorious. It also finds it inconceivable that it could ever be argued that the acts charged... namely, the rubbing of a knife against a woman's thighs and stomach, coupled with a threat to insert the knife into her vagina, once proven, are not serious enough to amount to torture.[124]

The appellant further questioned whether his liability for torture had been established. Furundžija argued that co-perpetration of torture had not been proved because there existed no direct connection between his questioning and the mental or physical pain of Witness A. Furundžija also asked for relief because there was no proof that he *intentionally acted in concert* with Accused B in questioning Witness A.

In denying both grounds, the Appeals Chamber affirmed, and ultimately interpreted, a broader factual scope of common purpose for the crime of torture than that articulated in *Furundžija* at the trial stage. The Appeals Chamber restated what the lower chamber concluded, that a co-perpetrator must participate in an integral part of the torture and partake of one of the prohibited torture purposes.[125] However, in referring to the intervening *Tadić* jurisprudence, the Appeals Chamber re-emphasized that there is no necessity for a previously arranged plan, since the common purpose 'may materialise extemporaneously and be inferred from the fact that a plurality of persons acts in unison'.[126]

Applying the appellate jurisprudence to the *Furundžija* facts, the Appeals Chamber held that there was 'no need for evidence proving the existence of a prior agreement'[127] wherein it was agreed that the appellant would ask the

---

[123] See the Trial Chamber sentence of 25 years in *Prosecutor v Duško Tadić*, Case Nos. IT-94-1-A and IT-94-1-A*bis*-R117, Sentencing Judgment, which was reduced to 20 years in *Prosecutor v Duško Tadić*, Case Nos IT-94-1-A and IT-94-1-A*bis*, Judgment in Sentencing Appeals, 26 January 2000.

[124] *Furudžija Appeals Judgment, supra* n. 12, at para. 114.

[125] Ibid., at para. 118.

[126] Ibid., at para. 119.

[127] Ibid.

questions and Accused B would inflict the physical harm. The events themselves precluded any reasonable doubt that a common purpose existed. The Appeals Chamber then stated that *all the circumstances* led to the inference that the named and unnamed accused participated in a common purpose. These included:

(1) The interrogation of Witness A by the Appellant in both the Large Room while she was in a state of nudity, and the Pantry where she was sexually assaulted in the Appellant's presence; and, (2) the acts of sexual assault committed by Accused B on Witness A in both rooms.[128]

Here the Appeals Chamber seemingly modified the Trial Chamber's holding that evidence of common purpose solely entailed identifying the joint prohibited purpose. Certainly, if two torturers acted to obtain information, or punish or coerce the same victim or a third person, such actions would point to a common purpose. Conspicuously, the Appeals Chamber extended the evidentiary scope to encompass intertwined actions, such as the fact that one torturer asks questions while the other demands that the victim undress. Under the second example, the Appeals Chamber appears to be of the opinion that common purpose is implied by the *very acts of sexual violence* performed by Accused B in the second phase of the interrogation, since the torture process was a continuum. The Appeals Chamber approach, reminiscent of the Trial Chamber's description of the operative, collective criminality of modern torturers, holds material *all* aspects of the torture process.

The concluding remarks leave little doubt that a myriad of factual circumstances may imply the presence of a plan or common purpose between co-perpetrators. The Appeals Chamber rejected the Appellant's argument, observing that:

Where the act of one accused contributes to the purpose of the other, and both acted simultaneously, in the same place and within full view of the other, over a prolonged period of time, the argument that there was no common purpose is plainly unsustainable.[129]

The more global factual analysis is particularly beneficial to collective acts of sexual violence. Stressing the collective conduct of perpetrators, such as simultaneity of acts, time span of acts, and acceptance that one torturer can contribute to the 'purpose of the other torturer', again underscores the fact that wartime sexual violence is often not restricted to physical perpetrators.

Under this analysis, the rapes committed by Accused B might have been ruled to be an extemporaneously materalized plan. Furundžija, by prolonging

---

[128] Ibid., at para. 120.   [129] Ibid., at para. 119.

the interrogation in the pantry and by forcing Witness D to watch the rapes, contributes to Accused B's intention to commit rapes. As evidenced by his acts, Furundžija could have intended the rapes to occur, although he was not and never intended to be the physical perpetrator. The *Furundžija* appeals analysis might also have supported the conclusion that the undifferentiated collective conduct of Tadić and the unnamed guards in the hangar made them liable as co-perpetrators for the sexual mutilation of the male detainees.

Nevertheless, a fuller and more legally astute articulation of the common purpose doctrine has been developed from this appellate jurisprudence. In a case that did not involve sexual violence, the *Kordić and Čerkez* judgment, two accused were convicted of participation in a common design to persecute non-Bosnian-Croats in the Lasva Valley.[130] Kordić, a politician, was found to have been involved in planning and preparing parts of the campaign,[131] while Čerkez, a mid-ranking soldier, commanded some of the troops involved in the campaign.[132] *Kordić* was significant for the application of common purpose to a high-level political and mid-level military leader. It is two subsequent cases, *Krstić* and *Kvočka*, that would provide the occasion to apply common purpose, categories two and three, to crimes of sexual violence.

E. Natural and Foreseeable Consequences in *Prosecutor v Krstić*

The Srebrenica massacre represents the nadir of the armed conflict in the former Yugoslavia. As poignantly stated in the *Krstić* judgment, 'the nine days from July 10–19 1995 defy description in their horror and their implications for humankind's capacity to revert to acts of brutality under the stress of conflict'.[133] Srebrenica, the United Nations-designated safe-haven for Bosnian Muslims in eastern Bosnia, was attacked and captured. While over 25,000 Bosnian Muslims, mainly women, elderly men, and children, were 'uprooted in an atmosphere of terror' and expelled behind the Bosnian Muslim-held lines, the Drina Corps of the Bosnian-Serb Army (the VRS) systematically executed over 7,000 military-age Bosnian males.

General Radislav Krstić was the Chief of Staff and then acceded to the position of Commander of the Drina Corps during the crucial time of the massacre. The Prosecutor did not indict General Krstić for the military

---

[130] *Kordić Judgment, supra* n. 88.

[131] Ibid., at para. 829.

[132] Ibid., at para. 831. What is notable in the convictions of Kordić and Čerkez, is that their participation consisted only of performing Article 7(1)-type tasks, ordering, planning, preparing, that could otherwise be viewed as modes of liability for the underlying acts provided for in Articles 2–5 of the Statute.

[133] *Krstić Judgment, supra* n. 13, at para. 2.

invasion of Srebrenica; rather, it indicted him for genocide[134] and for several provisions under crimes against humanity[135] because of his role in the aftermath of the invasion. The aftermath consisted of two distinct stages: the expulsion of the women, elderly men, and children; and the killing of the remaining men.

The second stage, the murder of the Bosnian-Muslim males, has, and rightly so, received the intense worldwide attention that these horrific events warrant. The Trial Chamber ultimately found that General Krstić, together with General Mladić and the VRS Main Staff, were co-perpetrators in a joint criminal enterprise, the alternative phrase of common purpose, to forcibly 'cleanse' the Srebrenica safe area. The findings conclude that in addition to forcible transfer of some Bosnian-Muslims, mainly women, the joint criminal enterprise undertook a campaign to kill the military-aged men and perman-ently eradicate the Bosnian-Muslim population from Srebrenica. After being satisfied that the execution had been proved, the Trial Chamber established that General Krstić knew that Muslim men were being killed at various locations and that the joint criminal objective of forcible transfers had evolved into a 'lethal plan' of destruction of the male population.[136]

In addition, the Trial Chamber held that General Krstić participated in the killing plan through the 'tangible and substantial assistance and technical sup-port'[137] given by the Drina Corps. Analogous to the multiple actors required to execute the torture process, the Drina Corps had been utilized for its 'resources and expertise for the complicated operations like ... detentions, executions and burials' in the territory it controlled. The Trial Chamber concluded that:

[B]eyond a reasonable doubt, General Krstić participated in a joint criminal enter-prise to kill the Bosnian Muslim military-aged men from Srebrenica from the evening of 13 July onward. General Krstić may not have devised the killing plan, or partici-pated in the initial decision to escalate the objective of the criminal enterprise from forcible transfer to destruction of Srebrenica's Bosnian Muslim military-aged male community, but there can be no doubt that, from the point he learned of the

---

[134] The provisions of the Convention for the Suppression and Punishment of Genocide, as incorporated into Article 4 of the ICTY Statute, are in part as follows:

2. Genocide means any of the following acts committed with intent to destroy, in whole or part, a national, ethnical, racial or religious group, as such:
   (a) killing members of the group;
   (b) causing serious bodily or mental harm to members of the group;
   (c) deliberately inflicting on the group conditions of life calculated to bring about its physical destruction in whole or in part;
   (d) imposing measures intended to prevent births within the group;
   (e) forcibly transferring children of the group to another group.

[135] Under crimes against humanity, General Krstić was charged with extermination, de-portation, persecution, and inhumane acts.

[136] *Krstić Judgment, supra* n. 13, at para. 622.

[137] Ibid., at para. 624.

widespread and systematic killings and became clearly involved in their perpetration, he shared the genocidal intent to kill the men. This cannot be gainsaid given his informed participation in the execution through the use of Drina Corps assets.[138]

General Krstić, as a co-perpetrator in the genocidal acts, incurred liability for the killings under Article 7(1). Moreover, the Trial Chamber's examination of the execution led it to hold that General Krstić was guilty for the ordeal suffered by the men who miraculously survived the massacre. The causing of serious bodily and mental harm, not death, to these men, constituted an act of genocide under Article 4(2)(b) of the Statute.[139] The Trial Chamber stated that while the agreed upon objective of the joint criminal enterprise was execution, the 'terrible bodily and mental suffering of the few survivors was a natural and foreseeable consequence of the enterprise'.[140]

The third category of common purpose is achieved when the co-participant who intends one criminal plan is aware, and assumes the risk, that the plan is likely to result in crimes beyond those originally intended. The Trial Chamber went beyond the factual allegations of genocide and addressed the further genocidal harm waged on the male survivors that fell outside of the scope of the criminal plan to kill Srebrenica men. Similar to the conviction of Tadić for the Jaskici murders, the *Krstić* Trial Chamber held that 'General Krstić must be aware of this possibility and he therefore incurs responsibility for these crimes as well'.[141]

With this holding in mind, we return to the first stage of events to examine how the third category of joint criminal enterprise functions in regard to collective sexual assaults. The events immediately following the Bosnian-Serb capture of Srebrenica can be described thus:

Late in the afternoon of 11 July 1995, General Mladić, accompanied by... General Krstić... and other VRS officers, took a triumphant walk through the empty streets of Srebrenica town.
...

Faced with the reality that Srebrenica had fallen under Serb control, thousands of Bosnian Muslim residents from Srebrenica fled to Potocari seeking protection within the UN compound. By the evening of 11 July 1995, approximately 20,000 to 25,000 Bosnian Muslim refugees were gathered in Potocari. ...

Conditions in Potocari were deplorable. There was little food or water available and the July heat was stifling. ...

On 12 July 1995, the situation in Potocari steadily grew worse ...

[A]s the day wore on, the already miserable physical conditions were compounded by an active campaign of terror, which increased the panic of the residents, making them frantic to leave. The refugees in the compound could see Serb soldiers setting houses and haystacks on fire ...

[138] *Krstić Judgment, supra* n. 13, at para. 633   [139] Ibid., at para. 635.
[140] Ibid.   [141] Ibid.

Killings occurred. In the late morning of 12 July 1995, a witness saw a pile of 20 to 30 bodies heaped up behind the Transport Building...Another testified that...he saw a soldier slay a child with a knife in the middle of a crowd of expellees. He also...saw Serb soldiers execute more than one hundred men in the area behind the Zinc Factory...

As the evening fell, the terror deepened. Screams, gunshots and other frightening noises were audible throughout the night and no one could sleep. Soldiers were picking people out of the crowd and taking them away: some returned; others did not...

That night, a Dutch...medical orderly came across two Serb soldiers raping a young woman...

Bosnian Muslim refugees could see the rape, but could do nothing about it because of Serb soldiers standing nearby. Other people heard screaming, or saw women being dragged away. Several individuals were so terrified that they committed suicide by hanging themselves. Throughout the night and early the next morning, stories about rapes and killings spread through the crowd and the terror in the camp escalated.

. . .

On 12 and 13 July 1995, the women, children and elderly were bussed out of Potocari, under the control of the VRS forces, to Muslim-held territory ...

The removal of the Bosnian Muslim population from Potocari was completed on the evening of 13 July 1995 by 22:00 hours. When UN soldiers visited the town of Srebrnica on 14 July 1995, they said they did not find a single Bosnian Muslim alive in the town.[142]

This first stage of events was frequently called the 'humanitarian crisis'[143] that preceded the expulsions and the killings. The Trial Chamber readily conceded that the primary crime in the joint criminal enterprise was the expulsion of the Bosnian Muslims out of the safe-haven. It found that General Krstić participated in this criminal enterprise of forcible transfer because he ordered the procurement of the buses that would transfer the Bosnian Muslims out of Potocari, as well as ordering his subordinates to secure the passage until they arrived in Muslim-held territory. In a televised message, Krstić assured the residents that they would be safely 'taken to a destination of their choice'.[144]

In determining the scope of the plan forcibly to transport the Muslims, the Trial Chamber held the ensuing humanitarian crisis in Potocari to be 'so closely connected and so instrumental, in the forcible evacuation' as to reside within the scope of the criminal plan. That the humanitarian crisis was germane to the criminal plan was the only plausible interpretation, given the conduct of the transfer and holding operation at Potocari, coupled with General Krstić's awareness and disregard for the alleviation of the crisis. The Trial Chamber therefore reasoned that General Krstić fully adhered to the creation of the humanitarian crisis as a prelude to the expulsion.[145]

The Trial Chamber, however, did not assert that each of the cruel acts inflicted during the humanitarian crisis also came within the criminal plan. On the contrary, the Chamber opined that it was not 'convinced beyond a

---

[142] Ibid., at paras 38–51.   [143] Ibid., at para. 615.
[144] Ibid., at paras 346–7.   [145] Ibid., at para. 615.

reasonable doubt that the murders, rapes, beatings and abuses committed against the refugees at Potocari were also an agreed upon objective among the members of the joint criminal enterprise'.[146]

The acts did not escape unpunished. The Trial Chamber, satisfied that General Krstić was aware of the inevitability of the crisis, declared:

[T]here is no doubt that these crimes were the natural and foreseeable consequences of the ethnic cleansing campaign. Furthermore, given the circumstances at the time the plan was formed, General Krstić must have been aware that an outbreak of these crimes would be inevitable given the lack of shelter, the density of the crowds, the vulnerable condition of the refugees, the presence of the regular and irregular military and paramilitary units in the area and the sheer lack of sufficient numbers of UN soldiers to provide protection.[147]

The *Krstić* Trial Chamber surmised that as a member of a joint criminal enterprise formed to execute forced transfers and to precipitate the transfer by creation of a humanitarian crisis, General Krstić was also guilty of the 'incidental murders, rapes, beatings and abuses'.[148] These incidental crimes that fell outside of the joint criminal enterprise were characterized as persecution, under crimes against humanity in Article 5 of the Statute.

The Trial Chamber, not placing any relevance on General Krstić's specific lack of knowledge about the sexual violence, reasoned that because of his acquiescence to the collective plan to cleanse the area he knowingly assumed the risk that other crimes, such as sex-based crimes, would occur. The Trial Chamber found that together with the random killings, the sexual violence and sexual terrorization were foreseeable and consistent with the presence of a massive, vulnerable refugee population, combined with the army and paramilitary presence. General Krstić therefore satisfied the *mens rea* requirement. For his participation, General Krstić received a global sentence of 46 years' imprisonment.

The *Krstić* pronouncement is one of first impression. That wartime sexual assault crimes are ostensibly characterized as the natural and foreseeable consequence of *other* violations is landmark jurisprudence. It reverses the inevitable conventional belief that wartime sexual abuse is either the unrelated, variant conduct of individual soldiers, or the consequence of soldiers obeying superior orders. The holding notably gives rise to the question—when are perpetrators on notice that sexual assaults committed by their co-perpetrators are a natural and foreseeable consequence of their own non sex-based war crimes?

In *Krstić*, the situational context primed the foreseeability of these crimes, even though they were beyond the scope of the original plan. Similar to the murders in Jaskici, the murders, terrorization, and sexual violence in Potocari

---

[146] *Krstić Judgment, supra* n. 13, at para. 616.   [147] Ibid.   [148] Ibid., at para. 617.

flowed from purposeful, criminal conduct. Prior to *Krstić*, only the *Blaškić*[149] Trial Chamber rendered a verdict of guilt for 'foreseeable' inhumane acts based on sexual violence, when the facts revealed that Colonel Blaškić had barracked HVO soldiers in a school where civilian females were detained. The Trial Chamber admonished Colonel Blaškić that he 'could not have been unaware of the atmosphere of terror and rapes which occurred at the school'.[150] His conviction did not examine common purpose or joint criminal enterprise liability.

Subsequent to *Krstić*, the common purpose doctrine formed part of the deliberation upon crimes, including sexual violence, committed at the Omarska camp in the *Prosecutor v Kvočka* case.

F. Detention Camp as Criminal Enterprise in *Kvočka*

The *Prosecutor v Kvočka*[151] case concentrates on the criminal conduct of five accused at the Omarska camp in the Prijedor region of Bosnia Herzegovina. Four accused were employees of the camp, Kvočka, Prcać, Kos, and Radić, and the fifth was a civilian Serb named Zigić, who abused detainees at Omarska and other nearby detention facilities. The five accused were possibly among the unnamed actors who terrorized non-Serb detainees at Omarska in tandem with Duško Tadić.

The Omarska camp riveted the world with images of emaciated, hollow-eyed detainees confined behind a perimeter of meshed wire. An atmosphere of sweeping impunity and consuming terror reigned inside the camp. Detainees passed through a gauntlet of guards who beat them on their way to and from the cafeteria, causing them to drop the insufficient but precious ration of bread.[152] Detainees suffered from lice, skin rashes, diarrhoea, and dysentery.[153] Detainees had to urinate and relieve themselves on the spot.[154] Dead bodies were left outside to fester for days. A stench enveloped the camp.[155]

Interrogations of detainees were conducted in a consistently cruel manner, seeding the atmosphere with dread. A stream of murders, torture, and other physical and mental violence became routine.[156] To celebrate Petrovdan, a Bosnian-Serb holiday, several detainees were thrown on a traditional bonfire and burned alive.[157] On another horrific occasion, two busloads of Muslim males from the village of Hambarine were brought to Omarska and summarily executed by a single bullet to the head.[158]

---

[149] *Blaškić Judgment, supra* n. 88. [150] Ibid., at para. 732.
[151] *Kvočka Judgment, supra* n. 14. [152] Ibid., at para. 54.
[153] Ibid., at para. 61. [154] Ibid., at para. 75. [155] Ibid., at para. 61.
[156] Ibid., at para. 92. [157] Ibid., at para. 93. [158] Ibid., at para. 95.

In addition, sexual violence was rampant. Among the 36 Muslim females detained at Omarska, the Trial Chamber heard that several were constantly raped and subjected to sexual abuse. Guards routinely removed women from their common sleeping areas, raped them, and then returned them to the rooms, terrified. Multiple perpetrators were not uncommon.

Witness U, however, testified that when she was detained in the administration building with the other women, a guard took her from the room several times at night to a room at the end of the corridor, where she was systematically raped by a string of perpetrators: 'He would rape me...he would leave, and then all the time, one after the other, others would come in, I don't know the exact number...they also raped me.'[159]

Given the totality of the crimes committed against detainees, the Trial Chamber held that Omarska 'functioned' as a criminal enterprise that was among the means to cleanse the territory of non-Serbs. The collective criminality, as viewed from the bench, did not constitute 'atrocities committed in the heat of battle', but rather crimes that were 'intentionally, maliciously, selectively and in some instances sadistically' perpetrated against non-Serb detainees.[160] The Trial Chamber was of the opinion that 'the primary means of sustaining and furthering the purpose of the criminal enterprise was by persecuting...through various forms of physical, mental and sexual violence'.[161]

Bearing in mind that the Tribunal's jurisprudence had condemned sexual assaults as persecutory acts,[162] the Chamber concurred, and found no barrier to declaring that persecution at Omarska entailed sexual violence and these acts appeared to be germane to this system of ill-treatment. However, the *Kvoćka* Trial Chamber simultaneously seemed to posit a fallback position— that the sexual violence was alternatively the natural *or* foreseeable consequence of Omarska's system of ill-treatment.[163]

Reminiscent of the humanitarian crisis language in *Krstić*, the *Kvoćka* Trial Chamber pointed out that the presence of female detainees and the unruly demeanour of the guards would presage the occurrence of sexual violence, insisting that such ingredients do not distort any logic, rather they lead to a foreseeable conclusion.

In Omarska camp, approximately 36 women were held in detention, guarded by men with weapons who were often drunk, violent, and physically and mentally abusive, and who were allowed to act with virtual impunity.

---

[159] *Kvoćka Judgment, supra* n. 14, at para. 102.
[160] Ibid., at para. 319.
[161] Ibid., at para. 323.
[162] See *Krstić Judgment, supra* n. 13.
[163] *Kvoćka* interprets the category three common purpose elements, natural consequences and foreseeable consequences, as alternatives, not cumulative requirements. *Kvoćka Judgment, supra* n. 14, at paras 326–7.

Indeed, it would be unrealistic and contrary to all logic to expect that none of the women held in Omarska, placed in circumstances rendering them especially vulnerable, would be subjected to rape or other forms of sexual violence. This is particularly true in light of the clear intent of the criminal enterprise to subject the targeted group to persecution through such means as violence and humiliation.[164]

Even though it was evident that collective sexual assaults formed part of the persecution inflicted at Omarska, Radić was the only named physical perpetrator among the accused. The Trial Chamber deliberated upon the testimony from several witnesses that Radić sexually assaulted them. Witness J recounted that Radić attempted to rape her and ejaculated over her.[165] Witness K testified that Radić had her led to an isolated room in Omarska where he raped her. Prior to that, Radić had attempted to coerce Witness K into having sex by threatening to have her children killed.[166] The accused's pattern of sexual coercion, replete with threats, was noted by the Trial Chamber. It held that Radić committed sexual violence via the sexual intimidation, harassment, and assaults[167] that were legally characterized as acts of torture and persecution.[168] However, Radić's sexual assaults fell within a larger pool of both sexually violent conduct and other criminal behaviour committed by multiple perpetrators.

A narrow reading of common purpose, category two (see pp. 176–7), asserts that co-perpetrators who maintain a 'concentration camp' participate in a 'concerted system of ill-treatment'.[169] Omarska, like systems of ill-treatment, bred the commission of myriad cruel acts by multiple perpetrators. As such, the *Kvočka* Trial Chamber held, for appropriate reasons, that the Omarska joint criminal enterprise did involve a plurality of persons:

Indeed, they could only have been committed by a plurality of persons, as the establishment, organization and functioning of the camp required the participation of many individuals playing a variety of roles and performing different functions of greater or lesser degrees of importance.[170]

The named perpetrators were certainly, in the Trial Chamber's eyes, only part of a larger group of unnamed accused. In determining the culpability of the named individuals, the Trial Chamber examined their precise authority, knowledge, and intentional furtherance of the system of ill-treatment, including the commission of specific crimes. Underscoring the jurisprudence of *Krstić*, the Trial Chamber held that crimes committed in furtherance of the criminal enterprise extend to *any one who knowingly participated in a*

---

[164] Ibid., at para. 327.   [165] Ibid., at para. 548.   [166] Ibid., at para. 551.
[167] Ibid., at para. 559.   [168] Ibid., at para. 761.
[169] *Tadić Appeals Judgment, supra* n. 11, at para. 228.
[170] *Kvočka Judgment, supra* n. 14, at para. 320.

significant way in the enterprise.[171] Moreover, it established that knowledge of the joint criminal enterprise could be inferred from the time an accused spent in the camp, the functions performed, and his contact with detainees or staff, and through ordinary senses. The Trial Chamber left little room for a participant who spent any significant time at Omarska to deny knowledge about the ill-treatment system. Further, it was of the opinion that:

Knowledge of the abuses could also be gained through ordinary senses. Even if the accused were not eye-witnesses to crimes committed in Omarska camp, evidence of abuses could be *seen* by observing the bloodied, bruised and injured bodies of detainees, by observing heaps of dead bodies lying in piles around the camp, and noticing the emaciated and poor condition of detainees, as well as by observing the cramped facilities or the bloodstained walls. Evidence of abuses could be *heard* from the screams of pain and cries of suffering, from the sounds of the detainees begging for food and water and beseeching their tormentors not to beat or kill them, and from the gunshots heard everywhere in the camp. Evidence of the abusive conditions in the camp could be *smelled* as a result of the deteriorating corpses, the urine and faeces soiling the detainees' clothes, the broken and overflowing toilets, the dysentery afflicting the detainees, and the inability of detainees to wash or bath for weeks or months.[172]

The Chamber thus held the accused, Kvočka, to be the functional equivalent of the deputy commander of the guard service;[173] Prcać to be an administrative aid to the camp commander;[174] Kos and Radić to be guard shift leaders;[175] and Zigić to be an interloper who entered Omarska and abused detainees at will. The accused were deemed to have satisfied the *mens rea* of the common purpose. Each was found to have had knowledge of the ill-treatment system. Additionally, according to the legal findings, each accused substantially participated in and intentionally furthered the ill-treatment system of Omarska by running or maintaining the camp, or directly committing crimes. The Chamber observed that that liability flowed from crimes that were within *and* outside of the scope of the plan if the latter were the natural and foreseeable consequences of the intended crimes.

As such, the Trial Chamber pronounced each accused guilty of persecution, a crime against humanity, for the combined murders, tortures, beatings, confinement in inhumane conditions, *and* sexual assaults, including rapes, sexual harassment, and humiliation, all components of the terror at Omarska.[176] Radić, like Accused B in *Furundžija*, physically committed sexual assaults that were, via the common purpose doctrine, ascribed to other accused. Unlike Accused B, Radić's sexual abuse was not necessarily committed in the presence of other accused, nor with their specific knowledge. Nevertheless, the Trial Chamber entered convictions for these and other

---

[171] *Kvočka Judgment, supra* n. 14, at para. 326 (emphasis added).
[172] Ibid., at para. 324.   [173] Ibid., at para. 372.   [174] Ibid., at para. 439.
[175] Ibid., at paras 485, 517.   [176] Ibid., at paras 452–766.

individualized charges, and imposed sentences that varied between five and 20 years' imprisonment, dependent upon the accused's knowledge of the system, together with his position and physical commission of individual crimes.[177]

Kvočka closes a significant liability gap, by capturing sexual violence under category two common purpose, *or* as a result of 'knowingly assuming the risk' under category three. It has thus importantly addressed liability in a frequent wartime scenario—the detention camp. It is the plethora of detention facilities in the former Yugoslavia that renders this judicial examination potentially powerful for future ICTY cases. Like acts committed during *Krstić's* humanitarian crisis, the predictability of sexual assaults in detention camps must be assumed by co-perpetrators.

Moreover, the common purpose doctrine now reads that whenever institutionalized persecution exists, it is a co-perpetrator's knowledge of the systemic ill-treatment, and not of each cruel act, that is material to his liability. This signifies a complex factual journey from *Furundžija's* narrow beginning of a single crime based common purpose to an enterprise of ill-treatment.

3. INTERMEZZO

This intermezzo or midlife phase of the ad hoc Tribunal for the former Yugoslavia coincides with the official development of an exit strategy in contemplation of the Tribunal's eventual closure.[178] The surrender of the Bosnian-Serb leaders and other outstanding accused has accelerated, attesting to the international community's political will to conclude this much heralded judicial experiment with solid achievements. Not the least striking is witnessing the ICC advance to the brink of its day-to-day operation. It is fitting in this intermezzo to note that the Tribunal has wrought a legal demystification of sexual violence prosecution.

Two seemingly primordial myths bind wartime sexual violence. The first is that sexual violence, and rapes in particular, are often construed as 'private acts' committed by soldiers who are motivated by lust and thus outside the reach of humanitarian law. The second myth deduces that the inevitability of sexual violence during armed conflict bodes against, not for, legal redress unless there is proof of a superior's order, or proof that rapes were numerous or systematic.

The first myth rests in the penumbra that feminist international legal scholars term the public/private dichotomy. It posits that women's concerns have been persistently waylaid by a public/private dichotomy that assigns gendered domains to international law.[179] International law regulates armed

---

[177] Ibid.

[178] See the Minutes from the SC, 4429th Meeting, 27 November 2001, S\PV.4429 (discussing the Prosecutor's 'exit strategy' for the ICTY and the ICTR).

[179] H. Charlesworth and C. Chinkin, *The Boundaries of International Law* (2000), at 56–9.

conflict and international crimes, such as genocide and crimes against humanity; yet these crimes, when committed against women, especially via sexual violence, are often decried as a detour, a deviation, or the acts of renegade soldiers. In other words, they are pegged to private wrongs that are not really the subject of international humanitarian law.

The illusory breadth of this private domain exists primarily because of the international community's churlish lack of enforcement of international humanitarian law, especially prohibitions of sexual violence. This is compounded by rape and other sexual assaults' explicit absence from the grave breaches provisions of the Geneva Conventions and the fundamental guarantees of Additional Protocol I. Sexual violence therefore occupies an uncomfortable, lesser legal rung within the international humanitarian law hierarchy.[180] However, much of this legal fallacy has been dispelled by the Tribunals' jurisprudence that has consistently interpreted condemnations of rape and other forms of sexual violence as coming within provisions of the respective Statutes.[181]

There remains a self-evident point. All international humanitarian law, or in modern terminology, the laws of armed conflict, is public, not private, law. To accentuate the obvious, war crimes, crimes against humanity, and genocide reside only in the *very* public domain that obligates state action and more recently galvanized the international community to establish ad hoc Tribunals and the ICC. This body of law is *never* categorized as a harm that pits only one individual interest against another. Even given the gendered analysis, these crimes reside within the patriarchal-sanctioned public domain.

The thoughtful jurisprudence of the ad hoc Tribunals affirms that what makes wartime sexual violence public, in the legal sense, pertains only to proof of rather precise jurisdictional elements of the *materiae ratione* or subject matter jurisdiction. An example suffices to illustrate the point. Crimes against humanity under Article 5 require that the following common or jurisdictional elements be proven: (i) there must be an attack; (ii) the acts of the perpetrator must be part of the attack; (iii) the attack must be directed against any civilian population; (iv) the attack must be widespread or systematic; (v) the perpetrator must know that his acts constitute part of the pattern of widespread or systematic crimes directed against a civilian population and know that his acts fit into the pattern.[182] Proof of these jurisdictional elements transforms the underlying enumerated acts of Article 5, murder, imprisonment, *or* rape, from ordinary crimes into crimes against humanity.

Consequently, in *Kvočka* and *Tadić*, the Trial Chambers had to establish that the accused knew of the larger attack on non-Serb civilians in the Prijedor

---

[180] Gardam and Jarvis, *supra* n. 8, at 99–101.
[181] See text accompanying nn. 51–6.
[182] *Kunarac Appeals Judgment, supra* n. 107, at para. 85.

region, including the setting up of Omarska camp. The non-sex-based crimes that they committed at Omarska, together with the sexual assaults committed by Radić, formed part of the attack. The Trial Chamber held that Radić 'was aware of the abusive treatment and conditions endured by the non-Serbs detained in Omarska prison camp... [and] that Radić physically perpetrated crimes of sexual violence against females detained in the camp'.[183]

Remember, in *Tadić*, the sexual assault evidence of Ramić served as proof of the attack against the civilian population, not the underlying allegations against Tadić. Hence, a facet of the attack, into which the crimes that Tadić committed fit, included the sexual assaults inflicted upon Ramić. The Trial and Appeals Chambers accepted her evidence as proof of the jurisdictional elements. The sexual assaults inflicted by unnamed perpetrators furnished the public context against which the named accused's acts were measured. These sexual assaults inhabited and embodied the public zone.

Moreover, the *Tadić* Appeals Chamber, in examining what relevancy, if any, personal motives, such as lust, hate, or revenge, exert on these jurisdictional elements declared that:

The Appeals Chamber agrees with the Prosecution that there is nothing in Article 5 to suggest that it contains a requirement that crimes against humanity cannot be committed for purely personal motives. The Appeals Chamber agrees that it may be inferred that the acts of the accused must comprise part of a pattern of widespread or systematic crimes directed against the civilian population and the accused must have *known* that his acts fit into such a pattern. There is nothing in the Statute however, which mandates the imposition of a *further* condition that the acts must not be committed for purely personal reasons.[184]

The *Tadić* Appeals Chamber concluded that it is not necessary to prove an accused's motive.[185] What renders sexual assaults public is not the physical location of the assault, nor the personal motive of the accused, but rather the establishment of the jurisdictional elements.

In a similar manner, the *Kunarac* Appeals Chamber was asked to examine whether the sexual nature of the perpetrator's intention was inconsistent with a finding of guilt for torture. The Appeals Chamber stated:

In this respect, the Appeals Chamber wishes to assert the important distinction between 'intent' and 'motivation'. The Appeals Chamber holds that, even if the perpetrator's motivation is entirely sexual, it does not follow that the perpetrator does not have the intent to commit the act of torture or that his conduct does not cause severe pain or suffering, whether physical or mental, since pain and suffering is the likely consequence of his conduct.[186]

---

[183] *Kvočka Judgment, supra* n. 14, at para. 571.
[184] *Tadić Appeals Judgment, supra* n. 11, at para. 248.
[185] Ibid., at para. 272.
[186] *Kunarac Appeals Judgment, supra* n. 107, at para. 153.

Jurisprudence from the common purpose or joint criminal enterprise doctrine also lends assistance to untangle the feminist public/privacy paradigm. As unmistakably demonstrated in *Krstić* and *Kvočka*, common purpose, particularly under category two, removes the 'inability excuse' to prosecute sexual violence under humanitarian law because of irrelevant notions about the 'privacy' of an individual's criminal act. The specific sex-based crimes of one accused can be part of a broader criminal plan of, say, persecution. Within the underlying crimes, lone acts become part of collective criminal acts. *Kvočka* holds alternatively that the sexual violence was part of the common design to persecute. Neither Radić's motives, the location of the acts, nor the fact that the other accused did not specifically know that Radić committed sexual violence were legally relevant. Hence there exists no renegade soldier as co-perpetrator of a common purpose or design whose acts can privatize sexual violence, whenever a myriad of sexual abuse could be an *actus reus* or the planned crimes of persecution, torture, or inhumane acts.

The second myth of wartime sexual abuse admits the possibility of legal redress, yet alleges that this inevitable sexual violence is not justiciable unless there is proof of a superior's order, or proof that rapes were systematic.[187] The common purpose doctrine trounces that myth. Sexual violence as a natural and foreseeable consequence of other crimes, comes close to being the legal description of the inevitable wartime sexual violence. When random or rampant sexual violence, such as that in the *Krstić* humanitarian crisis, happens, as long as a co-perpetrator knowingly assumes the risk of its occurrence, it lies within, not beyond, the reach of humanitarian law. The very formulation of foreseeable conduct for which the accused risks liability is not dependent upon a superior's order or the 'systematicity' of acts, although evidence of either could be proof of foreseeability.

Resolution 820's famous reference to systematic detention and rape often caused scholars and lawyers to mistake the adjective 'systematic' for a legal requirement in order to prosecute rape. The *Kunarac* Appeals Chamber clarified this misconception, noting:

> The consequences of the attack upon the targeted population, the number of victims, the nature of the acts, the possible participation of officials or authorities or any identifiable patterns of crimes, could be taken into account to determine whether the attack satisfies either or both requirements of 'widespread' or 'systematic' attack vis-à-vis this civilian population.
> ... Only the attack, not the individual acts of the accused, must be widespread or systematic.[188]

As such, under crimes against humanity, the attack against the civilian population must be systematic or widespread. The underlying acts must form part

---

[187] *Supra* n. 21.
[188] *Kunarac Appeals Judgment, supra* n. 107, at paras 95–6.

of the attack, but the acts themselves need not be widespread *nor* systematic, although that could be evidence of the existence and nature of the attack. Whatever the characteristic of the sexual abuse, if it is foreseeable, it is justiciable.

Under common purpose, it is precisely the inevitability that pulls such acts into the realm of an indictable offence. Whether as part of the ill-treatment system, or as a foreseeable consequence of that system, or as a single, one-act crime by multiple perpetrators, the common purpose doctrine provides an adept legal tool. Common purpose's tendency is to normalize sexual assault prosecution. Collective crimes of sexual violence that were in the public domain, yet were invisible or ignored, find a useful, lucid framework for joint liability.

4. CONCLUSIONS

In achieving the spirit of Security Council Resolution 808, the ICTY Appeals Chamber has ruled that no one who participates in a serious violation of humanitarian law escapes the Tribunal's jurisdiction. The ad hoc Tribunals' simultaneous attention to the *in personam* and *materiae ratione* jurisdiction has assured the sound growth of sexual assault jurisprudence. The development of forms of liability, a crucial part in satisfying individual criminal responsibility, has steadily accompanied, and at times been propelled by, deliberation upon evidence of collective sexual violence. The Tribunal is now beginning to try the political and military leaders,[189] supposedly the individuals the most responsible for the policies that erupted into international crimes in the former Yugoslavia. The Prosecutor's strategy relies upon alternative theories of liability, the most prominent being common purpose or joint criminal enterprise.

In *Prosecutor v Slobodan Milošević*,[190] the indictment alleges that the former President of Serbia ethnically cleansed Kosovo, having committed crimes recognized under Articles 2–5 of the Statute. By way of explanation:

[T]he word 'committed' in this indictment . . . does not intend to suggest that any of the accused physically perpetrated any of the crimes charged, personally. Committing in this indictment refers to participation in a joint criminal enterprise as a co-

---

[189] In *Prosecution v Biljana Plavšić*, Sentencing Judgment, Case No. IT-00-39 & 40/1-S, 27 February 2003, the former member of the Bosnian Serb collective presidency admitted guilt to one count of persecution, a crime against humanity, based upon her participation in a joint criminal enterprise. Among the criminal conduct that comprised the persecutory acts was sexual assault committed against men and women, 'including forced assaults by family members against each other, resulting in deaths in some cases'. Ibid., at para. 29.

[190] *Prosecutor v Milošević et al.*, Second Amended Indictment, Case No. IT-99-37-I, 29 October 2001.

perpetrator. The purpose of the joint criminal enterprise was, *inter alia,* the expulsion of a substantial portion of the Kosovo Albanian population.[191]

The indictment further alleges that:

The crimes enumerated in Counts 1 to 5...were within the object of the joint criminal enterprise. Alternatively, the crimes enumerated in Counts 3 to 5 were natural and foreseeable consequences of the joint criminal enterprise and the accused were aware that such crimes were the likely outcome of the joint criminal enterprise.[192]

A learned blend of the jurisprudence of *Krstić* and *Kvočka* has informed the pleadings concerning sexual assault evidence. As part of the common purpose, the Prosecutor alleges under Count 1, deportation, that the Serb forces deliberately created an atmosphere of fear and oppression, through the use of force, threats of force, and violence, including sexual assaults. Count 5 alleges persecution, 'stating that persecutions included, but were not limited to ... the sexual assault by forces of the FRY and Serbia of Kosovo Albanians, in particular women'.[193]

Milošević, a named co-perpetrator, is indicted for the multiple and collective sexual violence committed as part of and as a result of the deportation and persecution, such as

Some women and children were taken away by members of the forces of the FRY and Serbia and held in a barn in Cirez/Quirez. The women were subjected to sexual assaults, and their money and property were stolen. At least eight of the women were killed after being sexually assaulted, and their bodies were thrown into three wells in the village of Cirez/Quiroz.[194]

Milošević's co-perpetrators are far removed in space, and separated by the forms of participation—an active *actus reus* as physical perpetrators compared to Milošević's participation by way of 'committing'. Both, according to the Secretary-General's original intent and the rapidly evolving jurisprudence of the Tribunal, are guilty of sexual violence. Common purpose's ability to tie leaders to the acts of co-perpetrators might deliver the first conviction of a head of state for sexual violence.

[191] Ibid., at para. 16.
[192] *Prosecutor v Milošević et al., supra* n. 190, at para. 18.
[193] Ibid., at para. 68.
[194] Ibid., at para. 63(c).

7

'The Appeals of the Orient': Colonized Desire and the War of the Riff

NATHANIEL BERMAN[*]

1. INTRODUCTION

'The Appeals of the Orient': this was the title of the February 1925 issue of the French literary journal, *Les Cahiers du Mois*. It contained over 100 responses to a questionnaire sent by the journal to a wide range of literary and cultural writers. On the cover of the issue, under the title, the editors placed a phrase in Arabic, untranslated. The French reader not familiar with Arabic would have had to delve deep into the journal to learn that these exotic signifiers constituted an 'Arab proverb', translated as: 'Entice the Orient unto you, lest it be lured far away from you.' In keeping with this proverb, the journal's questionnaire reverberated with the anxieties about European supremacy circulating during the interwar period:

(1) Do you think that the Occident and the Orient are completely impenetrable to each other? ...
(3) Do you think that the influence of the Orient constitutes a grave danger for French art and thought? Or, do you think that we should seek to *enrich* our general culture and *renew* our sensibility through the 'knowledge of the East'? ...
(5) What do you feel are the Occidental values which make the Occident superior to the Orient, or, what are the false values which debase our Occidental civilization?[1]

The 'Appeals of the Orient' inquiry sets the stage for my study of a key episode in interwar debate about colonialism. In April 1925, just two months after *Les*

[*] I would like to thank Lama Abu-Odeh, Marie-Claire Belleau, James Fanto, Janet Halley, David Kennedy, Duncan Kennedy, Karen Knop, Martti Koskenniemi, Tayyab Mahmud, Julie Stone Peters, Anthony Sebok, and Steve Winter for their valuable comments. This paper was funded in part by the Brooklyn Law School Dean's Summer Research Stipend Program.

[1] 'Enquête', 9 *Les Cahiers du Mois* [hereafter '*CM*'] (1925) 240, at 240–1 (emphasis added) (all translations are mine, unless otherwise noted).

Cahiers du Mois's special issue, the 'War of the Riff' broke out between France and a group of Moroccan rebels led by Mohamed ben Abd el-Krim el-Khattabi (known popularly, if misleadingly, as Abd el-Krim). The Riffan rebels were fighting against increasing European encroachments in their region of Morocco.

In the last decades of the nineteenth century, Spain and France had gradually extended their control over most of Morocco. This control was formalized in 1912 with a division between French and Spanish zones, with France retaining the lion's share in the legal form of a 'protectorate'. The Riff region lay on the border between the French and Spanish zones and was recalcitrant to outside domination, whether by the Moroccan central government or by Europeans. In the early 1920s, Abd el-Krim's rebels fought against Spanish attempts to exert full control over their region. Their success against the Spanish Army in a series of battles traumatized the Spanish political scene and led to a right-wing *coup d'état* by Primo de Rivera.[2]

The fighting that began in April 1925 between the French and the Riffans lasted about a year and ended with the defeat of the rebels. The war was a major political and cultural event in France—much antiwar activity and furious public debate, as well as a Communist attempt at a general strike. There was also a great deal of international support for the Riffan struggle, from Latin America to India. Perhaps because the War of the Riff came to be viewed as foreshadowing the French debacles in Vietnam and Algeria, French writers often refer to it as the first modern anticolonial revolt—'something absolutely new, without precedent . . . the portent of a process that its contemporaries did not yet know how to name: decolonization'.[3] One may be tempted to dismiss such statements as francocentric, though equivalent hyperbole can be found in Arab nationalist writings.[4] Nonetheless, the international dimensions of the War of the Riff, at least, do make it appear to announce the great anticolonial struggles of the 1950s and 1960s—in its divisive effect within the colonial *metropole* and, especially, in the responses it evoked in a wide range of places around the world.

My study of the public discourse on this war focuses on the relationships among a variety of French images of the colonized world, a variety of notions of international legal order associated with those images, and a variety of images of anticolonial struggle claimed and evoked by Abd el-Krim. In this introductory section, I want to make two methodological points. First, in studying the French images of the colonized world, I highlight the ways they relate to a variety of libidinal desires and a variety of configurations of gender,

---

[2] See S. E. Fleming, *Primo de Rivera and Abd-el-Krim* (1991), at 94–108.

[3] D. Rivet, 3 *Lyautey et l'institution de protectorat français au Maroc* (1988), at 253.

[4] See e.g. M. Tahtah, *Entre Pragmatisme, Réformisme et Modernisme, Le rôle politico-religieux des Khattabi dans le Rif (Maroc) jusqu'à 1926* (2000), at 58–60.

in the tradition of the critique of 'Orientalism'.[5] Yet, unlike some of that work, I will focus on the diversity of the desires expressed by those libidinally invested in an array of 'appeals of the Orient'—including divergent configurations of gender and sexuality, as well as normative indeterminacies and political antagonisms.

My study takes as axiomatic that a demonstration that libidinal desires inform a normative position does not by itself constitute a critique of that position, though it may shed light on its complexity and intensity. I will not, however, present some general theory of the relationship between desire and normativity. Rather, by studying their multiple associations in a specific context, I hope to show how one can find a broader and often surprising range of political and cultural possibilities at a given historical moment. On another note, the libidinal focus highlights both the goals and perplexities of the actors in this drama, the ways their desires both impelled their articulated positions and simultaneously undermined the seamlessness of those positions. I refer to all the desires in this chapter as 'colonized desires', desires both opened up and frustrated by a world in which colonialism played a central role.

I also have a methodological concern about the place of this debate in international legal history. My interest in the War of the Riff originated in my study of international law's changing relationship to colonialism and nationalism during the interwar period. Nevertheless, the writers I emphasize in this chapter were cultural and political figures rather than lawyers. I will explain why understanding the relationship of colonialism to international legal history often requires that we move beyond law's disciplinary boundaries— and for historiographical, rather than 'interdisciplinary', reasons.

I will thus be using the language of desire and the language of law as two interpretive frames to understand the pronouncements on the war by a variety of cultural and political figures. I hope to link these interpretive frames, to show, for example, the libidinal desires informing legal, cultural, and political positions. Yet I also proceed on the understanding that desire, law, culture, and politics provide distinct interpretive frames that may all be used to understand an historical event, that these frames usually affect and implicate each other, but that one need not view any one of these frames as providing the privileged key to understanding the others.

A. Desire and Colonial Politics

The interwar period was a time of two seemingly contradictory developments in European attitudes toward colonialism, particularly in

---

[5] See E. Said, *Orientalism* (1978). I have also been influenced by a variety of critiques of Said's work, such as that of J. Clifford, *The Predicament of Culture* (1988), at 255.

France.[6] On the one hand, the period saw the consolidation of a broad consensus about the desirability, or at least the provisional inescapability, of what the French called the 'colonial fact'—a consensus that extended from the right-wing all the way to most of the non-Communist left. On the other hand, the period saw the spread of anxieties about the political, cultural, and moral dangers of colonialism—anxieties reflected so strikingly in *Les Cahiers du Mois*'s questionnaire.

These conflicting tendencies informed many of the essays that *Les Cahiers du Mois* received in response to its questionnaire. To give a sense of the cultural and political context of the journal's inquiry, I note first the undifferentiated nature of the Orient about which the editors were concerned. Among the writers whose views they solicited were specialists on everything from Russia to equatorial Africa—in short, on almost everything outside Western Europe. So wide a net was cast, in fact, that a full study of these responses would give a snapshot of the French intelligentsia of the period—a sign of the importance of the fears and fantasies evoked by the word 'Orient' in French self-understanding.

I want to cite a striking passage from one of these responses, that of the cultural historian Alexandre Embiricos. This response was representative of many of the others in its basic assumptions. It stands out, though, by virtue of the overtness of its expression—the turgidness of its vitalistic and gendered fantasies, in which the Orient provided energy and life and the Occident provided form and meaning:

The Orient has *fertilized* the Occident. Asia has always been the inexhaustible source which has flooded the Earth with its *vitality* and great *dynamic* visions. But it is the Occident . . . which has given *meaning* to this *formless* richness. Without the Occident the world would struggle in confusion and chaos, despite flashes of brilliance. But, on the other hand, how useless and emaciated the powerful Occidental framework would be if the *barbarian sap* didn't seethe and bubble within its inflexible dikes.

Asia is the *subconscious* of the world. . . . Its misdirected forces, left on their own, acquire all the *destructive* virtues of the blind elements. They destroy each other and, without *rational* channeling, they expend themselves in vain, *infertile*.[7]

This fantasy was Modernist, liberal, and imperialist. *Modernist*—in its paradoxical images of the Orient's seething energies, fertile and infertile, creative and destructive, masculine and feminine.[8] *Liberal*—in its qualified embrace of another culture, in its affirmation that it was the 'interpenetration of the

---

[6] See generally Semidei, 'Les socialistes français et le problème colonial entre les deux guerres', 18 *Revue Française de Science Politique* (1968) 1115; Girardet, 'L'apothéose de la "plus grande France": l'idée coloniale devant l'opinion française (1930–1935)', 18 *Revue Française de Science Politique* (1968) 1085.

[7] 'Alexandre Embiricos', 9 *CM* (1925) 272 (emphasis added).

[8] I intend the term 'Modernism' to evoke the culturally innovative movements of the first decades of the twentieth century. On the relationship of cultural Modernism, nationalism, and

Occident and the Orient that has made civilization',[9] in its ambivalently gendered celebration of the Orient as providing the vital fluids without which the Occident would shrivel up. *Imperialist*—in its prescription that the Occident should nevertheless currently 'repulse invading Asia without pity'.[10] This imperialism was of a provisional variety: at the right moment, the Occident should be ready to 'pass its scepter' to the Orient.[11] That moment would come when the Orient would learn from the Occident to 'dominate its furors'[12] and become worthy of international primacy: self-discipline as a prerequisite for bearing the international 'scepter'. A premature shift in power would lead to the overwhelming of the Occident by the Orient's 'disordered and violent forces'; a shift at the right moment, by contrast, would lead to the 'renewal of [the Occident's] youth'.[13]

Much of the French response to the Orient in this period can be understood as playing a set of variations on the themes laid out in this passage. Despite all their differences, those French writers I will discuss—liberal leftists,[14] radical leftists, and members of the avant-garde—saw the Orient in vitalistic and gendered terms (although, as we shall see, they expressed divergent configurations of gender and sexuality in the Oriental/Occidental relationship). Nonetheless, due to the period pervasiveness of anxieties about Western supremacy, it would be an error to interpret most of these writers simply as naive participants in the dominant ideology. On the contrary, the carnage of World War I had left many deeply sceptical about Western values, a scepticism expressed in terms ranging from liberal provisionalism to detached irony to bitter cynicism.

We are dealing with a highly self-aware moment. For an illustrative example, we could look at the response of the writer Roger Martin du Gard to the War of the Riff. He declared that he could not oppose the war because to do so would be to 'put on trial universal history and everything we conventionally call civilization'.[15] And this trial he refused to undertake—but not on normative grounds. Rather, he explained, 'it is by an *instinct of self-preservation* that I seek to defend myself against the disintegrating and clearly sterile anxiety that this war provokes in me'.[16] Such ambivalent stances in relation to

international law in the interwar period, see Berman, 'Modernism, Nationalism, and the Rhetoric of Reconstruction', in M. Loriaux and C. Lynch (eds), *Law and Moral Action* (2000) 108.

[9] Embiricos, *supra* n. 7, at 272.
[10] Ibid.
[11] Ibid.
[12] Ibid.
[13] Ibid.
[14] On this terminology, see *infra* n. 34.
[15] 'Réponse de M. Roger Martin du Gard', 76 *Clarté* (1925) 18.
[16] Ibid., at 19 (emphasis added).

colonialism—in this case, anxious and defensive 'support'—reinforce the notion that one must analyse them at the 'instinctual' level, to use du Gard's term, rather than solely at the level of normative argument.

The avant-garde, especially the Surrealists, carried disgruntlement with the Occident to its furthest extent. While they often articulated the familiar fantasies about the vitalism of the Orient, they expressed quite different desires than the liberals. They declared that they sought not to appropriate the Orient, but to be appropriated by it. André Breton's response to *Les Cahiers du Mois*'s questionnaire resonated with this other desire: 'I am not waiting for "the East" to *enrich* us or *renew* us, but rather, for it to *conquer* us.'[17]

Other avant-garde writers also declared their desire to make an alliance with the Orient as part of their general fury with Occidental civilization. As the Surrealist Louis Aragon declaimed:

Occidental world, you are condemned to death. We will make alliances with all your enemies, we have already signed a pact with that demon, the Dream . . . *Let the Orient, your terror, respond finally to our voice* . . . [18]

(To be sure, the last sentence of this passage suggests some of ambivalences in the avant-garde's relationship to its proclaimed Oriental ally—in this passage, an oscillation between submission and manipulation—to which I shall return at pp. 215–22 below.)

In marked contrast to many of the questionnaire's respondents, the Surrealists rejected all attempts to channel the forces of the Orient into the rational forms of the Occident, a rejection with aesthetic and political consequences. On the aesthetic level, Breton hoped that 'conquest' by 'the East' would lead to the reinstatement of 'art into its proper place, that of the *barbaric expression* of our sorrows'.[19] On the political level, the Surrealists gave a central place to anticolonialism. Through their support for anticolonial revolt, the Surrealists sought, in a variety of ways, to press the widespread Modernist fantasy of the Orient's exorbitant energy into the service of the avant-garde desire for total subversion of 'bourgeois society'.

Before leaving *Les Cahiers du Mois*, I would like to focus again on the title of the journal issue, 'The Appeals of the Orient'. The term 'appeal' connotes both an attraction experienced by the one to whom an appeal is made (as in, for example, sex appeal) and a challenge made by the one making an appeal (as in, for example, a legal appeal). The 'appeals' of the Orient which the French intelligentsia experienced in 1925 combined these senses of attraction *to* an Other and challenge *by* an Other. On the one hand, these writers expressed a European desire for an alternative to the culture that had brought about World

---

[17] 'André Breton', 9 *CM* (1925) 250, at 250–1.
[18] Aragon, 'Fragments d'une conférence', 4 *La Révolution surréaliste* [hereafter '*RS*'] (1925) 12, at 15.
[19] Breton, *supra* n. 17, at 251.

War I, a desire that led to the *active projection* of such an alternative in the exotic Orient. On the other hand, they expressed an *anxious reaction* to challenges to European rule coming from the colonized world, challenges posed by growing political and cultural contestation from India to North Africa. The range of interwar variations on the European fantasy of the life-giving, yet threatening, Orient emerged out of this combination of 'appeals'.

The response submitted to *Les Cahiers du Mois* by two writers, Etienne Dinet and Sliman ben Ibrahim, contained a telling use of this combination. Dinet was a French Orientalist painter who spent much of his life in Algeria and eventually converted to Islam.[20] Ben Ibrahim, an Algerian, was Dinet's lifelong companion and co-authored several works with him, including *The Orient Seen from the Occident*. It was this Oriental/Occidental couple from whose contribution the journal's editors took their cover-page 'Arab proverb'. In the midst of an essay praising the charms of Oriental culture, the two writers explicated the threat latent in the proverb ('Entice the Orient unto you, *lest it be lured far away from you*'). They declared that the reaction against non-European culture promoted at the time by the French right-wing constituted a new 'Crusade', which could 'paralyse French thought, destroy the centuries-old influence which [France] enjoys in the Orient, and, consequently, gravely compromise the future of France in its North African possessions'.[21] The authors suggested the range of sources from which the threat could come:

Crusades of this genre, conducted by writers and sectarian politicians, have been a hundred times more effective in the introduction of Bolshevism in Algeria than the excitations and subsidies from Moscow.
The Germans are more insightful.[22]

Bolshevism, German intrigue, and North African revolt: the entire panoply of interwar French nightmares—that were, indeed, aroused a short time later by the War of the Riff.[23] The two writers were warning France to respond to the 'appealing' charms of the Orient (praising, to this end, the naturalness, vitality, and 'convulsive passion' of Arab art, music, and dance),[24] lest the Orient shrewdly 'appeal' to other allies who could better make use of its cultural and, perhaps more threateningly, its geopolitical value.

A final note about the 'Appeals of the Orient'. The plural of the title, 'Appeals', seems to reflect the journal's implicit recognition that European fantasies about the exotic took many forms—despite the journal's rather undifferentiated view of the composition of the Orient that was the object of those fantasies. It is this diversity of the Orient's appeals to European and

---

[20] See generally D. Brahimi, *La Vie et l'Oeuvre d'Etienne Dinet* (1991).
[21] 'Etienne Dinet et Sliman ben Ibrahim', 9 *CM* (1925) 267.
[22] Ibid., at 268.
[23] See the statement by the French General de Castlenau quoted in the text, *infra* n. 121.
[24] Dinet and ben Ibrahim, *supra* n. 21, at 268.

non-European desires, and the attempts by Abd el-Krim to evoke and manage those desires, that will be my focus in looking at a challenge from a very specific Orient—the Riff, a mountainous region located rather to the south and west of France than to its east.

B. Disciplinary Boundaries and Intertemporal 'Law'

An analysis of international response to this war requires that we depart from a purely legal framework. A major event like the War of the Riff was beyond the purview of mainstream international law in 1925. No major French, American, or British international law journal published an article about this war. It was only when he was consulted by the French Human Rights League that a leading French international lawyer, Georges Scelle, explained this silence:

> In my view, the League of Nations has without a doubt no competence at all in the Moroccan affair.
> *The Rif, the Riffans, Abd el-Krim, have no international personality of any degree.* Morocco is a country under protectorate with two protecting States and the League of Nations has no capacity to intervene in the domain of a protectorate.
> ... *[L]egally, one cannot even say that there is a war—an international war, of course, because there is a war in the larger sense of the term* ...[25]

For Scelle, this major anticolonial revolt had no international legal existence —though, as a liberal, he found this situation 'regrettable'.[26] He wondered whether it would not be a good idea to transform the Riff into a League Mandate. He noted, though, that such a step would be difficult since it would require renegotiating all international treaties relating to Morocco and that Spain would have to take the initiative since the Riff was in its zone[27] (while neglecting to mention any need for the Moroccans to consent to this new abridgement of their still nominally existing sovereignty). As things stood, Scelle declared that international law was unable 'even [to] say that there is a war'. Or, more precisely, Scelle projected colonial affairs into a 'larger' domain ('war in the larger sense')—a 'non-legal' domain of cultural and political conflict.

My turn to cultural and political writers in this study is thus not some arbitrary interdisciplinary move. Rather, it was international law itself, in the authoritative voice of Georges Scelle, that projected the War of the Riff into a 'larger domain'. The localization of this 'larger domain' as outside law was itself a legal construction. Specifically, this boundary between law and non-law was an artefact of the discipline's interwar relationship to colonialism.

---

[25] 'Rapport de M. Georges Scelle', 25 *Les Cahiers des droits de l'homme* [hereafter 'CDH'] (1925) 496 (emphasis added).
[26] Ibid.
[27] Ibid.

When we look at the 'larger' domain to which Scelle directs us, we find the arguments, fears, and fantasies that would come to structure international law's response to anticolonial struggle when it was finally forced to acknowledge its existence three decades later. The 'non-legal' responses I am about to analyse thus constituted a sort of proto-legal or crypto-legal debate—the cultural and political 'outside' of law whose concerns would, especially during the decolonization decades, come to form the core of legal discussion.

The question of whether debate on the War of the Riff belongs within international legal history raises a methodological conundrum about the disciplinary boundaries of international law at earlier periods analogous to that posed, on a doctrinal level, by the question of 'intertemporal law'. Under that thoroughly ambivalent doctrine, the legality of actions, such as the acquisition of territory, must be judged by the law in effect at the time of the action—and yet their ongoing legal effects should be judged by the law as it develops.[28] At times, this doctrine has been interpreted in a conservative manner. According to this view, territorial titles, valid at the time of acquisition, should not be brought into question, since 'if old roots of title are to be dug up and examined against the contemporary rather than the intertemporal law there can be few titles that will escape without question'.[29] Yet it has also been interpreted in a manner conducive to revisions of territorial title, particularly in the colonial context. Thus, one writer argues that, under the doctrine of intertemporal law, 'the new law of decolonization arising out of the right to self-determination' can defeat territorial claims based on 'nineteenth century colonialist rules'.[30]

Transposed to the level of historical methodology, the conservative version of the principle underlying this doctrine would seem to command that we study the international law of a past moment within the disciplinary boundaries accepted at that time. However, in the context of the study of colonialism, that maxim would not merely be a neutral historiographical principle commanding the avoidance of anachronism. Rather, it would place the legal historian in an uncomfortable position in relation to colonialism.

---

[28] In its classic formulation by Huber: 'As regards the question which of different legal systems prevailing at successive periods is to be applied in a particular case (the so-called intertemporal law), a distinction must be made between the creation of rights and the existence of rights. The same principle which subjects the act creative of a right to the law in force at the time the right arises, demands that the existence of the right, in other words its continued manifestation, shall follow the conditions required by the evolution of law.' 'Island of Palmas Arbitration Award', 22 *Am. J. Int'l L.* (1928) 867, at 884.

[29] R. Y. Jennings, *Acquisition of Territory in International Law* (1963), at 53; see also Jessup, 'The Palmas Island Arbitration', 22 *Am. J. Int'l L.* (1928) 735, at 740.

[30] L. Berat, *Walvis Bay: Decolonization and International Law* (1990), at 164. For an overview of the debate about intertemporal law, see Grant, 'A Panel of Experts for Chechnya: Purposes and Prospects in Light of International Law', 40 *Va. J. Int'l L.* (1999) 115, at 166–75.

As a legal rule, the doctrine of intertemporal law in its conservative version can legitimate the retention of territory acquired through colonial conquest. Sometimes this legitimation operates through doctrines affirmatively legalizing colonialism; at other times, as in Scelle's pronouncement on the Riff, it operates through doctrines excluding colonialism from the international legal domain. As a historiographical maxim about disciplinary boundaries, an analogous application of the doctrine's principle could place historical scholarship in a similar legitimating role. In the case of the War of the Riff, the maxim would insulate international law from the taint of colonialism by erasing the conflict from legal history.

I will take my methodological guidance in part from the conservative version of the doctrine of intertemporal law and in part from its revisionist version. Accepting Scelle's dictum that the war occurred in a 'larger domain' beyond law, I will look to literary and political writings on the Riff. Yet I see these 'larger' debates as proto-legal or crypto-legal, forming an indispensable part of international legal history. My turn to the writings of non-lawyers, therefore, is not an engagement in interdisciplinarity for the sake of 'enriching' or 'renewing' legal history but, rather, is both required and forbidden by the historical materials themselves.

2. FOUR DESIRES

I am going to interpret a variety of French responses to the war, focusing on the left side of the French political and cultural spectrum. Specifically, I identify these responses as representative (though not unanimous) strands of opinion among: (1) liberal leftists,[31] specifically among Socialists and the mainstream of the French Human Rights League; (2) radical leftists, among left-wing Communists[32] and those close to the left-wing of the French Communist Party in rhetoric and politics; and (3) members of the avant-garde, particularly among the Surrealists. I interpret these responses as embodying three kinds of desire in the imperial *metropole*. I will then turn to an interpretation of the desire expressed in Abd el-Krim's public relations 'appeals'.

The liberal leftist, radical, and avant-garde responses shared an aspiration to change the prevailing international legal relationship towards colonialism through deploying the energy of the Orient against prevailing legal institutions—though with dramatically different intentions. They each projected a specific form of cultural otherness as a means of self-construction. To give a

---

[31] On this terminology, *see infra* n. 34.

[32] On the divisions among the French Communists about colonialism generally and the Riff in particular, see Slavin, 'The French Left and the Rif War, 1924–25', 26 *Journal of Contemporary History* (1991) 5.

sense of what follows, I describe these political projects here in extremely telegraphic form:

(1) Liberal leftists *presented themselves as* humanistic reformers of a prevailing international order based on mere sovereignty, *through a call for* a deeper colonial relationship under internationalist tutelage, *to be achieved through* cultural seduction of colonized peoples, imagined as freedom-loving yet anarchic.

(2) Radical leftists *presented themselves as* offering a radical replacement of an international system based on imperialism, *through a call for* a European-led revolutionary order, *to be achieved through* conscription of the colonized, imagined as muscular and violent yet mystified about their true interests.

(3) Avant-gardists *presented themselves as* subversive rebels against European bourgeois society, *through a call for* destruction of that society and its international legal framework, *to be achieved through* the uncontrollable barbaric energy of the colonized.

I interpret these political stances as embodying three kinds of desire, playing a set of variations on gender and sexuality: *the desire to seduce* (which I associate primarily with Socialists); *the desire to conscript* (which I associate with left-wing Communists and similarly minded writers); and *the desire to explode* (which I associate with Surrealists).

Lastly, just as I suggested that the 'Appeals of the Orient' inquiry should be understood in light of the attraction/challenge of the non-European world, so the varieties of French response to the War of the Riff should be understood, in part, in a complex relationship to Abd el-Krim's strategic self-presentation. Abd el-Krim engaged in a set of shifting public relations pronouncements, evoking a wide variety of often incompatible fears and fantasies. I call the desire that informs Abd el-Krim's strategy the *desire to disorient*—a term I borrow from Dinet and ben Ibrahim, in their 1921 comments on the broad array of contradictory descriptions of Islam in Occidental Orientalism.[33] This term is particularly apt for Abd el-Krim, who sought both to confound his adversaries and to make possible a reconfiguration of the Orient/Occident dichotomy for an anti-colonial alliance.

The three main French desires I analyse emerged, in part, in the wake of Abd el-Krim's project of disorientation. I use the qualifier, '*in part*', because it is not always clear that the French who imagined and responded to the war took the trouble to differentiate Morocco, let alone the Riff, from anywhere else in the rather expansive period conception of the Orient—whose precise geographical location was of rather subsidiary importance in the French

---

[33] E. Dinet and S. ben Ibrahim, *L'Orient vu de l'Occident* (1921) 16. See my discussion, *infra* at pp. 225–6.

imagination, as we have seen in connection with *Les Cahiers du Mois*. Abd el-Krim's shifting strategy should be seen as one element in a changing international situation, associated with a range of desires in the *metropole*, a range of responses to the 'Appeals of the Orient'.

A. The Desire to Seduce

I use the idea of 'the desire to seduce' to interpret the majority position among liberal leftists, particularly among Socialists and the mainstream of the Human Rights League—the body of opinion just to the left of the liberal government of the time.[34] This position originated in the Socialist leader Jean Jaurès's criticism of government policy during the ongoing French conquest of Morocco in the early 1900s. Though his position hardened over time, Jaurès did not object *in principle* to French colonial expansion.[35] Rather, he opposed the government's *methods*, contrasting its policy of 'military colonial expansion' with his own notion of 'peaceful and reasonable expansion of French interests and civilization'.[36] In short, to the bad colonialism of the government, Jaurès juxtaposed a good colonialism of 'peaceful penetration' of Moroccan society—'*la pénétration pacifique*'.[37]

To understand this dispute, it is necessary to mention an enduring stereotype about Moroccan political structure. This stereotype sees Morocco as split between the areas controlled by the central government (the '*Bled Makhzen*')

---

[34] To avoid confusion, I am using current political labels here, rather than those of 1920s France. The parliamentary majority between 1924 and 1926, which we would today call 'liberal', was at the time called the *Cartel des Gauches* (cartel of parties of the left). The government consisted of members of centre and centre-left parties, initially led by Edouard Herriot of the misleadingly named Radical Party, a centrist group. The Socialist party (then called the *Section Française de l'Internationale Ouvrière*, the SFIO) had recently taken a new political identity, which I call 'liberal leftist', after splitting with its radical leftist wing in 1920. The radical leftists, for their part, formed the French Communist Party and joined the Third International. In the 1924–6 period, the Socialists' relationship to the government was one of 'support without participation', generally voting with the government in the parliament without holding cabinet posts. Finally, the Human Rights League included a fairly wide range of political tendencies, ranging from those close to the centre of the French political spectrum (Herriot was a founder of the Lyon section of the League) to those sympathetic to the Communists. The League's mainstream opinion, at least as reflected in the editorial stance of its journal, *Les Cahiers des Droits de l'Homme*, was close to the Socialists on issues relating to colonial policy during this period.

[35] See Bruhat, 'Jaurès devant le problème colonial', 20 *Bulletin de la Société d'histoire moderne* (11th ser. 1956) 15, at 21. For a contention that Jaurès was gradually moving towards opposing colonialism in principle at the end of his life, see Semidei, *supra* n. 6, at 1123. My argument in this section implies that the debates over the Jaurèsian legacy are a product of his indeterminate conceptual framework.

[36] Jaurès, 'Au Maroc' (1903), in II *Oeuvres de Jean Jaurès* (1931) 40, at 48.

[37] E.g. Jaurès, 'Un Grand Danger' (1903), in ibid., 33, at 35.

and those controlled by tribes resistant to government control (the *'Bled Sibâ'*). International lawyers will remember that competing interpretations of this split by Morocco, Mauritania, and Algeria played a key role in the International Court of Justice's 1975 *Western Sahara Case*.[38] In the colonial era, this split posed a strategic choice to any outside power that sought to dominate Morocco through a divide-and-rule strategy: either an alliance with the government against the tribes, or vice versa.

The French governments that undertook the conquest of Morocco chose the first option, both as a matter of strategy and as a matter of the legal framing of French dominance. This strategy culminated in the establishment of a 'protectorate' over Morocco by the 1912 Treaty of Fez. In such colonial protectorates, the *'protégé sovereign'*, in this case 'His Majesty the Sultan', accepted the supremacy of the 'protector', in this case the 'Government of the French Republic'. Under the Treaty of Fez, the parties agreed to introduce 'a new regime including administrative, judicial, educational, economic, financial, and military reforms which the French Government shall judge useful to introduce on Moroccan territory'.[39] It also provided for French military occupation.[40] The strategic choice for dominance through the Sultan was underlined in the provision by which the French undertook to 'provide constant support to his Cherifian Majesty against any danger which might threaten his person or his throne or which might compromise the tranquility of his State'.[41] Those who justified French rule over Morocco continually cited the indispensable French contribution to firmly establishing the Sultan's rule throughout Morocco and ending the country's supposed age-old anarchy.

In short, the protectorate regime sought to reinforce the Sultan's rule over his own society, while placing him in humiliating subservience to the French. A 1901 Franco–Moroccan agreement required the Sultan to extend his authority over the tribes, effectively forcing him, as Jaurès argued, to declare war on many of his compatriots.[42] The French government's policy may be called a double strategy of *splitting and submission*—dividing the Sultan from the tribes though the promise of protecting his fetishized 'person', then sadistically reducing him to the status of an instrument of French domination of the countryside.

Jaurès vigorously opposed this strategic choice. Though Jaurès's articulation of his position shifted over time, he gave it its clearest and most interesting expression in 1903. Jaurès argued that France, the homeland of liberty, should oppose the Sultan and form an alliance with the tribes—those 'absolutely independent' tribes, 'refractory to the authority' of the Sultan, and possessed of

---

[38] See *Western Sahara Case (Adv. Op.)* [1975] ICJ Rep 12, at 44–5.
[39] *Treaty between France and Morocco*, signed at Fez, 30 March 1912, Article 1.
[40] Ibid., at Article 2.
[41] Ibid., at Article 3.
[42] Jaurès, 'Au Maroc', *supra* n. 36, at 44–5.

their own 'special regime'.[43] The policy of 'peaceful penetration', like its rival, was a double strategy, that of *splitting and seduction*: splitting the tribes from the Sultan, then seducing them into love for France through appeals to their freedom-loving culture.

This policy was the opposite of the protectorate strategy. Rather than identifying the centralized political authority of the country and humiliating it, Jaurès wanted to seek out the dispersed, anarchic groups and win them over. Such a decentralized approach inherently entailed a multiplicity of seductive activities, rather than a decisive act of subjugation. Thus, Jaurès argued that the government should 'try to *attract, one by one,* these autonomous tribes to France'.[44] 'Conquering these tribes to [France] by benevolent treatment' ('conquest' clearly used here in the sense of seduction) would be facilitated by the fact that the tribes 'desire nothing other than to get close to us'.[45] By encouraging this tribal 'desire', France would become 'the moral center of these politically *disseminated* tribes'.[46] France would thereby 'surround the Sultan with a belt of tribes devoted to France, won over bit by bit to French civilization'[47]—making the Sultan pliant to French demands by taking his place as the main object of the tribes' allegiance, rather than helping him to subjugate them. In the end, 'without violence, with the free consent of the tribes, France will have contrived to make the *penetration of its peaceful influences*' pervasive throughout Morocco.[48] Indeed, Jaurès argued that the protectorate strategy would, paradoxically, be less effective as a method of colonial domination, since its real result would be to render France an 'instrument of the Sultan'.[49]

Jaurès's 1903 polemic against the government's policy may be restated in terms of its consequences for a reform of the prevailing international law of colonialism. At the beginning of the twentieth century, as at the beginning of the twenty-first, international law reformers stressed the demise of an exclusive emphasis on *sovereignty* as the basis for international order. The government's strategy served as a perfect target for such reformism. The government focused on an inter-sovereign process: the subordination of the Moroccan Sultan to the French Republic. Jaurès, on the other hand, sought to establish a deeper kind of colonial relationship by appealing to the tribes' love of liberty in order to win their hearts for French culture. In Jaurès's time, as in our own, such attempts to replace inter-sovereign ties with inter-cultural ties culminated in a call for a greater role for international authority. Accordingly, Jaurès completed his strategy for winning over Morocco for France with a call for placing Morocco under an international trusteeship[50]—a moment in the Socialist side of the genealogy of the League of Nations Mandate idea.

---

[43] Jaurès, 'Au Maroc', *supra* n. 36, at 44.   [44] Ibid. (emphasis added).
[45] Ibid., at 45.   [46] Ibid., at 46 (emphasis added).   [47] Ibid., at 51.
[48] Ibid. (emphasis added).   [49] Ibid., at 49.   [50] Bruhat, *supra* n. 35, at 19.

Jaurès's dispute with the government may also be restated in light of its strikingly gendered language. The government sought to humiliate, dominate, and manipulate its image of Moroccan masculinity, the Sultan, by forcing him to consent to the protectorate regime of legal subordination. The Socialist position, by contrast, would be to seduce a feminized Morocco, establishing a 'direct, cordial understanding with the tribes', an understanding which would 'go to the heart of the natives'.[51] In this way, France would 'peacefully penetrate' Morocco, becoming the 'center' of her 'disseminated' body. Rather than serving as the Sultan's chaperone in his relations with the Moroccan interior, relations of dominance established by force, France would take his place, 'penetrating' through 'free consent'.

If we turn to 1925, we find this Jaurèsian framework emerging as a constant throughout the vicissitudes in the Socialist position on the Riff. The Socialist stance on war financing in the French parliament gradually shifted from support to abstention to opposition.[52] Nevertheless, throughout these shifts, most Socialists defended their views of the moment on the basis of the Jaurèsian good-colonialism/bad-colonialism framework. Indeed, the ambivalences of that framework and the indeterminacy of its key dichotomy when confronted with a concrete situation were an important part of the Jaurèsian legacy.[53] The oscillations in the Socialist voting posture may be viewed as a product of that indeterminacy—for example, the difficulties in the colonial context in clearly distinguishing between activities of 'conquest' in the coercive versus seductive senses, or in characterizing the Riffans as a collection of disparate tribes only held together by a coercive political leader versus viewing them as a unified people entitled to its own status.

Thus, a resolution passed by the French parliament in May 1925, as amended by the Socialists, called for qualified support for the government. The resolution supported French action on behalf of the 'the security of the . . . tribes placed under our protection by international treaties' (i.e., quelling the rebellion). Yet it expressed 'opposition in the name of both humanity and the national interest to any *imperialism of conquest*' (i.e., but not to a reformist imperialism).[54] The Socialists also called for League of Nations supervision.[55] Here the Socialists stamped a Jaurèsian good-colonialism seal of approval on a campaign that nonetheless already included a significant military component.

---

[51] Jaurès, 'Au Maroc', *supra* n. 36, at 46.
[52] C.-R. Ageron, 'Les Socialistes français et la guerre du Rif', in *Abd el-Krim et La République du Rif: Actes du Colloque International d'Etudes Historiques et Sociologiques* (1973) 273, at 275.
[53] See R. Girardet, *L'idée coloniale en France* (1972), at 166–7.
[54] 'Ordre du jour', as amended by the Socialists, (29 May 1925) (emphasis added), quoted in Kahn, 'La Guerre au Maroc', 25 *CDH* (1925) 291, at 297.
[55] 'Une Conférence Socialiste internationale', *Le Populaire* (1 August 1925) 1.

In July 1925, the Socialists announced a change in their position, but retained their underlying schema. Explaining the party's intention to abstain on the next war credits vote, the Socialist leader Léon Blum declared:

We love our country too much to disavow the expansion of French thought and civilization.... We affirm the right and even the duty of superior races to attract to themselves those races who have not arrived at the same degree of culture ...: but we have always repudiated a colonialism of war![56]

Blum here again succinctly articulated the Jaurèsian ideal: opposition to a 'colonialism of war', support for the 'expansion of French thought and civilization'. Blum also reiterated the Socialist rejection of an 'immediate evacuation of Morocco' by France; he declared that such an evacuation would ignore the *'fait acquis'* of French rule and lead to the massacre of European settlers as well as of Moroccans who had already been won over to France. Yet the abstention vote implied that the heightened French military campaign had by then crossed some intangible line of acceptable intensity, disqualifying it from an unconditional good-colonialism stamp.

Many Socialists ended up clearly opposing the war by the end, due to the increasingly brutal military means used by the government; a similar motivation had led Jaurès to oppose the original French conquest of most of Morocco a couple of decades earlier. Yet whatever their position, the basic Jaurèsian schema persisted among most liberal leftists. The following analysis by the editors of the journal of the Human Rights League used the Jaurèsian schema of splitting and seduction to interpret the conclusion of the War of the Riff:

If Abd el-Krim has surrendered, it is because the war has become impossible for him to continue. It has become impossible because the tribes, *one by one, have abandoned him*. Yet, ... the tribes only abandoned Abd el-Krim after being convinced that the French government was pursuing a policy neither of annexation nor of revenge.... '[French] policy has achieved a slow *disagregation* of the Riffans ... taking advantage of *useful fissures* among them.... The tribes ... have come to realize the peaceful intentions of France, and have *thrown themselves into submission* ...'[57]

True to Jaurès's advocacy of the seduction of 'disseminated' Moroccan tribes away from their merely political ruler, this interpretation of the French victory celebrated it as the fruit of the French seduction of the 'disaggregated' Riffan tribes—in this case, away from Abd el-Krim, rather than, as for Jaurès, the Sultan. 'One by one', the tribes, now distinguished from even their local political leadership, 'abandoned' Abd el-Krim and '[threw] themselves into

---

[56] 'Les Crédits pour le Maroc', *Le Populaire* (17 July 1925) 1.
[57] 'Pour le Combat: Au Maroc', 26 *CDH* (1926) 297, at 298 (emphasis added). In the passage in quotes, the editors are citing with approval an account of the end of the war in the newspaper *L'Oeuvre*.

submission to France'. In the end, despite the regrettable need to use force to accompany the French campaign, this writer on the liberal left endorsed its results: the enriching of the colonial relationship through the deep appeal of decentralized cultural seduction rather than the traditional legal form of sovereign consent.

This analysis suggests the contingency of the relationship between desire and politics on a number of levels. First, colonialism at its most general level does not depend on a particular gender projection. Rather, the analysis reveals a variety of equally, though differently, colonial desires: the masculinizing projection and sadistic desire of the protectorate strategy versus the feminizing projection and seductive desire of the tribal strategy. Secondly, incompatible positions on particular issues may result from a single type of desire—for example, the Socialist oscillations on the War of the Riff.

In broader historical perspective, the splitting-and-seduction strategy cannot be classified politically. It has been adopted across the political spectrum by many who have pursued a strategy of *disaggregation* in relation to other societies. Such splitters-and-seducers seek to make horizontal alliances between particular sectors of the strategist's own society with those of another. This strategy has been pursued by a wide variety of political actors: particular kinds of Marxists, feminists, liberals, and World Bankers, among others. And just as this strategy can take a wide variety of political stripes, so it can take a variety of libidinal stripes. French Socialist discourse, to be sure, stuck to a stereotypical deployment of gender roles to express this desire. Yet the very fact that this deployment appears to us as terribly unimaginative suggests that the intervening period has witnessed a wide variety of variations on this theme. The desire to split-and-seduce is no longer the monopoly of male Socialist chivalry.

B. The Desire to Conscript

I use the idea of the 'desire to conscript' to interpret the position on the war of many of those close to the left wing of the French Communist Party. One of my goals in this interpretation is to read afresh left-wing Communist rhetoric of the period about the alliance of the European proletariat and anticolonial fighters[58]—rhetoric which has long become difficult to read as anything but hopelessly hackneyed. Specifically, I want to read it libidinally, to attend to the

---

[58] For example, two French Communist deputies sent a congratulatory telegram to Abd el-Krim, in which they declared their hope that 'after the definitive victory over Spanish imperialism, he will continue, in alliance with the French and European proletariat, the struggle against all imperialisms'; quoted in Kahn, *supra* n. 54, at 293.

ways it plays variations on the high Modernist desire for an alliance between Oriental energy and Occidental form.

This version of Modernist desire took a highly elaborate form in the journal *Clarté*, a literary journal at that time very close to left-wing Communists. Its analysis of the war expressed the desire to press the energy of the Orient, imagined as exorbitant but irrational, into the service of a European project of revolution, imagined as rational but fatigued. Note how this analysis replaced the good-colonialism/bad-colonialism schema central to the Socialists with the dichotomy between good nationalism and bad nationalism:

> They will accuse us of . . . favoring panislamism, of supporting oppressive indigenous chiefs. Nothing is more false. A movement of national emancipation obviously makes its first appeal to the union of all national forces against the oppressor. The *national-nationalist prejudices [préjugés nationaux-nationalistes] subsequently disappear* when the economic life of the country is transformed—and this is precisely the case for the Riff. . . . The debilitated conscious proletariat of the European states, bourgeoisified by a century of democracy, bloodied by war, or enfeebled by hunger, has lost too much of its *revolutionary virulence* since 1914 to disdain the support offered by the world revolutionary movement, that of the colonial peoples. The battle lost in Germany two years ago—without combat—can be regained *in the Riff or in Shanghai.* . . . [T]he European proletariat has proven for the time being *impotent to make revolution.* Let it not oppose . . . the crushing of the immense revolts which are just now appearing among the *barbarian peoples.*[59]

This passage expresses a variant of high Modernist desire quite distinct from that of liberal leftists: here we have the European desire to conscript the fantasized energy of the Orient, in the guise of revolutionary energy, to infuse the 'impotent' and exhausted Occident, in the guise of a decadent proletariat that had lost its 'virulence'. In turn, this 'barbarian' energy would be channelled into a rational form: the anticolonial fighters would gradually lose their irrational 'national-nationalist prejudices' as they came to recognize the rational basis of their struggle, that of the world proletariat. The need for differentiation between good and bad nationalism, the 'prejudices' of 'indigenous chiefs' versus economic revolution, served to make Communist internationalist leadership of the anticolonial struggle appear indispensable—just as the Socialist claim for the need for differentiation between good colonialism and bad colonialism served as an argument for the establishment of liberal internationalist authority.

If we pay attention to the gender tone of the language, we can distinguish even more strikingly the left-wing Communist desire from its Socialist counterpart. The left-wing Communist desire to conscript looked to the Orient for the latter's masculinity, its ability to provide a replacement (a hormone replacement?) for the 'impotent' Occidental proletariat. In the place of the

---

[59] Fourrier, 'Ce que nous en pensons', 75 *Clarté* (1925) 1, at 4 (emphasis added).

Socialist desire for the feminized Moroccan heart, we find the left-wing Communist desire for the muscular native fist. And in the place of the chivalrous Socialist desire to save the damsel in distress, in the guise of the chaotic and fragmented Moroccan countryside, we find the homoerotic Communist desire to instruct 'barbarian' virility, in the guise of the urbanized Moroccan worker.

These images are all the more remarkable because the same issue of *Clarté* contained two articles mocking *Les Cahiers du Mois*'s 'Appeals of the Orient' inquiry, attacking its 'culturalist' interpretation of the struggle between colonizer and colonized. One article declared that one should not frame the issue as a struggle of 'Oriental against Occidental culture', but rather as the struggle of 'Humanity against the Imperialism of Capital'.[60] Nevertheless, in its own analysis of the Riff, *Clarté* presented a radical political variant of the familiar Modernist desire for revitalizing Oriental energy, similar in structure to that expressed in liberal cultural terms by many *Les Cahiers du Mois* contributors. To be sure, *Clarté*'s variant expressed a desire for the revolutionary energy of the Orient to reinvigorate an exhausted Occidental proletariat, rather than for the Orient's cultural energy to renourish a depleted Occidental civilization.

When we turn to Communists' relationship to international legal order, we find a recurrent ambivalence. One antiwar manifesto published in the Communist newspaper, *L'Humanité*, appealed to legal ideas like sovereignty and self-determination and called on the League of Nations to intervene.[61] But this manifesto was strongly attacked by another writer in *L'Humanité*:

We Communists, we reply: to turn towards Geneva, to the League of Nations, is to propagate the most dangerous illusion. The League of Nations is the association of imperialist pirates ... It is also a center of counter-revolutionary preparation against the Soviet Union.[62]

These two positions—the first calling for the League to expand its concerns, the second rejecting it wholesale—should be read together, reflecting ambivalence in Communist circles toward international legal order. I see this ambivalence as stemming from Communist *envy* in relation to the League, the Communist desire to replace the League with a rival institution—a replacement to be achieved in part through the conscription of Oriental energy. For many left-wing Communists, liberal reformers of international law, such as the Socialists, merely sought to tinker with a League of Imperialist Nations. By

[60] Eugène, 'Orient contre Occident, ou la révolte de l'Humanité contre l'Impérialisme du Capital', 75 *Clarté* (1925) 244.
[61] 'Appel aux Travailleurs intellectuels', reprinted in 76 *Clarté* (1925) 13. The manifesto did take a critical stance toward some other aspects of contemporary international law, declaring that rights such as self-determination should prevail over treaties 'imposed by violence on weak peoples'.
[62] A. Rose, *Surrealism and Communism* (1991), at 132.

contrast, left-wing Communists sought to create an alternative structure, constructed out of an alliance between Occidental reason, in the form of the Third International, and Oriental energy, in the form of the conscripted revolutionary energy of the colonized. If Socialists harboured hope for an idealistic reform of the League, Communists were jealous of the organization, seeking to create an alternative entity with Communist leadership.

The relationship between desire and politics was just as contingent in the Communist case as in the Socialist. First, as we have seen above, the fantasy of the Oriental as masculine could be compatible with the protectorate strategy as well as with the left-wing Communist strategy—though the desire toward that masculine was quite different in the two cases. Secondly, the Communist good-nationalism/bad-nationalism dichotomy was just as slippery in application as the Socialist good-colonialism/bad-colonialism schema. Not all Communists felt that the Riffans fell on the good side of this dichotomy, that they were appropriate objects of the desire to conscript. In effect, these critics of the left-wing Communist campaign were attacking the Orientalism of their pro-Riffan colleagues. They argued that the pro-Riffans had indulged in excessive romanticization of their heroes, an excess they called 'Abd el-Krimism'.[63] They contended that the pro-Riffans had mistaken an ambitious feudal strongman for a proletarian ally. Indeed, if Oriental nationalism was in need of Communist discipline, why should it not be judged in a particular case to fall on the wrong side of the disciplinary gaze?

Beyond their many differences, Socialists and Communists shared a will to legitimize European leadership. In both cases, it was the very indeterminacy of their central analytical dichotomies that legitimated an outside authority to decide on their application—specifically, the authority of an Occidental decision-maker to parse the subtleties of Oriental identity. And, in each case, the indeterminacies of the central dichotomy made possible incompatible positions on the war within the same political camp—support, abstention, and opposition among Socialists; a debate about the compatibility with the proletarian revolution of Abd el-Krim's nationalism among Communists.

In broader historical perspective, there was nothing necessary about the particular hierarchical configuration, any more than the gender distribution, of the radical fantasy of revolutionary native 'virulence'. Westerners who have desired the muscular energy of some revolutionary Other have positioned themselves in relation to the objects of their fantasy in a wide variety of ways: a desire to submit to a virile native revolutionary as well as a desire to discipline, a desire to be infantilized before an exotic teacher as well as a paternalist desire to instruct a primitive pupil, and so on. The past century has exhibited the entire catalogue of such desires in Westerners' relationships to a variety of

---

[63] Gallissot, 'Le parti communiste et la guerre du Rif', in *Abd el-Krim et La République du Rif, supra* n. 52, 237, at 251–3.

Third World heroes, heroes who have come in a range of political, cultural, and libidinal stripes.

C. The Desire to Explode

I use the idea of the 'desire to explode' to interpret the position of members of the avant-garde, particularly that of many Surrealists. The latter part of 1925 was a crucial turning point in Surrealists' understanding of the relation between art and politics. Breton later declared that the turn of Surrealism to overt political engagement in 1925 was directly due to the 'brutal, revolting, *unthinkable* fact' of the War of the Riff.[64] Near the start of the war, the Surrealists disrupted a literary banquet in Paris with various provocative cries, among them, 'Down with France' and 'Long live the Riffans'.[65]

In this section, I analyse three versions of the relationship between the avant-garde's general animus against French society and their celebration of the Orient—that I call the masochistic, strategic, and hysterical versions. I begin with a comment by the Surrealist René Crevel, which is quite representative of the attitudes of many in the avant-garde towards the War of the Riff. Note the way it casts the Riffan rebels in the role of the Orient for which Breton had hoped in his *Les Cahiers du Mois* contribution (the Orient that would 'conquer us')—and, especially, its animus against the prevailing international legal framework:

[T]he government's appeal to *the laws of men, to treaties, to conventions*—and we understand what they're really worth—forces us to state our contempt for the anti-Riffan enterprise. At a time when grasping hypocrites[66] denounce the 'Oriental peril', this odious European conduct makes us dream of some dynamite that could pulverize the institutions and methods of our precious country and its neighbors.

Maybe the benefit of this war will be the hastening of the debacle of what they call our civilization.[67]

Many Surrealists expressed versions of this hope that the war, and the Riffans themselves, would serve as the 'dynamite' that could 'pulverize' their own society, whose 'laws, treaties, conventions' were the object of avant-garde 'contempt'.

---

[64] A. Breton, *What is Surrealism?*, trans. D. Gascoyne (1974), at 51.

[65] M. Nadeau, *Histoire du Surréalisme* (1964), at 82–3.

[66] Crevel's term is 'Raminagrobis', a character from a fable by LaFontaine. Raminagrobis is a cat to whom the weasel and the rabbit turn for a judgment in a territorial dispute. The feline judge asks the litigants to come nearer so he can better hear their arguments. He then grabs them and devours them both. LaFontaine explicitly draws an analogy between this fable and the relations of great and small sovereigns.

[67] 'Réponse de M. René Crevel', 76 *Clarté* (1925) 24.

The manifesto against the war which the Surrealists co-wrote with the *Clarté* group contained a typical Surrealist spin on the pervasive period amalgamation of all non-Europeans into an undifferentiated Oriental mass: 'It is the turn of *the Mongols* to camp in our plazas.' From the Surrealist perspective, it was of little importance whether the fantasized 'dynamite' to blow up European society came from Asia or Africa—of no more importance than, in the Socialist fantasy, the provenance of the energy for the revitalization of that society, or, in the left-wing Communist fantasy, the provenance of the conscripts ('the Riff or Shanghai') for European revolution.

For an international lawyer, it is striking to learn the extent to which the avant-garde denunciation of European society in the name of the 'barbaric' Orient was explicitly lodged against international law, whose 'treaties and conventions' authorized the French hold on Morocco. The writer Henry Poulaille pithily summarized the avant-garde's position on international law, particularly in the wake of World War I:

The war in Morocco?
Obviously against.
Against all wars.
On the subject of this new 'last' war,[68] what happens to the question of *Law?*
Is the war in Morocco also a war of law?[69]
Then against law.[70]

Indeed, some Surrealists specifically directed their rage against the League of Nations, that hope of liberals, that envy of Communists. The Surrealist Robert Desnos especially condemned the League's fight against abortion, narcotics, and pornography—a rather different set of concerns than those expressed by the anti-League writer in the Communist *L'Humanité*. Desnos argued that these campaigns showed that the League's main goal was 'the struggle against liberty'. Combining three typical avant-garde impulses— contempt for bourgeois hypocrisy, desire for explosive sexuality, and classic gender typology—Desnos summed up his attitude to the League with a striking exclamation: 'League of Nations! Old whore!'[71]

The Surrealists' scorn for law and its institutions played a central role in their 1925 polemics with the *Clarté* writers. In these polemics, they associated the Communist revolution with a superficial reordering of society, a superficiality they designated with the adjective '*legal*'; the *Clarté* writers, in turn, accused them of a merely '*cultural*' rebelliousness. This polemic was strikingly expressed in this exchange between the Surrealist Aragon and Marcel Fourrier of *Clarté*:

[68] Official French propaganda called World War I the 'last war'.
[69] Again, official French pronouncements referred to World War I in this way.
[70] 'Réponse de M. Henry Poulaille', 76 *Clarté* (1925) 21.
[71] Desnos, 'Descriptions d'une Révolte prochaine', 3 *RS* (1925) 25, at 26.

Aragon: 'if [Marxists] find me closed to the political spirit, in fact, violently hostile to this dishonorable pragmatic attitude . . . it is because I have always placed the spirit of revolt *beyond all politics*. . . . The Russian Revolution . . . was, at most, a *vague ministerial crisis*.'

Fourrier: 'Aragon, a pure anarchist, willfully limits himself to the *cultural* plane.'

Aragon: '[You have] reduced the infinite cause of Revolution to the proportions of a *simple legal crisis*.'[72]

For Surrealists, the 'legal' was the name for that which co-opted revolutionary energy in order to effect superficial shifts in the elite power structure. Surrealists, by contrast, sought a 'spirit of revolt' that could more profoundly destroy 'the debacle they call our civilization'. And if Surrealists viewed even the Communist revolution as 'merely legal', their fury was at least as great when it came to the legal reformism of the Socialists and the Human Rights League—for example, scorning the two groups for their shared distinction between 'good and bad ways to colonize'.[73] To paraphrase Breton, rather than looking for an opportunity to reshape or even revolutionize legal relationships, Surrealists sought an energy which could destroy them.

In opposing the War of the Riff, therefore, Surrealists, unlike many Socialists and Communists, rejected the appeal of international law, whether reformed or revolutionized. Aragon, for example, attacked the antiwar manifesto published in *L'Humanité* in terms quite different than those of its Communist critic:

... let me reproach you ... for having used expressions drawn from nationalist language: *independence, national sovereignty, inalienable right of peoples to self-determination*. For me, *there are no 'peoples'*, I can barely understand this word in the singular.[74]

With the 1925 Surrealists, we find ourselves in a different world than that of liberal Socialists or radical Communists: no self-determination, no national liberation struggles, no 'peoples'—indeed, not even the leftist evocation of 'the people' in the singular. Instead, we find a fierce desire for an indiscriminate subversion of Occidental politics and culture. As the Surrealists declared in connection with the Riff:

We wish with all our might that revolutions, wars, and colonial insurrections will come to annihilate this Occidental civilization . . . . We seize this occasion to disassociate ourselves from everything French . . . . We find treason . . . more compatible with poetry than [patriotic activities] ...[75]

[72] 'Communisme et Révolution', 2 *RS* (1925) 32 (emphasis added). I should note that Aragon would soon abandon this stance and join the Communist Party. His pre-Communist polemics remain, however, classic avant-garde protests against doctrinaire leftism.

[73] Breton *et al.*, 'Ne visitez pas l'Exposition Coloniale' (1931), in J. Pierre (ed.), 1 *Tracts Surréalistes* (1990) 194, at 195.

[74] 'Réponse de M. Louis Aragon', 76 *Clarté* (1925) 24.

[75] Alexandre *et al.*, 'Lettre ouverte à M. Paul Claudel' (1925), in Pierre (ed.), *supra* n. 73, 49, at 50.

With this desire for the Orient to erupt into a frenzied and total destruction of their own society, we seem to find ourselves at the limit of colonized desire in the *metropole*, the point beyond which the Surrealist would simply submit to 'the mass of the Orient' as it 'swoop[ed] inexorably down' upon the Occident.[76] This desire would have much in common with the left-wing Communist desire for violent Oriental energy, but would substitute a masochistic desire to submit to that violence for the Communist desire to discipline it. The Surrealists seemed to express an unqualified desire to explode, in both the active and passive senses of that verb: a desire for the Orient to detonate and for the Occident to be pulverized.

In contrast with this version, another strand of Surrealist pronouncements suggests a much more critical stance in relation to Modernism's image of the Orient.[77] In some of these critical pronouncements, which persisted alongside their straightforwardly primitivist rivals,[78] Surrealists revealed their intention to manipulate prevailing Orientalist imagery as part of a calculated strategy of political provocation. Indeed, where Socialists' rhetorical authority depended on their claimed expertise in distinguishing between good and bad colonialism, and Communists' authority on the ability to differentiate between good and bad nationalism, Surrealist discourse produced its provocative effects in part by oscillating between affirmations of the reality and illusoriness of Modernism's Orient.

Thus, in some passages, Breton asserted that the word 'Orient' in Surrealist discourse did not refer to an actual source of subversive energy located in the geographical east. Rather than relying on a real Orient literally to destroy Occidental civilization, the Surrealist declared that it was the word itself, and not its mythic referent, which interested him. For example, in December 1926, Breton wrote that

> it is out of place to point out that we have contradicted ourselves in giving divergent senses to certain *buffer-words*, like the word 'Orient'. This word—which plays on one literal meaning and many figurative meanings, and of course on a variety of countermeanings—has been increasingly pronounced in recent years. It must correspond to a particular worry of this period, its most secret hope, its unconscious foresight. The insistence with which this word comes up . . . itself constitutes a good argument on its behalf. Today's reactionaries know this well, and they never miss an occasion to attack

---

[76] Eluard, 'La suppression de l'esclavage', 3 *RS* (1925) 19.

[77] For example, a few years after the War of the Riff, a group of Surrealists heaped scorn on the desire of 'bourgeois intellectuals' for the 'call of some "mystic Orient" or other'. Breton *et al.*, 'Murderous Humanitarianism', in N. Cunard (ed.), *Negro: An Anthology* (1934) 574, at 575. See also the critique of colonial French sexual desire in Crevel, 'The Negress in the Brothel', in Cunard, ibid., at 1.

[78] In 1948, Breton continued to write of his affinity with the 'resources of the primitive soul' and of the 'inseparability' of early Surrealism from its 'fascination' for Asian and Oceanic art. See Breton, 'Océanie' (1948), III *Oeuvres Complètes* (1999) 835, at 837–8.

the Orient. . . . Why, under these conditions, shouldn't we continue to *claim the Orient, even a 'pseudo-Orient', for ourselves*—an Orient in relation to which Surrealism would merely be an homage?[79]

In effect, Breton here declared that scholarly or political critics of his Orientalism were missing the point. He asserted that he privileged the word, 'Orient', simply as a discursive weapon to provoke French anxieties and delusions—rather than because of a belief in a vitalistic Orient, or in any literal Orient at all. What appeared to the Communists as a merely 'cultural' programme was a calculated Surrealist strategy of subversion, of throwing discursive 'dynamite' at the psyche of 'our precious society'.

Lastly, there is yet a third strand in Surrealist writings of this period, the hysterical strand. This strand expressed a desire for identification with the Orient—a desire not to submit or manipulate, but to *be* the primitive force whose eruption would shatter Occidental civilization. Thus, in their antiwar manifesto, the Surrealists declared that 'we are certainly Barbarians because a certain form of civilization disgusts us'.[80] Similarly, in another context, Breton wrote of 'our total primitivism', claiming a Surrealist embodiment of the primitive more powerful than any merely aesthetic representation of it.[81] In this self-referential primitivism, the Surrealist claimed for himself the role of the barbarian that he at other times projected on geographically distant others.

This strand competed with, and incorporated, both the masochistic version, in which the avant-garde longed for destruction of the Occident by a real Orient, and the calculated strategy version, in which the avant-garde waved the Oriental fetish in order to frighten its opponents. On one level, it incorporated the masochistic version because it retained the Frenchman's desire for the destruction of his own society. Yet it went beyond it due to the doubling of roles the Surrealist claimed for himself: Oriental *and* Occidental, explosive primitive *and* suave Parisian, dynamite *and* target, killer *and* suicide.

In this strand, Surrealist discourse presented itself as a series of *hysterical texts*—exhibiting the typically hysterical 'features of a discourse in crisis', marked by 'confusions of utterance' and 'splittings and displacements of the subject of the story'.[82] As I have noted, 'confusions of utterance' marked Surrealist discourse on the Orient which was characterized by 'divergent senses', of 'meanings and . . . counter-meanings'. Perhaps more significantly, 'displacements of the subject' also typified this discourse, in its shifts between projecting an aggressive Orient in an exotic locale and locating it within the Surrealists' own Parisian subjectivity, within the target of the desired Oriental aggression.

---

[79] Breton, 'Légitime Défense', 8 *RS* (1925) 30, at 35.
[80] Altmann *et al.*, 'La Révolution d'abord et toujours', 5 *RS* (1925) 31.
[81] Breton, 'Le Surréalisme et la peinture', 4 *RS* (1925) 16, at 17.
[82] C. Kahane, *Passions of the Voice: Hysteria, Narrative, and the Figure of the Speaking Woman, 1850–1915* (1995), at xiv.

To broach the gender tones that again insist here, the violent doubling of the Surrealists' identities in this strand of their anticolonial pronouncements points us to a classic Freudian explanation of the seeming incoherence of hysterical attacks.[83] Freud asserted that this outward incoherence can be attributed to the fact that the hysteric, through 'multiple identification', undertakes incompatible roles in a single performance. Freud gives the following characteristically gendered example: 'For instance, I have mentioned a case in which a patient tore off her dress with one hand (as the man) while she pressed it to her body with the other (as the woman).'[84] Indeed, Freud interpreted the seeming incoherence of the hysterical performance as the enactment of a violent conflict between a range of opposed sexual identities within the hysteric, male and female, homosexual and heterosexual, aggressor and victim.[85] Similarly, in their fantasy of playing both parts in an Oriental/Occidental explosion, the Surrealists presented themselves as classic hysterics in this Freudian sense, gender-doubled players in a violent sado-masochistic performance.[86]

On another level, this version of the Surrealists' relationship to the Orient also incorporated the calculated strategy version. The Surrealists' deliberate deployment of the signifier, 'Orient', played a crucial part in their hysterical performance—for their claim to the role of destroyers of the Occident depended on their posing as the Oriental aggressor. The Orient thus served to magnify the Occidental Surrealists' role not by providing some external source of energy, but by making possible the rhetorical technique of self-doubling without which they would appear as merely narcissistic or suicidal. Or, perhaps, in accordance with Breton's ruminations on suicide, the term 'Orient' enabled the doubling which would make cultural suicide discursively possible.[87] In this strand of their pronouncements, the Orient thus became something conjured up by the Surrealists in order to serve their project of

---

[83] S. Freud, 'Some General Remarks on Hysterical Attacks' (1908), 9 *Standard Edition* (1953) 229.

[84] Ibid., at 230. Xavière Gauthier uses this passage from Freud to interpret a painting by Magritte. See X. Gauthier, *Surréalisme et sexualité* (1971), at 259.

[85] Freud, 'Hysterical Phantasies and their Relation to Bisexuality' (1908), in S. Freud, *Dora: An Analysis of a Case of Hysteria* (1963) 145, at 150–2.

[86] Indeed, their desire to enact such a performance here would be anticipating the celebratory description of hysteria that Breton and Aragon published in 1928: 'We love nothing better than these young hysterics. . . . Hysteria is a mental state . . . characterized by the subversion of the relations between the subject and the moral world . . . Hysteria is not a pathological phenomenon and can, in all respects, be considered a supreme means of expression.' Aragon and Breton, 'Le cinquantenaire de l'hystérie' (1928), reprinted in M. Nadeau, *Histoire du Surréalisme* (1964) 284, at 284–5.

[87] As Breton wrote: 'Suicide is a misnomer; he who kills is not identical with he who is killed.' Breton in 'Enquête, Le Suicide est-il une solution?', 2 *RS* (1925) 8, at 12 (quoting Théodore Jouffroy).

internal cultural splitting and self-destruction. As suggested in the quotation from Aragon I cited earlier ('Let the Orient... *respond to our voice'*—see p. 200 above), the Surrealists were here manipulating an Oriental signifier in the service of an intra-Parisian agenda, even if that agenda was one of a performance of hysterical self-destruction.

From our historical distance of nearly eight decades, there is something that seems rather *too* deliberate in this self-presentation, something that seems to tarnish the power of the Surrealists' hysterical performance. The Surrealists seem in such passages to be feigning self-destructive hysteria, rather than undergoing it. They seem to lack the spasmodic energy which makes hysterical attacks such frightening and fascinating performances. The Surrealists seem rather like hysterics *manqués*, bad-faith presenters of themselves as the destroyer/destroyed of their Parisian habitat.

Indeed, the male writer's self-portrayal as a hysteric was a not uncommon trope beginning in the mid-nineteenth century.[88] By the Modernist era, 'mimicry of hysterical form' characterized the literary style of a range of writers.[89] These calculated representations of hysteria provided such writers with 'a way of speaking through the Other in order to explore their own phobic involvement in unsettling cultural ambiguities of desire and difference'.[90] By 'playing with this lack of control', with this 'tactic of dissociation', the Modernist sought to 'keep his authority intact'. In the Surrealists' case, it was the Orient that served as that 'Other' that enabled them to flirt with cultural, libidinal, and gender doubling and dissolution while simultaneously reinforcing their own power—specifically, their power to be provocative.

The seeming bad faith of their hysterical self-presentation may counsel scepticism about Surrealist anti-Occidentalism.[91] In broader historical perspective, it suggests a certain scepticism about all those in powerful *metropoles* who piously proclaim their identification with the primitive 'Other' and their wish for destruction of their own society—but who simultaneously seek to reap the cultural dividend of the hysterical performance, in all its gender-doubled fascination.

In the Surrealist case, however, things are rather more complicated—due to their sustained anticolonial political engagement, but also due to their sustained engagement with writers in the colonized world, particularly in the Caribbean. Encounters between Breton and Caribbean writers, for example, left an enduring, if ambivalent, mark on all sides.[92] In 1932, a group of

[88] E. Showalter, *Hystories* (1997), 95.
[89] Kahane, *supra* n. 82, at 127–50.
[90] Ibid., at 150.
[91] Cf. Scott, 'Dreaming the other: Breton, Césaire, and the problematics of influence', 42 *Romance Quarterly* (1995) 28.
[92] See generally Richardson, 'Introduction', in M. Richardson, *Refusal of the Shadow: Surrealism and the Caribbean* (1996), at 1.

Martiniquan students in Paris, many of whom later became key literary figures, regularly met with Breton and issued a manifesto declaring their allegiance to Surrealism;[93] this allegiance persisted through much of the 1940s for many Martiniquan writers.[94] In 1945, Breton lectured in Haiti and expressed his anticolonial politics and primitivist affinities.[95] The power of the Surrealist's performance deeply affected writers like the Haitian Paul Laraque, who adopted Breton as 'my dear Magus'.[96]

Yet the relationship between such Caribbean writers and their colleague from the colonial *metropole*, however avant-garde, could not but be fraught with tension. The Martiniquan René Ménil declared that the Surrealism practised by Caribbean writers was part of a 'colonial exoticism' that alienated them from themselves.[97] Aimé Césaire, perhaps the most well-known Caribbean writer often linked to the French movement, emphatically differentiated his own Surrealism from that of Breton. He declared that his compatriots who professed their Surrealist allegiance in the 1930s were 'too penetrated by assimilationism'.[98] As should be evident by now, of course, a full consideration of these complexities and ambivalences would considerably transcend the limits of a study of the War of the Riff.

D. The Desire to Disorient

Each variant of desire on the French left may be associated with the 'appeal' of an image of the colonized as exorbitantly vitalistic: primitive, freedom-loving tribes for Socialists; virile, muscular revolutionaries for left-wing Communists; cataclysmic forces of destruction for Surrealists. This exorbitance was *both* a creation of French desire, the projection of a wild Otherness to seduce, conscript, or explode, *and* an effect on French desire of the active resistance of the colonized. In the preceding sections, I looked at one side of this double phenomenon, that of the projection of French fantasy. I analysed the indeterminacy and contingency of the intersection of desire and normativity in the French debates. In this section, I turn to the other side of the double phenomenon and look at the active attempt by the Riffan leader to create his local and international identity through his many public pronouncements—letters, proclamations, and interviews addressed to audiences ranging

---

[93] '*Légitime Défense*: Declaration', in Richardson, *supra* n. 92, at 41.
[94] See e.g. Suzanne Césaire, '1943: Surrealism and Us', in Richardson, *supra* n. 92, at 123.
[95] See Breton, 'Discours d'André Breton à "Savoy"', 193 *Conjonction* (1992) 62; Bélance, 'Interview d'André Breton', 193 *Conjonction* (1992) 107.
[96] Laraque, 'André Breton en Haiti', 193 *Conjonction* (1992) 24.
[97] Ménil, 'On Colonial Exoticism' (1959), in Richardson, *supra* n. 92, at 176.
[98] Interview with Césaire (1967), quoted in G. Ngal, *Aimé Césaire* (1994), at 59.

from 'North African Muslims' to 'the American people', to 'Latin America', to the French parliament, to select European and American journalists. In this analysis, I focus on the oscillation between Abd el-Krim's mastery and bewilderment in relation to the multiplicity of his images on the various stages on which he chose to play—on his *desire to disorient* and on his own disorientation.

In examining the public discourse of Abd el-Krim, both contemporaneous and historical commentators have invariably been struck by the diversity of his characterizations of the Riffan struggle. At times he described the Riffan goal as establishing a 'republic', playing on all the modernizing, secular nationalist connotations of that term;[99] at other times, he described the struggle in terms drawn from an Islamic tradition of holy war.[100] As to the territorial scope of the struggle, he sometimes described his goal as the establishment of a Riffan autonomous area loyal to the Sultan; at other times, he spoke contemptuously of the submissive Sultan and allowed himself to be addressed in terms suggesting his aspiration to supplant him;[101] in yet another statement, he asserted that the Riff had a right to absolute independence, that it had never been a part of Morocco, and that the Riffans were racially distinct from 'all other African races, having mingled with the Europeans and Phoenicians hundreds of years ago'.[102] Abd el-Krim's followers addressed him by a correspondingly varied assortment of titles, which may be listed in ascending order of the Riffan leader's possible ambitions: leader of the holy war, emir of the Riff, *khalifa*, sultan, master, lord.[103]

Abd el-Krim's continually shifting self-presentation produced remarkable successes among an exceptionally diverse international audience far beyond France.[104] A few disparate examples: among his Islamic supporters, he inspired calls for solidarity based on the image of a transnational religious community extending to India,[105] or even Indonesia.[106] For his Swiss supporters, the campaign for Riffan independence seemed a reprise of William Tell's freedom struggle.[107] For his US and Latin American supporters, he appeared to take up the anticolonial cause in which their nations were born.[108]

[99] Tahtah, *supra* n. 4, at 157.
[100] Mohamed ben Abd el-Krim el-Khattabi, 'Appel à tous les musulmans du Maroc' (1925), reprinted in Tahtah, *supra* n. 4, at 174.
[101] Rivet, *supra* n. 3, at 260, n. 486.
[102] Mohamed ben Abd el-Krim el-Khattabi, 'Declaration of State and Proclamation to all Nations' (1923), reprinted in R. Furneaux, *Abdel Krim, Emir of the Rif* (1967), at 83.
[103] Rivet, *supra* n. 3, at 260.
[104] See generally T. Boutbouqalt, *La Guerre du Rif et la Réaction de l'Opinion Internationale* (1992).
[105] Rivet, *supra* n. 3, at 265.
[106] Boutbouqalt, *supra* n. 104, at 135.
[107] Rivet, *supra* n. 3, at 265; Boutbouqalt, *supra* n. 104, at 108.
[108] Rivet, *supra* n. 3, at 265; Boutbouqalt, *supra* n. 104, at 129–30.

For his German supporters, traumatized by the recent French occupation of the Ruhr, he seemed an ally in their perennial struggle against their European neighbour.[109]

One way to characterize Abd el-Krim's multiple public relations efforts is that he was animated by a *desire to disorient*, the term I have borrowed from Dinet and ben Ibrahim. I use the term 'disorientation' in two senses. First, I use 'disorient' in its conventional sense, to refer to Abd el-Krim's shifting characterizations of the Riffan struggle in a manner that complicated all attempts to categorize, praise, or condemn it. Secondly, I use the term to refer to his attempt literally to 'dis-Orient'—in the sense of refusing the European projection of the categories of 'Orient' and 'Occident' and reconfiguring them in the name of an anticolonial political project.

We can see the latter aspect of Abd el-Krim's strategy in an open letter that he addressed to 'North African Muslims', which was published, among other places, in the anticolonial Parisian newspaper, *Le Paria* (edited by the young Ho Chi Minh):

Just as, in the far West [*l'Extrême-Occident*], we have risen up to fight for independence, so China, with its 400 million inhabitants, has risen up in the far East [*l'Extrême-Orient*] to obtain the liberation of its territory. Let us form with the nations of the Orient a single group and let us rise up together ... [110]

Abd el-Krim's reference to the 'far West' was, on one level, simply a translation of the Arabic name for Morocco (*al-Maghreb al-Aqsa*, literally, the 'farthest west'). On another level, though, this rhetoric confounded and reconfigured the European usage of the Orient/Occident dichotomy. By claiming Morocco as 'the Occident', Abd el-Krim refused European projections of the colonized as an undifferentiated Oriental mass in which one can't tell the difference between Moroccans and Mongols, or between the Riff and Shanghai. Abd el-Krim's letter sought both to distinguish and unite a very different 'Occident' and a more specific 'Orient'—an alliance between the distinct struggles of the Riff and Shanghai.

The *desire to dis-orient and reconfigure*: this is the desire that emerges from the public pronouncements of the Riffan leader. Abd el-Krim sought to shake up the terms of the prevailing international discourse by exploiting the ambivalences and indeterminacies in Riffan, Moroccan, French, and international desires. Abd el-Krim's public discourse consisted of shifting attempts to manipulate these desires as he struggled to reconfigure identity on the cultural frontiers of Orient and Occident, Islam and Europe, modernity and tradition—even as he conducted a military struggle on the literal frontier between the French, Spanish, and Riffan zones.

[109] Rivet, *supra* n. 3, at 265; Boutbouqalt, *supra* n. 104, at 108.
[110] Mohamed ben Abd el-Krim, 'Aux Musulmans de l'Afrique du Nord', *Le Paria* (April 1926) 1.

Abd el-Krim was well-suited for such frontier strategies. He began his career writing the Arabic section of a local Spanish newspaper, then served as a Muslim judge within the Spanish colonial government. Among other pursuits, he studied modern nationalism and international law.[111] Like many other colonized intellectuals of the early twentieth century, he began his political life as a reformist of the good-colonialism/bad-colonialism school, another version of which I have analysed in discussing the French Socialists. In the young Abd el-Krim's case, the 'good colonialism' was that of Spain, the 'bad' that of France. Abd el-Krim urged his countrymen to look to Spain for help in cultural and economic modernization. In 1909, he condemned those Moroccans who opposed Spain as 'fanatics who understand nothing'.[112]

Eventually, of course, Abd el-Krim thoroughly rejected any European political control. His other political views, whether on the relationship between European and Islamic ideas, or among various versions of both, remain difficult to pin down. His stance on the relationship between religion and modernity, for example, has evoked a variety of interpretations, each attempting to reconcile his disparate pronouncements by using some mediating term or paradoxical phrase. He has been viewed as a religious modernizer, a secular nationalist, and even a puritan reformer.[113] One writer declared that the contradictions could be resolved by distinguishing Abd el-Krim's true allegiance, which was to secular nationalism, from his merely expedient appeals to the Riffan tribesman, which relied on religious imagery.[114] All of these explanations attempt to find a coherent logic in his multiple and divergent pronouncements, and attribute to Abd el-Krim an underlying mastery of this multiplicity.

I suggest, by contrast, that the desire to project mastery onto Abd el-Krim's shifting public relations efforts may itself be a byproduct of Abd el-Krim's disorientation project. Disoriented analysts may understandably seek a way out of their perplexity by projecting coherence onto the source of their confusion, as suggested in the passage by Dinet and ben Ibrahim from which I borrowed the idea of the desire to disorient. After noting the many contradictory descriptions of Islam in the writing of various Orientalists, the authors comment:

Completely *disoriented*, shouldn't we say, by the divergence of all these versions, the reader will find it difficult to form a precise opinion and *be left with only one desire*, to finally know the true Arab tradition.[115]

---

[111] Tahtah, *supra* n. 4, at 147.
[112] Ibid.
[113] Ibid., at 163.
[114] Ibid., at 155.
[115] Dinet and ben Ibrahim, *supra* n. 33, at 16 (emphasis added).

Dinet and ben Ibrahim, in the rest of their book, set out to satisfy that 'one desire' produced in the French reader, the desire to 'know the true Arab tradition'. Yet I suggest that that 'one desire to know' and its imagined object, the 'true tradition', as well as the authors' desire to present that object, were themselves byproducts of the disorientation. Complex cultures like 'the Arab tradition', or complex political events like the Riff, invariably both produce and frustrate desires to know a univocal truth about them. From this perspective, the authors of *The Orient Seen from the Occident*, precisely in so far as they sought to satisfy their readers' 'one desire', were just as disoriented as their audience. And, similarly, the notion that Abd el-Krim had full control over his conflicting pronouncements—a notion held by some contemporaries, historians, and Abd el-Krim himself—may have been an illusion produced by a related kind of disorientation.

One symptom of this disorientation may be found in Abd el-Krim's retrospective legal articulation of his ultimate goal. After his defeat, the leader whose ambitions included complex and shifting reconfigurations of Orient and Occident, tradition and modernity, Islam and secularism, the Riff and Morocco, and so on, explained the goal that animated his struggle in unexpected and modest terms:

I wanted to make the Riff an independent country on the model of France or Spain, to found a free state with sovereignty, not an emirate subject to the rules of a protectorate or a mandate.... I tried to make [the Riffans] understand that... their interest lay in unifying and in organizing a government in the modern style. I would have wanted them to understand that they have a country and a patriotic tie, not just a religion... We wanted a real independence and a government in possession of its rights, its economic movement, its alliances.[116]

Sovereignty, modern governmental style, separation of religion and state, membership in the club of states—worthwhile goals perhaps, the basic goals of many leaders of decolonization movements over the next few decades, but hardly up to the level of the complex and shifting discourse of Abd el-Krim during his rebellion. In this retrospective attempt at defining his historical role, Abd el-Krim would take his place as simply another reformer of international law, seeking to expand the club of states while retaining its prevailing structure. His multiple self-characterizations would all have been in service of a clear, limited goal of the achievement of European-style sovereignty. The numerous other ways his goals had been understood, both within and beyond Morocco, would all have been mere misunderstandings.

A consideration of this retrospective self-description by Abd el-Krim requires a re-examination of the relation between his tactics and his ultimate goal. I revisit once more the ambivalences found in contemporaneous and

---

[116] Tahtah, *supra* n. 4, at 158.

historical interpretations of the inconsistencies in the images he claimed and evoked. For his adversaries, these disparate images signified the Riffan's duplicity, his attempt to hide his true goals under a false exterior—though they were undecided whether this duplicity was of the modern, calculating, perhaps 'Bolshevik' variety, or of a primitive, reflexive, 'atavistic' sort.[117] Yet even this uncertainty paled behind the uncertainty about what his true goal was, about which of his various guises should be viewed as Abd el-Krim's true identity and which as propagandistic camouflage. For some, he was a feudal lord in disguise as the leader of a modern republic,[118] a 'vindictive and cruel Barbarian' either concealed by 'a refined appearance',[119] or 'dressed up in the current fashion' of Bolshevism and Communism.[120] For others, on the contrary, he was a Russian or German puppet costumed as a primitive tribal leader: 'behind [Abdel Krim's] burnous, one can detect the agitations of the bloody follies of Moscow and the unsatiated cravings of Berlin'.[121] The images of sartorial masquerade and hidden desire that recur in these descriptions, coupled with the uncertainty about which persona was the real Abd el-Krim and which the sham, suggest a gender ambivalence evoked by Abd el-Krim— an ambivalence that emerges more clearly in considering the more explicit discussions of the Riffan's power over his multiple images.

For Abd el-Krim's supporters and some historians, the disparate images were a product *either* of the Riffan's masterful stratagems, *or*, on the contrary, of the fantasies and nefarious schemes projected on him from near and far. For example, referring to the steady 'inflation' of the titles by which Abd el-Krim was addressed, one French historian wrote that this 'semantic crescendo' must have been 'controlled and perhaps organized by Abd el-Krim'.[122] Yet this same historian also wrote: 'The Riff is a phenomenon of moving mirrors, where everyone discovers the image that he was seeking.'[123] These two observa- tions—the first attributing to Abd el-Krim active 'control' over his image, the latter treating the Riff as a passive 'mirror'—might be viewed as setting forth as alternatives the two perspectives I have described: the Riff's image as a projection by others versus the Riff's image as a product of Riffan agency. They might also suggest a combination of the two explanations: the fantasy

---

[117] J. Ladreit de Lacharrière, *Le Rêve d'Abd el-Krim* (1925), at 255.

[118] E.g. 'Réponse de M. René Maran', 76 *Clarté* (1925) 279.

[119] Kahn, *supra* n. 54, at 294.

[120] See the statement of Augustin Bernard, quoted in Rivet, *supra* n. 3, at 257.

[121] *Echo de Paris* (June 1925), quoted in Rivet, *supra* n. 3, at 257. In evoking these comments, Abd el-Krim followed in his father's footsteps. His father was subject to this difficult-to-translate taunt by his fellow Riffans: 'Si Abdelkrim à la barbe de verdier, il était Espagnol, aujourd'hui il est devenu Allemand' ('Abdelkrim with the beard of a greenfinch, yesterday he was Spanish, today he's become German'). G. Ayache, *Les Origines de la guerre du Rif* (1981), at 233.

[122] Rivet, *supra* n. 3, at 260.

[123] Ibid., at 264.

images of Abd el-Krim could be viewed as projected not onto a blank and stable screen, but rather onto an active set of 'moving mirrors' that partly created the desires they might seem only to reflect.

Turning to the gendered imagery that again seems so insistent here: the commentators have been unable to decide between Abd el-Krim, the macho manipulator, and Abd el-Krim, the passive object of desire or plaything in the hands of devious patrons. Abd el-Krim, too, seemed bewildered by his historical position and by the difficulties posed by its apparent undecidability. He repeatedly declared that his fellow Riffans, as well as international observers, failed to understand him and, after his defeat, that he 'had come too early'.[124] Perhaps surprisingly, these statements almost exactly replicate those of a French anti-Abd el-Krim polemic of 1925, referring to him as 'a type of leader who is not in harmony with his time or his context'[125]—and, in a more overtly, if complicatedly, gendered manner, as 'an African example of *bovarysme*'.[126]

Pairing the Riffan rebel with Flaubert's provincial anti-heroine was not meant as a compliment. Nonetheless, Emma Bovary[127]—that gender-doubled hysteric, misunderstood on all sides, composed of equal parts of shrewd calculation and dreamy fantasy, borrowing her self-image from multiple literary sources in an attempt to escape from the intolerable identity imposed on her by the prevailing social structure—provides a wild, but not utterly misplaced, analogy to Abd el-Krim. A cunning tactician tempted by grandiose ambitions, trapped between Spain, France, and Morocco, torn between competing cultures and political visions, feeling misunderstood by his fellow Riffans and by the world at large, believing himself to belong to a different historical moment—Abd el-Krim sought to improvise his way out of his situation, trying on any number of identities for himself and his cause, drawing these identities from a variety of available ideologies (rather than romance novels). If contemporaries and historians have felt disoriented by his claims, unable to settle on one true interpretation of his identity, they have been sharing Abd el-Krim's own bafflement.

From this perspective, the difficulty of interpreting Abd el-Krim's tactics in light of one overall goal would not stem from mere misunderstandings, but from the implausibility, or even fictionality, of identifying such a unified goal. The sovereignty goal would take its place among all his other self-characterizations as yet another tactical fiction—another tactic without an overall strategy, in a campaign composed solely of tactics. Abd el-Krim's tactics, untethered from one organizing principle, were thus inherently in

[124] Tahtah, *supra* n. 4, at 165.

[125] Ladreit de Lacharrière, *supra* n. 117, at 263.

[126] Ibid., at 262.

[127] I draw the description of her character that follows in the text from Charles Baudelaire, 'Madame Bovary par Gustave Flaubert' (1857), in *Curiosités esthétiques, l'Art romantique* (1962) 643, at 648–649.

constant transformation. And since those tactics consisted of shifts of identity, his identity itself was inherently shifting, without any one element playing the role of true self and the others that of masquerades.

Macho master of manipulation or feminized object of desire, atavistic warlord or secular modernizer, Arab nationalist or German puppet, and on and on: Abd el-Krim moved constantly between all the identities claimed by him or imputed to him. He *was* his shifting tactics and identities, simultaneously creating and reflecting European and Moroccan desires, simultaneously disorienting and disoriented, veering between unexpected achievement and desperate powerlessness.

In the end, Abd el-Krim failed. At the simplest level of his literal military defeat, one can attribute this failure to the fact that he 'had come too early'. A band of tribal rebels operating very close to Europe could not defeat the combined forces of France and Spain in the 1920s. Abd el-Krim was exploiting and creating unprecedented possibilities whose scope and plausibility he could not gauge, experimenting with a variety of ideologies and political alliances whose consequences he could not predict. Far from mastering his alternative and incompatible rhetorics and tactics, he could only seek to manoeuvre within them as best he could.

Yet his failure may be located at a deeper level. The myriad tensions between the various ideologies invoked by Abd el-Krim are unresolvable conceptually and can work together only under very specific political and historical conditions. Not even the most masterful strategist could create or predict those conditions. And the tensions between the disparate ideologies would long outlive the struggle against formal colonialism. More than one post-colonial state has been thoroughly disoriented by the warring forces unleashed by the contradictory strategies of anticolonial resistance. At the end of the colonial day, managing the tensions among the programmes of Robespierre, William Tell, Kemal Ataturk, the Prophet Mohammed, Simon Bolivar, V. I. Lenin, and George Washington—let alone Emma Bovary—would become more than a matter of remembering to which newspaper one was giving an interview.

3. CONCLUSION

My analysis of varieties of colonized desire in relation to the War of the Riff rests on several axioms. First, it presumes that fears and fantasies about others, marked by shifting and ambivalent configurations of gender and sexuality, are an irreducible element of human experience. They cannot be replaced, except in utopian myth, by some unmediated, authentic encounter—especially in situations of great disparities of power and wealth, even leaving aside linguistic, geographical, racial, and religious difference. Secondly, it presumes that the grand dichotomies that have long structured discussions of the relationship of

Europe to the colonized and formerly colonized world—such as those between good and bad colonialism, good and bad nationalism, real and illusory
Orients—are both persistent and indeterminate.

These axioms do not entail a tragic worldview; on the contrary, they provide a
basis for exploring cultural and political possibilities that would otherwise
remain invisible. It is *not a critique* of Socialists, Communists, Surrealists, or
Riffans simply to describe the ways their constructions of the Moroccan conflict
embodied fears and fantasies about Orient and Occident—however gendered,
sexualized, or geographized. Rather, this description should be the beginning of
a series of questions—to what cultural and political alliances did such fears and
fantasies lend themselves? To what alliances might they have lent themselves?
Fears and fantasies do not *inevitably* indict the political positions taken.

For example, Abd el-Krim was not let down by his left-wing Communist
supporters due to their eroticized Orientalist fantasies—on the contrary, these
Communists would probably not have gone into the streets to protest the war
without those fantasies. From a Riffan perspective, the problem with the
Communists was rather that their ardour was not more widely shared and
that it flagged too soon. In fact, the critique of Orientalism within the
Communist Party took an anti-Riffan form: an attack on a specific form of
Orientalism the critics called 'Abd el-Krimism'. From an anticolonial perspective, then, French Communist Orientalism was too weak, rather than too
strong. The European fantasy of conscripting virile Riffans as trophy lovers for
a Third International disappointed with impotent European proletarians was
quite detached from political possibility. Antiwar actions in the streets of Paris,
by contrast, though driven by that fantasy, could have had an actual effect on
French policy if they had garnered sustained and wide support.

In short, this study is based on a rejection of ahistorical and rationalist
critiques of Orientalism. Just as it rejects an unequivocal link between Orientalist desire and particular political positions, so it rejects a view of such desire
as monolithic and unchanging, of its gender projections and sexual longings as
static and unimaginative. Historical inquiry based on a rationalist critique of
Orientalist desire often limits itself to the discovery and condemnation of a
seemingly inexhaustible record of a monotonous delusion. Empires come and
empires go, millions are born and millions die, yet the rationalist critic of
Orientalism sees only a tiresome, if uncanny, stasis—from Aeschylus to Bush
and beyond. Such a one-dimensional approach may be occasionally productive—if, for example, it succeeds at academic or political provocation. Yet,
beyond an initial polemical phase, this stance leads to flawed theory, impover-
ished history, and political paralysis—not to mention libidinal tedium. By
contrast, if we get rid of the rationalist prejudice, if desire is irreducible and
protean, then we can and should look for variety, instability, and ambivalence—uncovering the complex impulses that make change possible, even if a
troubling and unpredictable affair.

8

Toward an Understanding of Transnationalism and Gender

RUBA SALIH

As Zygmunt Bauman notes, 'access to global mobility' is becoming one of the most important factors in social stratification.[1] Yet 'access to global mobility' is also gendered.

The ethnography of Moroccan women in Italy presented in this chapter shows that the conditions for moving transnationally are not always available to women, or are limited or framed within a set of normative and culturally gendered rules. By example, the chapter suggests that as globalization stimulates a reformulation of time, space, and mobility, the political and social fields on which gender and human rights must be analysed are becoming transnational.

Unlike earlier migrants, current migrants are increasingly likely to participate in the political and social lives of two or more countries.[2] This phenomenon has led to a shift in the understanding of contemporary international migration. Whereas scholars traditionally concentrated on the adaptation of immigrants to their new society, the past decade has seen a growing literature on the ways that migrants live in 'transnational communities':[3]

... dense networks across political borders created by immigrants in their quest for economic advancement and social recognition. Through these networks, an increasing number of people are able to live dual lives. Participants are often bilingual, move easily between different cultures, frequently maintain homes in two countries, and pursue economic, political and cultural interests that require their presence in both.[4]

[1] Z. Bauman, *Globalisation* (1998), at 87.

[2] L. Basch, N. Glick-Schiller, and C. Szanton-Blanc, *Nations Unbound: Transnational Projects, Postcolonial Predicaments and Deterritorialized Nation-States* (1994).

[3] See Vertovec, 'Transnationalism and Identity', 27 *Journal of Ethnic and Migration Studies* (2001) 573, at 574–6.

[4] Portes, 'Immigration Theory for a New Century: Some Problems and Opportunities', 31(4) *International Migration Review* (1997) 799, at 812.

While these transnational practices are theorized as potential forms of resistance to the new socio-economic predicaments transmigrants are facing, the theoretical focus by and large has been on changes to the processes of nation-building and the conditions that these changes create for migrants. Nation-building now takes places within and across nation states—both the state of origin and of residence. For Linda Basch and co-authors Nina Glick-Schiller and Cristina Szanton-Blanc, the state of origin has therefore become deterritorialized. It should no longer be conceived of as a geographically bounded state with a diaspora, but as a state that is spatially coextensive with its people: 'The nation's people may live anywhere in the world and still not live outside the state.'[5] This reconception has been criticized by Robert Smith, who notes that nation states are territorial by definition in the Weberian sense. Nation states, Smith argues, exist when a state incorporates and forms the nation by fostering an imaged community sharing similar discourses, sentiments, and imagination within a given territory. Rather than seeing nation states as deterritorialized, we should, therefore, perceive migrants' increasing political, social, and economic involvement in their countries of origin as an attempt by the sending nation state to incorporate others outside its borders into the territorially based national political community.[6] Viewed from this perspective, the phenomenon is surely older than is commonly supposed, and indeed scholars have shown how diasporas dating back to the pre-colonial period have historically been linked with the construction of nationhood both at 'home' and abroad.[7]

Although offering important insights into the nature of transnationalism by showing how migrants are embedded within, and reproduce, nation-building logics, such analyses[8] do not address the tension between structure and agency and their articulation with gender. To what extent is the position of migrants produced by the state processes described by scholars of transnationalism, and to what extent do migrants have the capacity to choose and to resist? And does the answer differ for women and men? The focus on migrant women in this chapter highlights a specific type of embeddedness within nation states' hegemony[9] and, often, a different experience of transnationalism from that of their male counterparts.

This chapter aims at unravelling the different levels of transnational activities and movements Moroccan women are engaged with. As we shall see,

---

[5] Basch *et al.*, *supra* n. 2, at 269.

[6] Smith, 'Reflections on migration, the state and the construction, durability and newness of transnational life', in L. Pries (ed.), *Migration and Transnational Social Spaces* (1999) 187, at 213.

[7] Van der Veer, 'The Diasporic Imagination', in P. van der Veer (ed.), *Nation and Migration. The Politics of Space in the South Asian Diaspora* (1995) 1, at 1–17.

[8] Basch *et al.*, *supra* n. 2; Portes, *supra* n. 4; Smith, *supra* n. 6.

[9] See Joseph, 'Gender and Citizenship in Middle Eastern States', 26(1) *Merip* (1996) 4, at 7.

Moroccan women construct a 'home' which includes Italy and Morocco, since both these contexts provide them with complementary symbolic and material resources. However, their activities are also conditioned by a set of normative and cultural regulations based upon hegemonic interpretations of gender roles, which both in Morocco and Italy condition their activities, their identities, and their likelihood of moving across countries or staying put.

1. GLOBALIZATION, POST-INDUSTRIALISM, AND TRANSNATIONALISM: MOROCCAN MIGRANTS IN ITALY

At the end of the 1960s the number of Moroccans officially resident in Europe was around 160,000. In 1992, only some 23 years later, the number of Moroccans in Europe was estimated to be around 1,343,000. This is a substantial figure if we consider that the Moroccan population is around 20 million and growing at a rate of 2.6 per cent annually. In the course of the 1960s and 1970s, apart from France, other countries such as Germany, Holland, and Belgium started to become important destinations. Migration trends in this period followed the favourable economic situation of European industrial societies and were regulated by agreements between Morocco and the receiving states. Agreements that dealt with employment and other conditions regarding Moroccan manpower within European countries were signed with Germany and France (1963), Belgium (1964), and Holland (1969).

Italy became an important country of immigration only quite recently, and the presence of Moroccans started to be visible at the beginning of the 1980s. In 1970 there were 136 Moroccan citizens residing in Italy.[10] Between 1987 and 1990 (roughly the dates of two major amnesty laws), Italy saw a huge growth in the number of Moroccans, which rose from 15,705 to 77,971. By 1992 around 130,000 Moroccans were estimated to be living in Italy.[11] Concerning the Emilia Romagna region, Caritas' figures suggest 16,051 Moroccans regularly resident in the region in 1997. In contrast with previous migration to France, the majority of Moroccans in Italy were undocumented and acquired a *permesso di soggiorno* (residence permit) through three main amnesties in 1986, 1990, and 1996.

Moroccan women represent 20 per cent (equivalent to some 26,000) of the Moroccan population in Italy. About 11 per cent of them live between Bologna, Reggio Emilia, and Modena,[12] some of the areas where fieldwork

---

[10] M. de Bernart *et al.*, *Migrazioni femminili, famiglia e reti sociali tra Italia e Marocco. Il caso di Bologna* (1995), at 61.

[11] A. Bencherifa, M. Berciane, and M. Refass, *Études des mouvements migratoires du Maroc vers la communauté européenne*, GERA (groupe d'études et de recherches appliquées) (1992), at 20.

[12] Kuider and Calzolari, 'Les marocaines en Italie', in K. Basfao and H. Taarji (eds), *Annuaire de l'emigration* (1994) 423.

was conducted. Contrary to the common perception that portrays Moroccan women as by and large followers of their husbands, many women migrated to Italy as single migrants in the course of the late 1980s and the beginning of the 1990s. In 1994, data showed that 49 per cent of Moroccan women living in Italy had a residence permit for work reasons, while 44 per cent were in Italy for family reunions. The rest had a visa for tourism or study.[13] Other studies show that even in the context of family reunions, women are often involved in the family's strategy and decisions.[14]

At a general level, contemporary international migration flows to Italy occurred within a framework of changing socio-economic conditions as compared to the industrial expansion of the 1950s and the 1960s in France and other European countries. In the United States, Roger Rouse has defined this new stage in the relations of production as a 'reconfiguration of the landscape of socio-economic experience', symbolized by the shift in the strategies of capital accumulation from the multinational corporations, where self-contained processes of production were basically located in different countries, to the era of transnational corporations that distribute a single economic process in various countries and reduce the time of technological communication between the different places and phases of production.[15]

While European industrial societies in the post-war period were characterized by a high level of recruitment within an expanding Fordist industrial sector, in the 1990s the importance of the tertiary sector increased. Contrary to the industrial growth characteristic of the traditional immigration countries during the 1950s and 1960s, the Italian labour market manifests complex and contradictory traits, with deep internal differences. It is characterized by a high level of segmentation and, especially in the southern regions, of flexibility. This expands the demand for seasonal or precarious jobs which, because of their low salaries and very bad conditions, are not satisfied by the local labour supply.[16]

At the same time, in wealthy regions of northern Italy, such as Emilia Romagna, immigration has been described as more stable, and from the outset it has been characterized by a higher number of family reunions and of legal migrants with long-term projects of settlement.[17] Here, there is an increasing number of immigrant workers in permanent and stable jobs, especially in

[13] Kuider and Calzolari, 'Les marocaines en Italie', in K. Basfao and H. Taarji (eds), *Annuaire de l'emigration* (1994) 423.

[14] Schmidt di Friedberg and Saint-Blancat, 'L'immigration au féminin: les femmes marocaines en Italie du Nord', 131 *Studi Emigrazione* xxxv (1998) 483, at 496.

[15] Rouse, 'Thinking through Transnationalism: Notes on the Cultural Politics of Class Relations in the Contemporary United States', 7(2) *Public Culture* (1995) 353, at 366.

[16] Pugliese, 'Economie. Le marché du travail', in K. Basfao and H. Taarji (eds), *supra* n. 12, 432 at 432–3.

[17] L. Pepa (ed.), *Immigrati e comunità locali: azioni, interventi e saperi dall'emergenza al progetto* (1996).

small and medium-sized industries (SMEs). However, even in this case, the number of non-regular (*in nero*) or cash-in-hand workers amongst immigrant workers is very high.[18]

Moroccan women are mainly employed within the domestic and cleaning sectors and, in very few cases, in small industries. The majority of domestic workers in Italy are, however, employed without a regular contract (*in nero*).[19] The fast ageing of the local population, together with changes in women's employment outside the home, are amongst the principal explanations for migrant women's insertion within the domestic sector at the regional and national levels. Compared with Italy as a whole, Emilia Romagna shows a much higher rate of local women's participation within the labour market (43 per cent against 37 per cent nationally in 1986). However, the increasing participation of Italian women in the labour market has not brought about changes in the traditional division of roles within Italian families. Moreover, the rapidly increasing percentage of older people coincided with (and caused) a major restructuring of the Italian welfare system, which was a consequence of cuts in public expenditure. In this context, Italian families turn to migrant women for care-related jobs. Migrant women seem, then, to substitute for Italian women in their domestic roles.

In addition, in the last few years a new recurrent theme that emphasizes the advantages of migration is emerging in Europe and Italy. Demographic decline is perceived as a major risk for the future of the national economy and the welfare system. Politicians, economists, and demographers have started to maintain that migrant families and their higher fertility rates with respect to Italian families are, and will continue to be, a major resource for the country.[20] The ageing of the Italian population constitutes a serious problem since, it is argued, older people consume less and cost the state more. Moreover, as mentioned above, demographers maintain that within 20 years or so, the demand for labour will not be covered by Italian nationals. This argument relies heavily on the fertility rates of migrant women who are expected to reproduce the labour force for the national economy, and represents a shift with respect to the trend in Europe up to the 1970s when, to contain the public costs of maintenance of inactive members, the temporary migration of single males with a project of return was encouraged.[21]

This insistence on migrant families' productive and reproductive roles as resources for the economy and demography of the country suggests that the

---

[18] See Motturra, 'Immigrati e sindacato', in E. Pugliese (ed.), *Rapporto Immigrazione. Lavoro, Sindacato, Società* (2000) 113.

[19] J. Andall, *Gender, Migration and Domestic Service. The Politics of Black Women in Italy* (2000); G. Vicarelli (ed.), *Le mani invisibili. La vita e il lavoro delle donne immigrate* (1994).

[20] *La Repubblica*, 19 June 1998, 17 January 1999; *Il Sole 24-Ore*, 5 October 1998.

[21] Morokvasic, 'Fortress Europe and Migrant Women', 39 *Feminist Review* (1991) 21, at 69–83.

state is increasingly operating together with economic interests to cope with the contradictions caused by globalizing trends. These require a cheaper and easily exploitable manpower, and may eventually lead to a general depreciation of local labour costs. However, despite the increasing demand for migrants' manpower within certain sectors, the Italian government has strengthened the policy of control of its borders under the pressure of the construction of a 'Fortress Europe' sanctioned by the Schengen Agreement. The 1998 Law (known as 'Turco-Napolitano') has suggested that the integration of migrants already settled in Italy is contingent upon the state's capacity to prevent further (illegal) immigration.[22]

These contrasting attitudes of the Italian state suggest that the state is not a coherent and homogeneous body, but operates according to different and sometimes contradicting interests. Moreover, global forces do not simply weaken a nation state's power but may force it to adapt its strategies and roles to survive new challenges.[23]

2. MOROCCAN MIGRANT WOMEN: TRANS/NATIONAL SUBJECTS

It is my argument that we need to grasp the concurrent action of economic changes, cultural and normative regulations, and individual strategies in understanding both migration and the gendered nature of transnational movements between Morocco and Italy. The major theoretical approaches to migration present limitations in that they explain female mobility or immobility exclusively by structural factors, such as relations of production, by cultural factors, or by individuals' strategies. In order to understand gender selectivity in migration patterns, Sylvia Chant and Sarah Radcliffe instead propose a household strategy, which focuses both on economic factors, such as the gender division of labour and of relations of production, and on the reproductive roles and hierarchies within the household.[24] In emphasizing the relation between the two, the household approach discloses the interconnection between individual agency, cultural factors, and socio-economic

[22] This argument is not new and it recalls the situation in France during the 1980s, when illegal immigration was also constructed by the state as a challenge to the 'integration' of legal immigrants. As M. Silverman puts it, 'the consensus on integration and control (the success of the former dependent on the rigour of the latter) is at the heart of the illegalisation of immigration (immigration perpetuates the "problems" of integration)': M. Silverman, *Deconstructing the nation: immigration, racism and citizenship in modern France* (1992), at 138.

[23] Compare Rouse, *supra* n. 15; A. Ong, *Flexible Citizenship. The Cultural Logic of Transnationality* (1999).

[24] Chant and Radcliffe, 'Migration and development: the importance of gender', in S. Chant (ed.), *Gender and migration in developing countries* (1992) 1, at 1–30.

structures. Moreover, household approaches also consider wider determinants, such as civil and legislative issues, in accounting for gender selectivity and inequality in migration flows.[25] In her analysis of gender and migration in Europe, Annie Phizacklea also seeks to go beyond the structure/agency dichotomy. Drawing on Anthony Giddens' structuration theory, she maintains that structures are 'both constraining and enabling because they are both medium and outcomes of the practices they recursively organise'.[26]

Both these analyses are helpful in situating Moroccan women's migration to Italy, and I argue that a similar theorization is needed for an examination of the relation between gender and transnationalism. The household approach, as we shall see, is particularly appropriate when it comes to understanding a particular form of transnational activity, namely, women's reproductive roles as performed in the two countries. These approaches together thus constitute a useful framework for the conceptualization of Moroccan migrant women as plurinational subjects, who embody, but at the same time challenge, the multiple set of constraints, both in Italy and Morocco, which frame their movements back and forth.

Among Moroccan women, the rationales for migration are heterogeneous: some saw it as an opportunity to improve their lifestyle or to pursue their studies, while for others (although it was never explicitly stated) it seems that the project of getting married to fellow emigrants was amongst their goals. Other women migrated as a result of their marriage to emigrant men already settled in Italy who had returned to Morocco to find a wife. However, amongst women who migrated to join their husbands, the reasons were not simple and homogeneous but, as we shall see, complex and varied.

For women who had left Morocco as single migrants, an important aspect was the previous history of migration within their extended families. In most cases, women were not the first members of the family to migrate; migration does not represent a new experience, since it is, so to speak, integral to the social identity of some families whose migration story goes back one or two generations. Moreover, some women who came as single migrants had brothers or sisters already living in Italy. The presence of male kin often made women's migration more socially acceptable since it allowed a conceptualization of women's migration as a reunion with family members rather than as an individual adventure.

Along with socio-economic reasons, political issues played a role in the motivation to migrate. Many informants made it explicit on different occasions that one of the reasons that propelled them to take advantage of the opportunity

---

[25] Chant, 'Conclusion: towards a framework for the analysis of gender-selective migration', in Chant (ed.), *supra* n. 24, at 204.

[26] Phizacklea, 'Migration and Globalization: a feminist perspective', in K. Koser and H. Lutz (eds), *The New Migration in Europe: Social constructions and social realities* (1998) 21, at 26.

to migrate and to settle in Italy was the lack of democracy, the censorship, and the lack of freedom of information in Morocco. Suheila, a young former university student in Morocco, stated several times that she had had enough of Morocco, which she described as an 'underdeveloped country', meaning socially and economically. Suha stressed that in Morocco, 'you can't talk about the King, you can't smoke, you can't wear a miniskirt!', and others have stressed that 'there is no freedom, it is disordered and dirty, it is not like here, where, for example ... it is clean and silent, there the streets are dirty, it is not like Italy'.

However, discourses and reflections of those informants, women and men, whose migration to Italy was the result of an active decision, revealed that the possibility of leaving their country did not depend simply on their personal individual choice. Rather, both women who were keen to migrate and those who perceived migration as a necessary evil stressed that conditions for migrating emerge under particular economic, political, or social circumstances. Many Moroccans migrated in the late 1980s after they had heard from other fellow Moroccans already in Italy that the Italian government was issuing an amnesty law, which would regularize all undocumented immigrants able to prove that they had a job and that they had entered Italy prior to a certain date.

The Moroccan government, however, also provides opportunities. Settat, for example, a small town located on the road between Casablanca and Beni Millal, is a place from where many Moroccans migrated to Italy. The town has seen an extraordinary expansion and development. Many houses have been built and the main roads show luxurious shops and restaurants. A new and modern university together with a large library have recently been constructed. A golf club with a swimming pool and bar provides one of the social centres of the small town. Interestingly, my informants in Italy showed great astonishment when I informed them of my intention to visit Settat, probably because they still thought it a backward rural village of no particular interest. However, this town has a special status. Settat is the birthplace of one the Ministers of the now deceased Hassan II, who supported it in various ways, not least by favouring locals in the selection for migration by issuing them with passports. Likewise, when I was in Casablanca during summer 1997, people were talking about an 'opportunity to migrate to the United States' as a result of an agreement between the US government and King Hassan II. In this and other circumstances, it emerged that migration is also understood as a political-economic strategy of the Moroccan government unwilling and unable to provide alternatives to young people with no prospect of employment in their own country.

Having provided a framework for locating Moroccan migration to Italy, I would like now to present women's experiences and reflections on their migration, through some life histories which will shed light on the interconnections of the varied elements discussed so far.

A. Samia

Samia left Casablanca to come to Italy in 1989. When Samia was still a child, her mother was offered a job as a housekeeper for a diplomatic family in London. At that time, she was a widow and her sister, Samia's aunt, was supporting the whole family. Samia's mother enthusiastically accepted the job, but this meant that Samia and her brother had to be left with some relatives for a while until the mother could settle. Just before everything was ready for her departure, Samia's mother decided not to go because she was unable to resist the social pressures against leaving, including the criticism that she was abandoning her children. Samia's mother has always somehow regretted her choice. She imagines how her life could have been if she had had the strength to overcome the social pressures. Hence, when Samia decided to leave Morocco, her mother did not oppose her. Samia told me she left Morocco with the wish to do something new. At that time she was the owner of a hairdresser's shop which she closed and sold. Before opening the hairdresser's shop, she worked for many years in a factory that produced shirts.

When Samia left Casablanca she had no contacts other than the address of a woman living in a small town (Montecchio) near Reggio Emilia who, Samia was told, 'is a very nice woman who helps *extracomunitari*' (*extracomunitari* literally means from outside the European Union and is a derogatory term used in Italy to speak about migrants). Samia brought with her only a small suitcase and some money, because she was not sure about what would happen once in Italy, whether she would be able to settle or not, and whether she would like it or not. She stressed that, if things had turned out too hard for her, she had been prepared to go back to Morocco. For example, she would have never gone to a hotel by herself or 'sleep in the street'. Samia was lucky. Her contact referred her to another family, who hosted Samia for a couple of weeks. Eventually she found a job as the housekeeper and care assistant of an old woman. She lived with the woman and her family, who later helped Samia in finding a flat.

Once in Italy, she met a fellow Moroccan, Yusuf, married him and had two children. However, she could not find a place to live with her husband. She was living in Montecchio, while he was in Reggio Emilia. After having searched unsuccessfully for a flat for a long time, she took the initiative to go to the mayor to tell him her problem, explaining that she could not carry on being separated from her husband. Again, a solidarity chain was activated. The mayor sold an old property to Samia's host family who then rented it to Samia and Yusuf. Samia emphasized that things had been somehow easier then, since when she arrived in Montecchio in 1989, she thought she was probably the only Moroccan there.

However, when I first met her, Samia was unemployed and very depressed. She had attended more than one training course organized by the local trade unions and the municipality to become a professional care assistant, but despite this, the only job she had been offered was in a different town, one hour from where she lives, and the salary was as low as 900,000 Lire a month (around 450 Euros). Indignantly she refused the offer. Yusuf had also been unemployed for a long period when they first met.

Currently Samia has a job as a manual worker in the same factory where her husband found a job, but from time to time, she still works as a care assistant, when she has free afternoons from the factory shifts. However, this kind of life is made possible by the presence of her mother, who basically lives between Casablanca and Reggio Emilia, helping Samia with the house and the children.

B. Rima

When I first met Rima, she apologized for not being able to give much time to our meeting, as she was an extremely busy woman—she appeared sincere when she claimed that she would have loved to have done so. She is married, with three children of 17, 13, and 11, and a job that keeps her busy every day including Saturday mornings—she usually spends Saturday afternoons shopping for the rest of the week. On Sundays she is busy cleaning and ironing, and taking her children to visit their friends. Her husband, who is Italian, is only rarely present, as he has started a new job in another town.

Rima, the only daughter of a well-off family from Tangier, has been living in Italy for 18 years. Soon after she obtained her degree in literature in Morocco, she decided to come to Italy where she met her husband. The decision to marry an Italian was a crucial one in her life. After Rima decided to have a family with an Italian, her father excluded her forever from his life: 'He told me that if I had gone back to Morocco he would have taken my passport away from me.' Rejected by her family, Rima did not return to Morocco for many years. Rima's husband and children have never seen Morocco. Her 13-year-old daughter refused to accept her Moroccan half for a long time: 'Whenever she saw someone she recognized as Maghrebin she used to run away.' Rima bitterly claimed: 'My children are Italian ... they would come to Morocco as tourists, I can't accept this idea.'

Recently Rima visited Tangier for the first time after 18 years to attend the funeral of her father. Once there, she discovered that her mother had lied to family and acquaintances, asserting that her daughter had married a Tunisian in Italy. However, when Rima went back to Morocco, she found her mother in a state of nervous breakdown, not even able to recognize her daughter.

C. Ziba

Ziba migrated to Italy in 1993 to join her husband. Her sister moved early on to Spain, where she is now living with her husband and her grown-up daughters. Another sister is married to a Tunisian and lives in Tunisia. Her other three sisters and two brothers are in Morocco. However, Ziba did not leave Morocco straight after her wedding but decided to stay with her parents in Tangier. After some months she decided to leave because she was feeling under heavy social pressure and control. She did not enjoy the freedom she thought she would have as a married woman because she was still living with her parents. Moreover, she felt watched by the neighbours who were checking all her movements, although she said she was not doing 'anything wrong'. Eventually she decided to join her husband. Yet she is keen on proudly emphasizing that she never thought about Italy, she was not interested in migrating herself, and stated: 'I came for my husband.' When she first arrived in Italy she lived for four years in Piemonte, in the northwest of Italy, before moving to Modena.

In Morocco, prior to getting married, Ziba was working as a clerk in a branch of a ministry in Tangier. After completing her baccalaureate she went through a public competition to get the job, which she obtained thanks to a well-placed relative. In Italy she cleans rooms in a hotel where she is employed without a regular contract (*in nero*). Yet Ziba prefers to earn more in the clandestine labour market (in exchange for not paying taxes, employers sometimes pay higher wages to employees who work for them '*in nero*'), and is willing to renounce pension rights and contributions, for her project and that of her husband is to return to Morocco sometime in the future, where they have already bought land. The reason, moreover, is that she does not trust the Italian state to pay her pension once she is in Morocco. In fact, as far as she knows, there are no clear and fixed agreements between Italy and Morocco on these matters, and she is convinced that once she returns to live permanently in Morocco, Italian bureaucrats will try to defraud her and she would lose the pension anyway. Moreover, Ziba is obliged to be flexible and not subject to job rules, because she also needs to be free to travel to Morocco when she is required there. Indeed, after some time, Ziba had to leave her job. Her husband was complaining that, since she also had to work on Saturdays and sometimes on Sundays, he had to spend his free days taking care of their daughter. She also stated that she was struggling too hard to keep up with her other duties, and she had to pay a higher fee to leave her daughter for an extra two hours in the kindergarten. On top of these problems, when her mother in Morocco became ill, she had to leave the job in Italy in order to go to Morocco to take care of her. Since Ziba's daughter was not yet attending primary school, it was decided that Ziba was freer than her sisters who live in Tunisia and

Spain, and more flexible than her sisters who live in different parts of Morocco, who are busy with small babies, since Ziba could take her daughter with her and spend long periods of time in Morocco helping her mother.

D. Karima

Karima told me how she came to Italy by chance, although she has always been connected to Italy in various ways. Three of her sisters and a brother had been living in Rome before she migrated. They arrived during the 1980s, and they all found jobs with well-off families. One of her sisters is married to an Italian. Moreover, a special friend of her family is a former Italian army employee who lived in Morocco for many years in the past. During a visit to Italy to attend a wedding, Karima was offered a job as a housekeeper. She explained:

They offered me 14 salaries[27] and paid holidays, a first class ticket and a nice and new flat as accommodation. They said they knew I was very good and for this reason they wanted me at all costs. At the beginning I was confused, I was not sure. But my friends convinced me ... I have some friends here. They said they would have helped me with any problem and they added that whenever I felt homesick, I could take a plane and be home in three hours.

Karima is now working as housekeeper and baby-sitter for a famous Italian singer who is often away, and for this reason, Karima is left for most of the time alone with the child. She lives in the second floor of the flat, where she has her own room and bathroom with a little lounge. With her own savings, she has already bought a flat in Rabat. Karima is very keen on emphasizing that she has always worked with a regular contract (*in regola*):

I was always *in regola*, even when they employed me on trial for a short period; I was always *in regola*. You know, I cannot work without insurance, because I need the documents, the *permesso di soggiorno* [residence permit] to go home, to travel, since from time to time I travel, I have an aunt in France, in Paris, sometimes I go to see her, and to go to Paris I need the visa, to have the visa I need a job, the documents should be *in ordine* [in order]. I was always *in ordine*. The only time I had some trouble was with a job I had up in the mountains. It was a seasonal job; they told me that there was a lady who needed a care assistant. I went to see about this job and the lady's son told me he did not want to do the documents for me, he said he was going away for a trip and after he'd come back he would do the documents for me. When he came back, he refused to do my documents. I told him I would leave the job if he refused to employ me regularly. He answered that I shouldn't be afraid because it would be done soon. I waited four months and I ended up working for the sister of the lady.

[27] Italian law states that regularly employed workers earn 14 months' salary per year: two extra salaries are paid in the middle and at the end of each working year.

3. TRANSNATIONALISM, MIGRATION, AND THE NATION STATE

The previous stories provide various and different illustrations of how Moroccan women's migration and their potential transnational movements take place. They also shed light on the ways in which, in some cases, there is an interconnection between women's migration, how they are inserted in the labour market, and the formal and social constraints which actually impinge upon their likelihood of migrating and/or living transnationally.

For some women, migration was not an option since their migration and/or the potential to move transnationally was conditioned by hegemonic normative structures which they have internalized. Whereas some women like Samia and Karima have partly challenged these structures, other women are not in a position to counteract the normative and socio-cultural rules they are expected to observe. Women who came to join their husbands often express a mixture of resignation and acceptance towards their situation. In some cases, the expectations they had of their futures and careers have clashed with their current lives in Italy. This is especially the case for young educated women, who were performing well at school and whose dreams turned out to be illusions. Ziba's story, and those of other women not mentioned here, indicate that their migration to Italy was encouraged by their families and society in general, and contrasted with their aspirations. Ziba was compelled to migrate since she could not cope with the social pressures and the rumours that eventually started to affect her reputation, as a result of the fact that she initially had decided not to follow her husband to Italy and to remain to live with her family. Her roles and responsibilities in the domestic sphere in her transnational household, however, required her to fly back to Morocco when her mother became ill, leaving her flexible, badly-paid job as cleaner. Likewise, these are the same social constraints that 30 years ago Samia's mother did not dare challenge, preventing her from leaving the country.

Transnational movements are thus sometimes forged by the roles women are expected to perform in the domestic sphere and in the household. The fact that when legal and social status and conditions permit, daughters spend periods of time with their mothers in Morocco, and mothers temporarily join their daughters in Italy, bears witness to the emergence of what I term a 'transnational sphere of reproductive and care activities'. This aspect has been underlined by other scholars. For example, Fernandez-Kelly in the 1970s noted how:

Men, socialized to act as providers, are expected to send money and/or presents to their families in Mexico and to visit occasionally. Women, on the other hand, are expected to take full responsibility for the daily care of their children and their homes.

If they must migrate, they must also return to the homestead more frequently. Thus, the widespread ideological notion that 'man was made to work, and woman to care for the house' impinges upon the likelihood of crossing the border.[28]

Transnational movements are also highly linked to and conditioned by laws and regulations. Legality is the other crucial factor that influences the potential for crossing borders. For women who came alone, to have a job which fulfils the requirements to be *in regola* is essential if they are to be able to move. As Karima said, among the considerations that eventually convinced her to accept the job in Italy, the central one was the possibility of travelling back to Morocco in only three hours. But to be able to travel, she needs to be legal. In her case, to possess the documents becomes an embodied feeling, that of *being in order*, which pervades her identity. Women whose permit is linked to that of their husband, such as Ziba, on the other hand, are able to work '*in nero*' since they do not need to have a regular job to renew their permits. This flexibility, however, allows them to accomplish their reproductive and care roles transnationally.

However, not only women's legal status in Italy, but also the different kind of citizenship women experience in their country of origin might operate to condition their transnational movements. Italian private international law states that concerning personal status matters, migrants are ruled by their national laws, unless these are in open conflict with Italian legislation, producing a danger to the 'public order'.[29] For example, polygamous unions and repudiations are not recognized in Italy since they are considered a threat to the public order and a violation of human rights, as defined within the European Convention on Human Rights.[30] However, the national law is applicable only when the two spouses share the same citizenship. If the spouses have a different citizenship, the law which is applied is that of the state where the two spouses reside, or where their life take place, therefore Italy.[31]

Personal status laws in Morocco are collected in the Mudawana, a code based on the Maliki Islamic school of interpretation which, despite some reforms brought about in 1993, still maintains women in a subordinate

[28] Fernandez-Kelly, 'Mexican border industrialization, female labor force participation and migration', in J. Nash and M. P. Fernandez-Kelly (eds), *Women, Men, and The International Division of Labor* (1974) 205, at 213.
[29] Italian law n. 218/1995: 'a foreign law is not applied if its effects are in contrast to the public order' (in Italian: 'la legge straniera non è applicata se i suoi effetti sono contrari all'ordine pubblico'), cited in Campiglio, 'Famiglia e diritto islamico. Profili internazional-privatistici', in S. Ferrari (ed.), *Musulmani in Italia. La condizione giuridica delle comunità islamiche* (2000) 175, at 175.
[30] Although there have been cases where women who were married to the same man were accorded resident permits not on the basis of family reunification with their husband, but rather as single migrants.
[31] Articles 29–30, Italian law n. 218/1995. For a review of the legal situation of Muslims in Italy, see Ferrari (ed.), *supra* n. 29.

position. Therefore, a wedding celebrated according to Italian law between two Moroccan citizens is not valid for the Moroccan state if not registered in the Consulate. However, to be registered in the Consulate, the marriage has to conform to the Mudawana. This means that the marriage between a Moroccan Muslim woman and a non-Muslim, such as that of Rima, will not be considered valid and will not be registered in Morocco, according to the Mudawana which forbids marriages between Muslim women and non-Muslims. The Moroccan state has tended to safeguard the applicability of its laws to its citizens abroad, even in case of double citizenship (see, for example, the Convention Franco-Marocaine signed in 1981). Therefore, a marriage celebrated in France or Italy which does not conform to the Moroccan Personal Status Law would not be recognized in Morocco. Interviews I conducted within the Consulate of Morocco in Bologna revealed interesting insights in this regard. During a first encounter with officials in the Consulate, I was told by the official responsible for social services that a Moroccan woman who leaves her husband without referring to a court or, more specifically, without respecting the Mudawana's prescriptions on women's rights to divorce, would be forbidden entrance to Morocco. Bewildered by this statement, during a subsequent encounter, I sought clarification from the Halami, the notary, who specified that, if not Moroccan law, social rules would consider such an action unacceptable within Moroccan society and would ostracize women. This recalls Rima's case, who, after she married an Italian against the will of her father, could not and would not keep up links with Morocco for 18 years, to the extent that her children became in her own words 'Italian'.

4. THE LIVED EXPERIENCE OF TRANSNATIONALISM: THE DIALECTIC OF BELONGING AND LONGING

The embeddedness of Moroccan women's lives and transnational movements with normative rules and cultural constructions of gender roles operating in both national contexts does not deny the importance that transnational activities have in the accumulation of both symbolic and economic capital for migrant families, as well as in the construction of their identities.

An important aspect of transnational practices is the extent to which they enable migrants to rely on two countries to construct their social personhood by distributing not only economic but also symbolic resources.[32]

A pivotal moment in the life of many Moroccan women in Italy is the summer return that involves shopping, consumption, and displaying goods.

---

[32] See Goldring, 'The Power of Status in Transnational Social Fields', in M. P. Smith and L. E. Guarnizo (eds), *Transnationalism from Below* (1998) 165.

Through consumption practices, Moroccan women construct their home and social status by objectifying themselves in the commodities they bring back and forth. Particularly significant are the objects and consumer goods through which Moroccan women construct the space they inhabit, and through which they both negotiate identity ruptures and establish continuities between countries.

As well as to the cultural complexity deriving from the flow of ideas, cultural meanings, and commodities,[33] attention is here drawn to consumption as a domain of objectification and expression of social status. As Katy Gardner has shown in her study of Sylheti migrants, consumption and gift exchange across England and Bangladesh 'are part of the discourse of power between places'.[34] In the case of Moroccan migrant women, consumption emerges as a twofold practice. On the one side it represents a complex process whereby women appropriate and negotiate symbols of modernity by interpreting and attributing value to goods that flow from Italy to Morocco and vice versa. On the other side, it serves the aim of operating a distinction and affirming a difference with respect to those who remained in Morocco.

As other scholars have argued, it is not so much the flow of different things, in the form of goods, ideas, or cultural meanings, in itself that is significant.[35] Rather, we should look at the ways in which things are given new social and cultural meanings, and what kind of relations they produce, modify, or redefine in the social field in which they are received and consumed. A significant site of analysis in this regard is the way the flow of goods is articulated with the conceptualization of home. Home is here understood as both the physical space women and their families inhabit and as the symbolic conceptualization of where one belongs. I suggest that women articulate and give meaning to the spaces they inhabit through the objects they bring back and forth.

To most Moroccan women, the summer return is a very important event that involves a long period of preparation and shopping. Women start to arrange things one or two months before the date of leaving, although it can be said that, for some families, the whole way of life in Italy is functional and complementary to the summer return. The lifestyles migrants display when they are in Morocco for a short period are the result of a hard and difficult life for the rest of the year in Italy. Women's preparation revolves around buying presents for relatives, but also buying many things for themselves and their children. Typical goods of interest to women are items for the house, especially blankets, sheets, and towels, as well as domestic appliances to take both for

---

[33] U. Hannerz, *Cultural Complexity. Studies in the social organization of meaning* (1992).

[34] Gardner, 'Desh-Bidesh: Sylheti images of home and away', 28 *Man* (1993) 1, at 11.

[35] Appadurai, 'Introduction: commodities and the politics of value', in A. Appadurai (ed.), *The social life of things. Commodities in cultural perspective* (1986) 3.

personal use and as gifts. Clothes and shoes for themselves and their children are also amongst major expenses. Domestic appliances are particularly significant in underlining the expanded economic possibilities, also in view of the very high prices they have in Morocco. Women also tend to take with them to Morocco those goods with which they have become very familiar in Italy, such as baby food, nappies, or indeed Parmesan cheese, which are usually too expensive in Morocco and through which, moreover, they constantly remind themselves and others that their habits have changed.

On the other hand, homes in Italy are decorated with things that reflect the double belonging. Typical cheap, popular Italian furniture is displayed together with objects recalling the Moroccan and Muslim world, such as covers for sofas, pictures showing Quranic writings on the walls, and in some cases, calendars arriving from France with dates of Islamic celebrations and feasts, or posters of Moroccan women wearing the traditional dresses of different areas of Morocco. Food stored in the kitchen reflects a multiple identity. Together with Italian food, spices brought back from Morocco and particular ingredients are kept in big quantities. Some of them are used during Ramadan or on other special occasions. The typical Moroccan terracotta cooking pots used to prepare *tajin* (a way of cooking meat and vegetables using such special ceramic pots) were also present in many of the homes I visited in Italy. The importance of food in forging a sense of belonging and identity has been underlined by Gardner too, who showed how, for Sylheti people who are leaving their country to migrate to England, food 'not only nourishes members of the group, but its consumption is also a sign of belonging and socialisation'.[36] The consumption of Moroccan meals with guests is also a way of objectifying the Moroccan background, since the consumption of food is also a symbolic incorporation of the place it recalls.

In this way, Moroccan women construct a 'home' which includes Italy and Morocco, since both these contexts provide them with complementary symbolic and material resources. But is this transnational construction of 'home' enough to overcome Moroccan women's sense of rupture and discontinuity? Or, in broader terms, could we define Moroccan migrant women and their families as living *simultaneously* in two countries?

Whereas many scholars of transnationalism have tended to use a celebratory language to describe the phenomenon, my informants expressed a high sense of unease, the feeling of being trapped in a vicious circle. Their transnational activities signal and epitomize the tension between Moroccan women's multiple belongings and their needs: what Peter van der Veer has aptly defined as the 'dialectics of belonging and longing'.[37] Some women, especially those who do not have children and therefore invest predominantly in social

---

[36] Gardner, *supra* n. 34, at 6.
[37] Van der Veer, *supra* n. 7, at 4.

recognition in Morocco, overlooking the search for social recognition in Italy, manage to go through this process in a more balanced way. For other women, on the contrary, the continuous movements back and forth increase the need for rootedness and stability.

Indeed, a deep level of anxiety takes place around the feeling of transience in women's life caused by their continuous movements between Italy and Morocco, which paradoxically bear contradictory outcomes. On the one hand, up-to-date knowledge through ongoing visits creates the possibility of building 'social fields that link together their country of origin and their country of settlement'.[38] Moreover, through keeping networks and activities between Morocco and Italy, migrants are able to construct a social personhood that encompasses boundaries and territorialized differences.[39] Nonetheless, at the same time, transnational links do not have the power to overthrow the sense of rupture women experience as a result of attempts to maintain membership in both countries yet being ultimately 'of' neither. I would like to conclude by quoting Leila, whose words strive for security and stability against this sentiment of ephemerality:

> After we came back from Morocco this summer, my husband decided that he wants to go back and live there ... in Italy we are neither here nor there. We save all our money to go back to Morocco during the summer and we spend our time in organising the travel. Then, once we are back in Italy, we start working again and saving for the next journey ... we don't save anything for the future. I have to think about my son, about his future.

Decisions on where to invest, materially and symbolically, might then constitute a field of negotiation or contestation, since transnational practices eventually lead to deeper anxieties on where 'home' is, and thus where one is supposed to build a future for children, provide them with their education, and acquire something more than material objects, that is a long-term symbolic capital. Analysed from this perspective, transnationalism and continual movement do not seem to reconcile fractures, but rather exacerbate anxieties on the future and amplify insecurities. While keeping a simultaneous relationship with their country of origin, women paradoxically also increase their need for territorialization and secure identities.

5. CONCLUSION: PARADOXES OF TRANSNATIONALISM

In this chapter I have argued that, with few exceptions, analyses of transnationalism lack a theorization that sheds light on gender factors and on the

[38] Glick-Schiller *et al.*, 'Transnationalism: a new analytic framework for understanding migration', in N. Glick-Schiller, L. Basch, and C. Szanton-Blanc (eds), *Towards a transnational perspective on migration: race, class, ethnicity and nationalism reconsidered* (1992) 1, at 1.

[39] Cf. Rouse, 'Questions of identity, personhood and collectivity in transnational migration to the United States', 15(4) *Critique of Anthropology* (1995) 351.

relations between gender, structure, and agency in accounting for trans-national movements. My aim was to show how narratives and experiences of transnational migration vary according to gender, economic possibilities, and legal circumstances, and according to the configurations and interplay of these factors in individuals' lives.

On the one hand, transnationalism allows women to construct a 'home' which includes in a continuum both Italy and Morocco. Indeed, women's construction of 'home' between Morocco and Italy is a significant site whereby broader feelings and narratives of displacement and belonging can be grasped. These are expressed in the objects and consumer goods through which Moroccan women construct the space they inhabit and through which they both manage identity ruptures and establish continuities between countries.

The material presented above illustrates that Moroccan migrants may return to their countries of origin once a year, but the material and psycho-logical preparation to undertake this trip may be overwhelming, to an extent that we may say that some migrants conduct lives in Italy which are predomin-antly functional to their return (however, not a permanent return, as it used to be in the past). For some families, life 'here' and life 'there' become therefore complementary. For other Moroccan families, however, transnationalism may paradoxically involve mutually exclusive choices. Indeed, annual visits to Morocco imply sacrifices in Italy. These aspects are salient in Moroccan women's narratives that often revolve around the tension embedded in man-aging the family's budget. For many of them, transnationalism means strug-gling to distribute resources evenly between Italy and Morocco, satisfying children's needs in Italy and relatives' expectations in Morocco, operating a balance between the desire to display their success in Morocco and the concrete requirements of everyday life in Italy.

However, I have also suggested that Moroccan women could be seen as plurinational subjects to emphasize their embeddedness with multiple hege-monic structures operating at more than one national level which condition their potential to move, their identities, and their transnational activities in a gendered way. Moreover, the term 'plurinational' aims at emphasizing that modern institutions and ideologies—such as the nation state, citizenship, and identity in terms of internalization of hegemonic discourses—which post-modernist and optimistic scholars represent as superseded are actually very much part of the reality of Moroccan families in Italy.[40] Particularly in some specific spheres, notably in the control and discipline of migration, the nation state seems to be far from weakened. Analyses of diasporic groups and hybrids that ignore or overlook this very fact, I believe, account for a very partial

---

[40] Kearney, 'Borders and Boundaries of State and Self at the End of the Empire', 4(1) *Journal of Historical Sociology* (1991) 52; Y. N. Soysal, *Limits of Citizenship. Migrants and Postnational Membership in Europe* (1994).

picture of the nature of contemporary migration, and certainly fail to see how modern institutions still discriminate on the basis of gender.

The ethnography of Moroccan migrant women thus contrasts the celebratory stances that emphasize transnational agencies, and highlights how transnational spheres are not only contingent upon migrants' vulnerability which derives from the transformation of the global economy, but are inscribed in specific cultural and normative constraints. Not only, therefore, should the nature and quality of women's movements and practices be understood in the light of the nature and quality of their membership in the various contexts (that is the household, the state, or the society more at large), but transnationalism may challenge or reproduce inequalities between genders and between places.

Index

Abd el-Krim el-Khattabi 196, 222–9
Abortion 40–1
Abu-Odeh, Lama 60
Affirmative action 48–9
Ageing populations 235
Aldridge v Booth 148
American Convention on Human Rights (Pact of San José) 131, 139, 141, 142, 143, 144
Anti-feminism 59–60
Aragon, Louis 200, 216, 217, 221
Arendt, Hannah 97
Argentina 122, 144
Aristotle 89
Association of Women of Southern Europe (AFEM) 108
Astell, Mary 20
Asylum-seekers 95
Australian jurisprudence 148–50

Basch, Linda 232
Bauman, Zygmunt 10, 231
Beijing Conference 142, 147
Ben Ibrahim, Sliman 201, 205, 225–6
Bentham, Jeremy 32, 33, 36, 39, 42, 48
Black Power 92
Blum, Léon 210
Boyle's Law 62–3
Brazilian Constitution 121
Breton, André 200, 215, 217, 218, 219, 220, 221, 222
Butler, Judith 67
Byrnes, Andrew 143

Canadian Charter of Rights and Freedoms 121, 126
Caribbean writers 221–2
Catholic Church 149–50
CEDAW (UN Convention on the Elimination of All Forms of Discrimination against Women) 22, 37, 48, 49, 50, 51, 53–5, 120–1, 122, 136, 139, 141, 147, 148
Césaire, Aimé 222
Chant, Sylvia 236
Charity organizations 91
Charter of Fundamental Rights of the European Union 4–5, 84–8, 101–2, 106–10, 111–12
Child abuse 22
Childbirth 95
Citizenship 4
  commonality approaches 90–1
  critical positioning 96

duties and obligations 89–90
European Charter of Fundamental Rights, *see* **Charter of Fundamental Rights of the European Union**
European citizenship 83–4, 110–12
European Convention on Human Rights 103–6
heteronormativity 99–100, 105–6
identity 91–3
inclusion 94, 95, 110
legal construction of citizens as subjects of law 85–6, 88–9, 97–8
Maastricht Treaty (Treaty of the European Union/TEU) 83, 110–11
migrant communities 95, 108, 236, 244–5, *see also* **Moroccan migrant women**
multiplicity approaches 91–3
nobility titles 132–3
participatory approaches 93–6
public/private distinction 90–1, 104
resources 97
  access to 102–3
rights 98–9
sex and gender 99–102
statelessness 97
subject status and contracting citizens 89–90
voting rights 94, 95
warfare 92, 94–5
see also **Rights**
Codes of rights 4, 13
Collective remedial rights 48–9
Colombian Constitution 119–21, 139–42
Colonialism 8, 9, 63, 64
  interwar debate 195–6, 197–8
  War of the Riff, *see* **War of the Riff**
Communism 204, 205, 211–15, 230
  see also **Marxism; Socialism**
Constitution-making 119–21
  see also **International gender norms**
Constitutional amendment 121–3
Convention on the Elimination of All Forms of Discrimination Against Women (CEDAW) 3–4, 22, 37, 48–51, 53–5, 120–2, 136, 139, 140, 141, 142, 147, 148, 150
Convention on the Rights of the Child 143, 149
Cornell, Drucilla 17, 18, 44, 45, 47, 52
Cossman, Brenda 73
Costa Rican Constitution 123, 129–31, 136–7, 138–9, 143–4
Crevel, René 215
Critical race theory 41–2

Cultural feminism 23, 59, 61
Cultural practices 50–1

Dahl, Tove Stang 15
Danielsen, Dan 73
Davies, Margaret 100, 101, 102
De Rivera, Primo 196
Democracy 36
Desnos, Robert 216
Difference feminism 25–6
  beyond gender neutrality 26
  conceptual framework of legal reasoning 29–30
  constitution of the legal subject as male 27–8
  enforcement of laws 30
  images of women and men in legal
      discourse 28–9
  legal methods as masculine 28
  normative reconstruction 43
  substance of law implicitly reflects male point of
      view 27
Dinet, Etienne 201, 205, 225–6
Divorce 72, 95
Doctrine of common purpose 6
Domestic violence 6–7, 14, 22, 29, 30
Du Gard, Roger Martin 199
Duties 89–90
Dworkin, Andrea 21, 39–40
Dworkin, Ronald 20, 33–4, 36, 37, 39, 47

Ecological feminism 23
Embiricos, Alexandre 198
Equal pay 145
European citizenship 83–4, 110–12
  access to resources 102–3
  democratic deficit 87
  Charter of Fundamental Rights, *see* **Charter of
      Fundamental Rights of the European
      Union**
  legal construction of citizens as subjects of
      law 85–6, 88–9, 97–8
  migrant communities 95, 108, 236, 244–5, *see
      also* **Moroccan migrant women**
  rights 98–9
  sex and gender 99–102
European Convention for the Protection of
      Human Rights and Fundamental
      Freedoms (European Convention on
      Human Rights/ECHR) 4, 37, 103–6,
      122, 132, 133
European Court of Justice 102–3, 135–6, 145
European Women's Lobby 107

Fantasies 8–10
  Orientalism 198–202, 205, 218–21, 229–30
Feminism 3–4
  cultural feminism 23, 59, 61
  gender trait feminism 58–9

heteronormativity 67
injury to men 65–6
intellectual narrowness 65
internal criticism 59–61
moral perfectionism 66–7
paranoid structuralism 62–3
subordination hypothesis 61–2
  hybrid feminisms 63–4
victim mentality 8, 9, 10, 67–8, 74–5
will to power 65
Feminist legal theory
  continuities with other legal and social
      theories 19
  difference feminism, *see* **Difference feminism**
  feminist critique of rights frameworks 38–41
  historical background 13–15
    analytical and political ethical claims 16
    methodology 16–17
    sex and gender 15–16
  liberal feminism 19–20, 25–6
    accusations of privilege 41–2
    gender-neutrality 22, 24
    individualism 20–21
    liberal conceptions of freedom 21
    normative reconstruction 43
    public and private spheres 21–2
  Marxist and socialist feminism 25, 63, 64
  methodology and written style 17–18
  normative reconstruction 42–7
    affirmative action 48–9
    collective remedial rights 48–9
    group rights 49–50
    relational rights 52–3
    rights of being 51
    rights of equivalent worth 47–8
    rights to cultural membership 50–1
  radical feminism
    criticisms 24
    revaluing the feminine 23–4
  underlying theories of sexual difference 18
Fortress Europe 95, 236
Foucault, Michel 68, 75–7
Fourrier, Marcel 216
France
  interwar debate on colonialism 195–6, 197–8
  Orientalism 198–202, 205, 218–21, 229–30
  War of the Riff 196
    Abd el-Krim's public discourse 222–9
    avant-garde/Surrealist response 204, 205,
        215–22
    international legal existence 202–4
    liberal left/Socialist response 204, 205,
        206–11
    radical left/Communist response 204, 205,
        211–15, 230
Frankenberg, Günter 90
Freedom of speech 21, 29, 31, 32, 33, 47–8

French Constitution 122–3
Freud, Sigmund 220

Gardner, Katy 246
Gay identity politics 57
Gay Liberation 92
Gender-neutral language 4, 108–9
Gender neutrality 22, 24, 26
Gender norms 5, 15–16, 105–6
  see also International gender norms
Gender trait feminism 58–9
Geneva Conventions 153–4, 163, 168
Genocide 180–5
German Constitution 134–6
Giddens, Anthony 237
Gilligan, Carol 28, 52, 91
Glick-Schiller, Nina 232
Global Leader Summit 91
Group rights 49–50
Grzelczyk case 102
Guatemalan Constitution 142–3

Habermas, Jürgen 91
Haiti 222
Harassment 18, 29, 100
Harris, Angela 41
Hart, H.L.A. 32, 36
Hegel, Georg 88
Heteronormativity 67, 99–100, 105–6
Heyns, Christof 119
Hierarchical divisions 23–4
Higgins, Tracy 73
Hohfeld, Wesley Newcomb 31–2
Housework 101
Human rights 4, 35
  gender norms, *see* Gender norms;
    International gender norms
  judicial review of state action 36–8
Human Rights Act 1998 122

Identity-based citizenship 91–3
Immigration 95
  see also Migrant communities; Moroccan
    migrant women
Imperialism 64, 199
In vitro fertilization 143, 149
Incest 29
Inclusion 94, 95
Indian Constitution 125, 146–7
Individualism 20–1, 38
Inter-American Convention on the Prevention,
    Punishment, and Eradication of
    Violence Against Women 142
International Court of Justice 37–8
International Covenant on Civil and Political
    Rights (ICCPR) 119, 121, 131, 139, 141,
    149, 151

International Covenant on Economic, Social
    and Cultural Rights (ICESCR) 119,
    139, 149
International Criminal Tribunal for Rwanda
    (ICTR) 6
International Criminal Tribunal for the Former
    Yugoslavia (ICTY) 1–2, 6, 153–6
  collective liability 162–4
    Prosecutor v Furundžija 169–75, 178–80
    Prosecutor v Krstić 180–5
    *Prosecutor v Kvoćka,*185–9
    Prosecutor v Slobodan Milošević 193–4
    Prosecutor v Tadić 164–9, 175–8, 191
  evidentiary rules 159–60, 164
  individual liability 161–2
  male sexual violence 165–9
  Omarska detention camp 185–9, 191
  rape 170–1, 173–4, 186, 187
  Secretary-General's intent to punish persons
    liable for sexual assaults 156–62
  sexual violence as natural and foreseeable
    consequence of other violations 180–5,
    186–7, 192–3
  Srebrenica massacre 180–5
  torture 171–3, 178
International gender norms 5
  Argentina 122, 144
  Australian jurisprudence 148–50
  Brazilian Constitution 121
  Canadian Charter of Rights and Freedoms 121,
    126
  Colombian Constitution 119–21, 139–42
  constitutional domestication 113–18, 129,
    151–2
    assimilation 115, 118, 119–23, 137
    complementing constitutional
      parameters 115, 137–44, 147
    concretizing constitutional parameters 115,
      144–7
    constitution-making 119–21
    constitutional amendment 121–3
    expanding constitutional parameters 115,
      129–37, 144, 147
    interpretive adaptations 115, 119, 124–9,
      131, 137
    redefining structure of powers 115, 147–51
    supplementation 115, 118–19, 123–4, 129
  Costa Rican Constitution 123, 129–31, 136–7,
    138–9, 143–4
  French Constitution 122–3
  German Constitution 134–6
  Guatemalan Constitution 142–3
  Indian Constitution 125, 146–7
  South African Constitution 121
  Spanish Constitution 125, 132–3, 144,
    145–6
  supranational enforcement mechanisms 117

International gender norms (*cont.*)
Ugandan Constitution 121
UK law 122
US jurisprudence 127–9, 150–1
International Labour Organization (ILO) 139
Irigaray, Luce 17, 24, 45, 51, 52
Islam 205, 223, 225, 244–5
Italy
ageing population 235
immigrant workers 234–6
Moroccan migrant women, *see* **Moroccan migrant women**

Jaurès, Jean 206, 207, 208, 209, 210
Judicial review 36–8

Kalanke case 135
Kant, Immanuel 91, 108
Kennedy, Duncan 62
Kohlberg, Lawrence 91
Kosovo 9
Kymlicka, Will 92, 96

Labour law 101, 139, 145–6
Laraque, Paul 227
League of Nations 202, 209, 216
Legal rights *see* **Rights**
Liberal feminism 19–20, 25–6
accusations of privilege 41–2
normative reconstruction 43
Liberalism 14, 198–9
conceptions of freedom 21
gender neutrality 22, 24
individualism 20–21
public and private spheres 21–2
Littleton, Christine 47
Locke, John 36
Lorde, Audre 42

Maastricht Treaty (Treaty of the European Union/TEU) 83, 110–11
MacCormick, Neil 32
MacKinnon, Catharine 17, 18, 21, 29, 39–40, 61, 62
Male domination 62, 104
nobility titles 132–3
Marriage laws 11, 95, 130, 138, 244–5
Marshall, Thomas 88
Marschall case 135
Martinique 222
Marxism 18, 23, 39, 41, 42, 48
see also **Communism; Socialism**
Marxist feminism 25
Masculinity 58–9
McBain v State of Victoria 149
Ménil, René 222
Migrant communities 10–11, 95, 108

Moroccan women, *see* **Moroccan migrant women**
transnational communities 231–3
Military service 94–5, 101
Mobility-related rights 10–11
transnational communities 231–3, 236
Modernism 198, 212, 218, 221
Moller Okin, Susan 90
Moroccan migrant women 10–11
consumption practices 245–7
employment patterns 235
investment decisions 248
legal status 244–5
rationale for migration 236–42
responsibilities for transnational households 243–4
social recognition 247–8
statistics 233
transnational communities 231–3, 248–50
Morocco
French conquest 206–7
War of the Riff, *see* **War of the Riff**
Multiculturalism 94, 109

Naffine, Ngaire 17, 27, 38
Nagl, Herta 91
Nash, Kate 24
Nedelsky, Jennifer 52–3, 89
Nietzsche, Friedrich 68, 74, 75
Nobility titles 132–3
Norman, Wayne 96
Nuremberg Tribunal 163

Obligations 89–90
Olsen, Frances 23, 27
Orford, Anne 9
Orientalism 198–202, 205, 218–21, 229–30
Oslo school 15

Pact of San José (American Convention on Human Rights) 139, 141, 143
Paranoid structuralism 62–3
Pateman, Carole 90, 92
Phillips, Anne 90, 98
Phizacklea, Annie 237
Political morality 34–5
democracy 36
human rights culture 35
judicial review of state action 36–8
liberty versus equality 36
pre-social entitlements 35
Political participation 93–6
Pornography 21, 29, 39–40, 47, 100
Post-feminism 59–60
Postmodernism 26
Potter, Elizabeth 62–3
Poulaille, Henry 216

Pregnancy 109, 146
Prisoners 140
Public-private distinction 6–7, 11, 21–2, 29, 43, 90–1, 104
  wartime sexual violence 189–90

Queer theory 57–9
Quota laws 141–2

Racial hatred 30
Racism 63, 64
Radcliffe, Sarah 236
Radical feminism
  criticisms 24
  revaluing the feminine 23–4
Rape 22, 30, 68
  feminist discourse 71, 72, 74–5, 77
  substance of law implicitly reflects male point of view 27, 100
  wartime sexual violence, 6, 7, 8, 155, 157–8, 170–1, 173–4, 186, 187
Rawls, John 91
Refugees 95
Reproductive rights 138–9, 140, 143–4, 149
  abortion 40–1
Rich, Adrienne 99
Riffan struggle *see* War of the Riff
Rights
  citizenship, *see* Citizenship
  codes of rights 4, 13
  coercive framework of enforcement 39
  competitive assertion of entitlements 39
  critical race theory 41–2
  feminist critique 38–41
    objections to 41–2
  multiplication of rights 39
  normative reconstruction 42–7
    affirmative action 48–9
    collective remedial rights 48–9
    group rights 49–50
    relational rights 52–3
    rights of being 51
    rights of equivalent worth 47–8
    rights to cultural membership 50–1
  political morality 34–5
    democracy 36
    human rights culture 35
    judicial review of state action 36–8
    liberty versus equality 36
    pre-social entitlements 35
  theories 3, 30–1
    Dworkin's theory of rights as trumps 33–4, 39
    Hart's choice theory 32
    Hohfeld's claim rights 31–2
    interest theory and specially protected benefits 32–3
see also Human rights

Roiphe, Katie 59
Roosevelt, Eleanor 104
Rousseau, Jean-Jacques 89
Rubin, Gayle 57, 58

Sadomasochism 68–78
Scelle, Georges 202, 204
Sedgwick, Eve Kosofsky 67
Separatism 23
Sex and gender 15–16
Sexual difference 18
  legal discourse 28–9
  see also Difference feminism
Sexual exploitation 40
Sexual violence 22, 68
  in wartime 5–7, 8, 101
    Nuremberg and Tokyo Tribunals, 163
    public/private distinction 189–92
    Yugoslavia, *see* International Criminal Tribunal for the Former Yugoslavia
  Twyman v Twyman 68–78
  see also Rape
Smart, Carol 18, 39
Smith, Robert 232
Social conflict 92
Social subordination 61–2
  hybrid feminisms 63–4
Socialism 9–10, 204, 205, 206–11
  see also Communism; Marxism
Socialist feminism 25, 63, 64
Sommers, Christine Hoff 59
South African Constitution 121
Spain 196
Spanish Constitution 125, 132–3, 144, 145–6
Srebrenica massacre 180–5
Statelessness 97
Sterilization 138–9
Subordination hypothesis 61–2
  hybrid feminisms 63–4
Surrealism 200, 204, 205, 215–22
Szanton-Blanc, Cristina 232

Tasmanian Dam case 148
Tokyo Tribunal 163
Torture 171–3, 178
Treaty of the European Union/TEU (Maastricht Treaty) 83, 110–11
Twyman v Twyman 68–78

Ugandan Constitution 121
UK law 122
United Nations Charter 104
United States v Morrison 150–1
Universal Declaration of Human Rights 125, 132
US Bill of Rights 22
US Constitution 37

US First Amendment 29
US jurisprudence 127–9, 150–1
Utilitarianism 33–4
Utopianism 23, 42, 43, 44–5, 46

Van der Veer, Peter 247
Vance, Carole 57
Victim mentality 8, 9, 10, 67–8, 74–5
Violence Against Women Act 1994 150–1
Viljoen, Frans 119
Vishaka v State of Rajasthan 146
Vitorino, António 84
Voting rights 94, 95

War of the Riff 196
  Abd-el-Krim's public discourse 222–9
  avant-garde/Surrealist response 204, 205,
    215–22
  international legal existence 202–4
  liberal left/Socialist response 204, 205, 206–11
  radical left/Communist response 204, 205,
    211–15, 230
Warfare 92, 94–5

Wartime sexual violence 5–7, 8, 101
  Nuremberg and Tokyo Tribunals 163
  public/private distinction 189–90
  Yugoslavia, *see* **International Criminal
    Tribunal for the Former Yugoslavia**
Weiler, Joseph 110
Western Sahara 207
Williams, Patricia 17, 41, 98
Wollstonecraft, Mary 13–14
Women prisoners 140
Women's international human rights
  gender norms, *see* **International
    gender norms**
  influence of United States, 78–9
  status as research field 1–2
Women's movement 14
Work division 101
World War I 199, 200–1

Young, Iris Marion 92
Yugoslav conflict 8
    see also **International Criminal Tribunal
    for the Former Yugoslavia**